THE STORY OF THE OLD TESTAMENT

bju **press**®

Greenville, South Carolina

Note: The fact that materials produced by other publishers may be referred to in this volume does not constitute an endorsement of the content or theological position of materials produced by such publishers. Any references and ancillary materials are listed as an aid to the student or the teacher and in an attempt to maintain the accepted academic standards of the publishing industry.

THE STORY OF THE OLD TESTAMENT

Lead Writer
James H. Tuck Jr., PhD

Contributing Writers
Brian C. Collins, PhD
Kevin M. Collins, MDiv

Editor
Tim Endean, MA

Biblical Worldview Consultant
Brian C. Collins, PhD

Academic Oversight
Jeff Heath, EdD

Project Coordinator
Jennifer Ferguson

Cover and Book Design
Michael Asire

Page Layout
Maribeth Hayes
Bonnijean Marley

Illustrators
Jon Andrews
Zach Franzen
Chris Koelle
Del Thompson

Permissions
Sylvia Gass
Carrie Walker

Acknowledgments begin on page 304.

Photograph credits appear on page 307.

Based in part on original materials from *Bible Truths: Level B The Story of the Old Testament*, Fourth Edition, by Mark L. Ward Jr., PhD.

© 2018 BJU Press
Greenville, South Carolina 29609

Printed in the United States of America

ISBN 978-1-62856-241-5

15 14 13 12 11 10 9 8 7 6 5 4 3 2

CONTENTS

FOREWORD

Middle school is a crucial time in a person's life. I know this by experience. When I was in elementary school, I was aware that God loved me, that evil was in the world, and that I needed to live for God. But in my seventh-grade year, this awareness became an awakening. I didn't just know that evil existed, I felt it—even in my own heart. I wasn't just aware that I needed to live for God, I was overwhelmed with conviction that I ought to surrender my life to Him. At the end of that school year, God brought me to a breaking point. It was then that I gave my life to Him. It was then that I began to grow spiritually.

One of the first things that changed was my relationship to the Bible. It was no longer a book that sat on the shelf except for Sundays and Wednesdays. It was a book I read every day. As I read the Bible and prayed, my desires began to change. I wanted to please my parents, to get involved in ministry, and to be a good influence in my Christian school. I learned over the next couple of years that the Bible is a powerful book. If you let it loose in your life, it will change everything. It certainly changed me.

Things were very different for most of my friends. That year was for them the beginning of a downward spiral. Their relationship with their parents began to fall apart, and their behavior on the weekends was becoming shameful and dangerous. In time, some even got in trouble with the law. I learned that middle school isn't just the next step in life. It's the place where life forms a fork in the road. What you do at that fork determines the path you will travel. And in the end, Proverbs 13:15 will prove true: "The way of transgressors is hard."

I've often thought it was strange that many of my friends got on the wrong path while attending a Christian school. A Christian school is a place where everyone is a Christian, and everyone acts like a Christian, right? We all know better than that. In this fallen world, evil is found in every heart. And where it manages to take control, it turns everything to its will. My friends had many advantages in that Christian school, but they chose not to use them.

But there was one advantage they should have had but didn't. A challenging, engaging Bible class. Our teacher was a godly man, from what I could tell. But we didn't learn much about the Bible, and we didn't feel like we needed to either. The teacher basically read from a script, and we filled in blanks on worksheets. That Bible class was a missed opportunity.

What my friends needed was something like this course. The Story of the Old Testament is designed to help young people study the Bible for themselves, and it does so by focusing on a biblical worldview. It doesn't just cover the details of the Old Testament. It relates those details to one another, showing how the Bible fits together to tell one grand story. This course then demonstrates, lesson by lesson, how that story should shape a person's beliefs and values, and how those should lead to a changed life. That was what my friends needed many years ago.

It was what I needed too. God did change my life through His Word. But the change was for me a difficult struggle. I didn't know how to study the Bible, and I was confused about how the Bible was supposed to help me grow spiritually. I figured these things out slowly over time. Looking back, I wish I'd had some help.

That's the reason we put this course together. We want to help.

Of course, you'll need to do something too. Read the textbook, do your homework, be real when you complete a journal assignment. If you work hard, you'll find that this course does an excellent job leading you step by step through the Old Testament. It will show you how to read and understand God's Word. It will even confront you with God—His holiness, His power, and His grace. But you will have to be willing to take the next step. You will have to choose the right path at this fork in the road. If you do, you won't be disappointed. That's another promise from Proverbs: "The path of the just is as the shining light, that shineth more and more unto the perfect day" (Prov. 4:18).

Bryan Smith, PhD
Biblical Worldview Formation
BJU Press

UNIT 1

CREATION & FALL

The textbook that you have in your hands is designed to help you understand the story of the Old Testament and how it fits with God's larger story for creation. God's Word is the authority for knowing what is right and wrong, and a proper attitude will help you respond correctly to it. This unit introduces the skills needed to study God's Word. It also introduces Scripture's main story and examines how the story began. At first you will have a bird's-eye view of the whole Bible, and slowly we will zoom in closer and examine how each story fits in with the larger story of Scripture.

1.1 AUTHORITY & ATTITUDE

The story of the Old Testament is an epic account that tells of God's steadfast love for humanity and for the nation of Israel in particular. But that story covers more than just Israel's history. It also covers your history and mine. In the first eleven chapters of Genesis, we learn how God *created* the world, how Adam and Eve *fell* and caused problems for all their descendants, and how God sent a flood to punish the unrighteous and to *redeem* the righteous. Some of the people in those stories (Adam, Eve, Noah, and his wife, for example) are your ancestors. That's right. You are related to them. The story of the Old Testament is, in a sense, your epic story.

Though the Bible's historical accounts happened long ago in faraway places in unfamiliar cultures, its principles and truths are relevant today. The men and women, boys and girls, and even teenagers found in the Old Testament were sinners, just like you, in need of redemption. They faced the same types of problems you face. Some lived in times of peace. Some lived in times of war. Some lived in times when everyone did what he wanted to do regardless of the consequences. Some wondered aloud, "Why do wicked people prosper, while those who do right don't seem to prosper?"

But not all was bleak. There were those who showed kindness to others, expressed forgiveness, demonstrated meekness, despised evil, hated injustice, sang for joy, laughed, loved, and truly worshiped God.

We must remember that we know how their story ends. They didn't. Their future seemed to them as uncertain as ours does to us. God knew their uncertainty, and He made plans that would give them a future filled with hope (Jer. 29:11). These plans would be carried out because God has steadfast love for all who put their faith in Him.

Your future is also filled with hope, because God's plans of kindness extend to you if you put your faith in Him. Through Israel's promised Messiah, God has given you hope—not just a wishful hope, but a confident hope that He will redeem all things, including you.

Before we get to the story of the Old Testament, we need to understand a few things about God's Word and our relationship to it and to Him.

The Purposes of God's Word

To reveal God. God has revealed Himself through nature to everyone, everywhere, of all time. This is called general revelation. General revelation allows everyone to have a knowledge of God. But that knowledge is limited. It tells us only that God exists, a little of what He is like, and some moral laws He has written on our hearts (Rom. 1:18–20). Nature does not tell us anything specific about Him, nor does it reveal the gospel, which is the only way to know Him personally (Rom. 1:16–17, 21–25). God gives us special revelation—the Bible—so that we can know Him and His gospel.

To establish a relationship. Before Adam and Eve sinned, they had a relationship of favor with God, but after they sinned, they lost that special relationship. Everyone who came after them—and that is everyone—also lost that relationship with God. Simply knowing that God exists or knowing what He is like is insufficient to reestablish the relationship. Special instructions are needed, and God gave those instructions to godly men who wrote them down in the book we call the Bible (2 Tim. 3:16; 2 Pet. 1:19–21).

Many passages in the Bible tell us how to live. Much of the Bible is about men and women and their relationship or lack of relationship with God. You could call them stories. But these are not just any stories. They are true accounts of actual, historical events. Remember they might be in the past for us, but for the people in the stories, it was their present time. They didn't sit around the fire at night and talk about how cool it was to live back in Bible times. For them, these stories were their present lives.

These stories are also more than individual stories. Each story is part of the larger story. And that story tells us what God is doing to glorify Himself by redeeming His fallen creation. (In

Section 1.3 you'll see that this larger story has three elements: Creation, Fall, and Redemption.)

But the stories contained in the Bible accomplish more than giving us facts about people's lives or merely providing a generic user's manual for life. The stories reveal God to help you and me have a relationship with Him, with God who wishes to be known personally.

Authority

In today's society, each person wants to be his or her own boss. People want to make their own rules, live the way they want to live, believe what they want to believe, and trust only those they choose to trust.

Many people view authority negatively. They may have seen or experienced an authority taking advantage of being in charge. Some people simply don't like having anyone tell them what to do. Authority hinders them from doing what they want to do. For them, authority is automatically oppressive and tyrannical.

But God never intended for authority to be burdensome, to oppress us, or to keep us from doing good things. Authority is meant to enable us to freely do those things that are right and good—and what is right and good is determined by God's design for creation. Ultimately, life works only if you operate according to God's design. So God's authority exists to establish responsibilities so that you can be held accountable when you do wrong.

Obligations

God Himself is the ultimate authority. As Creator, He has the right to command our obedience. Since we are His creation, He alone has the right to set the standard for all areas of our lives. He has revealed that standard in the Bible, and it is that standard that obligates us to respond. When God gives us a command, we are to obey. When He gives us information about a future event, or about someone, or about anything, we are to believe Him. When He makes a promise, we are to trust Him.

When God gave Adam the command to not eat from the tree, Adam was expected to obey. When God told Noah to make an ark in order to

Benevolence
vs.
Tyranny

survive the Flood He was going to send, Noah was expected to believe God and to obey Him. When God told Abraham to sacrifice his son, Abraham was expected to trust God and to obey.

In other words, whatever God tells us to do, to think, to feel, to believe, to whatever, we are obligated to do it. Ignoring God's words or refusing to accept God's authority does not abolish or cancel His words or authority. God's authority is still there, and it still obligates us to follow His words regardless of how we view them.

God's authority gives Him the right to command our obedience through the Bible. The Bible shapes what we believe and how we act. This authority extends to all areas of life—both sacred and secular.

The Effect of the Fall

The Fall has affected everyone and everything. Fallenness resides within each human heart. It affects what we say, what we do, how we think, and how we react. It affects us in every way. Because the world is fallen, things aren't as they should be. God has given us His Word so that we can know how we should be and how we can help to make the world as it should be.

Christ told the lawyer that all the Law depends on the two commandments of loving God and loving your neighbor. Both of these commandments concern relationships. Since these commandments are the basis for God's entire law, then God's law is essentially about relationships. Everything we do affects somebody else—whether it is God or our neighbor. That means that right and wrong apply to every area of your life. We do not have the freedom to do anything we want, because our freedoms are limited by loving God and loving others.

Paul tells Timothy that the Bible is profitable (useful or to our advantage) "for doctrine, for reproof, for correction, [and] for instruction in righteousness" (2 Tim. 3:16). In other words, it teaches us what to do. It shows us our mistakes. It tells us how to correct them. And it instructs or trains us how to discipline ourselves to live rightly. It does all these things so that Christians can be equipped to do "all good works" (3:17). Basically, God has given us the Scriptures so that we can learn His principles for doing good works, and then we can do what God expects us to do regardless of the situation.

Bible scholar George Knight has put it well:

God has equipped "the person of God" to do what is "good," i.e., what he has indicated in his scripture should be done, since he himself is the norm of all good. Since God created Christians for good works and calls on them to do good works (Eph. 2:10; Tit. 3:1; 2 Tim. 2:21), he has given scripture to instruct them so that they may know in principle what God expects of them and thus be equipped to do that particular "good deed" called for in each situation.

Attitude

Obedience goes beyond following a set of rules and doing what you are told. Have you ever been told to clean your room or to do some other chore, and you did it with a rotten attitude? Instead of simply obeying, did you go about angrily throwing clothes into the closet or whining the entire time? You were obeying, but with your attitude you were disobeying.

Or perhaps you are the obedient child, and you know it. You go and clean your room with pride. You're proud of how well you obey. You too are obeying, and you too are disobeying with your attitude. In each case, the response is wrong. Maybe you are neither of the above, and you respond with a proper attitude.

Solomon talks about why people respond differently to God's Word. He says, "The fear of the Lord is the beginning of knowledge" (Prov. 1:7).

> "What the alphabet is to reading, notes to reading music, and numerals to mathematics, the fear of the LORD is to attaining the revealed knowledge of this book."
>
> —Bruce Waltke

What is fear? Is it something that involves only your mind? Or is it something that deals more with your emotions, your attitude? The answer is that both your mind and emotions are involved. You are smart enough to know not to walk out in front of a speeding car because you know that getting hit will hurt. Your fear of a speeding car involves your mind.

But notice the kind of fear that Solomon is talking about. It is the *beginning* of knowledge. Fearing comes before knowing.

What is the object of this fear? It is the Lord, the God of the Bible.

What type of fear is it? By looking at how the Bible uses the phrase "the fear of the Lord," you see that it is a trembling awe and respect before a vastly more powerful, perfectly holy, and utterly good being. It is not a fear where you cower in the corner, shaking uncontrollably. It is a fear that motivates you to conform to God's law and to please Him (Gen. 15:1; 26:24).

Knowing that God expects obedience from us actually allows us to avoid living in fear of Him. God's commandments were given to teach us what He expects of us. If we did not know

Awe vs. Paralysis

Proverbs says, "By the fear of the Lord men depart from evil" (Prov. 16:6). In other words, those who fear Him avoid evil. That is a healthy and liberating fear.

Conclusion

The story of the Old Testament is God's revelation to us. God has given us His Word to establish a relationship with us. In order to have a relationship with God, we must approach Him on His terms. He has the authority to make the rules, and His rules obligate us in every way. We must do what He says to do, believe what He tells us, and trust in His promises. And when we follow those obligations, we must approach Him respectfully and with a trembling awe.

To those who are living for God, a reminder of the proper balance of fear should cause you to walk rightly in the fear of God so that you can be preserved amid the trials of life (James 5:10–11; Ps. 124:7–8). To those who are lost and without God, you must realize the danger that you are in. "It is a fearful thing to fall into the hands of the living God" (Heb. 10:31). However, God has provided a way of hope to those who call on Him (Rom. 10:13; John 3:16).

Likewise, God's love and greatness give us cause to fear Him. This fear should be balanced between a terror of displeasing Him through our disobedience (Exod. 20:20) and a reverential respect demonstrated by our obedience.

what He expected, we would rightfully cower from the fear of never knowing if we have or have not pleased Him. But thankfully, we do know what He expects and how to make things right when we do not please Him.

The right kind of fear is healthy, and it comes through knowing God's Word. Moses gathered the people of Israel together to teach them God's words so that they might learn a proper fear of God (Deut. 4:10–14). Israel's kings were to read the Law to learn how to fear God (17:19). Fearing God is often associated with obedience to His commandments (5:29; 6:24; 13:4; 17:19; 28:58).

Thinking It Through 1.1

1. What are the two purposes of God's Word?

2. What is the purpose of God's authority? Why does God's authority exist?

3. Why are we obligated to God as our ultimate authority? Where do we learn about those obligations for what we should believe and how we should act?

4. According to Proverbs 1:7, what is the key for responding rightly to the knowledge of God's Word?

5. Compare and contrast a healthy versus an unhealthy fear of the Lord.

1.2 APPROACH & APPLICATION

Read Ruth 2:4–16
Memorize Proverbs 1:7

Solomon said, "The fear of the Lord is the beginning of knowledge" (Prov. 1:7). Two key words in this verse are *fear* and *knowledge*. In the previous section we looked at the phrase "the fear of the Lord." We concluded that this is a healthy fear that comes through seeking God (Prov. 2:1–5). The second phrase, "the beginning of knowledge," is directly connected with the first phrase. The first phrase involves your relationship with God, and the second phrase involves your interaction with the world around you. Having a true fear of the Lord shows that you have a right relationship with God. By fearing the Lord, you can know His will. You can know how He wants you to act and to respond. That knowledge allows you to think correctly about the world around you and to react properly to it.

God's words are available to us, and they are understandable. The issue is not merely to understand them but to understand them correctly.

Missed Observation, Missed Destination

Samantha had finally made it to vacation time. Even better, this was Christmas vacation, and she would be spending it on Grenada, an island in the southeastern Caribbean Sea. As she boarded her plane, thoughts of tropical breezes, warm ocean waters, and long walks down white sand beaches were going through her mind.

When the plane finally arrived, the captain welcomed the passengers and said that the temperature would be around thirty-four degrees. She quickly calculated in her head that thirty-four degrees Celsius would be around ninety degrees Fahrenheit. She was getting really excited to get off the plane, to smell the salty air, and to feel the warm breezes.

But as she emerged from the plane, she was met with a shock. There was no salty air or warm breeze. In fact, it was a frigid wind blowing in her face. It wasn't thirty-four degrees *Celsius*. It was thirty-four degrees *Fahrenheit*! Worse yet, she wasn't in Grenada in the Caribbean. She was in Granada, Spain—some 3,970 miles away!

How did this happen? It seems that when Samantha booked her flight, she forgot to verify the spelling of her intended destination. She just assumed that Grenada was spelled Granada. And she never thought there might be another similarly spelled place. Basically, she presupposed wrong. A simple verification of the spelling, asking the check-in clerk or boarding agent, or a number of other things could have prevented this mistake.

Another plane at her hometown airport *was* going to Grenada. Both jets started at the same place, but they ended up 3,970 miles apart.

Why?

Did the passengers or the plane by itself determine where it was going? No.

In each plane the pilot set the destination heading, and that determined where the plane would land.

How is this story relevant to Bible study?

Each one of us starts our Bible study in the same place with the same text. We're all at the same airport. But often, people end up with very different interpretations of a particular passage. Why is that? Because we take different approaches to Scripture. In our analogy, we take different airplanes. That is why we sometimes end up where we shouldn't be.

Sometimes the difference is very noticeable. Samantha immediately figured out that she was at the wrong location. Sometimes the difference is not as noticeable. Travelers have flown into Greenville and spent hours around town before they realized they were in Greenville, *North* Carolina, and not *South* Carolina. The city name was the same, but they were still almost three hundred miles from their intended destination.

Your method may not lead to your intended destination.

We can all agree that Samantha's intentions were good. She intended to go to Grenada. But her method of getting there led her to the wrong destination—Granada.

Three Steps for Studying Your Bible

Your purpose in approaching Scripture is to know God. Your "destination" is to reflect God. Bible study is the way to find out what God expects you to do, so that you can continue to walk with Him and have a personal relationship with Him. Your destination is to live your life in a way that pleases God.

So how do you keep from ending up where you don't want to go? If you're traveling, the answer is, "Don't get on the wrong plane." How do you avoid "getting on the wrong plane" when you start your Bible study?

The approach that this book takes to Bible study is a simple process that will keep you on the right plane. It is simple because it involves only three steps—observe, interpret, and apply. And you can learn to do each of the steps.

Observe

The first step is to observe. Observation is more than seeing. Observation is taking notice of what you see—being aware and alert. It is paying attention to what the text says. Like a sponge soaks up water, the observer soaks up facts about the story. When you finish observing, you should be able to recall basic facts from the story. You should know the who, what, when, where, and why of the story.

Who is in the story? Who is speaking? Who is doing the action? Who is not doing anything?

What are the characters doing? What are they saying? What objects are in the story?

When does the story take place? At night, in the morning, or afternoon? In what century? Under whose rule?

Where does the story take place? What country, city, or countryside? Is it outside or inside?

Why does the story take place? Does the text tell us? Does a later text tell us?

Each of these five questions represents a category vital to observing. When you observe the text, you are looking for information that everyone can agree is there. Every detail is important.

You must be aware, though, that observation is difficult work. Sherlock Holmes says, "The world is full of obvious things that nobody by any chance ever observes." So what do you need in order to observe these "obvious things"?

Bible scholar Robert Traina notes three things that are needed. First, you must be willing to observe. You must make a conscientious effort to observe. Skimming the text doesn't work. You will need to read the text with purpose, looking for facts and clues about what is going on.

Second, you must be exact when you observe. You must notice the details. The more attentive you are, the more accurate you can be.

Third, you must be persistent. Read the text multiple times even if you think you know the passage. For example, did God put the rainbow in the sky as a sign for us to remember the Flood or for Him to remember? Can you answer the question without looking it up? (See Gen. 9:8–17.)

Being willing, exact, and persistent are all necessary to prepare you to observe. The better you observe, the more you will know about the passage. But it doesn't stop there. You need to understand what you have observed.

Interpret

The second step is to interpret. Interpretation is understanding what you have observed. You can't interpret until you observe, but the more you observe, the more you can understand.

Basic interpretation begins with defining what you observed. This includes defining terms. For example, what does it mean to *redeem* something? You could use a Bible dictionary to look up the term. Basic interpretation also includes comparisons and contrasts. Once you gather the facts about Saul and David, you could compare and contrast their responses to God's commands.

Interpretation involves recognizing things that are implied. One aspect of recognition is to look at what a character says or does to determine what that character is like. When Naomi decides to go back to Bethlehem, she tells Ruth, her daughter-in-law from Moab, that she does not have to come with her to Bethlehem. Naomi says that it would be better for Ruth to return to her own mother's house rather than go to a foreign country. Ruth tells Naomi that she will go with her, worship her God, live with her, and die with her. Ruth does more than just talk. When they settle in Bethlehem, she goes out and works to bring home food for the two of them. Both her speech and her actions imply that Ruth is a kind individual. This is confirmed when Boaz explicitly compliments Ruth on her kindness to Naomi.

Interpretation is also about understanding why God has revealed what He has in Scripture. For example, why did God tell the serpent that the seed of the woman would crush his head? The reason is his role in the Fall. What is God's purpose for making the statement? To give hope of a promised seed who will make all things right in God's creation.

Once you have interpreted the text, you understand what it means. But this second step in Bible study is not the last step. For your Bible study to be complete, you must apply what you have already observed and interpreted.

 ## Apply

The third step is to apply. Application is taking the biblical truth found within the passage and putting it into action in your current situation. Sometimes this is easy, but sometimes it is difficult.

It is easy when your situation and the biblical story are very similar, or when there are biblical commands that directly pertain to your situation. For example, when your friend gets the latest iPhone or gaming system, and you're stuck with one that's a few years old, it can be tempting to want what he has. In fact, it can lead to an extreme desire to have what he has. You long for

it and it's all you think about. That's called coveting. And Scripture tells us specifically that we must not covet anything that our neighbor (our friend) has (Exod. 20:17).

At other times it's more difficult to find a passage that deals with your situation. Having the latest iPhone or gaming system brings its own set of temptations. The problem is that the Bible says nothing about the internet or video games. But it does have a lot to say about the temptations and problems often associated with the internet and video games. For example, the Bible has a lot to say about what you look at and how you talk to and about people. It also says a few things about managing your time well. Bible principles apply to every situation in your life.

All three Bible-study steps are necessary. If all you do is observe and collect facts, then you would make a great contestant on *Jeopardy!*, but that's about all. If you stop with interpretation, then you're just an educated Christian who knows a lot about the Bible. But if you observe, interpret, and then apply God's Word to your life, you will be a changed Christian. More than that, you will have a close relationship with God.

But you cannot do all this work alone. You need help. And you need more help than your teacher or parents can provide. They can teach you how to observe, interpret, and apply, but they cannot change you internally. To change inside, you must depend on God's guidance through His Spirit to help you in your study of the Bible. With the work of God in your life, you can be a proven worker who doesn't need to be ashamed before God.

Now that we have looked at the right attitude toward God and His Word (the fear of the Lord) and the approach for Bible study (observe, interpret, apply), we are ready to look at the story of the Old Testament.

Thinking It Through 1.2

1. What should be your ultimate purpose for studying the Bible? What should be your end goal or destination for studying the Bible?

2. List the three steps of the Bible-study method outlined in this lesson. Define each step.

3. Identify the three things that are needed to prepare you to observe well.

4. List at least one major thing you can do to help you interpret the text well.

5. When is application easy? When is it hard?

GOD'S BIG PICTURE

God **created** the world
and humans to rule it.

God's world **fell** into sin when
the first man disobeyed.

God promised to **redeem**
His fallen creation.

1.3 THE STORY OF SCRIPTURE: CREATION, FALL, REDEMPTION

Read See Exercise 1.3.
Memorize John 5:39

The Bible tells one story.

Just one.

It's a long story. And it took a lot of little stories to make up the big story. But it's just one story.

And it's not just any story. It is a true story. It involves real people, who had real feelings and emotions, and who really did the things that were written about them.

And the Bible is not just any true story. It is *the* true story of what God is doing to glorify Himself by redeeming His fallen creation. The story has three major parts, all serving one purpose.

Quite a lot of important things are left out of this lesson's little summary of the Bible's one story. However, every story points to Jesus Christ because He stands at the center of God's plan to redeem the world. It's important to add, too, that everything God does for His own glory is also done for the good of His people.

A summary has to be short if it is to be memorable. Every summary will leave something out because it can't be as long as the Bible! But a summary is important because with such a long book, we need something that will help us understand how all the smaller stories in Scrip-ture—Adam, Abraham, Moses, David, Paul—fit into the one big story.

Let's look at the three elements of our summary of Scripture. The first two point toward the last one, and they make a little acronym (like ASAP is for the phrase "**as s**oon **as p**ossible") that you can easily remember—**CFR**.

The Bible Tells One Story

Sometimes an author will be so popular that a number of his works will be collected into one volume. C. S. Lewis's books *The Problem of Pain*, *Mere Christianity*, and *The Great Divorce* are all put together under the title *C. S. Lewis Signature Classics*. Authors of children's books, too, might put many unrelated stories under one cover. But the Old Testament is not like that. It's not just a random set of stories put in no particular order. The books of the Bible can't be separated; they go together. The Old Testament is more like another of C. S. Lewis's series, *The Chronicles of Narnia*. The books come in a certain order, and they all tell one long, glorious story!

1. Creation

God's creation was originally what He called "very good." He created Adam and Eve, the first humans, in His own image and blessed them with the ability to multiply and to subdue the earth (Gen. 1:26–28). But their blessings were also tasks. Their job was to represent God to all of creation by ruling God's world as God would.

2. Fall

But they failed (Gen. 3). They believed the lies of the serpent, and they plunged both themselves and the world they cared for into what the Bible calls "bondage of [slavery to] corruption" (Rom. 8:21). Instead of being by nature submissive to God's rule, all people are now born in rebellion. Even animals suffer and die—and kill. Creation hasn't lost all its goodness, but it groans, waiting to be redeemed, waiting to be restored to the way God meant it to be.

3. Redemption

And creation didn't have to wait long for that redemption to start. God promised Adam and Eve that the "seed of the woman" would one day crush the head of the serpent (Gen 3:15). Good news! God was going to fix what Adam broke.

Abraham. Years later, God chose a certain idol-worshiper named Abraham to be His tool for that fix. The promised seed would come through him, God said. Abraham's family would be big, and they would get a land of their own (Gen. 12, 15, 17).

Israel. Abraham's family became the nation of Israel, God's chosen people. They were meant to do what Adam failed to do: represent God to the rest of creation (Exod. 19:5–6). God (through the prophet Moses) gave them laws to show them what it meant to be holy like He is (Exod. 20). He instructed them to sacrifice animals in order to teach them how seriously their sin offended His perfect holiness (Lev. 1–7).

But the story of God's chosen people is not a story of people getting better and better as they followed God's laws. Instead, they got worse and worse—and better and worse. And worse. They went up and down a lot—but overall, down. Adam's sin had infected them deeply. Even their

Why Study the Old Testament?

The story of Jesus doesn't start in a manger in Bethlehem. It starts long before that, "in the beginning." In fact, Jesus said so.

"Search the scriptures," He told a crowd of Jews. "They . . . testify of me" (John 5:39). And after His resurrection, He met two lone Jews (His disciples) on the road to Emmaus and explained a good deal more about what He meant. The Gospel of Luke says that "beginning at Moses and all the prophets, he expounded unto them in all the scriptures the things concerning himself" (Luke 24:27). He told them everything in "the law of Moses, and in the prophets, and in the psalms" about Himself (Luke 24:44). Every part of the Old Testament points to Christ.

prophets, priests, and kings failed them. They needed something better. Or maybe *Someone.*

David. In fact, Someone better was coming—and He would bring something better! God told one of Israel's kings, David, that someone from his line would sit on Israel's throne forever (2 Sam. 7). And God told one of their prophets, Jeremiah, that He was going to make a new set of promises to the people of Israel. He would write His laws on people's hearts so they wouldn't continue in their cycle of terrible sin (Jer. 31).

Have you ever read a story or seen a movie where one part ended without resolution? As the Old Testament closes, Israel is spiritually destitute, and the prophets are condemning them for their continuing sin. Countless poor decisions have created an air of tension and suspense that longs for a resolution.

But the Old Testament does not provide that resolution. There are still some big unanswered questions. How will God make something good out of Israel's mess? When will He bring David's heir to sit on the throne forever?

The New Testament

The very first words of the New Testament actually answer both questions: "The book of the generation of Jesus Christ" (Matt. 1:1). Jesus Christ

There is one more little piece of information you need to know before you jump into the story of the Old Testament: a lot of the Old Testament is left out of this textbook. You won't read about all the judges in Judges, all the kings in Kings, or all the numberings in Numbers. Not everything Moses and David and other Bible people did will appear in this book.

You may have heard the Jewish word *Tanak*. That's just an acronym that Jewish people use for the **T**orah, **N**eviim, and **K**etuvim: TaNaK.

- *Torah* is the Jewish word for the first five books of our Old Testament, Genesis through Deuteronomy.

- *Neviim* means "prophets," and it contains major and minor prophets (such as Isaiah and Jonah) along with a few history books including Joshua, Judges, Samuel, Kings and so on.

- *Ketuvim* means "writings," and it includes the special books of Job, Psalms, Proverbs, Ecclesiastes, Song of Solomon, and a few others.

Not all the books in the Ketuvim fit exactly in the story line of Scripture. Some of the Ketuvim (Proverbs, for example) aren't stories, but they complete the larger story. In other words, they *complement* the story line of Scripture.

The books of Proverbs and Ecclesiastes teach us about living and dealing with life within the story. The Song of Solomon is about fulfilling the Creation Mandate through marriage, and Lamentations is a counterpart to Jeremiah's prophecies. The book of Psalms likewise complements other books of the Bible such as Samuel and Chronicles. Many of the psalms are poetic expressions of God's acts that are recorded in other books. Some are the expressions of people who were experiencing those events. And there are other psalms that are expressions of thanksgiving or praise for God, His dealings, or His law.

Although some of these books don't exactly fit into the story of Scripture, we wouldn't want to study the Old Testament and leave them out. They show us how life should be lived in a world that God created to run according to His rules. They also show us what to think when the world doesn't seem to be following the rules! So the Ketuvim don't make sense apart from the story of Scripture, and the story is incomplete without them—even if they aren't stories. Special sections on five books (Psalms, Proverbs, Song of Solomon, Ecclesiastes, and Lamentations) from the Ketuvim will show up in this textbook at the points where they fit into the biblical story line. The rest of the Ketuvim have been integrated into the story line of Scripture and will have their own sections.

TORAH
Five Books of Moses

- Genesis
- Exodus
- Leviticus
- Numbers
- Deuteronomy

TaNaK

This is the traditional Jewish outline of what Christians call the Old Testament.

NEVIIM
Prophets

FORMER
- Joshua
- Judges
- Samuel
- Kings

LATTER
- Isaiah
- Jeremiah
- Ezekiel
- Hosea
- Joel
- Amos
- Obadiah
- Jonah
- Micah
- Nahum
- Habakkuk
- Zephaniah
- Haggai
- Zechariah
- Malachi

KETUVIM
Writings

POETIC
- Psalms
- Job
- Proverbs

THE FIVE SCROLLS
- Ruth
- Song of Solomon
- Ecclesiastes
- Lamentations
- Esther

OTHER BOOKS
- Daniel
- Ezra-Nehemiah
- Chronicles

The Kingdom of God

The kingdom of God is a central theme in the Bible. You and I are part of the kingdom of God. He is an eternal king whose reign is both now and in the future. The kingdom of God is often a confusing concept to many Christians. But it shouldn't be. God has chosen to fulfill His purposes through His kingdom. And because of that fact, it is important for you and me to understand what is meant by the phrase, "the kingdom of God."

A simple definition of the kingdom is "Christ's rule or dominion on earth." In Luke 4:21, Jesus read from Isaiah 61 and said that it was fulfilled that very day. But it was fulfilling more than His predicted coming; it also fulfilled His coming as the promised Messianic King. After Jesus ascended to heaven, the kingdom was taken from Israel's oversight and given to the Gentiles until Christ returns. The realm (the kingdom) doesn't cease to exist because the ruler has gone away for a while (Matt. 21:33–46). At His return, Christ will fully establish His kingdom on earth. The first phase of this kingdom will last one thousand years, and the second phase will continue into eternity and will be free from all opposition.

is God's answer! He is the resolution! Where all Israel's leaders and all humanity had failed, Jesus has succeeded. Jesus was a one-time sacrifice that could pay for all sins—unlike the lambs that the Jews had to sacrifice year after year. Jesus, from the line of David, was the great King that Israel needed, the King God promised to David.

Jesus, God in flesh, lived the perfect life no one ever could before. He died for the sins of God's sinful people Israel—and not just for *their* sins, but for the sins of everybody in the whole world.

After Jesus rose from the dead, He sent His Spirit to instruct and comfort His followers as they set up a new gathering of God's people, the church (John 16:1–15; Acts 2). This was the way Jesus chose to spread His rule over Jew and Gentile alike, through local groups of believers who come together to fellowship, pray, eat the Lord's Supper, and learn scriptural doctrine (Acts 2:42).

The New Testament explains and applies Christ's work to God's people. It reveals the Creation-Fall-Redemption story you've just been reading about.

The Future

The New Testament explains that God's people and the rest of creation can look forward to the day when Jesus will completely subdue the earth and have dominion over it (Gen. 1:26–28). Christ will restore His creation to the way He originally designed it to be: Arctic foxes won't steal and eat goose hatchlings. African lions will nestle together with little lambs. Jesus will renew and restore the whole earth, and His people will live under His wise rule in His city—the new Jerusalem—for all eternity (Rev. 21). People will fill the earth and subdue it as God first planned.

At the end of this age, Christ will hand all rule over to the Father, and God will be "all in all" (1 Cor. 15:28). That's where Creation, Fall, and Redemption all point—to God's glory. Your great goal in life, by God's grace, ought to be the same—to point to the glory of God.

The story of the Bible is the story of what God has done to save people like us who, far too often, make mistakes on purpose and are downright mean.

Thinking It Through 1.3

1. What is the three-point outline of the big story of Scripture?

2. According to the lesson, what is the major purpose God has in mind for all He's doing?

3. In one sentence, summarize what the Bible is the true story of.

4. How did God fulfill His promise to David that his heir would sit on the throne forever?

5. True or False. The Bible is a random collection of hundreds of stories for our moral instruction.

1.4 ADAM & EVE: MADE LIKE GOD

Read Genesis 1; Psalm 104
Memorize Genesis 1:26–28

Characters and Stories

The beginning of any story sets the stage for what follows. Often you not only meet the main characters but also find out what conflict is going to move the plot forward. Even Aesop's little fables work that way. The first sentence introduces you to the main characters: the tortoise and the hare. The next sentence tells you the conflict: they're going to race.

The Bible is no different. In the first two chapters, you meet the main characters: God and humanity. You also start finding out the focus of the plot when God tells Adam and Eve what He wants people to do: to fill the earth, subdue it, and have dominion over it. And in the third chapter, you discover the conflict that will drive the rest of the story: man rebels against the God who created him, and God is going to have to fix the world man broke—so that people can go back to doing what God originally wanted them to do.

You will want to pay special attention as you read the first three chapters of Genesis. They're the first stories in the Bible for a reason. They tell us how good things should be and how they got into the bad state they're in now.

The Image of God

It all started out so good. How could it have been any better? Not only did God make a beautiful world full of amazing things, but He paused, talked it over, and decided to create a being like no other. This being would carry His very image. This being—this *human* being—would receive abilities no animal has, abilities given straight from God Himself.

> "Human beings were . . . created with royal dignity and purpose."
>
> —Stephen Dempster

Humans were created to be like God in every way a creature can be. Only God and people (and angels too) can speak. Only God and people can feel complex emotions. Only these two categories of beings can make future plans, write out their thoughts, and invent technology. All the amazing things people can do come from God. That's because they were supposed to be His representatives to all creation. We are small mirrors of God's huge, infinite glory. We are made to be like God.

The Creation Mandate

After God made Adam, Genesis says that "the Lord God took the man, and put him into the garden of Eden to dress it and to keep it" (Gen. 2:15). The Garden of Eden needed to be "dressed." It was a little bit like you are in the morning before *you* get dressed. It needed to be put in order instead of left looking wild. Adam hadn't even had his first birthday yet and had never gone to school, but he already had a job.

But Adam and Eve's job was not limited to the garden. The verses you are memorizing for this section (Gen. 1:26–28) are very important because they show two big things about God's purposes for humanity:

1. People were (and are) supposed to fill the earth. Adam and Eve's descendants, at least, were supposed to spread out beyond the Garden of Eden and start to maximize its potential.

2. People were (and are) supposed to work. Work is something that God invented long before Adam and Eve fell into sin. God told them to subdue the earth and have dominion over it. And that takes work. To subdue your plot of ground and make it grow crops takes work. To build a road so farmers can get their crops to market takes work. To build a bridge for that road takes more work.

Work is a good thing, not a curse. It's a gift from God that gives purpose to our lives on this earth. To work any honest job is a good, God-pleasing thing. It's not only preachers and missionaries who are working for God. As Paul told the Colossians many years after Adam,

"Whatsoever ye do, do it heartily, as to the Lord, and not unto men" (Col. 3:23).

Whatever jobs your parents have (writing, mothering, building—whatever), they're fulfilling the purpose God programmed into Adam and Eve. And any job you take on (mowing, babysitting, waiting tables—whatever), you'll be doing the same. You'll be taking dominion over some small piece of this world just as God intended you to. We call God's command to subdue the earth and have dominion over it the Creation Mandate.

"After many thousands of years of accumulating human culture, the world we must make something of…is largely the world others before us have made."

—Andy Crouch

It's helpful to think of the Creation Mandate like this: We are supposed to make something of our world. God gave us this world, but He doesn't want us to leave it just the way it is. Our job is to make it more and more useful and enjoyable for the humans who are filling it. That may mean leaving some of the world as it is—like the beautiful, untouched wilderness of a national park. But it may mean changing things a lot—like digging a canal to connect the Atlantic and Pacific Oceans (that's what the Panama Canal does, for example). Canal builders are making something of their world.

The Image of God the Creator

One person who made something of his world and became famous for it was playwright William Shakespeare. His plays are widely thought to be the best literature the English language has to offer, and they're still performed all over the world all the time. His work helps people make something of their world in another sense—he helps them understand the way humans act. Shakespeare used his God-given gift of creativity in a way that has changed the world.

Shakespeare wrote approximately thirty-eight plays, and there's a famous and interesting thought experiment using those plays. Imagine, said one scientist, that a huge number of monkeys all sat typing randomly on keyboards for a huge amount of time. Eventually, he said, they might produce the entire works of Shakespeare.

Some scientists tried this with a few Sulawesi Crested Macaques, but the monkeys didn't get off to a very good start. They produced five pages consisting mostly of the letter S. Then, to spice things up at the climax of their play, they added about twenty-five lines of the letter Q.

After that, they started beating the keyboard with a rock. They had writer's block, apparently.

It's clear that even given an infinite amount of time and an infinite number of monkeys, no monkey or group of monkeys will ever write a play. But people disagree over why that is. Annalee Newitz, an American journalist and research fellow at Massachusetts Institute of Technology, thinks that the difference between monkeys and people is all in the minds of people.

The real question we should be asking ourselves is what we gain by claiming that humans are not animals. Does our special

Each worker is taking dominion over a small piece of the world.

status make us seem more powerful than we are? Does it make our lives more meaningful? Does is allow us to justify our behavior toward other life forms? . . . Ultimately, the only animals who buy the idea that humans aren't animals are humans themselves.

But the Bible paints a very different picture. The reason humans can create works of incredible beauty and monkeys can't is that creativity is an aspect of the image of God. The main thing God does in the first chapters of Genesis is create. So when He says in Genesis 1 that the male and female are made in His image, creativity is part of what that means.

Conclusion

Let's put this section together: God made human beings in His image. That means people have incredible power of thinking, feeling, and even creating. And we are supposed to use those powers to rule God's world as His representatives. We are supposed to make something of the world God has given us. That's a big blessing because this world is so full of joys. But it's also a big task because this is a big world.

You have God's image woven into the fabric of your being. And among the many things you are learning in school is how to make something out of God's world. You're learning to understand it and, one day, shape it by being an engineer or a homemaker—or any of a thousand other things.

Thinking It Through 1.4

1. Who are the main characters in the story of Scripture?

2. What does the main plot of the biblical story focus on?

3. What is the conflict that drives the rest of the biblical story?

4. Why did God create humans in His own image?

5. What are the two parts of the Creation Mandate?

1.5 ADAM & EVE: FALLEN, GRACED

Read Genesis 2:8–9, 15–17; 3:1–19
Memorize Genesis 3:15

Stories and Conflict

Just about every good story features a conflict that gets resolved in the end. Movies are often like that.

In the movie *McFarland, USA,* which is based on a true story, an all-Latino cross-country track team must overcome multiple conflicts throughout their season. Their school doesn't have enough money to adequately support a track team. The track members struggle to come to practice because of their jobs in the fields. They're physically smaller than their competitors. And if all that's not enough, the powers that be don't like the Latino kids winning the races. There is a lot of conflict in this story, and it is intense. But in the end, many of the conflicts are resolved.

Conflicts are sometimes painful to watch or read, but conflict is what drives a story and makes it interesting. And this example is just one story in which conflicts had to be resolved. Millions more stories can be found in books, movies, radio shows, and folk tales—and in real life. Storytelling is something humans do because they are made to be creators, like God. And they tell stories with conflict in them because they live in a world with conflict in it. There are disagreements, fights, even world wars.

Even the people who believe that we all evolved from nothing and are evolving toward nothing—even those people yearn for conflicts to end. They want peace. They want things to be fixed. So they tell stories in which that happens.

But if peace is what we all want (or say we want), why don't we have it?

Answers

A lot of people have given a lot of different answers to that question. It's the Democrats. It's the Republicans. It's the Communists. Or it's lack of education. It's poverty. It's the tensions between different social classes.

Those are (mostly) recent answers. Ancient people blamed jealous gods or some being in between the level of the gods and the level of people. Or they just said that good and evil are equal forces always striving for balance—sort of like the Force in the *Star Wars* movies.

The Bible has a definite answer for where human sin and conflict began: Adam and Eve. (It doesn't necessarily explain how the serpent became sinful—that's another story.) God told Adam and Eve that there was just one tree off limits to them, that eating from it would bring certain death. But the serpent tempted Eve: "Did God really say that? He just doesn't want you to be divine like He is . . ."

Eve's reasons for disobeying God sound so good: she saw that the tree was good for food, that it delighted her eyes, and that it could make her wise (Gen. 3:6). Those are all good things. Sin is the twisting and bending of good things so that they're pointing in the wrong direction. For Eve, that meant that the "wisdom" she was

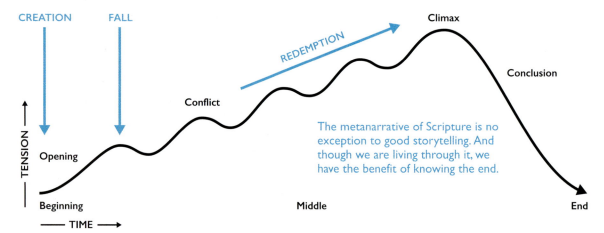

The metanarrative of Scripture is no exception to good storytelling. And though we are living through it, we have the benefit of knowing the end.

CREATION MANDATE	CURSES
FILL THE EARTH + WORK THE EARTH	PAIN + DIFFICULTY + DEATH

pursuing was one that didn't start with the fear of God. She was striking off on her own path.

Adam's first sin after eating from the tree is similar. He managed to twist a good thing: the truth. All his statements to God were true: "The woman whom thou gavest to be with me, she gave me of the tree, and I did eat" (Gen. 3:12). But these words all add up to a truth-twisting lie. Basically, Adam is blaming everybody but himself. It's the woman's fault for giving him the fruit. And ultimately, it's God's fault for giving him the woman.

But do you understand God's *response* to what Adam and Eve did? He responded in two ways: with curses and promises. These curses and promises are still in effect today, and they shape our world.

> "Ever since God made man in His own image, man has been trying to return the compliment."
>
> —Voltaire

Curses

When you really love someone, you do whatever you can to keep that person from being hurt, even if that means hurting that person in the short term. That's why your parents make you get shots. That's why they have disciplined you. That's why they've kept you from hanging out with certain friends, watching certain TV shows, or going to certain websites. It hurts to not be doing what the cool kids are doing, but your parents are only trying to help you avoid far greater harm.

When Adam and Eve violated the only rule in the whole world, God's response was loving, but it was also negative—and quick and firm.

We'll skip what God said to the serpent for a second, but think about what He said to Eve:
- You'll have great pain in childbirth.
- You'll have a desire to dominate your husband.
- But he will be the one who dominates you.

Eve's sin brought pain into the central relationships of a woman's life, her husband and her children. God's command and invitation to "be fruitful and multiply" would be difficult to carry out, all because of Eve's sin.

And think about what God said to Adam:
- The ground is cursed because of you.
- You'll have to work very hard to get food out of the ground.
- You will one day return to the dust from which you came.

Just like Eve's sin made it harder for her to do what God designed her to do, Adam's sin made it harder for him to subdue the earth and have dominion over it. The Fall makes bearing children and ruling the earth frustrating and difficult in ways they wouldn't be otherwise.

The New Testament reveals that Adam's fall did even worse things. It put the whole creation

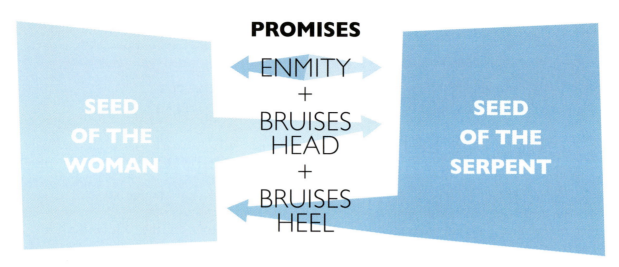

PROMISES

SEED OF THE WOMAN

ENMITY
+
BRUISES HEAD
+
BRUISES HEEL

SEED OF THE SERPENT

under slavery, slavery to corruption (Rom 8:20–21). People and animals get sick and die. Terrible accidents happen. Floods and hurricanes sweep life away in an instant. Things rot. Harmful bacteria and mold grow in unexpected places. Mosquitoes and roaches play around in people's houses and on their skin. It's very important—and very sad—to see that Adam's fall has touched every part of God's good creation.

The serpent, of course, got his own curses: God cursed him above all other animals and forced him to crawl on his belly.

Promises

But notice something. Even though we just looked at the curses that fell on Adam and Eve and all creation, the first thing God said to His image-bearers was actually a precious divine promise. This is one of those extremely import-

Seed and Offspring

Some translations of the Bible use the word *seed* in passages like Genesis 3:15. Some use the word *offspring*. Both terms have the advantage of being either singular or plural. You can say, "Hey, give me the last sunflower seed!"—that's singular. Or you can say, "I planted sunflower seed in my garden this year." That's plural because you're not just talking about one seed. Hopefully you planted more than one!

The same is true of the word *offspring*. It can be singular or plural. Your parents probably don't use that word to describe you unless they're trying to be a little funny. But if you're an only child, they can tell someone, "This is our offspring." Or if you're one of several children, they can say, "These are our offspring." Same word, but one use is singular, and the other is plural.

To make things even more interesting, *seed* and *offspring* can refer to an immediate descendant or a much later one—or a large group of later descendants. So think of your great-

great-great grandfather. You are his seed. So are lots of your cousins and aunts and uncles and people you've never met. And so was each of his children. The word *seed* is flexible.

All this is important because God used an ambiguous word—one that could mean either singular or plural, soon or much later—on purpose. There are good reasons for that choice, but you'll have to keep reading to find out what they are!

The word *seed* can refer to a whole pile of seed (plural) or to one seed (singular).

ant verses in Scripture that you can't afford to miss. It tells us what God is going to do throughout the rest of the Bible. And it points to Someone important—if you're paying attention.

Read again what God said to the serpent in Genesis 3:15:

> I will put enmity between thee and the woman,
>   and between thy seed and her seed;
> it shall bruise thy head,
>   and thou shalt bruise his heel.

This verse is often called the *protevangelium*. *Prot-* means "first," and *evangelium* means "gospel." This is the first mention of the gospel, the good news that Someone will come and fix what Adam and Eve broke so badly. Eve (and Adam) loved the vision the serpent created more than they loved God. And God's first promise is that He will make their relationship hostile again. That's a good thing. People should have "enmity" with the serpent.

But there's more. There's a hint of Jesus Himself. Did you catch it? Where do you see Him in this promise? Jesus is in the words *her seed*. God is saying that there will be a great conflict down through time between the seed of the woman and the seed of the serpent—between those who love God and those who do not. The seed of the serpent will injure the seed of the woman, no doubt. He will strike the heel of the seed of the woman. But the seed of the woman will do better: He will strike the serpent's head. A crushed heel is painful. A crushed head is fatal.

Satan, God says, will have access to the world. He'll fight against the seed of the woman down through the ages, and he will sometimes seem to be winning. But God promises that in the end the seed of the woman will win and the serpent will lie crushed before Him.

The Seed and the Story of Scripture

Jesus is in those words in Genesis 3:15 because Jesus is the one who will be bruised—on the cross—but will ultimately triumph over the serpent. But Adam and Eve didn't know all those details. For all they knew, the seed would come very soon.

If you were reading the Bible for the first time, you wouldn't know who the seed was either. You would probably catch a hint of His coming if you were paying attention, but you wouldn't know who He was. Try to read the story of Scripture as if you don't quite know what's going to happen.

Conclusion

We've looked at only three chapters of the Bible so far, and we've already hit all three points of the story of Scripture: Creation, Fall, and Redemption. You already read the most foundational things the Bible has to say about the creation of the world. You also read the most important passage on the Fall, the one describing how it happened and what resulted.

And you've read the first line out of the rest of the story, the story of Redemption. That's the story that flows through the rest of Scripture. God spends a great deal of time slowly but surely bringing Redemption to this broken world, and we're going to read a lot of the rest of that story.

Thinking It Through 1.5

1. Where did the root problem of all human conflict begin?

2. Describe what sin is or does according to the textbook's evaluation of Adam and Eve's actions and response to God.

3. According to the New Testament, why did Adam's fall result in worse consequences than Eve's? (1 Tim. 2:14; Rom. 8:20–21)

4. What was God's first promise of the gospel? Give the key Scripture reference.

5. Summarize the curses given to Eve and the curses given to Adam. How do those curses relate to the Creation Mandate?

1.6 CAIN: THE SEED OF THE SERPENT

Read Genesis 4
Memorize Genesis 4:7

What's That?

Some people are more inquisitive than others. But we all have been through the stage where we ask lots of questions. Perhaps you have a younger sibling or cousin who is always asking you a question. Some kids are in the "What's that?" stage. It seems that they constantly are asking you about everything you touch.

Some kids are in the "Why?" stage, always asking "Why?" to everything you say.

"Why is the grass green?"

"Because God made it green."

"Why did God make it green?"

"I guess because He likes green."

"Why does He like green?"

And it goes on and on.

And we all ask, "Why do kids ask *why* so much!" Well, they ask these types of questions because they don't know as much as we do. But they do know one thing: they know how to learn. They don't care if anyone else thinks they're dumb. They know they don't know big words or why things are the way they are, so they learn by asking lots and lots of questions.

Bible Reading Questions

Whenever you read in the Bible, you should ask a few questions first: Who wrote this? Who did he write it for? When did he write it? And why did he write it? For a narrative, you should ask another question: When did this happen?

For Genesis 4 and the account of Cain and Abel the answers are pretty easy:

• Moses wrote the book.
• He wrote it for God's people—particularly to help them understand who they were and where they came from.
• He probably wrote it while he was leading the Israelites from Egypt to the Promised Land.
• Cain, however, lived much earlier, and the events recorded in Genesis 4 took place near the beginning of the world—long before Moses' time.

There's one more question, though, that a lot of Bible readers fail to ask about accounts like the Cain-and-Abel incident: "Why is this here?" Sure, it's here because it happened. But a lot of other things happened that didn't get put into the Bible. In fact, most things that ever happened in the history of the world didn't make it in. They fell on the cutting room floor. So why did this story get chosen? What was so important about it that God determined it had to be told?

Context

The first step in answering the question of why something is included in Scripture is to think about the *context*. The context is what surrounds a passage. For the account of Cain, the description of Adam and Eve's fall comes before it in the context, and the story of Noah comes after it.

Two Bible Reading Hints

1. Some Bibles provide headings for paragraphs or sections within a Bible story. This feature is a valuable tool that can help you in your reading. You can use the headings—the bold or italicized words at the top of certain paragraphs—and get a quick idea of what you're about to read. It's simple. Above the paragraphs making up Genesis chapter 4, there's a heading in most Bibles that says, "Cain and Abel." By reading the headings over several pages, you can get a map showing you an overview of the Bible's story. It's like seeing a long hiking trail from far above in a helicopter before you get on the ground and hike it.

2. A good study Bible will also help you read the Bible better because it provides many notes meant to help you on the journey. Don't skip the introductions your study Bible gives to each book in Scripture! Those introductions will tell you the answers to the questions, "Who wrote this?," "To whom did he write it?," and "When did it happen?" Several good study Bibles are also available online.

And that ought to tell us something about the story of Cain. God places this story right after the one in which He shows Adam and Eve the consequences of their sin. Adam will have to sweat a lot to work the ground. Eve will have to endure great pain to give birth. And neither of them will be allowed back into Eden; it will be guarded by an angel.

But a burning question hangs in the air like the cherub's sword: Who will this promised "seed of the woman" be? Who is it that will crush the accursed serpent's head? You'd think it would be the woman's first child, Cain. But is it? Is Cain the seed of the woman?

Without context, we do not have a clear picture of what is happening.

The story of Cain and Abel gives a one-word answer to that question—no. He proves by his murderous anger that he's from the seed of the *serpent*, not the promised seed of the woman. And, sadly, in the first clash between the seeds, it's the seed of the woman who is crushed. The seed of the serpent just gets a mark.

The Story of Cain and Abel

So the story of Cain shows us how Adam's fall affected all his descendants—people God made to have dominion over His precious creation. It shows the beginning of a conflict between the two seeds: the seed of the woman and the seed of the serpent.

It's not a very pretty story.

But it's a pretty simple one. Cain and Abel made sacrifices to God. God was pleased with Abel, but not with Cain. Cain got mad. God rebuked him. But Cain wouldn't submit. His anger spilled out through his hands and onto his brother's throat, and Abel's blood spilled out onto the ground.

Cain didn't die, however. God let him live. And he ended up fathering many children and even founding a city.

The blessing and task of making something of this world didn't stop with Cain. The Creation Mandate worked itself out in his children. They invented livestock-herding, musical instruments, and metallurgy. They were doing just what God said to do, really. They were filling the earth and subduing it even if they didn't realize they were following God's plan. Remember, the mandate is a *blessing*, too. God programmed it into humanity. We can't help doing it.

"Am I my brother's keeper?"

—Cain

It's doubtful that Cain's children obeyed God on purpose because Cain's sinfulness—which he inherited from his parents—spread to his children. Cain "went out from the presence of the Lord" (Gen. 4:16), and the result was that his great-great grandson Lamech was a boastful, vengeful killer. There was (and still is) good in humanity because each person is made in the image of a good God. But Cain and his line started to show how deeply the human race is infected by sin.

The Promised Seed?

Eve, of course, must have been heartbroken over the first murder in the history of the world. She had the knowledge of good and evil; she knew that her sin was what made her the first grieving mother.

Context helps us understand the bigger picture.

But she still had a hope: maybe another son would take the place of Abel. And maybe that son would be the seed God had promised. That's exactly what she implied toward the end of Genesis 4 when she named Seth. Did you notice it? Cain wasn't the answer. Eve knew that. And it was too late for Abel. But maybe another son could fix this mess.

The Seed and You

The sinful mess Adam and Eve created is still with us. And so is the task and blessing of being God's representatives on earth. One major thing has changed, however. The seed that Eve was waiting for *has come*. And He stands at the center of the whole Bible.

But you won't care about what He did to fix Adam's sinful mess unless you agree that it's a mess, and a mess that touches *you*. Does the world sometimes seem unfair to you? Does your own body sometimes fail to work (or look!) the way it should? Do other people fail you, sin against you? Most importantly, don't you fall far short of the righteous person Scripture and your conscience tell you to be?

The story of Cain doesn't provide the solution, but the story of the Bible does.

Keep reading.

The Way of Cain

Turn on the news any time of the day or night, and you'll see sin—probably big sin. You'll see important politicians who have cheated on their wives or people who have stolen millions from their employers. You might even see the results of mass murder in some foreign country (or, through abortion, in the United States).

But most sins don't make the news. The sad truth about how sinful mankind is was probably on display in your own home this very morning. Did anyone do anything selfish? Did anyone hog the bathroom? Did anyone eat the last bit of someone else's favorite cereal? Did anyone say anything that was less than kind? Or is your family that perfect family, like the ones on really old TV shows?

The seed of the serpent is alive and well in our fallen world. The effects of the Fall haven't gotten any better over time. They worm their way into every part of life.

Thinking It Through 1.6

1. Define *context*.

2. How do we know that Cain isn't the promised seed of the woman? (Gen. 3:15)

3. How did Cain respond to God's rebuke of his sacrifice?

4. What are some ways that people in Genesis 4 worked out the Creation Mandate?

5. The seed of the serpent and the seed of the woman had serious conflict in Genesis 4, and the seed of the woman lost. What does this imply about the fulfillment of God's promise in Genesis 3:15?

1.7 NOAH: GOD'S COVENANT WITH ALL MANKIND

Read Genesis 5:29–9:17
Memorize Genesis 6:5

Many movies have tried to tell the story of Noah and the ark. It seems that each new movie about Noah is based more on the director's imagination than on the Bible. In fact, some renditions are so radical that it is difficult to recognize anything from the Bible other than a character named Noah, the ark, and the water.

Authors of children's books sometimes make similar mistakes in retelling the story. Usually their error is not in straying far from the Bible; rather, it's in their way of presenting the story. They romanticize it. In other words, they make it seem more appealing than it really was. Many also seem to focus too much on one aspect of the story or fail to tell the entire story.

The story of Noah is more than a story of how eight people survived the Flood along with a bunch of animals. The story is about God's judgment on the wickedness of man, which had become so great throughout the earth that "every imagination of the thoughts of his heart was only evil continually" (Gen. 6:5). In other words, even when people did "good," their intentions were always evil.

God's judgment of evil does not generate a pretty picture. We can only imagine the death and destruction that happened during the Flood. People drowned. Animals drowned. Buildings were destroyed. The earth sank down and mountains rose up. It was total destruction, and the repugnant smell of death and decay must have saturated the air.

But the story of judgment also boldly displays God's mercy—His steadfast love. The wickedness of humanity grieved the heart of the Lord, and the Lord was going to blot out humanity from the face of the earth. "But Noah found grace in the eyes of the Lord" (Gen. 6:8).

God's mercy was not something unique. As you progress through the Old Testament, many times you will see God send judgment upon His people, but you will always see Him give mercy to a remnant. He does this because He has steadfast love for His people.

Human Sin Reaches an Early Climax

Noah's ark is not a pleasant story because the depths of human sin aren't pleasant. They are repulsive. Humanity in Noah's day got so bad that anyone with eyes could see it. But God has eyes like no one else, and He saw deeper. He knew that sin had wormed its way down into every crack in the soul. He looked into mankind and knew that "every imagination of the thoughts of his heart was only evil continually" (Gen. 6:5). These people, still bearing the image of God, were incapable of good.

God Kills All on Earth Except One Family

But the Bible says that one man was different. "Noah found grace in the eyes of the Lord" (Gen. 6:8). It's worth pausing for a second to think about what that might mean. The Bible makes it very clear that people are responsible to choose to do right. And Noah apparently did. The next verses say that Noah "walked with God," meaning that he was righteous and blameless. So did Noah "earn" his salvation from the Flood?

> "[The world] God decided to destroy . . . had been virtually self-destroyed already."
>
> —Derek Kidner

Not exactly. The Bible does present God's choice of Noah as a response to Noah's righteousness. (See Ezekiel 14:14 and 20 if you want to do a little research on this question.) But where did Noah get that righteousness in the first place?

If the Bible is the story of what God is doing to glorify Himself by redeeming His fallen creation, then Noah can't take over the hero spot from God. Noah's goodness wasn't something he came up with independently. It's not as if the Fall had skipped over Noah and he was sinless. No, Noah needed redeeming just like all the rest of God's fallen creation. Hebrews 11:7 says it was "by faith" that Noah saved his household and that he "became heir of the righteousness which is by faith." You can only get righteousness—a right relationship with God—by faith, and Noah was no exception.

In any case, the rest of the world didn't receive God's righteousness through faith. We're not even told if Noah's wife and sons received that gracious gift from God. And don't miss what the Flood was all about: God killed everyone on the whole earth, animals included. That's how seriously God takes sin. Sooner or later—sooner for the people in Noah's world—sin brings death.

The Flood was kind of like God cleaning up the whole world and then re-creating it.

God Makes a Covenant with Noah and the Whole Earth

There's a powerful prayer in the little book written by the prophet Habakkuk: "O Lord, . . . in wrath remember mercy!" (Hab. 3:2). Though those words were prayed long after Noah, they describe exactly what God did in Noah's day. He spent His wrath; then He quickly turned to mercy, and creation began to return to normal.

He smelled the pleasing aroma of Noah's sacrifice and determined that He would not add to the curse He had already put on the soil. He said He would never kill every living creature again with a flood. He would let the seasons and the normal astronomical cycles of day and night continue.

Take a look at the words God used to promise these things: "I will establish my covenant with you" (Gen. 9:11). God calls these promises a *covenant*. And the story of Noah is the first place in the Bible where we see that very important word.

God's covenant with Noah (and humanity) made the earth a stable place for God to work out the plan of redemption. Without it, the earth would be facing one catastrophic judgment after another for sin.

God still has covenants with humanity, and this covenant is still in force. We'll learn a lot more about covenants as the story of the Old Testament goes on.

God Repeats the Creation Mandate

The reason the story of the Bible sort of restarts in the account of Noah is made clear by the other things God said after the Flood. He repeats the Creation Mandate that He gave to Adam and Eve. "Be fruitful, and multiply, and replenish the earth" (Gen. 9:1).

God intended for Noah and his seed to carry on the same tasks He had given to Adam and his. And because we are Noah's offspring, these tasks are our tasks as well. God added just one major difference. Adam's dominion didn't include the right to kill and eat animals; Noah's dominion did, as does ours. "Every moving thing that liveth shall be meat for you" (Gen. 9:3). We have every reason to take good care of animals and use them to help us do our work; there's nothing in here that justifies cruelty to God's creations. But we are allowed to eat them.

Noah Repeats the Pattern of Human Sin

God sent Noah away to start carrying out these plans for God's world. And they all lived happily ever after. The End.

Or is it? You might think that we have finally reached the seed of the woman who will crush the serpent's head. All the wicked people in the world are dead, and one righteous man and his family are left. Is Noah the seed of the woman God promised in Genesis 3:15?

To answer that question, we have to notice one other big difference between the children's version of the Noah's ark story and the biblical version. God doesn't put "The End" where a lot of children's Noah's ark storybooks put "The End."

After Noah and his family exit the boat, Noah plants a vineyard, harvests grapes, and makes wine. Later he gets drunk on the wine, falls asleep without his clothes on, and then curses the son of the one who saw him in that condition. It's *sordid*—that means just dirty and gross. It's kind of hard to put something like that in a children's storybook.

But it's an absolutely essential part of the story. This little incident stands at the end of the Noah account to show that the effects of sin were not wiped out by the worldwide Flood. Humanity didn't live happily ever after. Sin reared its ugly head immediately and began to infect God's world again. The ark carried all the kinds of animals and eight people from the world before the Flood to the world after. It also carried human sin.

Starting Over from Scratch with the Creation Mandate?

Genesis 4, which we studied in the last section, said that Cain's descendants became the "fathers" of all those who worked metal, herded livestock, and made musical instruments (Gen. 4:20–22). Apparently, Noah and his sons carried that knowledge with them from the time before the Flood and transferred it to people that came from them afterward. Shem, Ham, and Japheth all, naturally, became the fathers of many nations. Nations like us!

Thinking It Through 1.7

1. What two major themes about God's response to humans does the story of Noah and the ark display?

2. What motivated God to destroy the world with a flood?

3. Did God ever take away the Creation Mandate?

4. How did Noah obtain his righteousness?

5. What does the sordid account of Noah show to be true about humanity even after the Flood?

1.8 JOB: SINCERE FAITH & GOD'S SOVEREIGNTY

Read Job 1–2
Memorize Job 28:28

The Story of Job

Job is the story of a blameless man attacked by Satan—with God's permission! While Job is happily going about his God-pleasing life, Satan goes to God and accuses Job of loving God only because he gets good stuff out of Him. Did you catch the implied meaning of Satan's accusation? He claims Job's faith is insincere because it's bought—God is buying Job's worship. In essence, Satan is putting God on trial!

Integrity: God Is Genuine

So God lets Satan tempt Job in order to show that Job has sincere faith and that God has integrity. In an instant, all Job's riches are gone, and he loses his ten children. Then God lets Satan take away Job's health, leaving him with scratchy sores everywhere. Job's wife tells him to curse God and die, but he refuses. Four of his friends come to comfort him, only they don't provide much comfort. Three of them wrongly accuse Job, and one points to Job's real problem.

In the end of Job's story . . . Well, wait a minute for that.

We Don't Know as Much as We Think We Do

There's a lot we don't know about the book of Job. We don't know when it was that Job, the richest man in the East, suffered through the terrible trials described in the book that bears his name. We don't even know when the story of Job was written down. Since the book doesn't mention the Jews, and since Job makes sacrifices for his family like a priest, it seems as if his story may have taken place around the time of Abraham or even before. But we still don't really know.

There are some far more important things than these that we don't know, and the book of Job is in the Bible to tell us we don't know them. Job's story shows us that we simply don't know why, in any given case, God allows the innocent to suffer. Job is one of the few cases in world history (another being that of Jesus) in which we *do*

know why the innocent suffered. But Job himself didn't know. He was totally unaware of Satan's conversation with God. He suffered in innocence and ignorance. He and his friends thought they knew the whole picture, but they didn't know as much as they thought they did.

If you live long enough, you will suffer pain. And you'll watch it closely in others' lives. That can be even worse than suffering yourself. Sometimes you'll suffer because you did wrong. You might bend the rules at school and lose your privileges to hang out with friends. But sometimes you and your loved ones will suffer in a way that just doesn't seem fair. "God, my grandmother loves you more than anyone else I know, and she works harder for you than anyone! How could you possibly give her cancer when there are so many nasty people out there who deserve it?!" Or maybe you'll be the one who gets cancer. Or your tiny baby brother. This is the way our fallen world is. And like Job, we won't always know why someone is suffering.

Misunderstanding Suffering

But Job's friends, Eliphaz, Bildad, and Zophar, thought they knew for certain why people suffer: it's because they do bad things. And they were certain why Job was suffering: same reason. Job's friends followed a simple, uncomplicated logic. They reasoned that good things happen to those who are righteous, and bad things happen to those who are evildoers. So, they looked at Job and reasoned:

1. All suffering is the result of sin.
2. Job is suffering.
3. Therefore, Job's suffering is a result of sin.

The second point was a simple and obvious fact. Quite true. But Job's friends have made a logical error. Do you know what it is? They assumed that *all* suffering is a result of sin. It is true that sin results in suffering, but it is not true that suffering is always a result of sin. They did not even consider that there could be other reasons for suffering. They were wrong in their reasoning. Evildoers aren't the only ones in God's world who suffer.

That's a relief, right? "Phew . . . it's nice to know God isn't getting me back. That's not why I have this cancer. I don't have to feel guilty in addition to feeling physical pain."

Or is it a relief? You might start to think, "Well, if I didn't deserve this cancer, why in the world would God put me through so much pain?" A lot of people in our world refuse to believe that God could have any good reason for handing out pain and death like cancer. They want to say that God simply must not be powerful enough to stop suffering.

Elihu—a Voice of Reason

Not all of Job's friends were so rash in their thinking. Elihu, Job's fourth friend, had a passion for God. Elihu's arguments may have weaknesses, but, overall, he seeks to defend God's reputation. In fact, he burned with anger at Job because Job "justified himself rather than God" (32:2). This was Job's real problem.

Elihu was the youngest of the four men, but he was a good listener. Not only did he hear what the others had said, but he also gave them his attention and thought through what they were saying. Elihu actually quotes Job's words back to him and corrects him.

Job says, "I don't deserve this" (33:8).

Elihu responds, "God is greater than anybody. He alone is sovereign" (33:12–13).

Job says, "God is unjust in how He is treating me" (34:5–9).

Elihu responds, "God is always just" (34:10–12).

Job says, "I know that I am righteous" (35:2–3).

Elihu responds, "God is the one who is righteous" (35:4–16; 36:2–3; 37:23).

Job says, "God treats me like an enemy and is cruel to me" (33:10–11).

Elihu responds, "God is good" (36:22–23).

Each time Elihu responds, he defends God and shows that Job has spoken foolishly. Elihu also argues that suffering is not always the result of sin. It could be for other reasons. In his defense of God, he is unlike the three friends

who claimed that Job must have sinned since he is suffering.

The God of Job

The God of the book of Job is a God who rules this world so completely that even Satan can't do anything without His permission. God could have stopped Job's suffering at any point; He did so at the end of the book, in fact, and He restored all of Job's fortunes.

But before that, He had a few things to ask Job:

Where were you when I made this world? Have you ever walked on the bottom of the ocean? Can you feed all the animals? Did you design birds to be able to fly? Can you make it rain?

For four chapters God keeps throwing challenging questions at Job. Job answers them all correctly—by shutting his mouth. God allowed Job to ask questions. The Great King of the Universe didn't blame Job for crying out to Him in anguish or for asking Him hard questions about why evil things happened to him. But in the end, Job still had to sit silently and humbly before the only one with the answers.

Was God being cruel to Job in his misery? God's biggest answer for suffering people seems to be, "Trust Me. I'm powerful, and I'm good—in ways no human could ever be." God had good purposes behind Job's suffering. One of them was to help people who are suffering today.

Many people do look at the suffering of innocents in the world and refuse to believe that God is good. But if God is big enough to be blamed for our suffering, He has to be big enough to have reasons for that suffering that we can't know. The King of all the universe doesn't allow us into His courtroom to check up on His decision-making. God isn't required to tell you why your family doesn't have enough money to get the thing it seems you need the most. You may never know until you get to heaven. We've got to trust Him.

Job Alludes to Jesus

Halfway through the book of Job, Job is increasingly frustrated with his "friends." No one seems to listen to him. He wishes that before he dies his words were written in a book, or better yet, that they were written in stone for everyone to read forever (19:23–24). He realizes that he needs someone to act on his behalf. So he says something remarkable—something that points forward to Jesus.

> I know that my redeemer liveth,
> 　and that he shall stand at the latter
> 　　day upon the earth:
> And though after my skin worms
> 　destroy this body,
> 　yet in my flesh shall I see God:
> Whom I shall see for myself,
> 　and mine eyes shall behold, and not
> 　　another;
> Though my reins be consumed within
> 　me. (Job 19:25–27)

Notice his first words. He *knew*. Job was confident that what he was saying was true. He had struggled to believe that he was getting justice on this earth. He knew that his friends weren't giving it to him. But he had confidence that someone, his Redeemer, would act on his behalf and plead his case with God.

Job knew that the Redeemer would vindicate him. He doesn't expect this to happen in his life, but he does expect to see God when he dies. And he confidently expects to be redeemed.

Job never specifically states that this Redeemer is Jesus, Israel's Messiah. But his statements show that the Redeemer is God and that the Redeemer will vindicate him. What Job expected his Redeemer to do for him is exactly what Jesus would one day do for all His people.

Reading the story of Job's life provides us with a perspective that Job didn't have. Job didn't know about God's conversation with Satan, but we do. Job didn't know what Redeemer he was talking about. But we do.

Lessons from Job

You need to be ready for suffering before it comes, but the book of Job is more than a message about how to suffer valiantly. The book is about the relationship between God and people. It is about our faith and God's worthiness. It is about the sovereign God and our trust in Him—even when things are going horribly and life is at its worst. Job says that our days are few and "full of trouble" (14:1), and you and those you love will, unfortunately, face trouble and sorrow within your lifetime. You need to know what the book of Job says about God so you can build your house on the rock before the rains and the floods come. So let's put some lessons from Job together:

Spurgeon on Suffering

The great British preacher Charles Spurgeon saw how hard it would be to live if we didn't believe God was in control of our trials and suffering: "It would be a very sharp and trying experience to me to think that I have an affliction which God never sent me, that the bitter cup was never filled by his hand, that my briars were never measured out by him, nor sent to me by his arrangement of their weight and quality. Oh, that were bitterness indeed! . . . Our heavenly Father fills the cup with loving tenderness, and holds it out, and says, 'Drink, my child; bitter as it is, it is a love-potion which is meant to do thee permanent good.' The discerning of the hand of God is a sweet lesson in the school of experience."

1. God is sovereign and will do as He pleases.

2. God's sovereignty means that He rules over Satan and suffering. He does not send suffering just because He can; He sends it for good purposes.

3. We are ignorant of God's vast ways. We shouldn't think that we know for certain why things happen.

4. Because of our ignorance, we must be careful what we say and how we speak about God during times of suffering.

5. We, like Job, should realize that our only hope is a Redeemer.

Thinking It Through 1.8

1. What two things was Satan challenging?

2. Why did Job's three friends think that Job must have sinned?

3. Why did Elihu believe Job needed to be corrected?

4. What did God intend to prove to Job by His questions?

5. Why was Job confident that he would be vindicated?

UNIT 1 REVIEW

Scripture Memory

Proverbs 16:6	Genesis 3:15
Proverbs 1:7	Genesis 4:7
John 5:39	Genesis 6:5
Genesis 1:26–28	Job 28:28

Understand the Story

1. Summarize four ways in which the Bible is profitable for helping us to be rightly related to God.

2. Explain what application is. Explain why it is sometimes easy and sometimes hard to figure out what the application should be.

3. In one sentence, summarize what the Bible is the true story of.

4. What do we call God's command to fill the earth and to work it?

5. How did the Fall affect both men and women in their abilities to carry out the Creation Mandate?

6. How do we know that Cain isn't the promised seed of the woman? (Gen. 3:15)

7. Look up Genesis 8:20–9:17 in your Bible and list the promises of God's covenant with Noah.

8. True or False. The book of Job is primarily about humanity's trusting relationship with a sovereign God.

Develop Observation Skills

9. List the three steps of the Bible-study method outlined in Section 1.2. Define each step. Explain why the order is important.

10. What are five categories of questions used to gather basic facts about the story?

11. What observation skill would you use to evaluate Satan's statements to Eve in Genesis 3:1–6 about what God said? (cf. Genesis 2:8–9, 15–17)

    a. Look for statements that are alike/unlike.

    b. Look for statements that are emphasized.

    c. Look for statements that are true to life.

    d. Look for statements that are related.

12. Define *context*.

13. Identify one major difference between the Creation Mandate promises in Genesis 9:1–7 and those in Genesis 1:26–30.

14. Why are different approaches or methods of Bible study important?

Connect the Story to the Big Story

15. What conflict will constantly appear in individual Bible stories, driving the conflict of the larger biblical story?

16. How does Genesis 3:15 relate to the big story of Scripture?

17. The seed of the serpent and the seed of the woman had serious conflict in Genesis 4, and the seed of the woman lost. What does this imply about the fulfillment of God's promise in Genesis 3:15?

18. What is the bigger story behind God's allowing Satan to tempt Job?

Lessons for Life

19. Give examples of ways people can take dominion in the world today.

20. Choose one lesson from the book of Job and explain how you could apply it to your own life difficulties.

    a. God is sovereign and will do as He pleases.

    b. God's sovereignty means that He rules over Satan and suffering. He does not send suffering just because He can; He sends it for good purposes.

    c. We are ignorant of God's vast ways. We shouldn't think that we know for certain why things happen.

    d. Because of our ignorance, we must be careful what we say and how we speak about God during times of suffering.

    e. We, like Job, should realize that our only hope is a Redeemer.

UNIT 2

GOD'S COVENANT WITH ABRAHAM

As you read Unit 2, you will see how God is working through particular individuals to bring about His promise of redemption. God chooses Abraham and promises that his seed will bless the world. The story is now about God's fulfilling these promises to Abraham. As the story of Scripture continues, the promised seed is endangered multiple times. And each time, God provides a way for it to continue. When the unit closes, the seed of one individual stands out among all others. His seed is a kingly seed. His brothers' children and even other nations will come and obey this prophesied one.

The seed of the woman would come through the seed of Abraham, Isaac, and Jacob.

2.1 ABRAHAM: CALLED OUT OF IDOLATRY

Read Genesis 12
Memorize Genesis 12:1–3

Before Abram Became Abraham

You know Abraham as the great father of the Jewish nation—or at least you may have heard of him—the one who had kids when he was really old.

But what was he like at his first appearance in Scripture? If you have a good memory, you'll know that he used to have a slightly different name—Abram. You'll know that he was married to his half-sister Sarai—God later changed her name too. You might even remember that he and his father, Terah, came from a place called Ur of the Chaldees.

But what made Abraham so special that God selected him out of all the other people in the city of Ur?

The answer to that question is probably something you don't remember because it's kind of hidden away in a story that happened long after Abraham died. The answer actually comes from Joshua, who led the Israelites into the land God promised Abraham (we'll get there). As an old, battle-hardened leader about to die, Joshua gathered the Israelites together and told them how their story as a nation started:

Thus saith the Lord God of Israel, Your fathers dwelt on the other side of the flood [the Euphrates River] in old time, even Terah, the father of Abraham, and the father of Nachor: **and they served other gods**. (Josh. 24:2)

So what was Abraham doing that got him elected to the job of "father of the Jewish nation"? He wasn't elected because he was running for the office. He was too busy worshiping idols.

There were some people in Abraham's day who worshiped the one true God. Abraham later met one of them—Melchizedek, who not only worshiped the Lord but was a priest and king. We'll talk about this godly man later, but Melchizedek didn't get chosen. Abraham, the idol-worshiper, did. If we are right in guessing that Job lived around the time of Abraham, it's worth noticing that Job and his friends didn't get chosen to be the fathers of God's chosen people either. No, God chose Abraham.

God's Election and God's Promise

What can we learn from this? That God in His grace chooses some people to receive blessings that others don't get and that God in His grace chooses to bless some people who don't deserve it (Exod. 33:19).

We also learn that the gracious promise God gave to Adam and Eve—that the seed of the woman would crush the head of the serpent—is starting to grow into something very real. Genesis traces the seed of the woman through Seth down to Noah, and then from Noah down to Terah, the father of Abraham. Abraham, an idolater, was still in the main line of the seed of the woman. And now Abraham will become the father of the Seed who will fulfill God's promise to Adam and Eve.

> "Once again we learn a principle that operates right through the Bible: God does not choose people on merit."
>
> —Vaughan Roberts

Stop and consider your own life for a minute. Do you deserve the good things you have? Do you deserve a Christian education for which your parents sacrifice their time and money? Do you deserve parents who love you and teach you the ways of God? Think of the many things you have that many take for granted (hopefully you don't)—a home, food, clothes, books, electricity, clean water, and many other things that make daily life more comfortable. A lot of people in the world, about a billion of them, are so poor they can hardly imagine living like you do—even if you don't think of yourself as rich.

You don't have to feel guilty for having the nice things you have or, more importantly, for the spiritual blessings you enjoy. No, you *don't* deserve them. But by God's goodness, you have them. If you're one of His children, it's no surprise that you have so many spiritual blessings in particular. Fathers love to give gifts to their children. If, however, you aren't one of God's children, you should fear. You are either unaware of who has given you all that you have, or worse, you are so focused on what you have that you are an idol-worshiper like Abraham once was. Either way, you're grabbing all your stuff and turning your back on the God who gave it to you.

Take a close look at Abraham if you're in that category. He will show you what to do to get out of it because the Bible calls him "the father of all them that believe" (Rom. 4:11).

The Call of Abraham

We first meet Abraham at the very end of Genesis 11, where we're told that he is a descendant of Noah's son Shem. Abraham soon becomes the main character of Genesis. About 50 percent of the book focuses on him; that figure rises to 80 percent if you include his family.

In the passage of Scripture you read for this lesson, Genesis 12, and in 13:14–18, God made some special promises to Abraham. Did you notice them? There were three main promises. Here's a list (we will start with chapter 13 first):

1. Land: I will give to you and your children all the land that you see (13:14–18).

2. Seed: I will make you into a great nation (12:2).

3. Blessing: I will bless you and make your name great, so that you will be a blessing to all the earth. I will bless those who bless you, and I will curse anyone who dishonors you (12:2–3).

These are easily remembered as *land*, *seed*, and *blessing*.

Wow! Imagine walking down the street in your hometown and all of a sudden getting a visit from God and promises like these! They would seem unbelievable—but not to Abraham. He believed.

> "In Genesis 12 God begins to forge a chain of redemption whose last link will be Jesus."
>
> —Victor P. Hamilton

Liar

But now take a look at the second half of Genesis 12. We just saw Abraham, seventy-five years old, respond in faith to God's command to leave his home and go wherever God told him to go. What a good example! Right?

Abraham
- idolater
- liar
- chosen by God

Isaac
- lied about his wife being his sister
- chosen by God

Jacob
- self-serving
- deceiver
- chosen by God

Judah
- plotted against his brother
- immoral
- chosen by God

Then Abraham, at age seventy-five, goes into the land God shows him and hears God reaffirm His promise. But right after that, Abraham falls. He shows that there is still some idol-worshiper left inside him. He worships the god of his own safety. The Fall's effects didn't end when God appeared to him back in Ur, or even later when he built altars to the Lord. Abraham lies to Pharaoh to protect himself from being killed even though God had promised him he would live (otherwise, how could he have children?). What a bad example Abraham was!

Abraham's bad example should be a reminder to you. The Bible is not a book about heroes. The Bible doesn't create a perfect character, list all of his or her accomplishments, and say, "Be like so-and-so!" No, the Bible is about real people who had real problems. Some of them turned to God for help, and some didn't.

It is unfortunate, but every one of those who turned to God did wrong at some point in life. Each was a sinful human—just like you.

Abraham's success—his wholehearted faith in God—should be a model for you. But his failure—his faithless lie to Pharaoh—should be a comfort. Abraham committed stupid sins sometimes, just like you do. And yet he was still clearly God's child by faith. Just like you?

God chooses idol-worshipers, and He doesn't give up on liars. He simply expects us to respond in faith and obedience. There are many people who claim to be God's children who have serious reason to doubt their own claim. But the existence of sin in your life is not necessarily a sign that you don't know God. God's children in this fallen world do sin, just like Abraham did. The difference is that God's children do not continue in sin. They turn to God, just like Abraham did.

Thinking It Through 2.1

1. Why was Abraham chosen to be the father of the Jewish nation?

2. How will Abraham fulfill the promise that God made to Adam and Eve?

3. State the three promises God gave to Abraham in Genesis 12 in as few words as possible.

4. Why do you think God would include a story of Abraham's failure right after a story of his success?

5. How should the children of God respond when confronted about sin in their lives?

2.2 MELCHIZEDEK: THE LIKENESS OF A GREATER PRIEST

Read Genesis 14
Memorize Psalm 110:4;
Hebrews 7:24–25

When you think of Abraham, what type of person do you picture in your mind? Do you picture an old person with a long white beard, leaning on a staff, barely moving along? Do you think about the fact that he was a great person who was the father of a great nation? If you just look at his name, it points to his greatness—Abram means "exalted father," and Abraham, the new name that God will give him, means "father of a multitude" (Gen. 17:5).

What about a warrior? Do you picture Abraham as a great warrior leading hundreds of men into battle against multiple kings to make a daring rescue of a family member? That one probably didn't cross your mind, did it?

When Abraham (God hadn't changed Abram's name at this point, but to make it easier, we'll refer to him as Abraham) left his home country of Ur to go where God led him, he took along his nephew Lot. Abraham traveled along with Lot, and eventually they ended up in a small place between Bethel and Ai. In fact it was too small for both of their families and flocks to live peacefully. When things got heated between the families and their servants, Abraham decided that for the sake of peace it was best to separate. One would go one way, and the other would go the other way.

Abraham allowed Lot to choose first which way he would go. Lot looked around, found the well-watered land, and settled there. Abraham went the other way and settled. Now the two families could live in peace. Or so they thought.

Lot had not chosen wisely. He had placed his tent near the city of Sodom, and he ended up living in Sodom—where he found himself in the wrong place at the wrong time.

The King Who Picked On the Wrong Guy

Genesis 14 tells about a great king named Chedorlaomer (pronounced KE-dur-LAH-o-mur) who ruled over Elam. He was so great that for twelve years many other kings served him and paid tribute to him. But then in the thirteenth year, they rebelled against him. This of course didn't sit well with Chedorlaomer, and he quickly established an alliance with three other kings. He marched on six different cities and one by one defeated each of them. Then, he turned his armies toward Sodom and the surrounding cities.

Instead of sitting in their cities waiting to be captured, the king of Sodom and four other kings joined together to defend their cities. The five kings and their armies marched out to join in battle against Chedorlaomer in the Valley of Siddim.

But it wasn't much of a battle. Chedorlaomer and his three allies quickly defeated the five kings. Chedorlaomer and his allies continued their march into Sodom where they took captives and all the possessions of Sodom and Gomorrah. And that is where Chedorlaomer made his mistake—he captured Lot, Abraham's nephew.

It didn't take long for one of the captives to escape, find Abraham, and tell him what had happened. Abraham gathered his trained men, 318 of them, and pursued Chedorlaomer and his allies. Abraham wisely divided his forces and attacked the four kings from two angles. Those kings never stood a chance. Abraham and his men defeated them, recovered all the stolen possessions, and rescued those who had been taken as prisoners.

A Blessing and a Tithe

When Abraham returned, the king of Sodom and the king of Salem came out to meet him. Melchizedek, the king of Salem, brought food and drink, and then he blessed Abraham. Abraham responded humbly by giving Melchizedek, the priest of the most high God, a tenth of everything he had recovered.

The king of Sodom offered to let Abraham keep all the material things he had recovered. Abraham refused because he did not want others to say that the king of Sodom had made him rich. Abraham returned those he had rescued and their possessions.

So what?

So, Abraham is also a great warrior who defeated four kings who had defeated numerous cites and armies. What is the significance of this story? Why does God include it in Genesis? How does it fit into the main story of Scripture?

To find the answer we have to go to the book of Hebrews in the New Testament. But the answer has little to do with Abraham and more to do with Melchizedek—or rather, to the one he was "made like."

Who Is Melchizedek?

Before we jump into the Hebrews passage, let's stop and see what we know about Melchizedek. If you go back and read through Genesis 14, you can observe several facts about him. First (and most obvious), you see that his name is Melchizedek. If you were to search for that name in the rest of the Bible, it would appear in several other key passages. Second, he is the king of Salem. If you were to look up Salem in a Bible dictionary, you would find that Salem is eventually called Jerusalem. The third thing you can observe is that Melchizedek is the priest of God Most High. Fourth, you notice that he blessed Abraham. Fifth, you should be aware that Abraham tithed (gave a tenth) of his possessions to him, and that Melchizedek took the tithes. That is all we know from Genesis—five things.

If you search for the word *Melchizedek*, you will find that the name occurs once more in the Old Testament. In Psalm 110:4, the psalmist says that there is one who is "a priest for ever after the order of Melchizedek." The phrase "after the order" simply means that the individual is "in the likeness of" or "patterned after" Melchizedek. So, we know that Melchizedek is a "pattern" for an individual who will be a priest forever.

If you're counting, we now know six things about Melchizedek. And that's it. That is all the Old Testament tells us about him.

In the book of Hebrews, the writer states that he has many things to say about Melchizedek (5:11), and he tells his audience that it is hard to explain because they are "dull of hearing" (they are too lazy to pay attention). Hopefully that doesn't describe you! So, pay attention!

A Symbol of Someone Else
(Hebrews 7:1–3)

Hebrews 7 is an excellent example of how New Testament authors used Scripture to make sense of complex issues. In this case, the author is examining how Christ, who is from the tribe of Judah, could be a priest when the Old Testament is clear that only someone from the tribe of Levi could be a priest (Exod. 29:9). The author chooses to look at Psalm 110:4.

> "The Lord hath sworn, and will not repent, Thou art a priest for ever after the order of Melchizedek."
>
> —Psalm 110:4

Psalm 110:1–7 talks about a great ruler who will sit at the right hand of the Lord. He will rule with a mighty scepter, and he will be a priest in the likeness of Melchizedek. That means that he will be a king who is also a priest.

In Hebrews 7, the author starts by telling us about Melchizedek. He retells the story of how Melchizedek blessed Abraham and received tithes from him. He actually points out a few things that we didn't think about when we read Genesis 14. He tells us that Melchizedek's name means "king of righteousness" and that Salem means "peace"—king of peace (Heb. 7:2).

The author points out that the Old Testament says nothing about Melchizedek's ancestry—not even who his mother and father were. It doesn't mean that he didn't have parents. It just means that the Old Testament doesn't tell us about them. If you flip through the Bible, you will find more than forty genealogies listing hundreds of names, but you will never find anything about Melchizedek. This is especially surprising since he was a king and a priest. Both lines of work were often based on who your parents were. This shows that Melchizedek was not a priest because of his ancestry. He was a priest because he was called of God.

Who Is the Important One?
(Hebrews 7:4–10)

The author moves beyond observing facts about Melchizedek and begins to draw conclusions from the details. He tells us to "consider how great" Melchizedek was (7:4). But he also reminds us of how great Abraham was. Abraham is the patriarch who had the promises given to him. So who is the greater of the two?

Well, Melchizedek blessed Abraham. So who is the greater, the one who blesses or the one who is blessed? Clearly, "the less is blessed of the better" (7:7). In other words, the superior person blesses the inferior person. Melchizedek wins this one.

But something else happened after the blessing—Abraham gave a tithe to Melchizedek. The author makes an interesting point. The only reason the people tithed to the Levites was because the law commanded it (Deut. 14:22; cf. Num. 18:21, 24). But there was no law requiring Abraham to give Melchizedek tithes, yet he did. Melchizedek wins this one too.

So Melchizedek is greater than Abraham. What difference does that make? Well, if Melchizedek is greater than Abraham, then he is logically greater than Abraham's descendants.

And that includes the Levites who were the only ones who could be priests in Israel. If Abraham paid tithes to Melchizedek, then in a sense, Abraham's children (the Levites) who were not yet born ("yet in the loins of his father," 7:10) also tithed to Melchizedek. So we know Melchizedek is greater than the Levites.

What's the Big Deal?
(Hebrews 7:11–18)

What's the big deal? Why does it matter that Melchizedek is greater than the Levites?

It matters because the Levitical priesthood was not perfect. As you read the Old Testament story, the priests become corrupt; they fail the people. Instead of guiding the people in holiness, the priests guide them in wickedness. The Levitical priesthood was only a shadow of something greater that needed to come. That something greater was a priesthood like Melchizedek's.

Only God-authorized priests can stand between God and man. The big deal is that Jesus is called our high priest, but He was from the tribe of Judah. Nowhere does the Old Testament authorize someone from the tribe of Judah to be a priest. In fact, King Uzziah, who was from the tribe of Judah, intended to do the work of a priest by trying to burn incense on the altar before God. But that didn't go so well. God

struck him with leprosy, and the priests had to rush him out of the temple to save his life (2 Chron. 26:16–21).

Then why is Christ different from Uzziah? Why is He authorized to be our priest? And how does someone from the tribe of Judah become authorized to be our priest?

Something preceding the Levitical priesthood authorizes Christ to be our priest. That something is the pattern of the Melchizedek priestly line. Melchizedek symbolized one who could never lose his priesthood. Christ is the one whose priesthood will continue forever. Basically, Christ can be a priest because He is what Melchizedek symbolically was. In contrast, the Levitical priesthood was temporary. It only existed as long as the Mosaic law was in force, but the Mosaic law and Levitical priesthood ended (Heb. 8:13).

What Type of Priest Is Needed?
(Hebrews 7:19–27)

The Levitical priesthood was not able to give the worshiper permanent access to God. Levitical priests would die (Heb. 7:8). The Levitical priesthood was not able to perfect anyone (Heb. 7:11, 19). But we need that permanent access to God and that perfection. In order to get it, we needed a different kind of priest—one that was not from the order of Aaron.

Not just any kind of priest would do. We needed one who, like Melchizedek, was authorized by God—chosen by God with an oath—and not like the many who met only the requirements of the temporary law (Heb. 7:20–21, 28). We needed one who would continue forever, not the many who would eventually die (Heb. 7:24–25). We needed one who could bring us a better hope and give us access to God by always interceding for us, not the many whose sacrifices had to be given over and over again without ever bringing us closer to God (Heb. 7:27).

In Psalm 110:4 we find that one we so desperately need. The Word states that God has chosen a priest, and He will not change His mind. But weren't the Levites chosen by God's Word? Yes, but this new priest is different. He brings with Him a better hope. He is better because of the way He became a priest—God's Word and His oath. He is better because He will not be hindered by death—He has conquered it. His ministry continues on forever. We know that it will—because the Lord has sworn an oath that His priesthood will be forever, and God will not change His mind.

Thinking It Through 2.2

1. Why did Abraham refuse the spoils of war offered by the king of Sodom?

2. List all the things we know about Melchizedek.

3. What did Melchizedek and Abraham do that demonstrated that one of them was greater than the other? Which one was greater?

4. Why do we need another priesthood other than the Levitical priesthood?

5. In what ways is the priesthood of Christ better than other priesthoods?

2.3 ABRAHAM: HEIR OF THE PROMISE

Read Genesis 15
Memorize Genesis 15:5–6; 17:1–2

The Big Picture Narrows

We started this textbook with a three-point outline of Scripture: Creation, Fall, and Redemption (CFR). We're focusing mainly on the Old Testament, but already we've covered the first two points. Creation and Fall are done, but the effects continue.

Redemption (the restoration of God's good creation) has begun, but just barely. All we know so far is that God promised Adam and Eve that it would begin. And now, hundreds of years later, comes the next step. He is choosing one man, Abraham, to be His tool for restoring the world.

If you know the rest of the story of Abraham already, Genesis 12 doesn't come as any shock. But if you can try to imagine you're reading it for the first time, it's surprising. Why all these promises all of a sudden? And to this particular guy? A land? A nation? A blessing? But pay attention and you might catch a glimpse of someone else's name . . .

The Promises

There are four places in Genesis where God makes special promises to Abraham, and these are extremely important for you to remember and understand. You'll have to apply your knowledge of these promises in order to read the rest of the Bible with any true understanding. They form a big part of the big picture.

We can boil these promises down to the three basic categories: land, seed, and blessing. And the blessing part has two subpoints: God will bless Israel, and Israel will be His tool for blessing all the other nations of the world.

Reading these promises is like reading the table of contents for the rest of the story of Scripture. You're not sure how all these things will happen, but you have a basic idea of some of the most important things that are coming. Abraham will get a particular piece of land. He is going to have multiplied seed (many descendants), and that nation will receive God's blessings and share them with others. Just think *land*, *seed*, and *blessing*.

Genesis 12 & 13	Genesis 15	Genesis 17	Genesis 22
1. I will give to you and your children all the land that you see. 2. I will make you into a great nation. 3. I will bless you and make your name great, so that you will be a blessing. I will bless those who bless you, and I will curse anyone who dishonors you. In you, all the families of the earth will be blessed.	1. Count the stars. Your seed will be like that. 2. I give this land to your seed, from the Nile to the Euphrates Rivers.	1. You will be the father of a multitude of nations (this is where Abram's name changes to Abraham). 2. Kings will come from you. 3. I will establish my covenant between Me and you and your seed throughout their generations for an everlasting covenant, to be God to you and to your seed. 4. I will give to you and to your seed the land you have been staying in, all the land of Canaan, for an everlasting possession.	1. I will bless you. 2. I will multiply your seed like the stars of heaven. 3. Your seed will conquer the cities of his enemies. 4. In your seed all the nations of the earth will be blessed.

"[Abraham's] descendants will be numerous . . . , victorious . . . , and influential."

—Victor P. Hamilton

Abraham falls asleep during the covenant-starting ceremony in Genesis 15. What does that say about whether the covenant is conditional or unconditional?

The Abrahamic Covenant

All of these promises add up to something big, something Genesis 15 calls a *covenant*. We already saw that word describing God's promise to Noah to not flood the earth again, but with Abraham it steps up to the next level. God's covenant with Abraham will change the whole story from now to the end of the Bible. And from the end of the Bible up to right now, today. And from today to the end of time!

"[In God's promises to Abraham] God's rescue plan for humanity is revealed."

—Paul R. Williamson

The rest of the story of Scripture—the story of what God is doing to redeem His fallen creation—is going to go from covenant to covenant, all based on this one with Abraham. (More on this important covenant will come in the next section.) So let's take a moment to notice something about those promises, the difference between conditional and unconditional.

The difference is simple. Here's an unconditional promise your parents might give you: "Kids, we're going on a vacation next summer to the Rocky Mountains!" Here's a conditional promise: "Kids, if each of you is able to save fifty dollars of your allowance money to help pay for it, we'll go on a vacation next summer to the Rocky Mountains!" There's a big difference between those two promises. The second one has conditions. The first one doesn't; it's unconditional.

Now look carefully at Genesis 15 and the promises God gives Abraham there. Are they conditional or unconditional? How about the promises in Genesis 17:1–2? Both chapters contain God's promises about Abraham's future seed and land. But chapter 15 doesn't ask him to do anything. That part of the covenant is mainly about God's promises, not Abraham's responsibilities. Abraham is actually asleep during the covenant-starting ceremony God puts on in Genesis 15! God is the subject, the one acting, making promises. Abraham (still called Abram at the time) was the direct object; he was just there to receive God's gifts.

But in chapter 17, things are different. God tells Abraham to be blameless. And He tells him to circumcise every male child in his line forever (17:10). These are responsibilities God demands to confirm His promises.

So is the Abrahamic Covenant overall conditional or unconditional? It was unconditional in Genesis 12 and Genesis 15—so does adding responsibilities more than a dozen years later (in chapter 17) make it conditional all of a sudden?

Pause. Does this even matter? Yes! Because if Abraham gets all the promises by being good, then you and I are in trouble—because we're not good! We'll never be good enough to deserve God's promises to us. And the truth is, neither was Abraham. Remember Abraham, the liar (Gen. 12:10–20)? And if Abraham and all his descendants (his seed) had to stay good in order for God to fulfill the land promise to Abraham and his descendants, they would've dropped out of history by now. The effects of the Fall are so deep in every person that no one is truly righteous, not even one.

Covenants

There are at least four ways of enacting a covenant in the Old Testament.

1. Oath (Gen. 26:26–31)

2. Handshake (Ezek. 17:13–18)

3. Giving of a shoe (Ruth 4:7–8)

4. Blood sacrifice (Gen. 15:9–18)

In the Old Testament, a covenant was a mutual agreement between two parties to do or to refrain from doing certain acts. The covenant bound the two parties who would agree on promises, conditions, privileges, and responsibilities. The following covenants show several different ways to make a covenant during Old Testament times.

Some covenants were straightforward and resemble agreements in our time. Isaac swore an oath to Abimelech that no harm would come to him or his family (Gen. 26:26–31). Nebuchadnezzar and Zedekiah made a covenant of peace with each other and shook hands to seal the agreement (Ezek. 17:13–21). Zedekiah, however, broke the covenant by attacking Nebuchadnezzar. God said that because Zedekiah broke the oath, he would die. As you see, a handshake was an important way to enact a covenant!

Some covenants were made in ways that seem strange to us. In the book of Ruth, Boaz goes to the city gates to talk with the other kinsman to redeem Naomi's land and obtain the right to marry Ruth. The kinsman decides it is best if he does not redeem the land or marry Ruth. He then removes his shoe and gives it to Boaz. This was a sign that he was giving up his right to walk on the land.

The blood covenant is another way that may seem strange to us. It was the strongest way of saying that a covenant was to last forever. The two parties would come together and agree on the terms of the covenant. They would then sacrifice an animal and divide the carcass into two parts. The two parties would stand in front of the sacrifice, restate the terms, and then walk between the two parts of the carcass. The blood of the sacrifice bound them to the covenant.

The blood covenant is important for two reasons. First, sacrificing the animals signified that if either party didn't fulfill his part of the agreement, then he would be killed in the same way the animals were. The penalty for breaking the covenant was death. Second, once the two parties walked between the sacrificed animals, they could not change the covenant. It became permanent.

When God chose to make a covenant with Abraham, He chose the blood covenant because it was the strongest way of saying that this covenant would be permanent and eternal. God then had Abraham choose five different animals to sacrifice (a cow, a goat, a ram, a dove, and a pigeon). Any one of those would have been good enough to make the covenant permanent. But God wanted five animals—the five animals that would one day be the only acceptable sacrificial animals in the Levitical law—to show the great importance that He placed on fulfilling the covenant.

When it came time for God and Abraham to walk between the five split carcasses, Abraham was in a deep sleep. God alone spoke, and then He alone passed between the pieces. And the covenant between the Lord and Abraham was made. Because God alone passed through the pieces, it is He alone who is responsible to fulfill the promises of the covenant. This means that God will fulfill the promises despite what Abraham or his descendants do.

The Seed

The Abrahamic Covenant brings us back to the question that's been hanging in the air since Genesis 3:15. Who is this seed of the woman who will crush the serpent's head? Is it Abraham? Apparently not. But is it his seed? Apparently so. In Abraham's seed all the nations of the earth will be blessed. God is going to do good for His world despite its sin, and He's going to do it through Abraham's seed.

Remember, though, that *seed* (your translation of the Bible might have *off-spring*—same thing) is ambiguous, or capable of more than one meaning. *Seed* could be either singular or plural, and it could be either sooner or later—even much later. If you read the promises to Abraham, they make it look like the seed is a huge group of Abraham's descendants. So it's plural and it's coming in the future, not right away.

But there is still some ambiguity left over. God promised to Abraham that his seed would conquer the cities of "his enemies." That sounds singular! Is God trying to be confusing on purpose? You'll have to keep reading the story to find out how God's plan works out—and it will be a while before you see the answer.

Paul on Abraham

So—conditional or unconditional? There are some key answers to this problem in the text of Genesis itself, but Paul in the New Testament helps us make sure we're understanding things correctly. In Romans 4 Paul quotes both Genesis 15 and Genesis 17—the unconditional and seemingly conditional parts of the Abrahamic Covenant. And he makes a simple point: Genesis 15 comes first. The unconditional promises came before the commands God gave Abraham.

Otherwise Abraham would have something to boast about (Rom. 4:1–5): his obedience would be the reason he got the great promises of the Abrahamic Covenant. But Paul says, "No!" It was Abraham's faith that counted with God first. And faith is not a work; it doesn't "earn" you anything.

This should matter to you very deeply because your own salvation depends on it. Paul says so when he calls Abraham not just the father of the circumcised (that is, the Jewish nation), but the father of all who "walk in the steps of that faith of our father Abraham" (Rom. 4:12). The promises to Abraham did not come through his obedience to God's law, but through his simple faith that God would do what He said He would do.

Sonship

Statistics tell us that if you are reading this book, you are approximately 99.99 percent likely to be someone's son or daughter. There's a mix of the conditional and unconditional in the relationship you have with your parents. The fact that you will always be your father's son or your mother's daughter—that's unconditional. And though your parents aren't perfect, their love and concern for you should continue unconditionally throughout your life no matter what trouble you get into.

But your privileges are conditioned on fulfilling your responsibilities: your curfew, your internet time, your TV time, or whatever your parents decide. In other words, the *quality* of your relationship is conditional. If you continually rebel against your parents, your relationship will suffer. The good times will go away. They might even someday kick you out of the house. Their unconditional love hasn't ended; but you've violated the conditional parts of your relationship. Likewise, we'll see as the story of the Bible goes on that Abraham's seed were eventually kicked out of the land God promised them (more on that later).

But God calls believers His "children." We (if you're a believer) are sons and daughters of the Most High. So was Abraham. That relationship will never end; it's unconditional. But the blessings of good fellowship with God, the privileges of someone who walks with God and fears Him—these things are conditional. If you're really God's child, you will always want them. You'll never be able to get away with sinning. It will always bother you. Most kids, deep down, do want to please their parents instead of making them angry or upset. God's kids are no different.

Justified by Faith: Paul's Lesson in Observation

The story of Abraham is more than the story of God's choosing an unknown man and giving him great promises. The story is also about faith and works, and it is about how those two things relate to our being justified, or declared righteous.

In Paul's day, many Jews considered Abraham to be the perfect example of someone who was justified by works. One Jewish writer goes so far as to say that God justified Abraham because he was "perfect in all his deeds with the Lord" (Jubilees 23:10).

This is an important issue. If Abraham was justified because of his works, then he could boast about it, and we too could be justified because of our works. And we too could boast about it. But Paul says that no one is justified by works, and that faith rules out boasting (Rom. 3:27–28).

How does Paul know that Abraham was justified by his faith and not his works? The answer might surprise you. Paul simply observed, interpreted, and applied the passage that you read today.

In your reading today, you read Genesis 15:6, "And [Abraham] believed the Lord, and he counted it to him as righteousness." That's the Old Testament way of saying that Abraham was justified. In order to show that Abraham was justified by faith, Paul had to use his observation skills. So he asked a simple observation question, "How was it then reckoned? when he was in circumcision, or in uncircumcision" (Rom. 4:10). Or in other words, "When did God justify him? Before or after he had done the work of circumcision?"

Paul read Genesis 15 in context with the surrounding chapters (do you remember the importance of context?), and he looked at the order of events in Abraham's life. In Genesis 15 and 17, Paul finds out which happened first: justification or works. In Genesis 15 Abraham is justified, and in Genesis 17 Abraham is circumcised. So, Abraham was justified before he had done the work of circumcision. In fact, it happened years before he was circumcised in Genesis 17.

Paul then interprets the passage and concludes that Abraham was justified by faith and not by works. Next, he applies it to us. We who are Gentiles and do not have the sign of circumcision are also justified by faith (Rom. 4:11–12). Paul even says that Genesis 15:6 was written for both Abraham's and our sakes (Rom. 4:23–24).

Observe, interpret, and apply.

Because of our sin, we will often make God angry or saddened. He'll never stop loving us, but He does chasten us when His Spirit is grieved because of our sin. We'll never be perfect sons and daughters. But through Abraham, God is beginning to make a way for even the most rebellious sons and the most stubborn daughters to come back into His arms.

Thinking It Through 2.3

1. Go back through the big chart in this lesson and underline every promise related to the seed or nation. Draw a box around every promise related to the land. Circle every promise related to God's promised blessings for Abraham and the world.

2. What is redemption?

3. What is a biblical covenant, and what details does it include?

4. Is the Abrahamic Covenant conditional or unconditional?

5. Why was the blood sacrifice the strongest way of saying that a covenant would last forever?

2.4 ABRAHAM AND HIS COVENANT SON ISAAC

Read Genesis 22:1–18
Memorize Genesis 22:16–18

God Is Not Slack

You have needs. We all do. Some of those needs can be intense, like if your dad gets laid off and needs a job. If that's never happened to your family, just try to imagine what it would be like. What would your family do? If your parents are Christians, you would all pray. And pray. And pray. And you would all probably worry—worry about whether you'll have to give up your house, whether your mom will have to look for a job, whether you'll have to start going to a public school. But you would try to take your worries to the Lord. Every day would seem like an eternity, especially when you were waiting to hear back from a company your dad had an interview with.

When your dad finally did get a job, your family would all celebrate! What a relief! But after the joy faded, you might find yourself asking a few questions: *Why did God make us wait as long as He did? If Dad was going to get a job anyway, why not give it to us before we had to deplete our savings?*

There are a few answers the Bible could give to questions like that. One of the simplest is that God wanted to build your endurance (Rom. 5:3; James 1:3). But don't expect to ever know all the reasons. God is allowed to do things we can't fully understand—or even things we can't understand at all. Our job is to trust that He is doing what is best for His glory (Acts 9:16) and our good (Rom. 8:28). It's not wrong to ask God, "Why? Why is this happening to me?" That's what Job did. But God's true children won't turn *away from* Him to find answers outside of Him. They will turn *to* Him (Job 42:1–6).

People who don't know God come to a different conclusion when they have to wait for things to get better. Peter summarizes it like this: "There shall come in the last days scoffers, walking after their own lusts, and saying, Where is the promise of his coming? for since the fathers fell asleep, all things continue as they were from the beginning of the creation" (2 Pet. 3:3–4). In other words, some people say, "You believers claim God's going to come and fix all the problems in the world, but He sure has waited a long time! Maybe He's hanging out with Santa Claus and the Tooth Fairy!"

You might get a similar feeling yourself as you read the story of Scripture. Why did God wait so many hundreds of years after Adam and Eve sinned to give these promises to Abraham and get redemption rolling? Peter says two things in 2 Peter 3 that can help us:

1. God sees time a little differently than we do: with Him, a thousand years is the same as a day, and a day is the same as a thousand years (2 Pet. 3:8).

2. God is actually being patient with humanity, giving us all time to repent. God's plan does not move quickly. And we have to trust Him that He meant what He said, that His waiting is a mercy to mankind (2 Pet. 3:9).

A Little Boy Named Laughter

Time went slowly for Abraham too. After God's promise, his wife stayed barren for twenty-five long years, like she always had been. And it looked like she was just too old to have a child. He and Sarah even tried to fix things for God by having a child with Sarah's handmaid Hagar, instead of with Sarah. Once again Abraham showed that he wasn't a perfect hero. He had major flaws. It's no accident that right after the story of Hagar and the son she bore Abraham (whose name was Ishmael), God first demanded that Abraham be blameless and then gave him more covenant promises (in Genesis 17, which you read in a previous section). The promises didn't go away because of Abraham's sin; instead God insisted to Abraham he would have a son by Sarah, not Hagar or anyone else.

But what if you tried doing what God did? March into a nursing home near you and proclaim to the little old nonagenarian ladies (that means they're in their nineties), "One of you will bear a son this time next year!" If they don't laugh, it's probably because they didn't quite hear you. ("What, sonny? I'm going to carry a gun some time in my ear?")

> "It was a laughable idea; it is impossible for a ninety-year-old woman to give birth. But it happened. Right at this early stage we are being taught that it will take a miracle for the gospel to be fulfilled."
>
> —Vaughan Roberts

Abraham and Sarah weren't too old to hear, so they did laugh. Both of them. What a good name for that son, then—Laughter. That's what *Isaac* means in Hebrew.

And the happy new mother, as old as a great-grandmother, shows pretty quickly that she's not a perfect example any more than her husband is. When Isaac was little, they threw a party for him, and Sarah noticed that someone was laughing who shouldn't have been, at least in Sarah's opinion. It was Ishmael, the son Abraham had through Hagar. Sarah got angry and demanded that Abraham get rid of Hagar and Ishmael. Abraham didn't want to do this at all, but God instructed him to go ahead and do it. The promise God gave to Abraham worked for Ishmael, to a point—he would become a great nation, just like Isaac would.

Do Bible Names Tell You Something About the People Who Had Them?

Abraham means "father of nations." *Isaac* means "laughter." *Jacob* means "heel grabber" and "supplanter" (one who tricks someone else to take something good that he has). *Moses* means "drawn out," as in drawn out of the Nile from his basket of reeds. Do all Bible names have a hidden meaning that tells you something about the person or his character?

The simple answer is no. How could the parents of little babies in Bible times know what their kids would turn out to be like? Only God knows what character a tiny infant will grow up to have.

The more complicated answer is that God does sometimes give a baby a name—or arranges circumstances so that he gets a name—that predicts his future character. And a few times in the Bible God changed people's names.

God is the one who gave Abraham his new name because He knew He was going to make Abraham fit his name. Isaac's name is different: God gave it to him because his parents laughed when they found out they were going to have him. That doesn't mean he somehow had the character of a comedian. Jacob's name is a little more interesting. He got his name because as he was being born he grabbed his twin brother's heel (*Jacob* sounds like the word that means "heel" in Hebrew). But only God knew that one day Jacob would grab his brother Esau's heel in a bigger way, tricking him out of something valuable to him.

> "Is not he rightly named Jacob? for he hath supplanted me these two times."
>
> —Esau

It may be interesting to know what someone's name means, but the Bible text will tell you if the meaning of a person's name is actually significant. Don't look for secret meanings there; the Bible will always let you know.

There's one name in Scripture that is incredibly significant, more than any other (Matt. 1:21; Phil. 2:9). Every page of Scripture points to that name, and you already know it—don't you? But do you know what it means? It means "the Lord is salvation." The story we're reading in Genesis is the beginning of the story of how God proves that that simple meaning is deeply, wonderfully true.

The Sacrifice of the Son

So Abraham had his miracle child. But did God really have Abraham? Sometime later God, who knows all things, decided to give a test that would reveal the depth of Abraham's faith. He told Abraham to take the miracle son—his only son, the son he loved, the one he had waited so long for, the one in whom all his hopes lay—and offer him as a burnt offering. That meant slaughtering Isaac and burning his body as a sacrifice.

Would the Abraham who had left his home in Ur go in faith this time? Would the Abraham who had had to give up Ishmael give up another son in faith?

> "Testing shows what someone is really like, and it generally involves difficulty or hardship."
>
> —Gordon Wenham

The text simply says that Abraham rose early, got ready, and went. It never describes his feelings. But we already know he loved his son. This must have been the hardest thing he ever did. It only became harder when his son—who was maybe thirteen or so, we don't know—asked him, "My father, where is the lamb for a burnt offering?" When your beloved son asks you that question as you trudge up a mountain to his death, what do you say? Abraham said, "My son, God will provide himself a lamb for a burnt offering."

And, of course, He did. As Abraham raised the knife to slay his son, bound on the altar and no doubt incredibly scared, the angel of the Lord called out to him to stop.

And now we find out the reason for the test: God wanted to confirm His covenant with Abraham once and for all. Abraham had fully proven that he feared God, that anything God asked for, even his most beloved possession—his son—God could take from Abraham's open hands.

Covenant Confirmation

This time, God doesn't just promise; He swears an oath, which reemphasizes that there's absolutely nothing Abraham can do to keep these things from happening. Here are the promises in the oath. They all fit into the categories you've studied—land, seed, and blessing:

- I will bless you.
- I will multiply your seed as the stars of the heaven and the sand on the seashore.
- Your seed will conquer the cities of his enemies.
- In your seed all the nations of the earth will be blessed.

Isaac's Own Covenant Confirmation

After Abraham died, God confirmed the covenant to Isaac too. It's in the first paragraph of Genesis 26. God tells Isaac the same things He told Abraham. God specifically mentions His oath to Abraham and says He will establish it firmly. Isaac was definitely the one through whom God meant to carry on the official family line of blessing.

Substitutionary Sacrifice

We often hear about how difficult it must have been for Abraham to obey God and sacrifice his son—the son that God promised him in his old age. And we read about how relieved Abraham must have been when the angel stopped him and when he saw the ram caught in the thicket.

But have you ever read it from the perspective of Isaac? Can you imagine what Isaac must have thought as a son, when his father began the sacrifice and he was it? Or how relieved Isaac must have been when the angel appeared and when his father saw the ram? I'm sure that he was very relieved to have an animal take his place, to be his substitute.

That's exactly what the ram was for Isaac, a substitutionary sacrifice.

In our modern society, we think of a substitute as someone who teaches when our usual teacher is not here. Or, we think of the player on the bench who subs (substitutes) for the starter to give her a breather. We seldom, if ever, think of a substitute meaning another who is sacrificed instead of me. But that's exactly what the Israelites had to think each time they offered a sin offering to God.

When an Israelite came to offer a sacrifice for his sin, he did not simply give the animal to the priest and idly stand there or walk away. He, the offeror (a person who brought an animal to the tabernacle or temple and offered it as a sacrifice), was deeply involved in the sacrifice.

There were at least five things that happened when an animal was sacrificed. Notice all the things that the offeror actually did.

1. The offeror would choose from his herd or flock the animal to be sacrificed. This animal had to be a male who was perfectly pure without blemish.

2. Next, the offeror would present his sacrifice and lay his hands on the animal's head. This symbolized that the animal was a substitute and would take the place of the offeror, who was a sinner. The offeror most likely would confess his sins at this time.

3. Then the offeror, not the priest, would slaughter the animal (most likely by slitting its throat). In this way, the offeror would be reminded that death is the penalty for his sin. During the sacrifice, the priest would capture as much of the blood as possible.

4. After that, the priest would normally sprinkle or apply the blood of the sacrifice to the altar.

5. Finally, the priest would burn the sacrifice on the altar until all the flesh and fat pieces were consumed.

This was done on a regular basis. Each sacrifice reminded the offeror that the animal was a substitute for him. The offeror was guilty. The animal was innocent. The offeror lived. The animal died.

When Abraham found the ram and unbound Isaac, Isaac truly understood the meaning of a substitute. In the New Testament, Paul saw Abraham and Isaac as being types (pictures) of God the Father and Jesus. But when Jesus was going to be sacrificed, no one stepped in to take his place. He died.

In Genesis 22:16–17, God told Abraham, "Because thou hast done this thing, and hast not withheld thy son, thine only son: that in blessing I will bless thee." Little did Abraham know that his actions were a shadow of something coming. God "spared not his own Son, but delivered him up for us all" (Rom. 8:32). And that Son was His "only begotten Son," Jesus (John 3:16).

The ram that Abraham sacrificed did not take away his or Isaac's sins. Neither did the countless sacrifices made in the tabernacle and temple take away the sins of the people who offered them (Heb. 10:1–4, 10). These sacrifices were but a glimpse of "the Lamb of God, which taketh away the sins of the world" (John 1:29).

You and I deserve punishment for our sins, and that punishment is death and banishment from God. Nothing we do in life, no amount of good works and no amount of money, can cancel out the sins we have committed against God. We can't even die for ourselves. We are that wretched.

But God knew all that from eternity past, and He provided a substitute to stand in our place and take our penalty. That substitute is Christ. His death on the cross was a substitutionary sacrifice on our behalf.

Isaiah said it best, "All we like sheep have gone astray; we have turned every one to his own way; and the Lord hath laid on him the iniquity of us all" (Isa. 53:6). If you are a believer and have repented of your sins, you have the assurance that your sins were placed on Christ when He was on the cross. And as a believer, His once-for-all substitutionary sacrifice ensures that you are forgiven of your sins.

So What?

So what? Why should you care about the promises to Abraham? The promises God made to Abraham God didn't make to you. You might never have any seed, and you almost certainly won't see your grandkids become kings. God hasn't promised you a land, either.

Or has He? In the New Testament, Christians aren't promised a particular land, exactly, but they are promised rest. Having a land is not much good, in fact, if you don't have peace and rest there. The modern state of Israel has the land, but they don't have peace because their neighbors want the land and are willing to kill for it. According to the book of Hebrews, Christians can look forward to a time when they will rest from their earthly work, just as God did from His (Heb. 4:10).

And Christians will actually get land too. In fact, they inherit the whole new earth, not just one part of it (Matt. 5:5; Rev. 21:1–3). You, if you're one of God's children, will get to rest in the land of the new earth (Heb. 4:9). And that land will be bigger than Abraham ever dreamed. Abraham's biological descendants will get their land too. No one in God's family will be left out (Heb. 11:16).

Ishmael: The Fulfillment of God's Promise to Hagar

Because Ishmael is Abraham's seed—though not the promised seed—God promises to make a great nation out of Ishmael too (Gen. 21:13; cf. 16:10–11). Abraham need not worry. God has a plan for Ishmael. And He will make sure that Ishmael's life is preserved so that His plan for Ishmael will come to pass. Although Abraham tries to provide for Hagar and Ishmael's preservation, God must intervene to preserve their lives (Gen. 21:14–20). He reconfirms his promise to Hagar (Gen. 21:18) and providentially cares for Ishmael as he grows into a man (Gen. 21:20–21). This story shows that God is gracious even to Gentiles who are not a part of His special, chosen people of Israel. He provides for the general welfare of all people—even the unsaved—as a part of His fulfillment of the Noahic Covenant (Gen. 8:21–22; Matt. 5:45).

Thinking It Through 2.4

1. How long did Abraham have to wait for the promised son, Isaac?

2. Based on 2 Peter 3, why does it seem that God waits so long to fulfill the promises of His unfolding plan of redemption?

3. Why did God ask Abraham to sacrifice Isaac?

4. What is a substitutionary sacrifice?

5. True or False. The Bible text will tell you if the meaning of a biblical person's name is actually significant.

2.5 ISAAC & REBEKAH: A DISPLAY OF GOD'S STEADFAST LOVE

Read Genesis 24
Memorize Genesis 24:60

Have you ever asked your parents about how they met? Or your grandparents or maybe your aunt and uncle? Some of the stories are romantic. Some are rather mundane and boring. Some can be hilarious or dramatic. Each of them points to God providentially working behind the scenes to bring the two together, but some stories seem to show how God intentionally brought the couple together.

Abraham—Blessed in Every Way

When Genesis 24 opens, it is a rather sad time for Abraham and Isaac. Sarah, the beloved wife and mother, had passed away at 127 years old. It had been almost three years since her passing, and Isaac was 40 years old. He was the promised son to Abraham, whom God blessed in every way, yet Isaac was unmarried. If Abraham wished to see the promised grandchildren, then he needed to find a wife for his son.

The Servant's Oath

Abraham didn't want just any woman to be his son's bride, and he especially didn't want a Canaanite woman to be his son's wife. He wanted someone from his home country and from his family.

Abraham was too old to make the trip back to his home country, and he did not want Isaac to go there. So he decided that he would send his most trusted servant (most likely Eliezer from Genesis 15:2) to find a wife for Isaac. But Abraham's mind was made up. There was to be no Canaanite daughter-in-law. So he made Eliezer "swear by the Lord, the God of heaven, and the God of the earth," (24:3) to leave Canaan to find Isaac a wife among his relatives who were living in Abraham's home country.

Swearing an oath is a big deal. If in some way Eliezer failed to follow through on his part, then he would face severe consequences for breaking his oath. You can imagine what was going through his mind. Eliezer immediately asked what would happen if a potential bride refused to come back with him. Maybe he could bring Isaac to persuade her and her family. Abraham

instantly replied that taking Isaac back there was out of the question. There is no way he would allow Isaac to go all the way to the home country. But Abraham reassured Eliezer that the Lord would send an angel, just like He had done for Abraham before, to help him carry out his oath.

Abraham also reassured his servant that God would help him because God had sworn to Abraham personally that his descendants would live in this land. If Eliezer found a woman and she was not willing to come, then he would be free from his oath. But he could not take Isaac back there.

The Servant's Journey

Eliezer began to prepare for the journey. It would be a long journey of about five hundred miles over mountains and through deserts. If he made good progress each day, he and his fellow servants could make the journey in about a month. He prepared ten camels and loaded them with a variety of good things, some of which were gifts for the bride-to-be and her family.

When he arrived in Mesopotamia, he stopped to let the camels rest near a well outside the city. As the camels and the men rested, Eliezer prayed that God would grant him success in his journey and show kindness to his master, Abraham. He asked specifically that God would show him which young woman was to be the one. When he asked her for a drink, he would know that she was the one if she gave him a drink and offered to draw water for his camels. If she did this, then he would know that God had shown kindness to his master.

Before Eliezer had finished praying, a young woman came to draw water. He saw that she was very attractive and unmarried. When she came up from the spring, he ran over to her and asked her for a drink. She gave him a drink and then offered to draw water for the camels.

Eliezer was speechless. Could this actually be the answer to his prayer?

When she finished watering the camels, he gave her many gifts of jewelry and asked her who she was. Her name was Rebekah, and she was from Abraham's family.

An Explanation of Ḥesed

Twice in his prayer, Eliezer used the word *kindness*. In some translations you might find the word *loyalty*. The word *kindness*, or *loyalty*, is translated from the Hebrew word חסד (*ḥesed*—pronounced KHES-ed). In the Hebrew mind, the word *ḥesed* carries a deeper meaning than our words *kindness* or *loyalty*. Sometimes, *ḥesed* is translated "mercy." In fact, it is difficult to explain with only one English word. That is why some translations use the phrases "steadfast love," or "loving kindness."

Suppose that it's forty degrees outside and raining. You are driving down the road and see a stranger walking in the rain, and he looks directly at you. So, you stop the car and give him a ride to his destination. That is what we call *kindness*. You were under no obligation to stop and give him a ride. But you did, because you are kind. But suppose you continued on and you saw your grandmother walking down the road in the freezing rain, and she looks up and sees you. No matter what, you're going to stop the car and give her a ride to get her out of the rain. That is loyal kindness. There is a *relationship* between the two of you. And relationship is the basis for that loyal kindness. She is family, and you have an obligation to stop and help her no matter what the cost.

God had made promises to Abraham. One of those promises was that Abraham would become a great nation. And this is the first time in Scripture that *ḥesed* is used to show God's kindness toward Abraham. Eliezer is asking God to keep His obligation to Abraham—to show His *loyal kindness*, His *steadfast love*, to Abraham because He has a *covenant relationship* with him.

This could actually be the answer to his prayer!

He immediately thanked and praised God because He had not forgotten to show "mercy" (*ḥesed*), that is, steadfast love, to his master Abraham.

At the Father's House

When Eliezer finished thanking God for prospering his journey, he and Rebekah headed to her father's house. Her brother Laban saw Rebekah with all the new jewelry on. He immediately went to find the man that gave it to her. Laban invited Eliezer and the men to stay with them, and he provided food and water for their camels.

When they sat down to eat, Eliezer was so excited that he couldn't eat until he had told Rebekah's family everything that had happened. He told them who his master was and how Abraham and Sarah had borne a son when they were old. He told them about the oath he had made to Abraham. He also told them about his prayer and how God had answered it even before he had spoken it. He then asked Laban and his father to "deal kindly" (*ḥesed*) with his master.

Laban and his father agreed that this was from God, and they had nothing good or bad to say about it. They would gladly allow Rebekah to go with him. Laban and Rebekah's mother requested only that he give her at least ten days to prepare.

Eliezer was eager to return to Abraham and Isaac, and ten days was too long to wait. He wanted to return immediately. They would agree to this only if Rebekah agreed. And she did.

Before they left, Laban blessed Rebekah and said,

> Thou art our sister, be thou the mother
> of thousands of millions,
> and let thy seed possess
> the gate of those which hate them.
> (Gen. 24:60)

Return to Canaan

Then Rebekah and her nurse went with Eliezer to return to Abraham and Isaac. As they drew near to the tents, Isaac was meditating in the fields and looked up and saw them coming. It seems that Isaac and Rebekah saw each other at the same time. She asked Eliezer who the man was in the field. He replied that the man was his master, Isaac. Rebekah covered her face and prepared to meet her new husband.

Isaac and Rebekah were soon married. Although he wasn't the one who chose her, he loved her. And through this love, he "was comforted after his mother's death" (24:67).

just so happened to be related to Abraham and to be part of the family. She just so happened to be single. She just so happened to . . .

No, it didn't "just so happen"—it *happened just so*. In other words, it wasn't a coincidence. Eliezer was specific in what he asked of God. And God was specific in answering his prayer.

Notice Eliezer's response. At first he was silent. He was speechless. He was most likely somewhat stunned at how soon God answered his prayer and at how specifically God answered his prayer. It took him a while to figure out if this was really happening. Was God really answering his prayer?

He responded to the answered prayer by blessing God and giving Him the credit for being faithful to His promises that He had made to Abraham. In Eliezer's own words, "I bowed down my head, and worshipped the Lord, and blessed the Lord God of my master Abraham, which had led me in the right way to take my master's brother's daughter unto his son" (24:48). The answer of prayer led him to worship God. God's show of kindness led to His being worshiped.

Sometimes we pray and God quickly answers—often in a surprising way. We should never attribute those answers to "coincidence." With each answer to prayer, we have reasons to give thanks to God:

We do not want to ignore His response to us.
We want Him to answer other prayers.
We should develop our gratitude.
We should take prayer seriously.

Conclusion

Indeed, this is an unusual story of how a couple met and were married. It's not every day that a servant travels to a foreign land, returns with a bride for his master's son, and the two of them have a successful marriage. The marriage gave hope that the promise of a nation would occur. God was indeed showing His kindness, His steadfast love, to Abraham because of their covenant relationship.

Application

Did you notice the prayer that Eliezer prayed? His prayer was not only for a successful mission but that God would show Abraham kindness—steadfast love—by honoring the promises He had made to Abraham.

Did you notice when the prayer was answered? It was being answered "before he had done speaking" (24:15). Wow! While he was praying, God was answering that prayer. That is kindness. That is *ḥesed*!

What an amazing coincidence! A girl just so happened to come to the well. She just so happened to offer Eliezer and his camels a drink. She

Thinking It Through 2.5

1. What motivated Eliezer's prayer for a successful journey?

2. What is the basis for God's loyal kindness, His steadfast love?

3. How does God prove His loyal kindness?

4. How did Eliezer respond to God's answer to prayer?

5. Why should we give thanks for answered prayer?

2.6 JACOB THE HEEL GRABBER

Read Genesis 25:19–35:29
Memorize Genesis 35:2–3

Will the Seed Grow into a Nation?

It seemed the story of Scripture almost stopped when Abraham was going to sacrifice Isaac. What if Isaac had really died? Then the line of the promised seed would have been cut off. "In Isaac shall thy seed be called," God told Abraham. That meant, "No Isaac, no seed; no seed, no answer to the problem of human sin." Remember, it was the "seed of the woman" that God said would crush the head of the serpent.

But Isaac lived and was married to Rebekah. But for twenty years they had no children. What would happen to the seed God promised?

It finally came when Isaac was sixty. Rebekah actually gave birth to twins. Finally, Abraham's family tree was starting to spread. The seed was doubling. Soon it would double again, triple, quadruple—until it became a vast nation.

Or would it? Rebekah, pregnant in a time before ultrasounds, wondered why so much was going on inside her womb. And God told her that "two nations" were in there, two peoples who would someday be divided. And then God said something strange: "The elder shall serve the younger" (Gen. 25:23).

That's not the way things were done in Isaac and Rebekah's day. The oldest child got the best part of the inheritance. The younger served the elder. And how is it that there were two nations in Rebekah's womb? Why not two members of one nation?

Those two sons, Jacob and Esau, didn't get along inside the womb, and things didn't get any better after they were out. Family favoritism was part of the problem: Rebekah's favorite was the younger one, Jacob; Isaac's favorite was the older, Esau. And the two sons were very different. Esau was a rough guy covered with hair. Jacob was not rough, nor was he hairy. But more importantly, Esau seemed to be a straightforward tell-it-like-it-is kind of guy, while Jacob was more deceptive.

Unappealing Character Traits

Jacob was not the model of godliness. In fact, he had many unappealing character traits. He was what we call a manipulator. He had no problem taking advantage of other people to get what he wanted. He was the kind of person who wriggles himself in and out of trouble all the time, because once again, it seems that he was always trying to get what he wanted. We could call him a self-serving person—always scheming to get what he wants. Jacob was self-serving, manipulative, and deceitful.

He tricked Esau into giving away his birthright. He tricked Isaac into giving him the blessing meant for the firstborn son. Later in life he tricked Esau into thinking that their relationship was renewed by telling Esau that he would follow him south to Seir, but then he took off to Succoth in the north. When someone finally tricked *him* (with about the worst trick possible, giving him the wrong wife) he took revenge by playing more tricks. Or at least he thought he was getting even.

Jacob's Actions Reflect His Character

Your Bible textbook is calling one of the most important characters in the Bible, one of the patriarchs of God's chosen people, self-serving, manipulative, and deceitful. What made the authors come to this conclusion? If you look at how Jacob acted throughout the book of Genesis, you will see. Here is a sample of some his actions:

- Jacob manipulated Esau out of his birthright (25:27–34).
- Jacob deceived his own father into giving him Esau's blessing (27:1–40).
- Jacob tried to manipulate the breeding of his flocks to outwit Laban (30:25–43).
- When fearing an attack from Esau, Jacob placed Rachel and Joseph, who were his favorite wife and son, last of all to give them the most protection (33:1–2).
- Jacob thought only of himself and his own safety while ignoring the honor of his daughter Dinah (34:30).

despite his tricks rather than because of them (Gen. 31:12).

Not much time passed before Jacob was getting wealthier and wealthier, and Laban's sons were complaining about it. Conflict was coming with his father-in-law, and at this point God actually told Jacob and his family to just get out of there. Laban chased after them to bring them back, but the Lord warned Laban not to hinder Jacob.

The Abrahamic Covenant Again

Here's another place where it will help us to understand that the Bible isn't supposed to be read as "God's Big Book of Heroes." Instead of trying to figure out a way to explain how Jacob's behavior was actually godly, it's more realistic to just laugh at how foolish people can be when they're trying to run their own lives apart from God.

Jacob didn't win his battles with Laban because of being so godly (or so sly). The story of the sheep and goats demonstrates beyond doubt that Jacob "won" despite being a bit foolish. Clearly, a divine hand was sorting sheep for his benefit. Was God letting Jacob get away with foolishness?

The answer is found in God's promises to Abraham, Jacob's grandfather. God had repeated those special covenant promises to Isaac. And back when Jacob fled from a murderously mad Esau to go to Laban's house, God repeated the promises to him too. There is no indication in the life of Jacob to that point that he was following the Lord. But at Bethel the Lord appeared to him in a dream, told him He was the God of Abraham and Isaac, and started listing off the promises of the Abrahamic Covenant: land, seed, and blessing.

All of Jacob's foolish actions before that time didn't keep God from making these promises, nor did all of Jacob's sins after that change God's mind. The line of Abraham, Isaac, and Jacob was going to be blessed, and they were going to be a blessing.

That revenge was one of the most cunning things Jacob did. After his favorite wife, Rachel, finally gave birth to a son (Joseph), Jacob wanted to stop working for his father-in-law, Laban. He wanted to leave. But Laban didn't want him to go. He knew that the Lord was blessing Jacob, and he wanted to keep getting a piece of that good luck by making Jacob stick around.

So Jacob agreed, but he came up with a plot. He told Laban to keep all the animals with solid-colored coats; Jacob would take all those that were speckled and spotted. Laban probably couldn't believe his good fortune: all he had to do was send the speckled goats and sheep away with his sons, leave the solid-colored animals in Jacob's care, and it would take Jacob years to get many speckled animals for himself. Laban knew shepherding, and he felt lucky to get this deal.

But as usual, Jacob had a scheme up his sleeve. He would simply place strips of branches in front of the animals as they were mating, and that would make them produce speckled sheep.

In the light of what we know about genetics, Jacob's method was just a superstition. But the more important issue is that instead of trusting the Lord to prosper him, Jacob was banking on his own ability to trick his uncle. Strangely enough, however, the plan *seemed* to work quite well! Jacob may have been congratulating himself because God felt it necessary to reveal the truth to him in a dream later: God blessed Jacob

What the Bible Calls "Election"

Isaac wasn't Abraham's only son. But he was the only one through whom the line of God-given seed would continue. Isaac's half brother Ishmael was left out.

Jacob wasn't Isaac's only son. But he was the only one through whom the line of God-given seed would continue. Jacob's brother Esau was left out.

But why? Did you ever wonder about that? Why did they get left out of the official family line, the one God promised to bless? Descendants of Ishmael and Esau have never been part of the Jewish nation, God's chosen people, even though Ishmael and Esau were descendants of Abraham.

Paul raises this question very directly in the New Testament, in Romans 9. He starts by pointing out that not everybody who was physically in the line of Abraham was part of God's true people. Paul notes that only "the children of the promise are counted for the seed" (9:8).

Then Paul raises the question of why. Why would God leave some people out of the line of promise? Why did He tell Rebekah, even before Jacob and Esau were born, that the older would serve the younger?

Here's how Paul answers the question he just raised:

For the children being not yet born, neither having done any good or evil, that the purpose of God according to election might stand, not of works, but of him that calleth. (Rom. 9:11)

Did you catch that? Obviously, if Jacob and Esau hadn't even been born yet, they couldn't be guilty of doing good or evil. So God's choice (election just means "choosing") of Jacob was not based on how good he was or how good he was going to be. You just read the story of Jacob. How good was he? Did he really deserve God's special blessing? No, because he was a heel grabber, a conniver, and a deceiver. Esau wasn't any better, but when he meets Jacob again later in life, he actually comes across as a nicer man than Jacob. And yet he wasn't the one chosen, even though he was the older son in the family.

Paul says as clearly as anyone could that it was not Jacob's works that mattered, but "the purpose of God according to election." God's call went out to Jacob and not to Esau, to Isaac and not to Ishmael. And it was in order to show that God's choices are what really, ultimately matter in this world.

God gave Abraham eight sons in all (Abraham's marriage to Keturah after Sarah died gave him six more), and He gave Isaac two sons. In each set of brothers, God picked only one. It really seems as if God organized the family tree of the patriarchs to make a point about what Paul calls "the purpose of God according to election."

And what is God's purpose? God is at work to glorify His own name. God receives glory for His sovereignty, His control over man's activities. God's righteousness is exalted when He demonstrates His power in judging the wicked, and God alone receives great glory when He blesses unworthy sinners.

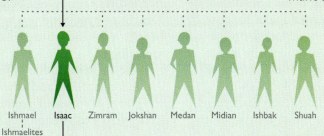

Abraham

Ishmael — Ishmaelites | Isaac | Zimram | Jokshan | Medan | Midian | Ishbak | Shuah

Esau — Edomites | Jacob/Israel

"The Lord's selection of Jacob over Esau is not based on merit but on grace, not on performance but on promise."

—Victor P. Hamilton

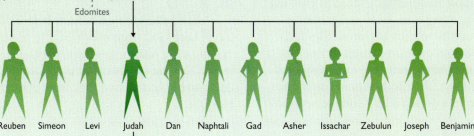

Reuben | Simeon | Levi | Judah | Dan | Naphtali | Gad | Asher | Issachar | Zebulun | Joseph | Benjamin

Jacob Wrestles with God

But twenty years later that didn't mean God was going to let Jacob off the hook for his foolishness. The Lord appears to him again in a dream and explains everything: God had taken over Jacob's genetics experiment (Gen. 31:11–13). He was the one who made sure Jacob became wealthy. Jacob was willing to admit this. But something inside him remained unbroken—until that very strange night when God stepped down to earth and wrestled with the patriarch.

> "It is not until the midnight battle that Jacob finally abandons his own resources and clings with desperation to his God."
>
> **—Stephen Motyer**

The guy who had always wriggled his way to the top could not wriggle fast enough this time. Here's the man who had always schemed to get his way, and now the best he could do was hold on. Near the end of that all-night wrestling match, God broke him. By the time it was over, he was still holding on—not to win or even to defend himself but to get a blessing. He knew he was wrestling with God. Years earlier, even before he had married Leah or Rachel, Jacob had made a vow saying that the Lord would be his God (Gen. 28:20–21), but it seems that nothing really changed. Only after wrestling with God does Jacob finally call the Lord his God, and not just the God of his fathers (Gen. 33:20). In that night of wrestling, it was as if the God he had pushed away was forcing the patriarch to take hold of the blessings He wanted to give him.

Out of this wrestling match Jacob came broken, blessed, and newly renamed. He was now Israel, the father of a nation that would bear his new name.

Jacob was like one of his own sheep, wandering around and going his own way. And you, because of the Fall of Adam, are the same way. All of us need to come to recognize how lost and tiny we are. With one touch, God dislocated Jacob's hip. This was an act of mercy because God could have done much worse. It would be better for you to admit your weakness while you're young than to have to wait till God wrestles that truth out of you. Some people don't admit it till they reach hell and perhaps not even then.

Thinking It Through 2.6

1. What circumstance in Isaac and Rebekah's life challenged the seed promise?

2. List at least two things Jacob did to demonstrate his self-serving, scheming character.

3. Did Jacob give up his place in the Abrahamic Covenant because of his sinful trickery? Explain your answer.

4. What was the result of Jacob's wrestling match with God?

5. What does election mean? How do we know it's not based on human works?

2.7 JOSEPH: GOD PLANNED IT FOR GOOD

Read Genesis 37; 39–45; 50:15–26
Memorize Genesis 50:20

The Providence of God

The story of Job taught us that we do not always know why things are happening to us. Sometimes we think we know, but we really do not know why things happen the way they do. Often, we're left wondering why God would allow certain things to happen to us—especially when we feel that we did nothing to deserve them.

You can imagine that Joseph spent many hours thinking about all the things that had happened to him. If any person had the right to claim that suffering and happiness were by chance, it was Joseph. But nowhere do we find that Joseph (or even Job) ever doubted God's control over any circumstance in his life. Even if you know the ending of Joseph's life, you could look at all the things that happened to him and (humanly speaking) think that he was very lucky for such an unlucky-guy.

It appears that he was always in the wrong place at the wrong time, which always seemed to put him in a circumstance where he would be in the right place at the right time. But did it really have anything to do with luck? Or was someone controlling these things?

Often when something good happens in a person's life, you will hear someone say, "It was the providence of God that took care of him." But what about the bad times in a person's life? Isn't that also the providence of God at work?

The providence of God is simply God's guiding and ongoing involvement with His creation to accomplish His purposes in history. Providence reveals God's sovereignty and is not limited to just the good things that happen in our lives. It includes the not-so-good things too. When things are going well, it's easy to accept God's providence. When things are not going so well, it's not so easy to accept God's providence. But sometimes God plans for us to go through some bad things because He has decided to put us in a situation where we can carry out His larger plans.

That is exactly what happened to Joseph. God planned for him to go through some bad things in order to carry out His larger plans.

If we observe Joseph's life, not from the beginning but from the end, we can clearly see how God accomplished His larger plan to protect Jacob's entire family. This is called reverse chronology because we're working our way backward through Joseph's life.

We'll save the very end of the story for later. So, we'll start right before the end begins—right when the ten brothers show up in Egypt.

- Joseph's family is fed because they bought grain from Joseph during a famine (41:50–42:5).

- Joseph was the one who sold grain to them because he was the governor over the land (42:6).

- Joseph was the governor because he had interpreted Pharaoh's dream and gave him a solution to the famine (41:14–49).

- Joseph was chosen to interpret Pharaoh's dream because the chief cupbearer remembered that Joseph had interpreted his dream two years earlier in prison (40:1–41:57).

- Joseph was in prison because he was falsely accused of trying to rape his master's (Potiphar's) wife (39:1–23).

- Joseph was Potiphar's servant because Potiphar bought him from some Midianites (37:36; 39:1).

- Joseph was owned by the Midianites because his brothers had sold him for twenty shekels of silver (37:27–28).

- Joseph was sold by his brothers because they hated him for being their father's favorite and because he had told them his dreams about them bowing to him (37:3–11, 18–26).

- Joseph was his father's favorite because his father loved Joseph's mother Rachel more than his other wives (37:3; cf. 29:30).

- Jacob loved Rachel more because . . .

Because why? Well, the "because whys" could continue on and on. But you get the point. Joseph was where he needed to be when his family needed him the most. Joseph didn't just happen to be chosen to control all the grain in Egypt. God in His sovereignty worked things out for good—both for Joseph and his family.

Truth and Nonfiction

Truth can be stranger than fiction in the world God rules because He is a more creative writer than any of the big names on the bestseller lists. His story—history—includes billions of characters and every place there is or was, and recounts thousands of years.

Just reading backward through the story of Joseph, you can see the amazing twists and turns it takes—and its incredible ending.

There is hardly a more exciting and interesting story in the Bible than the account of Joseph. It reads like a masterful novel. But that's a problem for some people. It includes so many "coincidences" that it seems unbelievable. Jacob's favorite son becomes a slave, gets thrown in jail, rises to be second in command of Egypt, then meets his brothers twenty years later—but they don't recognize him?

Coincidences?

You've read the story, and it would be impossible to retell it here half as well as Moses tells it in the first place. So let's just dig into what we can learn from it: why all the seeming coincidences and these amazing surprise twists?

Joseph reveals the answer in two places almost at the end of the book of Genesis. His own flesh-and-blood brothers had sold him as a slave and lied to his father, saying he was dead. But when they were reunited, Joseph wasn't vindictive. He didn't want revenge because he walked close enough to God to see a divine hand in his life story. He told his brothers not to be mad at themselves for selling him into slavery: "It was not you that sent me [here], but God" (Gen. 45:8). Why did God do it? "God did send me before you to preserve life" (45:5).

But what life? This is important. Whose lives are important enough that they are worth sending Joseph into slavery for? Joseph explains, "God sent me before you **to preserve you a posterity in the earth**" (45:7). The reason for everything in Joseph's amazing story is that God wanted to preserve the lives of His chosen people, Abraham's seed. God's promises to Abraham were driving the story of Abraham's grandson and great-grandsons. The lives of Abraham's family were so important that they were worth extraordinary efforts to preserve.

Way back when Joseph was a young teenager, he had dreams about the time when his

God worked throughout the various stages in Joseph's life to preserve His people.

family would come and bow down before him. Even his father, who treated him like a favorite, dismissed the dreams. But hidden in them was an amazing plan of God.

> ## "The dreams of an unlikely Israelite show that Yahweh is determined to bless the nations."
>
> —Stephen Dempster

Joseph's brothers never did seem to get it, though. Years later, after their father Jacob died, they were again afraid that the powerful Joseph was going to take revenge on them. So Joseph repeated himself: "As for you, ye **thought** evil against me; but God **meant** it unto good, to bring to pass, as it is this day, to save much people alive" (Gen. 50:20).

Now you'll have to pay close attention to this. These words were translated out of Hebrew, and in Hebrew the bolded words *thought* and *meant* are translations of the same word, *ḥashav* (חשב). It's a word often translated "plan," as in, "I'm planning to finish my project tonight." This means that the evil Joseph's brothers planned for him was also God's plan. The difference was the purpose: the brothers planned evil; God planned good. Whose plan won? The answer is obvious.

By His very nature, the Author of world history rules all circumstances, and He is pointing them to a good end for His people. "We know that all things work together for good to them that love God" (Rom. 8:28). There will be evil along the way, but God will never have to go to Plan B. Evil is like a bad note in the orchestra that God somehow weaves into the symphony, somehow making it even more beautiful by doing so.

God's Rule over Your Life

We're on the edge of some great mysteries here. No human being can explain how God can plan good out of evil—or all the reasons why He would want to. But there *is* something you can do. You can trust. You can depend on the God who rules over good and evil. Joseph's firm belief

in God's sovereignty freed him from the terrible chains of anger and bitterness that bind many people even today.

Believing and resting in God's loving rule can liberate you too. If you really believe that God rules the world, then you won't stay forever angry at the bully who terrorized you in third grade or the brother who is never nice to you. You won't forever worry about how your hair looks, or how tall or short you are, or even how muscular you are. Everything that happens to you and every dimension of your body was given to you by a good God. If you're one of His children, you can lean on Him and not on your own understanding. He will direct your paths in every detail. He's already doing it.

Joseph, Judah, and Jesus

The seed of the woman—the one who will crush the serpent's head—will come through one of the sons of Jacob. But which one? Joseph seems like the obvious answer. God used

Joseph in the Hall of Faith

Hebrews 11, often called the Hall of Faith (instead of the Hall of Fame), contains one little mention of Joseph. "By faith Joseph, when he died, made mention of the departing [the Exodus] of the children of Israel; and gave commandment concerning his bones" (Heb. 11:22).

This is talking about the very last paragraph of Genesis, where the dying Joseph makes the sons of Israel promise to preserve his bones so that they can be carried out of Egypt someday. But what does the writer of Hebrews mean when he says that Joseph did this "by faith"? What did Joseph have faith in?

Genesis 50:24 tells us. Joseph knew and had faith in the promises of God to his father, grandfather, and great-grandfather. He knew that the Israelites would one day leave Egypt because he knew that God had promised them another land. The very next book of the Bible, Exodus, tells the story of how Jacob's descendants finally did leave. (Did they remember to take Joseph's bones? Read Exodus 13:19 to find out.)

Jacob's Promises to His Sons		
Name	Description	Promised Future
Reuben	my firstborn, my might, the beginning of my strength, the excellence of dignity and power, unstable as water	He will not excel because of his past immorality.
Simeon	close brother to Levi, instrument of cruelty	He will be divided and scattered in the land.
Levi	close brother to Simeon, instrument of cruelty	He will be divided and scattered in the land.
Judah	like a lion	His brothers will praise him and bow to him; he will defeat his enemies; the scepter will not depart from him; he will prosper in the land.
Zebulun		He will be near the sea and be a haven for ships with his borders extending to the major Phoenician seaport of Sidon.
Issachar	like a strong donkey burdened down with labor	He will dwell in a pleasant land but in order to maintain peace must serve others.
Dan	like a serpent that bites	He will judge or defend his people by striking out at those who pass by.
Gad		He will be overcome at first but in the end will overcome his enemies.
Asher		He will produce an abundance of food from the fertile land and will enjoy the dainties of kings.
Naphtali	like a deer that freely roams	He will give of his prosperity.
Joseph (Ephraim & Manasseh)	like a fruitful bough	He will be prosperous; God will protect him from enemies who hate him; God will greatly bless him—surpassing all who came before.
Benjamin	like a ravenous wolf	He will devour his enemies and divide their spoil.

Joseph to preserve Jacob's family and keep the seed promise alive. But God is not indebted to anyone, not even Joseph. God recognized and praised Joseph's deep faith, but the honor of being the ancestor of the serpent-crushing seed would not be granted to Joseph. That honor would go to another son of Jacob, someone who points to God's amazing grace.

Thinking It Through 2.7

1. Define providence.
2. How did Joseph's trust in God keep him from being bitter?
3. Why did God lead Joseph through all his experiences of seeming coincidences and surprise twists?
4. In what way does the story of Joseph fulfill God's promise that all the nations of the earth would be blessed through Abraham's family?
5. Even though you may not be able to explain the mysteries of the plan of God in the circumstances of your life, what can you do?

2.8 JUDAH: A LION AMONG HIS BROTHERS

Read Genesis 38
Memorize Genesis 49:10

Why Is This Here?

If you were paying extra close attention during the Scripture reading for the previous section, you may have noticed that the reading assignment skipped Genesis chapter 38. It's the story of Jacob's son Judah.

Way back in the Cain and Abel section, you read that there's an important question that a lot of Bible readers fail to ask about Bible stories: "Why is this here?" Yes, Genesis 38 is here because it happened. But a lot of other things happened that didn't get put into the Bible. In fact, most of the things that happened to Jacob's sons didn't make it in. So what was so important about this particular incident in Judah's life that God decided it had to be told? And why is the Judah story here, stuck right in the middle of the Joseph story? You could skip Genesis 38 (you just did) and not even notice that it was missing. It doesn't seem to connect to Joseph at all.

Many Bible readers fail to ask these questions. But that's why you're taking a Bible class! One major goal of a good Bible education is to teach you how to read Scripture for yourself, and a huge part of that is just learning what questions to ask.

Judah in Genesis 38

The Bible doesn't say much about Judah before Genesis 38, and we don't find out much more after that. But what we do find out about Judah is very significant. Somehow, Judah manages to be the second-most important character (after Joseph) at every major stage in Joseph's story. When Joseph gets sold into slavery in Genesis 37, Judah is the one who makes the sale happen. When Joseph accuses his brothers of thievery, Judah is the one who pleads for the life of Benjamin, which convinces Joseph to reveal his identity. And by the end of Genesis, Judah even seems to rise above Joseph in the blessings handed out by their father, Jacob.

But we still need to figure out why the story of Judah in Genesis 38 gets told. The events

happened in the twenty years between Joseph's departure into Egypt and Jacob's journey to join him there. And the stories are pretty messy. Judah's first two sons, Er and Onan, didn't turn out very well at all. The Lord killed both of them for their wickedness. But Judah didn't see it as the Lord's hand. He apparently thought his daughter-in-law Tamar was bad luck for any husband who tried to have her. It was her fault that

Strange Marriage Customs

Before you can understand what the Bible is saying to you in the twenty-first century, you have to understand something of what life was like in Bible times.

So did you notice that it was a little weird that Judah's daughter-in-law Tamar married her dead husband's brother? And that she expected to marry the next brother after the second one died?

This practice was called "levirate marriage" (all that means is marriage to your brother-in-law, which is *levir* in Latin). Basically, if your brother died without children, you were supposed to marry his wife to keep the dead brother's family line going.

Why would such a custom arise in the first place? Ancient people weren't stupid or weird—at least, not any more than we are. Without strong national economies raising the standard of living for everyone, poverty and starvation were very real threats. Whatever wealth people had they wanted to keep within their own families so it didn't get divided up and shrunk.

So for Tamar to lose her husband meant she might go hungry (fortunately for her she could go back to her father's house). And for Judah to have no grandsons meant his wealth might go to someone he didn't want to have it. Add to this the fact that marriages were not made for love as much as for economic or political advantages—and now levirate marriage makes a bit more sense.

his sons had died, he seems to have thought. So when it came time to give his third son, Shelah, to Tamar, he went back on his word.

Tamar was not pleased about this, and she set a trap for Judah that ended up changing the course of history. She pretended to be a prostitute, somehow anticipating that her father-in-law would hire her—she must have known he was short on character. He left his personal seal and staff with her as a pledge that he would later send her a goat as payment. But later when he sent his friend Hirah with the goat, Hirah failed to find her and Judah gave up quickly. He figured there was no need for others to know what he'd done.

But soon everyone would know.

Judah

Judah could have lied when Tamar confronted him with the evidence. She was, in fact, pregnant and had his personal seal and staff in her possession, but he could have said that Tamar stole those things. Yet he admitted he was wrong, and not with the kind of halfway apology we've all used before. He even used the word *righteous* to describe Tamar. Was he admitting that he might have sinned against God? It's hard to tell yet.

The text also says that Judah did not commit immorality with Tamar again. And he apparently took full responsibility for rearing the two sons of Tamar—Perez and Zerah (Gen. 46:12).

The fact that Judah didn't resort to his father's trickery when he was caught suggests that something has changed inside him. The impulse to lie is so strong in that situation—especially after he had just hypocritically demanded that she be burned to death! What stopped him from denying everything? The text doesn't say. That's the beauty of a story. We just know something is different; this is not quite the Judah we used to know even a verse ago.

Judah and Joseph

By the time Judah meets up again with Joseph, it seems as if Judah has become the leader of the eleven brothers. The Bible even refers to them as "Judah and his brethren" (Gen. 44:14). And now we get to see Judah tested again. Has something inside him really changed? Or is he shifty like his father was? Or a traitor to the

family like the Judah who sold Joseph into slavery and pretended he was dead?

We get a strong hint that Judah has changed when he pledges to Jacob that he will get Benjamin safely to Egypt and back. Reuben tried promising the same thing, but Jacob didn't buy it. But Judah succeeds (perhaps Jacob trusts him more than he trusts Reuben).

But then, after they show up in Egypt a second time and get their next installment of grain, the hardest test comes. Joseph has his silver cup placed in Benjamin's sack, and he calls the brothers back to him to account for the cup they have "stolen."

Joseph is putting pressure on the most sensitive point in the family: Jacob's love for Benjamin. Jacob's special love for Joseph is what drove his jealous brothers almost to kill him. And now they have an easy opportunity to take revenge on their father again for his favoritism. Will Judah and his brothers do to Benjamin what they did to Joseph? The weight of responsibility falls on Judah, and he is the one that speaks: "What shall we say unto my lord? what shall we speak? or how shall we clear ourselves? God hath found out the iniquity [guilt] of thy servants" (Gen. 44:16).

What is Judah talking about? What guilt? Judah knew he hadn't stolen the cup. He's talking about their guilt in selling Joseph into slavery so many years before. God, Judah says, is now punishing them for that sin. Judah then offers all the brothers to become Joseph's slaves, and when Joseph says that only the guilty one (Benjamin) will need to stay, he is pressing hard on that same sore spot that years before had resulted in his being sold into slavery. The brothers can do to Benjamin, the new favorite, the same thing they did to Joseph. Will they?

Judah, at least, really has changed from what he used to be. He unselfishly offers to stay in Egypt himself and become Joseph's slave—so Benjamin can go back to Jacob in Canaan. Judah's act of selflessness is what pushes Joseph over the edge. He can wait no longer. He reveals his true identity to his brothers.

There are few more dramatic stories in all of Scripture—or even all of world literature. Joseph plays a central role, but standing right beside him at the center of the story is Judah.

Reuben

Simeon

Levi

Judah

Zebulun

Issachar

Dan

Gad

Asher

Naphtali

Joseph

Benjamin

Judah as a Lion's Cub

Years later, Jacob lay dying in Egypt, and he called all his sons together. Genesis 49 tells us what he said, and the heading in your Bible over that chapter probably says something like "Jacob Blesses His Sons." That may not seem quite right: some of the things he says don't sound like blessings. But remember that all of them get to stay in the covenant family. Every one of the twelve has it a lot better than Ishmael or Esau.

Reuben, Jacob's firstborn, gets to stay in despite the fact that he committed immorality with Jacob's concubine (Gen. 35:22). But because of that sin, he will not keep his preeminent spot among his twelve brothers.

This is significant because one of those twelve is going to be the father of the line of the seed of the woman, the one who will crush the serpent's head. Which brother will it be? Who will take the preeminent spot?

It ends up being none other than Judah. Judah, the son who stands with Joseph at the center of the story of Jacob's sons. His blessing from Jacob is much longer than anyone else's except Joseph's. And Judah's blessing includes some promises that set it apart. Joseph dreamed that his brothers would one day bow down to him. They did. But now Jacob predicts that all the brothers will bow down to Judah instead (Gen. 49:8).

And Jacob goes further. He compares Judah to a lion, the king of beasts. He says that "the scepter [the symbol of authority held by a king] shall not depart from Judah" (49:10) until a day in the distant future when, Jacob says, someone will come who really owns that scepter. (Can you catch the hint of a certain person?) Jacob then promised that different nations would come to "obey" Judah.

Apparently, a change in Judah that you would never have expected leads to his tribe becoming the kingly one in Israel.

> "God changes Judah and then rewards him for changing."
>
> —Bryan Smith

So What?

It's always useful to ask "So what?" after reading a section of the Bible. In other words, how can you use the truths in this passage? Yes, you ought to be like Judah who took responsibility for his sin and accepted its consequences—both in front of Tamar and in front of Joseph. In God's world it's always better to confess and forsake sin. God promises you'll receive mercy you wouldn't have if you tried to hide your wrongdoing (Prov. 28:13).

But remember that the Bible isn't mainly about giving us good and bad human examples (though it does do that). It's about what God is doing to redeem His fallen creation. The most important way to "use" the story of Judah is to start getting excited about the way the Bible's story is coming together even before the first book is done. The story is shaping up: one family is going to be a source of blessing for the whole world. And one tribe in that family, the tribe of Judah, is going to be the special focus of that blessing. But how will God do it? How will God bring that blessing all the way from Judah?

Here's another hint—this story has been pointing to Him.

Thinking It Through 2.8

1. List the sins of Judah mentioned in Genesis 38.

2. List the evidences of spiritual change in Judah.

3. Why is Genesis 38 stuck right in the middle of the Joseph story? What does Judah have to do with that story?

4. How do we know that Judah is going to be the top brother and not Reuben or Joseph?

5. Explain levirate marriage.

UNIT 2 REVIEW

Scripture Memory

Genesis 12:1–3   Genesis 22:16–18
Psalm 110:4   Genesis 24:60
Hebrews 7:24–25   Genesis 35:2–3
Genesis 15:5–6   Genesis 50:20
Genesis 17:1–2   Genesis 49:10

Understand the Story

1. What can you learn from God's choice of Abraham instead of those who seem more righteous?

2. Who are the only priests qualified to stand between God and man?

3. Why is it significant that Abraham was asleep and God alone walked through the five split animal carcasses in Genesis 15?

4. What is the significance of the offeror laying his hands on the sacrifice's head? What is the significance of the offeror, not the priest, slaughtering the animal sacrifice?

5. How does the story of Isaac and Rebekah display God's steadfast love?

6. True or False. God chooses people because He can look ahead and see how faithful they will be to Him.

7. True or False. Only the good things that happen to you in your life are providential.

8. Judah definitely changes in the course of his life, but most would agree that Judah doesn't come across as a more faithful or deserving person than Joseph. If this is the case, why did Judah gain the top spot among the brothers?

Developing Observation Skills

9. Read Genesis 12:1–3. Circle the three major promises that God gave to Abraham.

10. Read Genesis 15:1–6. What is the main topic of the conversation and to which of the three major promises to Abraham does it relate?

   In the conversation, how did you figure out what the main topic was?

   a. The narrator announced the topic of their conversation.

   b. The topic was repeated throughout their conversation.

11. How did Paul use observation skills to come to the conclusion that Abraham was justified by faith and not by works?

12. Read Genesis 22:11–12, 15–18. Circle all the references to the Angel of the Lord (including pronouns). How do you know that the Angel of the Lord is God?

13. Read Genesis 28:20–22. What words in Jacob's vow indicate that Jacob isn't submitted to God yet?

14. What observation method was used in the textbook to demonstrate how God carried out His providential plan in Joseph's life?

Connecting the Story to the Big Story

15. Why is a priesthood like Melchizedek's necessary to Christ's fulfillment of God's redemptive plan? (Ps. 110:4)

16. Several events in Jacob's life prove that the Abrahamic Covenant is unconditional. List several of them and explain how each one proves that point.

17. In what way does the story of Joseph fulfill God's promise that all the nations of the earth would be blessed through Abraham's family? (Gen. 12:1–3)

18. Explain why the Abrahamic seed blessing passed through the line of Judah and not through Jacob's firstborn, Reuben.

Lessons for Life

19. How should the failures of God's chosen people be encouraging to us?

20. What quality did every one of God's chosen people (the ones he chose to pass on the Abrahamic seed promises) eventually demonstrate, making possible their covenant relationship with God? What must you demonstrate that you have in order to be in a covenant relationship with God?

UNIT 3

GOD'S COVENANT WITH ISRAEL THROUGH MOSES

God promised Adam that the seed of the woman would crush the head of the serpent, and He promised Abraham that his seed would bless the whole world. And now the sons of Jacob are having families of their own. But the new pharaoh doesn't remember Joseph, and he decides to stop treating the Israelites as guests. They will now be slaves. But God remembers His people, and He makes a covenant with them so that they will walk in His ways and be His people.

God redeemed Abraham's
seed from Egypt.

God made a covenant with the
Israelites and gave them His law.

3.1 MOSES AND THE NAME OF GOD

Read Exodus 1–2
Memorize Exodus 3:13–14

At least four centuries have passed since the events at the end of Genesis (Exod. 12:40–41; cf. Gen. 15:13; Gal. 3:17), and things have changed for God's chosen people, the seed of Abraham. Joseph is long dead. The Egyptians who exalted Joseph to a high position and welcomed his whole family have now turned against them and enslaved them. Why has this happened?

For one very simple reason: God's promises are working. God had told Adam and Eve to "be fruitful and multiply," and He had promised Abraham that his seed would do just that. They would grow. But the Israelites' rapid growth scared Pharaoh because they grew so much that they filled the land of Egypt and became exceedingly strong (Exod. 1:7).

God had also promised Adam and Eve that He would put "enmity"—hostility, hatred, contention—between the seed of the woman and the seed of the serpent. They would have conflict. And the conflict between Pharaoh and the Israelites is just one example in the long history of that enmity.

Abraham's Seed in Slavery

It's impossible to know if any Israelites knew anything about the conflict God promised between the seed of the serpent and the seed of the woman. All they knew was that they were being crushed under a great weight of Egyptian slavery and that maybe their God could help.

The kind of total slavery the Israelites were under is an offense to God because all humans are made in His image and therefore have certain privileges. But there were many slaves in the world when Moses headed back to Egypt to help the Israelite ones. No doubt many slaves that year cried out to God—or the gods, at least—to save them. But there was one group of slaves on earth who had a special relationship with God. Those slaves had a covenant with God.

So when those slaves called out to God, Scripture records that He listened. If Abraham's seed was going to inherit a land and be a blessing, they would have to come out of Egypt.

> "God remembered his covenant with Abraham, with Isaac, and with Jacob."
>
> **—Exodus 2:24**

Moses the Great Hero?

God's first step toward delivering His people happened before they even asked. He prepared a tiny baby to become their future leader. And when they did ask, He began to move more obviously. He appeared to Moses, now an eighty-year-old shepherd in the wilderness, and told him it was time for him to move back to Egypt. Moses' job was to go speak to Pharaoh and tell him to let God's people go.

When you start reading Exodus, it seems like the Bible is setting up Moses to be a great hero—a lot like Joseph. Finally, someone will miraculously arise and powerfully save God's people from slavery!

But then the great hero runs away and hides in the desert for forty years. And even when God approaches him in the burning bush, Moses doesn't exactly sound like a potential hero. He seems like he'd rather just stay an old shepherd. His questions to God are really objections and delay tactics. "Who am I to do this?" he asks. And then he basically says, "Well, even if I do go, what am I supposed to tell the Israelites about who sent me? What is Your name?"

preserved at birth

raised by Pharaoh's daughter

a prince in Egypt

God uniquely prepared Moses to lead His people.

a shepherd

The Very Name of God

There are titles and there are names. A title can point to a person who holds a specific, official role—like the *president*. But a name is the specific person in that role—it is personal. Many men have held the title *president of the United States*, but there has been only one George Washington who served as the president. The word *God* is not God's name. It is his title. Much like *president* was George Washington's title and not his name.

When God appeared to Moses and revealed His name, He didn't give His title. He went deeper, to His very name. But that name sounds confusing: "I AM WHO I AM." Is God trying to avoid Moses' question? That doesn't sound like a name.

God is actually doing something very special. He's giving Moses His name *and* giving Him some of the deep meaning of that name. The root word for "I AM" is the same as the root for the Hebrew name you know as "the Lord." (We pronounce the name as "Yahweh.") So when God says His name is "I AM WHO I AM," He is digging deeper into the meaning of His name "the Lord."

That doesn't mean we now have it all figured out. "I AM WHO I AM" is still difficult to understand. It seems to be revealing two aspects about God's character: (1) God is free and (2) God is self-existent. In other words, God does whatever He wants (of course whatever He wants is always consistent with other aspects of His character), and God's existence doesn't depend on anyone else's.

Moses didn't have to be afraid because by knowing God's name (that He is free and hence all-powerful), he could have assurance that God would accomplish His plan. Moses also could know that God's name shows He has the authority to carry out His plan. So Moses was only a messenger communicating God's orders.

(1) **"I AM WHO I AM."** "No one else can make Me be or do something else."

The God of the Bible isn't sitting on His hands, waiting for people to do what He says. The God of Scripture is all-powerful. He made one of the greatest kings in the history of the world eat grass for seven years! And at the end of that time, that king said, "He doeth according to his will in the army of heaven, and among the inhabitants of the earth: and none can stay [stop] his hand, or say unto him, What doest thou?" (Dan. 4:35).

(2) **"I AM."** "Everyone else *is* only if I say so, but I exist even though no one ever created Me and no one keeps Me alive."

God doesn't have to prove His existence to anyone. He just *is*. He always is what He always was and what He always will be.

In the next verse after the "I AM" statement, God calls Himself "the Lord, the God of your fathers" (Exod. 3:15). But "He is" for the Israelites only after He exists for Himself. As the Bible later says, all things are from Him and for Him and through Him (Col. 1:16–17). He doesn't need anyone else; it is simply the overflow of His goodness that leads Him to love and rescue a people such as those in the line of Abraham.

So What . . . Again?

When you read Scripture, it's good to ask, "What is the Bible saying to me right now?" The Bible is a very practical and useful book. But very often you have to ask another question first before you can know how to "use" in real life what you read in the Bible. You have to ask, "What is this telling me about God?" Only if you answer that question will you know what to do with the truth yourself. The Bible even says that just looking at God—really fixing your gaze on His glorious perfections—*changes* you (2 Cor. 3:18). If you want to be more like God, you have to start by watching Him.

So knowing what God's name means may make no obvious, practical difference in your life tomorrow. You might not even think about it. But if you've paid attention to this section, and if you're a child of God, you've been drinking in a view of God that *will* change you.

Pharaoh's Challenge—God's Answer

Pharaoh was not one of God's children. Moses did finally approach him in Exodus 5, and he demanded in the name of Yahweh that Pharaoh let the Israelites go. Pharaoh shot back with a challenge: "Who is the Lord, that I should obey his voice to let Israel go? I know not the Lord, neither will I let Israel go" (Exod. 5:2).

Pharaoh knew many gods, but he didn't recognize Yahweh. Who is the Lord? Pharaoh was about to find out.

Thinking It Through 3.1

1. Why did God hear and respond to the Israelites' cry for help but not, presumably, the cries of all the other slaves on earth at that time?

2. Why would it be wrong to say that the Bible presents Moses as a hero?

3. "I AM WHO I AM" seems to be revealing two aspects about God's character. What are those two aspects?

4. Explain how the meaning of God's name could have helped Moses with his mission.

5. Jesus of Nazareth in the New Testament tells a group of Jews, "Before Abraham was, I am" (John 8:58). Now that you know about God's name that He revealed at the burning bush, what do you think Jesus meant by this statement?

3.2 PHARAOH'S HARD HEART AND THE GLORY OF GOD

Read Exodus 7:14–12:36
Memorize Romans 9:17–18

A Difficult Passage

The Bible is inerrant. That means that God's Word does not contain any errors. But it doesn't mean that it's always simple to understand. There are difficult passages in the Bible. Some passages of Scripture seem to contradict others. But the mistake is not in either passage, but in our own understanding.

When you come upon an apparent contradiction in the Bible, thorough observation and accurate interpretation of the text will help you clear up misunderstandings. The more you observe, the better your interpretation will be; and the better your interpretation, the better your application will be.

Well that all sounds nice, but what does it actually mean? It means that sometimes you will think there's a contradiction in the Bible. For example, how can God harden Pharaoh's heart but still hold him accountable for having a hard heart? As you progress through this lesson, you will see that sometimes we need to observe more—like reading what Paul has to say about the issue. Sometimes we are interpreting the text wrongly because it doesn't fit what we think is fair.

Sometimes we simply cannot understand God's dealings with people when it comes to "fairness." That's because we don't know the big picture. We don't know all the facts. And that's why God said concerning His mercy,

> For my thoughts are not your thoughts, neither are your ways my ways, saith the Lord. For as the heavens are higher than the earth, so are my ways higher than your ways, and my thoughts than your thoughts. (Isa. 55:8–9)

Sometimes we don't know as much as we think we do. And more often than not, we're not as smart as we think we are. In those times, we must accept God's Word by faith and pray for understanding.

God hardened Pharaoh's heart.

What Was God's Purpose?

Exodus 7–15 raises a tough question. God told Moses in Exodus 4 to go do a bunch of miracles in front of Pharaoh and to tell him to let the Israelites go. Moses was already nervous about this, and what God said next couldn't have helped his nerves very much. "I will harden his heart, [so] that he shall not let the people go" (Exod. 4:21). A soft heart is one that is sensitive to pressure; someone with a soft heart listens and is ready to give in. But someone with a hard heart has a rock in his chest. Talking to him is like talking to a piece of granite. God said He would make Pharaoh like that. What was God's purpose?

Paul on Pharaoh

Do you realize that we're not the first ones to ask these kinds of questions about this passage in the Bible? In fact, the Bible directly addresses this question. You should always remember to look at other Bible passages to explain the difficult Bible

Pointers for Difficult Passages

Very few people like to be told they've made a mistake. Even fewer like to be told they are wrong. In fact, it's hard to think of anyone who likes to be told he's mistaken or wrong. But we are human, and we make mistakes. A lot of them.

So it is no surprise that sometimes we make mistakes when we interpret Scripture. But make no mistake, the Bible is without mistake.

Every time we accuse the Bible of a contradiction or of making a mistake, it is we who have misinterpreted the Bible. Fortunately, those misinterpretations are easily remedied. When we misinterpret Scripture, we can make several mistakes. These are the most common:

1. **Assuming what you cannot explain is not explainable**

   Sometimes you come across a passage that you simply cannot understand. You should never think that because you can't understand it, no one can understand it. At times you simply need to study the passage and look at what other people who have studied the passage say. This type of mistake is often corrected by going to Bible dictionaries and commentaries.

2. **Presuming the Bible wrong until proven right**

   No one likes to be condemned as guilty and have to prove they are innocent. How would you feel if every time you took a test, you had to prove to the teacher that you didn't cheat? You would soon resent the teacher and the process of taking a test. In a sense, the Bible should be treated in the same way that you like to be treated. You should assume that the authors of the Bible are telling the truth. The burden of proof is on those who claim the authors are not telling the truth.

3. **Thinking your interpretation is more accurate than God's revelation**

   The Scriptures are God's breathed-out words to humanity. As such, they are without error. But your interpretations are not without error. You make mistakes. We all make mistakes. That is part of being human. Part of being God is that He doesn't make

mistakes. You must remember that your interpretation is an opinion, not the final say. When there appears to be a contradiction, you should always submit your opinion to God's Word.

4. **Ignoring the context of the passage**

   Ask any real-estate agent what the three most important things in real estate are, and he will tell you, "Location, Location, Location." Ask any theologian what the three most important things in interpreting a passage are, and he will tell you, "Context, Context, Context."

   For example, the Bible says, "There is no God." Even the Bible acknowledges that God doesn't exist. But wait, where is that found? This particular quote (and there are several like this) comes from Isaiah 44:6 where the Lord speaks: "Beside me there is no God." In other words, God is saying He is the only God and there is no other God but Him. Big difference!

5. **Thinking that the Bible approves of all it records**

   The Bible records lots of things. Among these things are sins that people have committed. The Bible records murders, people stealing things, idol worship, and many other sins. It even records lies that people spoke. The Bible is true in that it accurately records what was said, what was done, or what was thought—even if those things were sins. It doesn't mean the Bible condones them; it merely means that the Bible truthfully records them.

6. **Not looking for passages that explain the difficult passage**

   There are some passages that are difficult to understand but are actually explained by another passage. In Genesis 22:2, God told Abraham, "Take now thy son, thine only son Isaac." But what about Ishmael? He was born several years earlier. Did God forget about him? No. If you go back one chapter, God said that Abraham's descendants would be traced only through Isaac (21:12). This is also clarified in Hebrews 11:17–18.

passages (see pointer 6 from the previous page). Read Romans 9:15–23 to find Paul's answer.

In his letter to the Romans, Paul answers the question of why God made Pharaoh stubborn by pointing back to God's own explanation in the Old Testament. God said to Pharaoh, "For this cause have I raised thee up, for to shew in thee my power; and that my name may be declared throughout all the earth" (Exod. 9:16; cf. Rom. 9:17).

> "Everything that Pharaoh had, the Lord had given, including the breath he used to say no to the Lord."
>
> —Dorian Coover-Cox

We must also remember that Pharaoh starts not as an innocent person but as a sinner who has been oppressing God's covenant people. He deserves judgment. He also challenges God from the first meeting: "Who is the Lord, that I should obey his voice to let Israel go? I know not the Lord, neither will I let Israel go" (Exod. 5:2).

Every time Pharaoh's heart and the hearts of his servants harden, God gets another opportunity to (a) make His power known and (b) declare His glorious name over all the earth. Every hardening means another chance to answer Pharaoh's taunt by letting him know who God is.

The ten plagues showed Pharaoh, Egypt, and the whole world who the Lord is. And each plague increased in power and intensity over the previous one. The first three plagues (Nile to blood, frogs, gnats) were basically brief inconveniences. And the Egyptian magicians were able to mimic the first two. But then God started to show His strength. The next plague, flies, ruined the land (Exod. 8:24). The fifth one killed off very valuable horses, donkeys, and camels—animals people relied on to live.

Finally, God started touching the Egyptians themselves. In the sixth plague they received painful boils. And as they lay suffering from the boils, God sent hail to destroy their crops and then locusts to eat up whatever the hail hadn't demolished.

It sounds a little weird, maybe, that the ninth plague was darkness. That's not so bad, right? Only little kids are afraid of the dark. But have you ever been in a pitch-black cave? Can you imagine how terrifying it would be to be stuck in there for three days with (perhaps) only a couple of small candles? And this was after eight other frightening plagues. There's only one thing worse.

And God was about to do that, too.

Salvation by Substitution

In the biblical record, every major "salvation" God brings, He brings through judgment. Noah and the animals were saved through the judgment of most of humanity. Lot was saved as fire fell from heaven on the city he'd been living in. As one author put it, "When God saves his

The Ten Plagues				
1 Nile to blood *Exodus 7:14–25*	**2** Frogs *Exodus 8:1–15*	**3** Gnats (lice) *Exodus 8:16–19*	**4** Flies *Exodus 8:20–32*	**5** Plague on cattle *Exodus 9:1–7*
6 Boils *Exodus 9:8–12*	**7** Hail *Exodus 9:13–35*	**8** Locusts *Exodus 10: 1–20*	**9** Darkness *Exodus 10:21–29*	**10** Death of the firstborn *Exodus 11:1–12:36*

people, he delivers them by bringing judgment on their enemies."

But we shouldn't think that God is random in His judgment. He actually told Abraham that one of His reasons for leaving Israel in Egypt so long was that the people they were going to conquer in Canaan, the Amorites, weren't yet guilty enough to be destroyed ("The iniquity of the Amorites is not yet full," Gen. 15:16).

When the countless sins committed by the Egyptians have finally filled the cup of God's wrath nearly full, God sends Moses to warn Pharaoh that every single firstborn, man and animal, in all Egypt is going to die. The Lord hardens Pharaoh's heart, and he still refuses to let the people go.

> "Salvation always comes through judgment."
>
> —Jim Hamilton

And then the story is interrupted. God needs to give some final warnings and instructions to the children of Israel before He carries out the tenth plague. Exodus 12 reminds the Jews that even though they are God's chosen people, Yahweh's holy wrath stands against Jewish sin just like it stands against Egyptian sin. They weren't chosen because they were good and the Egyptians were bad. Even the Jewish firstborns will die if someone doesn't die in their place. So God commands Israel to slaughter lambs and paint

the blood on their doorposts. Lambs will die; firstborns will live.

> "The Israelites are being taught an important principle: God saves by substitution. His people deserve to die for their sin, but another dies instead."
>
> —Vaughan Roberts

The New Nation's First National Anthem

Now, after 430 years, God delivers the Israelites so that they might serve Him. And one big promise to Abraham has been fulfilled. The Jews are no longer just an extended family like they were when Jacob came down to Egypt to see his son Joseph. The Jews are a nation—like the sand on the seashore.

Moses gathers Joseph's bones, the Egyptians shower their former slaves with gifts, and the people head across the border. As if His other miracles weren't enough, God literally parts the sea in front of them. Having slaughtered the firstborn Egyptians just days before, now God drowns Pharaoh himself and his whole army (Ps. 136:15). All the Israelites have to do this time is be silent and watch God save them (Exod. 14:14).

What do you do when your team comes from way behind and wins the game in the last two seconds? You can't help yourself—you jump up and down and scream! You might even start singing your team's fight song! But the Exodus from Egypt is far more important than any game, so the joy these people feel is far greater too. They're not slaves anymore! They burst out singing what we now call the Song of Moses (Exod. 15:1–18). But the song is not, of course, about Moses at all. It's about the greatness, power, and faithful love of the Lord. The Exodus put these things on display for the whole world to see.

Hardening of Hearts

If God hadn't hardened Pharaoh's heart, we wouldn't have this display of God's glory. And this is what Paul is getting at in his explanation of this theological problem.

Think of it like this: when you look very closely at a mosaic, you don't see a pattern. You just see tiles. They might be cracked; they might even be ugly. That's like what God sees when

He looks at wicked things like Pharaoh's hard heart. God didn't rub His hands with glee when Pharaoh drowned in the Red Sea or when the Egyptian milkmaid's firstborn son lay dead at her feet. "I have no pleasure in the death of him that dieth," God said later (Ezek. 18:32).

But while we limited humans are usually stuck staring at little colored tiles, God is able to step back and see the whole beautiful mosaic. The ugliest tiles combine with the most attractive ones to form a glorious picture of God's glory. This is a picture that God can look on with pleasure.

This textbook is trying to help you step back, too, and look at the long-term plan of God to see the beauty of that big picture. You, too, can view that picture with pleasure. And if you do, it will change the way you look at all the other pictures in your life. The frustrations and disappointments you experience, the temptations and trials, even your acne and that kid who just won't leave you alone—they're all part of a bigger picture that God is making. And somehow they will make the final product more beautiful.

Thinking It Through 3.2

1. Why did God deliver His people?

2. What was God's purpose for the plagues and for hardening Pharaoh's heart? (Exod. 8:10, 22; cf. 7:5, 17)

3. What is the really tough question that Exodus 8–15 makes us think about?

4. Read Exodus 9:13–17. Quote and explain the phrase from the passage that tells *how* Pharaoh became king over Egypt at this time.

5. Read Romans 11:33–36. (a) How does this passage describe God and the things God knows or thinks? (b) What phrase from this passage describes the ultimate purpose for all things?

3.3 THE ISRAELITES: STILL SLAVES

Read Exodus 15:22–16:36
Memorize Exodus 15:26

There's clearly something wrong with the descendants of Jacob. Just days ago they were slaves, but slaves who got to watch more amazing and obvious miracles from God than almost anyone in history. And now they are complaining. It would be sort of like winning a free smartphone, exactly the one you've been wanting, and then turning around and grumbling because you didn't get a free case along with it. No, that's not good enough . . . Try this: It would be like God shining a light out of heaven and sending angels to sing a glorious chorus as they present you an awesome smartphone that hasn't even been invented yet, right in front of all your friends. And then you start complaining that the heavenly light hurts your eyes.

But don't start feeling superior to these Israelites. Their problem was not a Jewish problem; it was a human problem. Every descendant of Adam has been scarred deeply by his Fall into sin, and there are no exceptions outside the one who we've been catching a glimpse of throughout this book.

And there's another reason not to feel superior. These former slaves were in religious kindergarten. We don't know what they knew about the Lord while they were slaves. But they were slaves! Slaves don't get theological education—no Bible classes, no memory verses, no church services.

The Israelites hardened their hearts despite all God had done for them.

> "After the first great victory came the first big test."
>
> —Douglas Stuart

So they failed their first test. But how did you do on yours? You were just a kindergartener; it's okay if you wrote your capital *E* backward. Or perhaps you misspelled a few words. It's hard to know how to judge the Israelites.

God, at least, seems very patient with them. He basically says, "Just listen and obey, and you won't suffer the diseases I put on the Egyptians" (Exod. 15:26). There is an implied threat in this. The Israelites are showing that they're not much better (if at all) than the Egyptians, and someday God may punish them the way He punished the Egyptians. But there's hope too. God said, "I am the Lord that healeth thee" (Exod. 15:26). And He proves it: He sends meat, and He sends bread, which the Israelites call "what's that?" (*manna*) because they've never seen it before.

Free food from heaven isn't enough for the Israelites, though. Soon they're complaining about not having enough water. And their complaint turns nasty. They basically say to Moses, "You just brought us out here to kill us all!"

And still the Lord is patient. They get the water they ask for. But God doesn't fail to notice that the people He's testing turn around and test Him back. "Is the Lord among us, or not?" (Exod. 17:7). That's what they want to know.

EXTERNAL SLAVERY	INTERNAL SLAVERY
God freed the Israelites from bondage to the Egyptians.	Christ frees us from bondage to our sin.

And what a ridiculous question! Is the Lord among us?! What more does it take to prove God's presence than the huge string of amazing miracles they've just seen? They should realize that God has done great things for them in the past. These works of God should give them a basis for trusting Him in their difficult circumstance.

You

There are several takeaways from this story. The first one is kind of simple, but it shouldn't be missed: don't complain. Why? Because, if you're one of God's children, even your hardest trial is nothing compared to the change God has performed in you. If you're a Christian, you've been freed from slavery just like the Israelites, except that your slavery was far worse because it was internal. Only God can break chains that are inside you.

And that's one way to keep yourself from complaining. When you can feel the whiny, "Aw, Mom!" about to escape your lips, ask God for grace to really believe and feel the blessings you have—blessings that far outweigh having to take out the trash during your after-homework screen time.

Another takeaway has to do with whether you really believe God's blessings are from God. Not every middle schooler or junior higher who goes to church every week and has regular Bible classes really believes what he's being taught. You are getting to the age—if you're not there already—when a lot of people start questioning what they've always heard. This is not necessarily bad or wrong. True Christianity is one religion that you can't be born into; at some point in your life you'll have to choose whether you as an individual believe it or not. Maybe that point has already come. Maybe not.

In either case, learn a lesson from the deep fallenness of the Israelites. Don't test God. Don't say, "God, if you perform a miracle for me, I'll

The Second Sabbath in Recorded History

God took a day of rest after He created the world. Genesis 2 says that "God blessed the seventh day, and sanctified it: because . . . in it he had rested from all his work." But whether anyone on earth ever knew or cared about that special day we don't know for sure.

But after the Israelites came out of Egypt, God showed that He still remembered and still cared. One day a week is supposed to be set aside as a day of rest. The Hebrew word that Jewish people use even now for that day is *Shabbat*—Sabbath. And the first time that word appears in the Bible is here in Exodus 16.

God took it seriously enough that, once a week, He miraculously made the manna last two days so that the people could cease from work.

believe in You. Umm . . . make this rock disappear!" Don't even demand that your grandmother's cancer disappear—or that your dad's job *reappear.* Don't test God like that. Just like with the Israelites, God has good reasons for His choices. And anyway, the Israelites of Moses' day refused to believe even though they did see incredible miracles. Many others in the Bible were the same way. There's no guarantee that you'd be an exception. (In fact, you'd probably be like the rich man's brothers in Jesus' story in Luke 16:31: "If they hear not Moses and the prophets, neither will they be persuaded, though one rose from the dead.")

Former Slaves Still Enslaved

The effects of the Fall are so deep that people often do and say things that don't make any sense. Clearly, the Israelites are not—or at least not yet—going to be the seed of the woman that crushes the head of the serpent. These former slaves have a problem that goes deeper than slavery. In fact, they're in need of more saving than they've already received.

The Wilderness of Sin

This place sounds like it has that name for a reason! It was because the Israelites sinned there, right?

No, it's actually just a coincidence that the English word *sin* is spelled the same as the Hebrew place name *Sin* (סין in Hebrew—pronounced like "seen").

There are indeed some words that are the same in Hebrew and in English. But almost all of them are either names, like *Nathan*, *Sarah*, and *Adam* or religious words like *hallelujah*, *amen*, and *hosanna*. Perhaps the only exception is the simple word *sack*, as in a sack of potatoes.

So there's no secret message in the name Wilderness of Sin. The Bible doesn't hide what it's really saying with silly word tricks. And think about it. If the Bible were playing a word game here, wouldn't English-speaking people be the only ones to get it? The Spanish equivalent, *Desierto de Sin,* literally means "Desert of Without."

Thinking It Through 3.3

1. According to the Bible reading for this section, what sins did the Israelites commit several times?

2. List several factors that could have contributed to the Israelites' failures, and highlight the most significant.

3. How did God respond to the Israelites when they sinned during this period between the Exodus and the giving of the law?

4. Based on this section, why shouldn't you complain?

5. Reread Exodus 16:1–17:7, noting how God responds to His people's demands. Now read Psalm 95 to see what attitude God expresses toward the nation of Israel. Focus on verses 8–10. (Note: Psalm 95 is referring to several events.) (a) Distinguish between God's responses in the psalm and in the Exodus account. (b) Why do they seem different?

3.4 THE ISRAELITES: A HOLY NATION

Read Exodus 19:1–8; 20:1–20
Memorize Exodus 19:5–6

God made several promises to Abraham. And do you remember the three categories they fell into? Land, seed, and blessing. By the end of Genesis, Jacob's sons are not in their own land, but the seed is growing a little. It's beginning to poke its head out of the soil. As for blessing, by the time the book of Exodus opens, it seems to be hiding somewhere outside Egypt.

But the Exodus event has changed Jacob's seed from an underclass in Egypt into the world's newest nation. The seed has grown in a big way. Now some two million strong, they stand at Mount Sinai—the place where the bush burned and the place God promised Moses He would bring them back to for them to serve Him (Exod. 3:12). It's like they're standing on the edge of their new land, but Sinai blocks their way.

But this is a people that doesn't seem to deserve a trip to the Promised Land if you look at how they've been acting recently.

The Israelites show at least one good sign. They assemble before the Lord and promise that they're ready to do whatever God has commanded. They say very boldly, "All that the Lord hath spoken we will do" (Exod. 19:8; 24:3).

But no one in the human race, let alone the Israelites, has a very good track record of doing whatever God commands. Adam and Eve had only one command to worry about, and they were perfect people—and yet they still chose to go their own way. Even the great heroes of the faith, such as Abraham and Noah, failed in key ways. They certainly didn't do *everything* God said. Will the Israelites do any better?

A Kingdom of Priests

God wants them to do better because He's still bent on blessing the whole world through the family of Abraham. The words He uses at Sinai shouldn't be overlooked because they show how He wants Israel to bless the world:

> Ye have seen what I did unto the Egyptians, and how I bare you on eagles' wings, and brought you unto myself. Now therefore, if ye will obey my voice . . . and keep my cov-

enant, then ye shall be a peculiar treasure [or treasured possession] unto me above all people: for all the earth is mine: and ye shall be unto me a kingdom of priests, and an holy nation. (Exod. 19:4–6)

A kingdom of priests. A holy nation. That's the vision and plan God has for the people of Israel. But they have a responsibility to fulfill: they must obey God's voice and keep His covenant.

What covenant? Not the Abrahamic one but a new one God is about to create. We'll get there in the next section. But first we have to understand what a "kingdom of priests" and a "holy nation" are. What does God want Israel to do, and what does this have to do with the story of the Old Testament?

Priests are something the followers of many religions in the world are familiar with. Because of their sinfulness, people don't get automatic access to God (or the gods). So priests "mediate"—they stand in between people and God.

Priests are set apart from normal people to bring messages to and from God. A priest has about three basic options he can tell people: (a) you owe God, (b) God owes you, or (c) everything's good on both sides. Category (a) is probably the most common.

A spiritist "priest" (usually called a *shaman*) in Papua New Guinea might tell people that their dead ancestors require certain offerings—a little food probably. So if someone confesses telling a lie, his local shaman may instruct him to sprinkle some ground taro root over the grave of his grandfather and then the liar gets to move into category (c). Everything's good again. Hindu gods in India regularly get food as well, and priests help officiate the transaction.

The Israelites were supposed to be set apart as priests were—just like your prized photograph gets set apart in a special frame. The God who owns all nations ("All the earth is mine") put only one nation in a special frame, a place where people could watch them. That gives us a clue to what it means for Israel to stand in between God and humans as a "kingdom of priests." One Bible scholar who has written a helpful book on Exodus suggests that this means four things:

- Israel would be an example to Gentiles (non-Jews). They would be impressed and want to know more about Israel's God.
- Israel would tell Gentiles of God's truth and invite them into the covenant.
- Israel would bring God closer to man by being the one people who stayed in fellowship with Him.
- Israel would hold on to God's words in writing.

And there's one other passage in Scripture that helps us understand what a "kingdom of priests" is supposed to be. In Deuteronomy 4, an aging Moses tells the Israelites,

> The nations . . . shall hear all these statutes, and say, Surely this great nation is a wise and understanding people. For what nation is there so great, who hath God so nigh unto them, as the Lord our God is in all things that we call upon him for? And what nation is there so great, that hath statutes and judgments so righteous as all this law, which I set before you this day? (Deut. 4:6–8)

Many ancient peoples developed systems of laws. The law codes of Hammurabi are a famous example. But what nation would have laws as just and as well written as those that came straight from God? The chosen people would have laws

that could give them a just society. And those laws could do even more: they could bring God near to them and let them call on Him.

> "Priests stand between God and humans to help bring the humans closer to God and to help dispense God's truth, justice, favor, discipline, and holiness to humans."
>
> —Douglas Stuart

These are all positives, of course. But priests sometimes have to come to people and say, "You owe God," like category (a). So Israel was also often a means for God's judgment. We will see that when they finally set foot into Canaan, they will do it with swords drawn and will kill many people who owe God deeply for their sins (Gen. 15:16).

A Blessing to the Nations

If Israel can do all this, they will be living out God's promise to Abraham that his family would be a blessing to the nations. The nations were without God. They didn't know His words. They didn't know what He's like. Israel could show them.

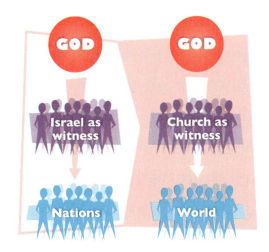

Most of the world at the time of the Exodus, including most of the Israelites, lived in spiritual darkness. They didn't know much of anything about the one true God. But God went public in a big way with the Exodus, and as we'll see, other nations definitely heard about the Lord and were afraid (Josh. 2:9–13). And now God wanted Israel to be a permanent, public billboard advertising His greatness. The way they filled their land, subdued it, and took dominion over it was supposed to be a model to all the peoples of the world. God was patient with them because they were His chosen way of bringing blessing to every man, woman, and child on earth.

> "Israel was the kingdom of priests called to mediate Yahweh's saving grace to the world."
>
> —Eugene H. Merrill

The Fear of God

It's after Israel hears this plan of God that they proclaim confidently, "Yes, we can do all this." But the Israelites aren't actually as able as they think they are. That's the point of Exodus 19 (see also Josh. 24:19). It's a fearful thing to serve the living and true God. He is so holy that all sinners ought to tremble when they approach Him. To the Israelites' credit, they do tremble—and they don't even want to approach Him because He is so fearsome. God tells them to cleanse themselves and warns them not to even touch the mountain. The flames, thunder, and lightning

Christians as a Holy Nation

Jesus' disciple Peter wrote something in the New Testament that alludes directly back to Exodus 19. He told God's people the church—including you, if you're a Christian—that they were "a chosen generation, a royal priesthood, an holy nation, a peculiar people [a people for His own possession]; that [they] should shew forth the praises of him who hath called [them] out of darkness into his marvellous light" (1 Pet. 2:9).

This doesn't mean that the church replaces Israel (Rom. 11:1, 23–26) but that we take on some of the same roles they had. Like them, we are to represent God to the world. That's why Jesus expects your good works to cause other people to notice, to make them glorify God whenever they see your light shining (Matt. 5:16).

God chose to give Israel very special advantages. He has done the same for the church. But He has never stopped loving the whole world. He wants His light to reach out through us to all of them.

coming from Mount Sinai terrify the people. Basically they tell Moses, "You talk to Him for us and tell us what He says! If we listen to Him, we'll die!" (Exod. 20:19).

But Moses says they shouldn't fear God like that. God has come to test them—not to kill them. He doesn't wish to drive them away from Him. He has come to instill in them a fear that keeps them from sinning, and as a result, draws them closer to Him.

Thinking It Through 3.4

1. How do you know from this section that God hasn't forgotten about His promise that Abraham would be the father of many descendants?

2. What does God want the nation of Israel to be according to Exodus 19?

3. What makes a priest different from everybody else?

4. Which of God's promises to Abraham is most closely connected to Exodus 19:5–6?

5. How do the Israelites respond when Moses first tells them what God wants them to be? (Exod. 19:8)

3.5 MOSES AND THE COVENANT

Read Exodus 19:1–8; 20:1–20
Memorize Deuteronomy 4:6–8

The Mosaic Covenant

God has rescued Israel from slavery and is now telling them the purpose of their existence as a nation. Israel, God's special possession, is supposed to be a kingdom of priests and a holy nation. But God says all this in a sentence that starts with the crucial little word *if*.

"*If* you obey My voice, *if* you keep My covenant—then you will be a holy, treasured possession that spreads My blessings to all the nations of the world" (see Exod. 19:5).

So which covenant is Israel supposed to obey? Here it comes, and almost everybody has heard of it, at least its most famous part. It's usually called the Mosaic Covenant, and the part most people have heard of is called the Ten Commandments. Those commands are all found in a chapter you should remember—Exodus 20. There are a lot more commandments in the chapters after it, but these are the most important ones. The Ten Commandments are very straightforward, simple enough for even a child to understand.

We won't take the time to explain them in detail—even though it would be a good thing for you to think through some of their implications. (See the box "The Flip Side of the Coin" for some examples.)

You probably can figure out how these commandments apply to you today. "Don't steal" means just what it did when you were three years old: "Don't take stuff that isn't yours." That's not too hard to understand. Even people who break that law all the time understand it perfectly—like the teenagers who download free music and movies from shady websites. Even they (often) admit that what they're doing is stealing; they just say, "Those rich people in Hollywood and Nashville already have plenty of money, so it won't hurt anyone if I grab these. Everybody does it."

Everybody does it—that may be true. Every culture has a way of covering up some of God's laws, making some of them seem too strict. We all need to make sure we're not being fooled by our culture into disobeying God. But if you understand what it means to murder, lie, and commit adultery, what more do the Ten Commandments have to teach you?

The Purpose of the Law

There is definitely more. There's some rich spiritual food to feed on here. And it comes to those who ask a simple question: what is the purpose of the law? Not just the Ten Commandments, but all the rest of the laws God gave Israel through Moses (all 613 of them!). Why did God give them in the first place?

The Flip Side of the Coin

The Ten Commandments are full of don'ts—but every one of them has a positive side, too.

1. Don't have any other gods before the Lord.	1. Put God first.
2. Don't make any images of the Lord.	2. Worship God the way He says to worship Him.
3. Don't use the Lord's name in an empty way.	3. Use God's name respectfully and fearfully.
4. Set aside one day a week to rest.	(Commandments 4 and 5 are already positive.)
5. Honor your parents.	
6. Don't murder.	6. Protect life.
7. Don't commit adultery.	7. Be faithful to your spouse.
8. Don't steal.	8. Respect others' property.
9. Don't lie.	9. Tell the truth.
10. Don't want things you're not supposed to have.	10. Set your heart on things that are truly valuable.

God surely means for us to practice the positives, not just avoid the negatives.

Some people think that God gave Israel the law so that His people could learn the rules they needed to keep in order to go to heaven when they died. But obeying these laws is not a way to earn salvation. The law had multiple purposes, but its most important purpose was to teach God's people how to love and obey Him.

Another important reason for believing that God's laws given at Sinai are not the way for Israel to earn salvation is what that would do to the Abrahamic Covenant. God made promises to Abraham about land, seed, and blessing. What if Israel fails to obey these new laws? Will they lose the promises God already made?

The answer is a bit complicated, but it boils down to "No!" The new laws Israel is getting don't replace the promises God made to Abraham. Instead, the Abrahamic Covenant is like the foundation of the Mosaic Covenant. Moses builds a new structure on top of Abraham's foundation. The laws on this first level don't destroy the foundation underneath them. Neither can they destroy the bedrock underneath even the foundation—God's promise that the seed of the woman would crush the head of the serpent. (See Gal. 3:17–18.)

This doesn't mean that an individual could do as he pleased. If an Israelite broke the law, that person would come under the covenant curses and would lose the covenant blessings. So on a national scale, Israel could not lose the promises, but an individual could lose them if he continued in disobedience.

Think of it like this. Your parents chose to give birth to you. They love you and care for you more than anyone else in the world does. And that's actually why they make rules for you. *Do your homework; wash the dishes on weeknights; no dating until you're thirty!* Stuff like that. Breaking all those rules would never change the fact that you're their child. But the love that they have for you leads them to make rules to guide, protect, and shape you.

Your parents love you; that's why they give you rules and even why they teach you table manners.

The special love and care Yahweh has shown for Israel is a privilege, but it also brings responsibilities. Now that they are God's "treasured possession," the laws tell them what a "holy nation" and a "kingdom of priests" looks like. This, in turn, will let all the nations around know something about the Lord. Through the nation of Israel, Yahweh puts Himself on display for every family on earth.

"In both testaments the command to be holy stems from the prior saving activity of God."

—Graeme Goldsworthy

This is why it was so important that Israel know and obey God's laws. If they didn't, they would be like a picture of God that had holes and stains.

Tabernacle & God's Presence

When the Lord met with Moses on Sinai, He said something amazing to Moses: "And let them make me a sanctuary, that I may dwell among them" (Exod. 25:8). For God to dwell with the Israelites was a blessing that no other nation enjoyed. In fact, it was a blessing that no one had enjoyed since Adam and Eve were expelled from the Garden of Eden.

When Adam and Eve lived in the garden, it seems that God regularly met with them in the garden (Gen. 3:8). But after Adam rebelled, they were exiled from the garden (Gen. 3:24). Their sin separated them from God. This was the most serious of all the consequences of Adam's sin. God would at times meet with people like Noah or Abraham or Moses. But He specially blessed the nation of Israel by having the people set up a tent for Him in the middle of their tents as a symbol of His continued presence with them.

God designed the furniture of the tabernacle to symbolize His presence with the people and the people's presence with Him. The two cherubim on the top of the ark symbolized the Lord enthroned between the cherubim (Ps. 99:1). This is the place from which God will meet with Moses (Exod. 25:22). There was no image of God, however, because God is never to be imaged (Exod. 20:4–5). The table of shewbread also symbolized God's presence with Israel. *Shewbread* could also be translated "bread of the Presence." The twelve loaves of bread, which were laid out each week, symbolized the presence of God with His people, and when the priests ate the bread, the meal also symbolized a meal of fellowship with God (Lev. 24:5–9). The lampstand was shaped like a tree, and it may have symbolized the tree of life in the Garden of Eden. The lampstand may also point ahead to Jesus, who says that those who follow Him will have "the light of life" (John 8:12).

But the design of the tabernacle also pointed to the barrier that still existed between God and humanity. In the tabernacle courtyard the altar and the laver symbolized the atonement and the cleansing that was still needed for humans to approach God. Only the priests could enter the holy place and the high priest alone could enter the holy of holies only on the Day of Atonement. The people were symbolically brought into God's presence by the high priest. He wore stones etched with the names of the twelve tribes of Israel on his shoulders and his breastplate. He symbolically brought the holy place and the holy of holies out to the people by wearing garments with the same colors as the interior curtains of those rooms.

These symbols were replaced with the real thing when Jesus was born. The angel told Joseph that the virgin birth of Jesus fulfilled Isaiah's prophecy of a virgin-born son identified as Immanuel, meaning "God with us" (Matt. 1:23). The apostle John also recognized that Jesus was the fulfillment of the tabernacle and the temple. He wrote, "And the Word was made flesh, and dwelt among us, (and we beheld his glory, the glory as of the only begotten of the Father,) full of grace and truth" (John 1:14). The Greek word for "dwelt" is similar to the Greek word for "tabernacle." So you can say that Jesus "tabernacled" with us. The tabernacle was also the place where God showed His glory (Exod. 40:34–35).

In the first century God was present not merely through a symbol but in person. God really lived with, walked with, and talked with Israelites in the person of Jesus Christ. They saw His glory (Exod. 34:6–7). In Jesus' life and ministry, they saw God's mercy to sinners and to the blind, crippled, and suffering. They saw His graciousness and long-suffering as He ministered to crowds of people. And in Jesus' death God showed that He would not clear the guilty without atonement.

Jesus is now ascended back into heaven, but this is not a step backward in God's plan to restore His presence to His people. Jesus told His disciples that it was good for Him to ascend into heaven, because He would send the Holy Spirit to them (John 16:7; cf. 7:39). Instead of God being with His people, now God would dwell within His people (John 14:17). Jesus' work on the cross removed the barriers that existed in the tabernacle and temple. Now God's people themselves are the temple. Paul says that the church is "a holy temple in the Lord" (Eph. 2:21; cf. 1 Cor. 3:16). And the body of each Christian is the temple of the Holy Spirit (1 Cor. 6:19).

But the best is yet to come. Ezekiel prophesied of a future in which Jerusalem would be called by the name "The Lord Is There" (Ezek. 48:35). In his vision of the new Jerusalem descending from heaven, the apostle John heard a voice declare, "Behold, the tabernacle of God is with men, and he will dwell with them, and they shall be his people, and God himself shall be with them, and be their God" (Rev. 21:3).

The tabernacle and temple look forward to that final day when all the barriers sin erected between humans and God are swept away. In that day God's people will rejoice in the glory of dwelling in His presence.

Sacrifices

Descendants of Adam, however, are rarely more than a few minutes from making a hole or getting a stain. We are born with sin in our hearts pushing us in the wrong direction—over and over, every day, all our lives.

So one of the other purposes of the law was to tell Israel how to handle that problem. The very first law *after* the Ten Commandments is one about what to do when you've broken one of the Ten Commandments. God tells the Israelites how to make an altar to sacrifice burnt offerings when they sin (the next book of the Bible, Leviticus, talks about sacrifices in much greater detail).

The Mosaic Covenant created an absolutely unique relationship between God and people, one that had never existed before. And there had to be some way of fixing that relationship when people broke it. That's what the sacrifices were.

God's Character

The law also gave insight into Yahweh's character. What kind of person is God? What can we expect Him to do; what is He like? The law tells us.

For example, God is *not* the kind of person who could say, "Thou shalt steal." He also couldn't have said, "Thou shalt commit adultery." He most certainly could not say, "You can choose one other god to put before me, possibly two if they are related, but no more." All those things would violate God's character. He is one who doesn't steal or lie, who is never unfaithful, and who could never let any other god have a higher position—because He already has it.

Every law shows us how holy God is or how truthful, how loving, or how wise.

Human Character

There's one final purpose of the law that you also ought to understand because it has to do with you—the person reading this book

When You Break God's Law

When you break the laws of God, what do you do? Israel was told that they were to sacrifice animals. But how does that help? You can sacrifice an animal while still hating your enemy. You can secretly worship false gods like Baal or Molech even while you're in God's tabernacle.

God knows this. Much later in the history of Israel, He basically tells the Jews, "I'm so sick and tired of your sacrifices! I can't stand them!" (Isa. 1:13–14). But then He tells them this: "Despite how bloody you are with your sin, I can clean you up and make you white as snow!"

Wait a minute—if the sacrifices didn't already do this, what can? *Every story points to the one who can.*

right now, today. When fallen people like you look at God by looking at His laws, you ought to fear. Very clearly, none of us lives up to His perfect standards. Every one of us has lied, and we started it before we can remember. We've all coveted what wasn't ours. And we've all committed the biggest sin of all: putting something other than God first in our lives. Our hearts have gone after all sorts of idols.

The law is here to tell us clearly: "You're guilty!" It's through the law, Paul said, that we even know we are sinning (Rom. 3:20). There's no way now to say we didn't know.

The Ten Commandments also hint very strongly that sin isn't just skin deep. It's not always something people can see. You can covet all day without anyone noticing. You can worship other gods in your heart. You can disrespect your parents behind a smile and a "Yes, ma'am!"

The laws in Exodus are not the path to salvation because no one can keep them all perfectly.

Thinking It Through 3.5

1. Where in the Bible can you find the Ten Commandments?

2. What is the most important purpose of the law?

3. Define conditional and unconditional covenants.

4. Is the Mosaic Covenant conditional or unconditional? How do you know?

5. How does the law give insight into Yahweh's character?

3.6 THE GOLDEN CALF AND THE DEATH OF THE FIRST GENERATION

Read Exodus 32
Memorize Exodus 34:6–7

One of the secrets that good readers know is something that seems obvious: look at the table of contents before you start to read a book. It's like looking at a map before you leave on a trip. When you have some idea of the big picture, the details fall more quickly into place.

That doesn't help with the Bible, however, because the names of the books don't tell you very much. Instead, you might try just looking through the headings in your Bible. Sometimes study Bibles have a detailed outline in the introduction to each book—that's worth checking out too.

If you look through the headings of the parts of Exodus we skipped after the last section (Exod. 21–31), here are some of the things you'll see:

- Laws About Social Justice
- Laws About the Sabbath and Festivals
- Conquest of Canaan Promised
- The Covenant Confirmed
- The Tabernacle

It's not very exciting to read headings, but it does give you a quick idea of what's there. Basically, God gave a number of laws on different topics, He promised that the people would enter the land He had shown to Abraham, and He and the people performed a formal ceremony agreeing to the Mosaic Covenant (Exod. 23:20–24:18). At that point Moses went up the mountain by himself to speak with God, and he was gone for almost a month and a half.

While Moses was talking with God, he received instructions for building the Israelites a mobile worship center called the tabernacle. Back when God created the world, He was able to live with mankind in peace. But since the Fall, God had never "lived" anywhere near humanity. Now, in the tabernacle, God is finally establishing a place on earth where He will live—where He will manifest His presence. This will be "God's house." And it's an amazing privilege for the Israelites to have it in their land. It points to the end of time, when God will fully establish His rule over all the earth. The whole earth will be His house.

The Golden Calf

But Israel was already doing its best to ruin everything. After forty glorious days with the Most High God, the great Holy One, Moses was told he had to go back down the mountain because the people were doing something Moses needed to stop.

Moses rushed down the mountain and grabbed Joshua on his way (Joshua must have been lower down the mountain). As they approached the camp of the Israelites, they heard a loud noise. At first it sounded like a battle, but as they came closer they could tell it was singing.

The Israelites were having a riotous, raucous party and worshiping a golden idol! The people had gotten impatient because Moses was gone so long. They demanded new gods! Aaron apparently

tried to compromise by making a statue of Yahweh—but even this was very obviously against the second commandment. When Moses sees what they are doing, he is so angry that he breaks the tablets of stone with the covenant law on them. His action is a picture: the Israelites have already broken the covenant.

> "Even as Moses was receiving the covenant stipulations, the Israelites were breaking them."
>
> —Paul R. Williamson

The Lord seems ready to kill the whole nation and start over with Moses, but Moses successfully persuades Him to relent. How? He appealed to God's public reputation. He pointed out that the Egyptians would notice if God brought Israel out of slavery only to destroy them. It would seem like God was breaking His promise to Abraham (Exod. 32:11–14). In fact, Moses himself was a descendant of Abraham, so God could have fulfilled the Abrahamic Covenant through Moses alone. But Moses' reasoning wins God over.

Of course, God knew all along what He was going to do. This conversation with Moses accomplishes two things: (1) It shows that God's grace has changed Moses. Moses himself has done some things that are rash; now he's being very patient with these people himself. (2) This conversation also helps us know how to pray. You yourself could pray, "Lord, I want your name and your fame to spread throughout all the earth! Please keep me from sin so that no one has reason to doubt your power to save people!" Or you might pray, "Most Holy God, the legislation going through Congress will make it more difficult for Christians to shine their light before others, making it harder for them to see You! Protect Your name!"

Moses' intercessory prayer made a difference in the aftermath of the golden calf fiasco because he based it on God's reputation (32:12) and His character (32:13). God listens, and very few Israelites die for their sin. By the final chapter of

Intercession

Moses saw that God was going to destroy the people because of their sin. Moses stepped in and prayed that God would forgive their sin. His prayer was one of intercession. An intercessory prayer is a prayer offered on behalf of another person. In fact, Moses' action was similar to what Christ does for the believer on a continual basis in His role as priest (Rom. 8:34; Heb. 7:25). He is continually before God making specific requests and petitions to God on behalf of the believer (Heb. 9:24). Moses was not perfect, but with Christ, the believer has a perfect man, the God-man, who is continuously praying and glorifying God through intercessory prayer. It is important to note that only one man could fill this role. That man is Christ, and He alone is our **mediator** to God (1 Tim. 2:5).

Mediator: One who stands between two parties in an attempt to reconcile them.

Exodus, the people have repented and renewed the covenant. They have built a beautiful tabernacle. And the last words of the book tell how the heavy glory of the Lord filled the tabernacle they had made. They are ready to enter the Promised Land.

The Book of Numbers

So the book of Numbers opens with (you guessed it!) numbers—the list of how many warriors each tribe has ready to fight. These are the men who, if all goes according to plan, will destroy the Canaanites that now live in the land God is going to give to His people. God has clearly fulfilled His promise to Abraham because Israel has a large number of fighters: 603,550. (That's actually larger than the current number in the active fighting force of the US Army.)

The numbers tell us that Jacob's predictions about Judah and Joseph are proving true: Judah's tribe is the biggest, with almost 75,000 soldiers. But even the two half-tribes of Manasseh and Ephraim—the two sons of Joseph—have at least 30,000 soldiers each. It's hard to say what this means for the whole Israelite population, but it's at least getting close to two million. (Most soldiers would have wives and children, and probably most would have living mothers and sisters.)

After a year at Mount Sinai, Israel is ready to leave. But if you're one of those people who skips to the end of a book to see what happens, the ending of this story might shock you: out of the 603,550 fighting men counted at the beginning of Numbers, only two of them make it into the Promised Land.

You may know the story of how twelve spies, one from each tribe, search out the land. Ten bring back a bad report: "The people there are too strong! We can't win!"

Two of them (Joshua and Caleb) disagree: "The Lord is with us! Don't fear those people!" (Num. 13:25–14:10). In this case, the Israelites are very democratic—they go with the faith-less majority. As a result, the book of Numbers actually records how Israel managed to come gloriously out of Egypt and then fall dead in the wilderness one by one over a period of forty years. By one estimate, they were averaging forty-two funerals a day—and that is only for the soldiers!

The beginning of the book of Joshua recounts how the people of God finally begin to enter the land of promise. Of the men of Israel, the number who would make it in would include only the two spies and all those who were not yet adults at the time of the Numbers 14 rebellion.

The Weight of Mount Sinai

There's probably one major lesson in this for us: the Mosaic Covenant makes Israel's sins more serious. In other words, knowing God's law and being in covenant with Him are weighty matters.

So before the Mosaic Covenant, Israel murmurs and complains. And God responds leniently. After the covenant, Israel murmurs and complains—and the places where they did it become known as *Taberah* ("Burning") and *Kibroth-hattaavah* ("Graves of Craving"). Israel defeated the Amalekites before Sinai. After that, the Amalekites defeat them instead (Num. 14:39–45). Even Moses and Aaron don't get to go into the Promised Land after they get sinfully angry in front of the people.

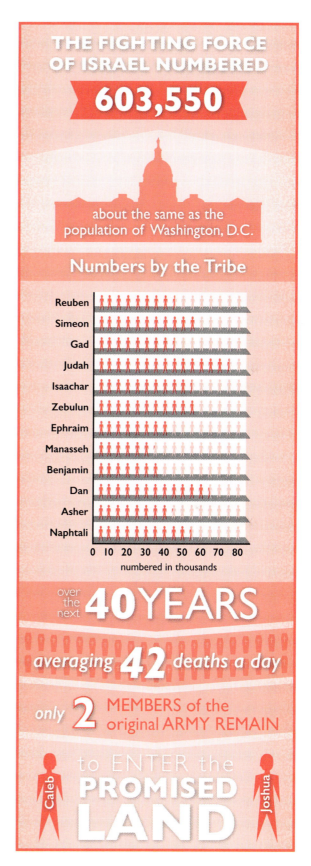

The Lord, the Lord God!

Think about the angry God who's ready to wipe Israel off the face of the earth and start over with Moses. This may not be a picture of God that you like very much. But that's only because you—like all fallen human beings—have a hard time taking sin as seriously as God does.

And yet there's an amazing verse after the golden calf story that gives a fuller picture of the Lord. Moses asks to see God's glory, and the Lord agrees to let him see part of it. As He passes by Moses, He describes Himself for us all:

> The Lord, The Lord God, merciful and gracious, longsuffering, and abundant in goodness (ḥesed—steadfast love) and truth, keeping mercy (ḥesed) for thousands, forgiving iniquity and transgression and sin, and that will by no means clear the guilty; visiting the iniquity of the fathers upon the children, and upon the children's children, unto the third and to the fourth generation. (Exod. 34:6–7)

God presents a careful balance: He starts with His mercy and grace, His steadfast love and truth, and His willingness to forgive (resulting from His steadfast love). But He ends with His very serious hatred of sin. It's not that children pay for their parents' sins, exactly. Instead, just think of any kids you know whose parents are deeply sinful. Simply by living with their parents, they share in the consequences. At the very least, they often pick up the sinful habits their parents have modeled for them.

The covenant made it so that Israel couldn't claim ignorance of God's law and God's ways. It ends up making their stubbornness clearer than ever. God's law has a way of revealing human sin.

The Fear of the Lord

God's plan will work; the Israelites can't stop it, no matter how bad they become! God will bless the whole world through Abraham's seed.

But reading stories like the ones you've read in Exodus and Numbers should lead you to conclude that no one can get away with sin. These stories ought to increase your genuine fear of the Lord. Here's a God who takes sin seriously and could righteously execute judgment at any time.

C. S. Lewis paints a fantastic word picture of this when the Pevensie children first hear of Aslan in the Chronicles of Narnia.

> "Ooh!" said Susan. "I'd thought he was a man. Is he—quite safe? I shall feel rather nervous about meeting a lion."
>
> "That you will, dearie, and no mistake," said Mrs. Beaver; "if there's anyone who can appear before Aslan without their knees knocking, they're either braver than most or else just silly."
>
> "Then he isn't safe?" said Lucy.
>
> "Safe?" said Mr. Beaver; "don't you hear what Mrs. Beaver tells you? Who said anything about safe? 'Course he isn't safe. But he's good. He's the King, I tell you."

Thinking It Through 3.6

1. What did the nation of Israel do to first break the covenant? Which of the Ten Commandments did they break?

2. Why didn't God wipe out the nation and start over?

3. Why did the Israelites wander in the wilderness for forty years until a whole generation died out?

4. Why did God deal more harshly with the nation after the covenant was established at Mount Sinai?

5. Should you be afraid of God? Why or why not?

3.7 LEVITICUS: GOD'S PROVISION & ISRAEL'S RESPONSIBILITIES

Read See Exercise 3.7.
Memorize Leviticus 10:10; 26:12

Be Ye Holy for I Am Holy

Holiness is an important concept in the book of Leviticus. In fact, the verb, noun, and adjective forms of the word *holy* occur almost 150 times in the book. In Leviticus, *holy* normally refers to that which is set apart for God's use. A related word is *sanctify*, which basically means to consecrate yourself or keep yourself holy. When the Lord tells the Israelites, "I am the Lord your God: ye shall therefore sanctify yourselves, and ye shall be holy; for I am holy" (Lev. 11:44), what exactly does He mean? What does God mean when He says, "Sanctify yourselves," and, "Be holy"? How would they know what it means to do those things? What exactly do you have to do to "sanctify" yourself or to "be holy"? Good news, God answers those questions.

> "Sanctify yourselves therefore, and be ye holy: for I am the Lord your God."
>
> —Leviticus 20:7

The Purpose of the Law

The purpose of the law is to tell God's people how "to sanctify" themselves and how they can "be holy." God didn't tell the Israelites to be holy and then just sit back and let them figure it out on their own. Could you imagine the confusion and fear that would result? Everyone would be asking his neighbor, "What do we do?" "Am I doing this right? I don't want to be punished for doing something that I didn't know I shouldn't be doing."

No, God does not operate like that. He wanted to have a relationship with His people. He wanted to dwell in their midst. In order to do that, they had to be a holy people. That meant that they would have to do certain things. It meant that they would have to separate from certain things, and it meant that they would have to be different from the other nations. They would be distinct.

The law was to be their teacher. It would tell them how to make atonement for their sins. It would tell them what they could not do and what they should do in order to please God. Without the law, Israel would not know what it meant to be holy. The law was essential to knowing what it would take to live a holy life for God.

A holy life is necessary to have a relationship with God. God told His people, "I will walk among you, and will be your God, and ye shall be my people" (Lev. 26:12). This is exactly what God did with Adam in the Garden of Eden. Evidently, God would in some way walk in the garden and talk with Adam. The last time this happened, Adam was hiding because he had sinned. His relationship with God was broken, and he didn't want to face God the way he was.

God had to banish Adam from the garden, and the daily walks in the cool of day came to an end. It had been some time since God could come and walk among His people. He wanted that fellowship. In His statement, He was telling the Israelites two things. First, by being their God, He would provide for and protect them. Second, by being His people, they had some responsibilities, and if they didn't fulfill their responsibilities, there would be penalties to pay.

I Will Be Your God

Part of God's being Israel's God meant that He would provide for them. The Bible says that God would give them His provision, protection, and presence (Lev. 26:4, 6, 11). It is God who does all this for them.

Provision

God promised that He would send rain "in due season." Unless you're a farmer, you probably take rain for granted. And unless you're a farmer, you probably don't know what it means for rain to come "in due season."

Rain is vital for crops. But the wrong amount at the wrong time can be disastrous. In the Middle East, when the crops are first planted in October

Levites and the Priests

Did you know that not all Levites were priests, but all priests were Levites? There were certain requirements in order to be a priest. The first was that one had to be a male from the tribe of Levi. Second, one had to be a descendant of Aaron. That's right. Only Aaron's sons and grandsons and so on could be priests.

Priests were responsible for keeping the people faithful to God's law by mediating between the people and God. They were responsible for offering sacrifices and helping the people make atonement for their sins. They also had other duties, such as judging between two parties and teaching the people.

The main duties of the Levites were to guard the tabernacle (or temple) and the priests. The Levites were made up of three different clans or families. Each of them had their own responsibilities regarding the tabernacle.

Gershon: The Gershonites were responsible for the cloth sections that were on the inside and the outside of the temple. They lived on the western side of the tabernacle and protected it from any attack from that direction (Num. 3:23–26).

Kohathites: They were responsible for the furniture and things inside the tabernacle (ark of the covenant, table, lampstand, etc.). They lived on the south side of the tabernacle and protected that side from attack (Num. 3:29–32).

Merarites: They were responsible for the frames, the bars, and anything that helped to hold up the tabernacle. They lived on the north side and protected that side from attack (Num. 3:35–37).

There was one other qualification for being a priest besides being a descendant of Aaron. You could not have any physical blemish (being blind or lame or having a deformed hand or foot or any other defect). You could still eat from the donations given to priests, but you could not approach the tabernacle (Lev. 21:16–24).

Those same types of defects disqualified the sacrifices too. So, any priest that had a defect could not approach the tabernacle, and any animal that had a defect could not be brought to the tabernacle.

Why was God being so picky? Because He demands perfection, and not just any perfection, but the highest quality of perfection that is possible. And the people were supposed to be a picture of that perfection. If you're thinking, "Nobody's perfect and nobody could meet His standard," well, you're right. None of the priests were as perfect as what God wanted. Except for one—the one the book of Leviticus is pointing to. And He's not only the perfect unblemished priest, He's also the perfect unblemished sacrifice.

---

and November, they need heavy rains. Light rains would not allow the crops to grow well. But in early spring (March–April), the crops don't need as much water. A heavy rain at this time could ruin the crop. The right amount of rain at the right time means an abundant crop. And that is exactly what God promised Israel—"rain in due season."

And this is no ordinary abundance of crops. There would be so much grain that they would not be able to finish threshing it all until it was time to gather grapes, and then it would take them so long to gather all the grapes that it would be time to sow more seed. God promises them that the harvest will be so great, that they will eat until they are full. In fact, they will not be able to eat up the entire harvest. When the new harvest comes in, they will have to get rid

of the last year's harvest to make room for the new harvest (26:10).

Protection

Anyone who lived during that time knew that a great harvest didn't mean you were guaranteed to live in peace. There were some clans that were lazy. They didn't farm. They didn't harvest. And they didn't store grain. But they had no problem attacking nations that did farm, that did harvest, and that did store grain.

That is exactly what the Philistines did to Keilah, a small city in Judah (1 Sam. 23:1–5). The farmers in Keilah worked all year, harvested their grain, and stored it so that they would have food for the winter. But the Philistines came in and robbed them. David asked the Lord if he could attack the Philistines for what they had done. God told him to go, attack the Philistines, and "save Keilah."

God protected Keilah through David when David went and slaughtered the Philistines and "saved the inhabitants of Keilah" (1 Sam. 23:5). That protection was one of God's promises in Leviticus (26:6–8).

God's promise would enable Israel to live in peace. They wouldn't have to worry about wild beasts attacking them. They could sleep at night without having to worry about their enemies attacking them. And if their enemies did attack them, the Israelites would overcome them with ease. David would one day be living proof of that promise.

God's blessing would also be on their families. He would make them fruitful and multiply them. This is precisely what He had promised to Abraham—"I will multiply thy seed as the stars of the heaven, and as the sand which is upon the sea shore" (Gen. 22:17).

Presence

Abundant crops with lots of food, peace from their enemies, no wild beasts, and many children—these were wonderful things that God had promised. But there was something better. God would set His tabernacle among them. In other words, God Himself would dwell among them and meet with them. He would walk among them, watch-ing over them, caring for them, and being with them.

You Will Be My People

All these things wouldn't *just happen* to Israel. They had responsibilities too. When God said that He would be their God, He also said, "You shall be my people." Being God's people came with responsibilities. In the first part of Leviticus 26, God said, "If ye walk in my statutes, and keep my commandments, and do them; Then I will give . . ." (26:3–4).

"Then."

Did you catch that? God said, "Then." In computer programming, this is called an "if . . . then" statement. *If* something happens *then* the program will perform a specific action. If A then B. B will not happen unless A happens. In God's statement, the "A" was for them to walk in His statutes, keep His laws, and do what He had told them to do. The "B" only came when they did what they were supposed to do.

IF Israel obeys THEN
God will bless them.

Holy Living: A Life of Discernment

God told the Israelites to walk in His statutes. In the Old Testament, walking is often used to portray life. In modern times, we often call life a journey. You see pictures online that say something like "Enjoy the journey," or "Enjoy the ride on the journey of life." We call it a "ride," they called it "walking." And as they walked along

---

That Which Is Sacred

Holy (sacred)—something set apart for sacred use

Common—something used in normal, everyday life, something ordinary

Clean (pure)—that which is pure

Unclean (impure)—unable to approach the sanctuary

Explanation: Everything that is sacred is pure, and some of what is common is pure. The sacred and the impure never contact each other. Some of what is pure is sacred, and some is common. The impure is always common, never sacred. Dotted lines (dividing sacred from common and pure from impure) indicate subjective areas—areas that require discernment to identify what they actually are.

[Taken from Jacob Milgrom, *A Continental Commentary: Leviticus: A Book of Ritual and Ethics* (Minneapolis: Fortress Press, 2004), 95.]

life's journey, they would encounter things every day where they had to decide between right and wrong. How would they know which way to go? The psalmist said it best: "Thy word is a lamp unto my feet, and a light unto my path" (Ps. 119:105).

By reading and listening to God's Word, they would know which decision was best.

Earlier in Leviticus, God tells the priests all the things they needed to be aware of to make sure the people were holy before God. But there comes a point when God has to say, "Use discernment. I can't list everything out for you. Take these principles that I have given you and apply them to every situation." God tells the priests they need to be sober because they need to be able to know the difference between "holy and unholy, and between unclean and clean" (10:9–10).

The priests had a lot of responsibilities. They had to look at all kinds of skin disorders and know what to do for each one. If someone vowed something to God, they had to tell him how much the offering was worth. They had to be judges for the people. They had to figure out who was right and who was wrong. On top of all that, they had to teach the law to the people and make sure they understood it.

Their responsibilities required discernment. More importantly, the priests were representing God. Discernment was essential. *The American Heritage Dictionary* defines discernment as "the act or process of exhibiting keen insight and good judgment." Most people can discern

The Day of Atonement

Leviticus 16 is one of the most significant passages in the Old Testament. God instructs His people in great detail about how to perform the ceremonies and ordinances of the Day of Atonement. The ceremony is not merely about what Aaron did thousands of years ago; it is also pointing to the one who would perfectly perform what the Day of Atonement symbolized.

The Day of Atonement was a special day. This was the only day of the year that the high priest was allowed to enter the most holy place. And on this special day, the high priest would perform his most special duty—he would act as a mediator between God and the people.

Two events occurred on the Day of Atonement. First, the high priest, in this case Aaron, would offer a sacrifice for himself and his family. He had to do this because he was going to enter the place of atonement, the place of God's manifested presence. The second event was a sacrifice for the people of Israel. This was not for individuals; rather, it was for the nation itself.

The Day of Atonement offering for the people covered two types of sins. The first type was those sins that were knowingly and willingly committed. The law provided many different types of sacrifices for various sins, but it did not provide a sacrifice for intentional sins. So if a person intentionally committed a sin, he had no way to ask for forgiveness. The sacrifice in the Day of Atonement provided such a sacrifice.

The second type of offering in the Day of Atonement was for those sins that the people committed unknowingly. They were unaware that they had committed a sin and never gave an offering. If left unhandled, unknown sins would be unforgiven. They needed a way to handle this situation. So God provided the Day of Atonement.

God prescribed a specific order for the events on the Day of Atonement. Here are the major events with a brief description of why they had to do each one.

1. The high priest must bathe and then put on white undergarments and a white tunic. He was not allowed to wear his normal ceremonial clothing of the high priest. Bathing was to remove any physical contamination, and wearing common clothes signified that he too was a sinner and had no superior rank above the people (16:3–4).

2. The high priest was to bring two goats for a sin offering and a ram for a burnt offering (16:5). The two goats together would form a sin offering. The ram would be a burnt offering for the high priest and his family (16:6).

3. The high priest would cast lots for the goats: one for the Lord to use as a sacrifice, the other for the Lord to use as the scapegoat (16:7–8).

between right and wrong. But only a very careful person is able to tell between right and almost right. Or between better and best.

But that's what the priests had to do. Look at the diagram on page 95. It was easy for them to determine that which was sacred versus that which was impure. But it took discernment to figure out those things that were near the dotted line (pure or impure; sacred or common). It also took discernment to figure out those things that were pure but not sacred.

Keen insight and good judgment are what the priests needed, especially for teaching the Israelites about God's commandments. The better they taught the people, the better the people's ability to discern between right and wrong would be.

The people needed discernment because there was a warning statement—an "else" statement in God's "if . . . then" statement. Programmers call it an "if . . . then . . . else" statement.

Penalty

"If A Then B *Else* C." Remember A? It was obedience. If (A) they obeyed then (B) God would bless them. Well, C is what would happen if they didn't do A. When they don't obey, the "else" happens.

IF Israel obeys THEN
God will bless them;
ELSE
God will punish them.

The "else" of Leviticus 26 starts in verse 14, and it is severe. God says that they would be

4. Before the high priest slaughtered the goat, he was to offer the ram. He was to put a handful of incense on the fire. He would take the blood and sprinkle it on the mercy seat seven times (16:11–15).

5. The first goat that was to be offered was to be used as a sin offering. The high priest would slaughter it and take its blood to sprinkle on the mercy seat. By doing this, he would make atonement for the holy place, the tabernacle, and the altar (16:9, 15–19).

6. The high priest would lay both of his hands on the second goat, the scapegoat. He would then confess over it the wickedness and rebellion of the Israelites. By laying both hands on the live goat and not on the one being sacrificed, he signified that intentional sins were being transferred. Also, it was the high priest and not any other individual performing the act. This signified that

the whole nation was being represented (16:20–21).

7. The high priest would send the goat into the desert in the care of a man appointed for the task. The destination was a solitary place, far away. It was meant to show there was no possibility for sin to return. Thus, the guilt was forgiven and taken away (16:21–22).

8. Then the high priest was to come into the tabernacle and remove the linen garments and leave them there. He was to put on his normal priestly clothes, and then offer the burnt offerings (16:23–25).

The slain goat represents the people for whom atonement was made. This first goat illustrates propitiation—the act of turning away God's wrath. The sending of the second goat into the desert represents the removal of Israel's sins to a place where it could never return. David poetically states what this means:

As far as the east is from the west, So far hath he removed

our transgressions from us. (Ps. 103:12)

The second goat illustrates expiation—the cancellation, or removal, of sin.

Together, the two goats illustrate that atonement is a combination of propitiation and expiation of our sin. The two goats also point to something more important—the work of Christ. In the Old Testament, the Day of Atonement was a yearly ritual. Every year on the tenth day of the seventh month, the high priest was to make atonement for the people (Lev. 23:26–32; Num. 29:7–11). This was an ongoing, never-ending process. But when Christ came as our High Priest, He entered the most holy place through His own blood, once for all, "having obtained eternal redemption for us" (Heb. 9:12).

Christ does not have to do this over and over every year. If He had to do that, He would have to die over and over, again and again. But because it was His own unblemished blood from His own sacrifice, He was offered once to "bear the sins of many" (Heb. 9:28).

terrified. They would be sick and waste away. Their seed would not grow into crops, and if it did, their enemies would eat up whatever it produced. Their enemies would defeat them and rule over them. The Israelites would be so scared that they would run even when nobody was chasing them. The beasts of the field would torture them, and all their farming would be in vain.

Everything that God promised as a blessing would turn into a curse. And it would be worse—seven times worse!

"But . . ." There is something after the "else." Something called an escape clause. God created an escape from the "else"—from the punishment. If in their punishment they repented and asked for forgiveness for their sins and those of their fathers, then God would remember His covenant with Jacob, with Isaac, and with Abraham.

IF Israel obeys THEN
        God will bless them;
    ELSE
        God will punish them;
    {ESCAPE if Israel repents}.

God would not reject them. He would not destroy them. Why? Because He is their God, and they are His people.

Conclusion

Peter tells us that we are called to be holy, and so we must be holy in everything we do. Why? "Because it is written, Be ye holy; for I am holy" (1 Pet. 1:15–16).

It's not easy being holy, but God has given us His Word to help us know what to do in order to "be holy."

You ask, "But what about those times when God's Word doesn't exactly tell us what to do? Have you ever done a Bible search for the word internet or texting? What about looking up referee or TV?" And that is true: the Bible doesn't specifically say how to deal with an unfair referee or how to use the internet. Those are things a lot of us deal with each day.

But listen to what Paul says: "Be not conformed to this world: but be ye transformed by the renewing of your mind, that ye may prove what is that good, and acceptable, and perfect, will of God" (Rom. 12:2). The phrase "prove what is" basically means to "figure out" or "discern."

Like the priests who had to have discernment to help the people distinguish between the sacred and the common and between the pure and impure, we too as Christians have to have discernment. How do you get it? The best way is by reading and studying God's Word and asking God to help you understand. The psalmist said, "Wherewithal shall a young man cleanse his way? by taking heed thereto according to thy word" (Ps. 119:9). In other words, how do I make sure I'm doing right? By obeying God's Word.

Then, as a Christian, how do I keep from doing wrong? By renewing your mind through the Word of God. The psalmist said, "Thy word have I hid in mine heart, that I might not sin against thee" (119:11). The more familiar you are with Scripture and the principles it teaches, the better you will respond when it is hard to tell what is right and wrong. Sometimes you may need to seek help from other people like your parents, your teacher, or your pastor.

Peter concludes his epistle by encouraging you to resist the devil, and to take comfort in the fact that God, who has called you by Christ, will one day "make you perfect, stablish, strengthen, settle you" (1 Pet. 5:10).

Thinking It Through 3.7

1. What does *sanctify* mean? How would the people know whether they were sanctifying themselves?

2. What does it mean for God to tell Israel that He will be their God? What does it mean for God to tell Israel that they will be His people?

3. On the Day of Atonement, why was a second goat sent off into the desert after the first goat was sacrificed?

4. What is discernment? How can you gain discernment?

5. What is God's "escape clause" from punishment? Why did He give this "escape clause"?

3.8 BALAAM: A PROPHET FOR HIRE

Read Numbers 22:1–21
Memorize Numbers 24:17

Balak Summons Balaam

The pagan prophet Balaam actually seems like a good guy when you first meet him. When the Moabite king Balak tries to hire Balaam to curse Israel, the prophet insists that he can say only what God tells him to say (Num. 22:18). But he might be lying. Does he really say only what God wants him to?

Yes—in fact, what Balaam says and how often he says it provide the outline of the story as he delivers four "oracles," or messages from God.

God made it very clear to Balaam that his job was to say only what God told him to say. And the biblical account leaves no doubt that the four messages Balaam delivers really are divine oracles. The text even says that God's Spirit came on Balaam (Num. 24:2–3). Balaam's oracles are words straight from the throne room of God (Num. 23:5).

So Balaam is a good guy, right? Not an Israelite, but certainly still a hero, right?

Balaam's Donkey and the Angel

Despite all the things that Balaam apparently does right, the most famous story about him gives us a clue about what's really going on in his heart.

In the Bible only one animal talks (aside from the serpent in Eden): Balaam's donkey. And she only speaks on one occasion.

Balaam is riding along, on his way to deliver an oracle for King Balak, who wants to curse Israel—but then the Lord gets angry and sends an angel to block Balaam's way. The donkey is the only one to see the angel, so when she stops, Balaam gets upset. He starts to beat the donkey—until the donkey talks back!

The donkey is like Balaam. Just as God gives the donkey speech, God will put words in Balaam's mouth. So the fact that he speaks God's words doesn't necessarily make him a good guy.

In fact, the New Testament tells us why God was angry with him. God knew exactly what

Balaam wanted: money. Peter says that Balaam "loved the wages of unrighteousness" (2 Pet. 2:15). In other words, he loved to make money from doing wrong. As long as he got his money, he didn't care what he had to say—God's words or the ones King Balak wanted. Somehow he just knew whose words would win.

> "This is a hilarious put-down of Balaam's pretensions. The international expert on magic cannot see the angel, but his donkey can."
>
> **—Gordon Wenham**

So Balaam is an example of how God can and will use anyone to do His bidding. It's not correct to say that God only uses pure vessels—mainly because there are none. But in one sense, God "uses" everyone. "A man's heart deviseth his way: but the Lord directeth his steps" (Prov. 16:9). Humans have no authority to tell God whom He can and cannot use.

Balak and the Abrahamic Covenant

The wicked Moabite king Balak, who wants the wicked prophet Balaam to curse Israel, tells Balaam why he has hired him. He's afraid of Israel, and he believes that Balaam's words are powerful: "He whom thou blessest is blessed, and he whom thou cursest is cursed" (Num. 22:6). Do those words sound familiar?

Where have you heard those words before? In God's promises to Abraham. "I will make of thee a great nation, and I will bless thee, and make thy name great; and thou shalt be a blessing: And I will bless them that bless thee, and curse him that curseth thee: and in thee shall all families of the earth be blessed" (Gen. 12:2–3).

Moses (who wrote the book of Numbers) quotes these words from Balak to set up the story. This is a chance for God to show what He'll do when someone tests Him on this promise. What will God do to Balaam and Balak for cursing Israel? Answering that question is what the story of Balaam is really about.

Balaam's Oracles

The history of Israel since the Exodus has been a huge string of disappointments punctuated by only a few successes. Numbers tells how the people rebel, God promises judgment, the priest Korah puts together a rebellion, and Aaron and Miriam die, along with other pieces of bad news.

And now they're into their fortieth year of wilderness wandering. What is going to happen to this nation that has been given so much and yet has rejected God's kindness time and time again? They have failed to trust Him over and over. Are God's promises to Abraham worth anything anymore?

The pagan prophet Balaam is here to tell us what God says to these questions.

Oracle 1

From the ridge they're standing on, Balaam and Balak can see the people of Israel sprawled out on the plain below, and the words God puts in Balaam's mouth all echo the Abrahamic Covenant. "Who can count the dust of Jacob?" he says (Num. 23:10). That was exactly God's promise.

Not a single word of cursing.

Oracle 2

And in case anyone is still wondering whether God intends to fulfill the Abrahamic Covenant, Balaam says in his second oracle, "Has he said, and will he not do it? Or has he spoken, and will he not fulfill it?" (Num. 23:19).

Not a single word of cursing.

Oracle 3

And if anyone still doesn't get it, Balaam declares to Israel at the end of the third oracle, "Blessed is he that blesseth thee, and cursed is he that curseth thee" (Num. 24:9).

Obviously, there's not a single word of cursing here either.

Oracle 4

Balaam's last oracle is even more amazing:

There shall come a Star out of Jacob, and a Sceptre shall rise out of Israel, and shall smite the corners of Moab (Num. 24:17).

So the king of Moab ends up paying for Moab to get cursed. And Israel, instead of a curse, gets the ultimate blessing—the promise of a king who will crush its enemies.

Balaam Takes Israel Down

Finally, it looks like the seed of Abraham is going to rise above its sin and take the land God has promised. Balaam's prophecies are incredibly hopeful!

But (and this is why reading the history of Israel can be very depressing) in the very next paragraph, we find out that the people of Israel turned right around and started worshiping the false god of the Moabites!

Though Balaam failed to curse Israel, we find out later that this trap was originally his idea.

"Just get your women to go after their men," he had told King Balak, "and they'll be treacherous to their God" (see Num. 31:15–16). (For this reason God's people later kill Balaam [Num. 31:8].)

How depressing! But Balaam's oracles show that no matter how bad Israel gets, the God who's in covenant with them will *not* set aside His promises.

Seven hundred years later through the prophet Micah, God is again reminding the Israelites, who are about to be taken captive, that God turned Balak's curse into a blessing (Mic. 6:5). And a full thousand years after Balaam lived and died, Nehemiah brings up the story for the same purpose (Neh. 13:2).

This story really is comical. Balaam gets hired to curse Israel, but every time he opens his mouth, blessings come out instead. Finally Balak just says, "Neither curse them at all, nor bless them at all!" (Num. 23:25). Just be quiet! But the end of Balaam's story is anything but humorous. When the Lord takes vengeance on the Midianites for leading His people astray, Balaam dies a violent death with them (Num. 31:8).

Conclusion

God is on a mission to bless Israel. And it's not because He doesn't care about Moabites. The blessing Israel gets will in turn be a blessing for the whole world.

We now have that blessing. It came in the King that Balaam predicted. And yet we ourselves are frequently as bad as or worse than Israel. We have blessings they never had and knowledge they couldn't know. And we still sin against our God. If God was this faithful to them, we can certainly rely on that same character and that same unstoppable intention to graciously bless His people.

Thinking It Through 3.8

1. Who was Balaam and where did he come from?

2. Describe Balaam's initial responses to Balak's offer and his final decision. What does 2 Peter 2:15 tell us about Balaam's true motivation for going?

3. Why did God allow Balaam to go work for a king who wanted to curse Israel?

4. Reread the oracles of Balaam (Num. 23:7–10, 18–24; 24:3–9, 15–19). List all the statements that refer back to promises made to Abraham (Gen. 12:1–3; 17:1–8), and identify the promises. (For your headings use *Land*, *Seed/ Nation*, *Blessing/Cursing*, and *Kings*.)

5. Since Balaam couldn't curse Israel, how did he try to destroy Israel?

UNIT 3 REVIEW

Scripture Memory

Exodus 3:13–14	Deuteronomy 4:6–8
Romans 9:17–18	Exodus 34:6–7
Exodus 15:26	Leviticus 10:10; 26:12
Exodus 19:5–6	Numbers 24:17

Understand the Story

1. Give one of the two explanations for God's name "I AM" or "I AM WHO I AM."

2. Why did God command the Israelites to slaughter lambs and paint the blood on their doorposts?

3. Why was God so patient with the complaining Israelites before they got to Sinai?

4. What were the four tasks that Israel was supposed to carry out as a kingdom of priests?

5. How does the conditional Mosaic Covenant relate to the unconditional Abrahamic Covenant?

6. Why does the Mosaic Covenant make Israel's sins more serious?

7. True or False. Everything that is sacred must be pure.

8. Why isn't Balaam a good prophet even though he speaks God's words?

Developing Observation Skills

9. What are the key elements in the narrative genre of literature that you should be careful to observe?

10. Choose one of those key elements to observe in Exodus 1–2.

11. Summarize at least two pointers for observing and interpreting a difficult passage of Scripture.

12. Read Exodus 15:22–27. Gather basic facts by asking and answering at least three who, what, when, where, why, or how questions.

13. Read Exodus 19:5 and observe the key relationships between words and phrases. Identify two keywords: the keyword that introduces a condition and the keyword that introduces a following promise.

14. Read Exodus 32:1–6. Gather basic facts by asking and answering at least three who, what, when, where, why, or how questions.

Connecting the Story to the Big Story

15. Why did the groanings of the children of Israel cause God to respond?

16. What role does the church have that is similar to the role that God intended for the children of Israel?

17. On what basis did Moses intercede for the people, convincing God not to wipe them out?

18. Reread the oracles of Balaam (Num. 23:7–10, 18–24; 24:3–9, 15–19). List all the statements that refer back to promises made to Abraham (Gen. 12:1–3; 17:1–8), and identify the promises. (For your headings use *Land*, *Seed/Nation*, *Blessing/Cursing*, and *Kings*.)

Lessons for Life

19. Compile a list of at least five ways in which you can represent God as a "priesthood of believers" to those in your community (1 Pet. 2:9–12).

20. List at least five areas of your life for which Scripture does not give direct commands. Write a plan for how you would handle those areas with biblical discernment.

UNIT 4

THE WEAKNESS OF THE OLD COVENANT

If you open up the book of Judges hoping for good news about God's chosen people, you'll be disappointed. Judges is one of the lowest points for the Jews in all of Scripture. It actually starts out great. The Israelites continue to conquer their land even after the death of Joshua. But the Israel-ites start having trouble expelling the Canaanites from the Promised Land. And it wasn't always because they couldn't. They made poor choices and failed to do what God commanded. But keep reading because God has a purpose for recording these stories in the book of Judges.

God brought His people into the land
He had promised their forefathers.

The judges were themselves
a judgment on Israel.

4.1 MOSES: THE NECESSITY OF A NEW HEART

Read See Exercise 4.1.
Memorize Deuteronomy 30:6

A Corrupt Heart

In medical science the heart is a hollow, muscular organ that circulates blood. But in reality, we use the word *heart* to mean much more than the physical organ.

We use the word *heart* to represent a range of emotions and actions. We convey feelings with the word when we say things like, "He doesn't have the heart to do it," or, "Take heart." We sorrow for people with a "heavy heart." We use the heart to represent our wills or our minds: "I had a change of heart," or, "I knew the test by heart." We use it to talk about attitude: "Her effort was half-hearted."

Some people are mean and have a "hard heart." Others are too sympathetic and have a "bleeding heart." And we all know that "home is where the heart is," but Grandma's is where we get to eat our favorite food "to our heart's content."

You get the idea. You probably can think of a lot of different ways we use the word *heart*. The Israelites were a lot like us. They too used the word *heart* in a lot of different ways. The box on the next page tells you about the various ways they used *heart*.

In the Old Testament, the heart represents our physical beating heart, our attitudes, our feelings, our desires, our will, and even our minds. It seems that the heart represents everything about an individual.

This is why God desires for His people to have a special kind of heart that would cause them to fear Him and keep all His commandments (Deut. 5:29). He even commands them to love Him with all their hearts and to keep His commandments on their hearts (6:5–6). But God knows that their hearts could be deceived (11:16), that their hearts could be hardened (15:7), and that their hearts could be greedy (15:9–10). He knows too that their hearts could be weak (20:3) and scared (20:8).

And it is their hearts that fail them. Because of their hearts, the Israelites can't keep their covenant responsibilities. So if they are to keep those covenant responsibilities, God—and not them, for they cannot do it—will have to change their hearts. In fact, He will have to give them new hearts. In other words, something internal will have to happen—they will have to be regenerated (made alive again). They will have to be saved. And only God can do that.

A Good Story

There are very few stories out there in which the hero dies. People don't tend to like stories where the hero fails. It just doesn't feel right. The main character is supposed to win. The guy gets the girl. The underdog team wins the championship. It makes people unsettled and even angry if that doesn't happen.

At this point in our survey of the Old Testament, the main (human) character of the Bible's story is actually a whole nation: the seed of Abraham. And it hasn't exactly been winning. The generation of former slaves died off in the wilderness. But maybe now Israel will win! Maybe they'll make it into the land, wipe out their enemies, and bless the whole world by crushing the serpent!

Deuteronomy

Deuteronomy is basically one long sermon that Moses gives to the second generation of Isra-elites as they all stand at the border of the Prom-ised Land. Moses is reminding them of everything that happened to their parents—the Exodus, the law, the reason the previous generation died.

Even if you read the sermon carefully, though, you may not be sure whether to feel hopeful or afraid for Israel. Toward the beginning of Deuteronomy, Moses reminds the people of their past failures. And he warns them not to think they're getting the land because they deserve it:

> The Lord thy God giveth thee not this good land to possess it for thy righteousness; for thou art a stiffnecked [stubborn] people. Remember, and forget not, how thou provokedst the Lord thy God to wrath in the wilderness: from the day that thou didst depart out of the land of Egypt . . . , ye have been rebellious against the Lord. (Deut. 9:6–7)

Ouch. And toward the end of Deuteronomy, it gets worse. Moses basically predicts that the Israelites will ruin their beautiful land by worshiping other gods (Deut. 29:22–28).

The Human Heart

The Old Testament uses the word *heart* in numerous ways. It can mean the physical organ (Exod. 28:29). Sometimes it is the word used to mean the *midst* of something—such as the sea (Jon. 2:3). Sometimes, it means to be kind or friendly. For example, Ruth tells Boaz that he has spoken "friendly" to her (Ruth 2:13). The word *friendly* in this passage is the same Hebrew word for *heart*. It can mean courage. Amos says the *courageous* (those who have heart) will flee in the day of the Lord (Amos 2:16). It can also mean desire. Nehemiah uses *heart* to show that the people had a *desire* to work (Neh. 4:6). Several times it refers to a person's will—to the choice to do something. For example, Joash decided to repair (i.e., "with *heart* he repaired") the temple (2 Chron. 24:4).

The Hebrews saw people as rational beings. For them, the heart was central to feelings, to desires, to thinking, to reasoning, and to choosing to do something. You could say that the Hebrews saw the heart as representing the most important part of a person. In fact, it represented the person.

God says that their hearts are in need of circumcision, which means that each person's whole being is in need of repair, because sin has tainted every aspect of their lives. Early in Deuteronomy, God tells the people, "Thou shalt love the Lord thy God with all thine heart, and with all thy soul, and with all thy might" (6:5). Humanly speaking, this is impossible to do twenty-four hours a day, seven days a week. God promises that in the New Covenant He will give them new hearts. And when He gives them new hearts (30:6), loving Him will be the result.

And if that weren't enough, God says it very directly Himself. God tells Moses that after his death

this people will rise up, and go a whoring after the gods of the strangers of the land . . . , and will forsake me, and break my covenant which I have made with them. Then my anger shall be kindled against them in that day, and I will forsake them, and I will hide my face from them, and they shall be devoured, and many evils and troubles shall befall them. (Deut. 31:16–17)

> "Israel is constitutionally incapable of choosing the way of life."
>
> —J. G. McConville

How would you feel if you were an Israelite and God said these things about you? Even as a reader, it's unsettling to see the people you were rooting for fail—and fail so miserably.

The Lord—Gracious and Compassionate

But we should never have expected that the hero of the Bible—the serpent crusher who is to restore the world to the way it ought to be—would be another fallen human like Adam. Apparently, putting together a whole nation of fallen humans (like Israel) only makes the problem of sin worse, not better.

If the Bible is the story of what God is doing to redeem His fallen creation, then the true hero of the Bible has to be God Himself. Even the most blessed people in the world are still stuck in their sins. Even getting their own land and special laws straight from the finger of God isn't enough to save them. They still need more saving than they received in the Exodus because they're still slaves—slaves to sin.

Possible Route of the Israelites

As the messages in the book of Deuteronomy are presented, Israel is standing at the border of the Promised Land, ready to enter and conquer.

So our merciful God gives them a special promise. They will fail, yes, and God will push them out of their land and scatter them around the world for breaking His covenant with them. But God won't leave them on their own outside the land. In His love and faithfulness, He will eventually bring them back and fix the broken thing that is causing all their problems—their own sinful hearts. Near the end of Deuteronomy God reveals just a glimpse of the work that Jesus will do in the New Covenant:

And the Lord thy God will circumcise thine heart, and the heart of thy seed, to love the Lord thy God with all thine heart, and with all thy soul, that thou mayest live. (Deut. 30:6)

> "Deuteronomy recognizes the need for God to act within the heart if Israel is to achieve faithful obedience to God's covenant."
>
> **—Paul Barker**

The real, fundamental problem of all people is that they do not love the Lord with all their hearts. They love themselves. They love sin. Their hearts are twisted in the wrong direction. But God can untwist them. God will change their hearts. That's what Israel really needs, and someday God will do it.

Your Heart

That's what you need too, of course—if you haven't already experienced it. That's why some readers have to drag their eyes across these pages like pulling a wheelbarrow up a mountain. In their deepest heart, they just don't care about all this stuff, because they don't love the God who is the main character of the Bible.

You can't just make yourself love something you don't already love. Wanna try it? Okay, on the count of three, love spinach. Okay, now stop. On the count of three, love God. Okay, now stop. It doesn't work. Love can't be turned on and off because it comes from your inmost nature. And just as God would have to change your tongue to like a food you hate, God has to change you deep inside if you're going to love Him.

Thinking It Through 4.1

1. In the Old Testament, what does the term *heart* represent?

2. In Moses' final sermon to the second generation as they are about to enter the Promised Land, why does he insist that they will fail to keep God's covenant law?

3. What is God's solution to the problem of Israel's failure?

4. How will God accomplish this solution to the problem?

5. Why does God give Israel the land?

4.2 JOSHUA: PROMISES FULFILLED

Read Joshua 6:1–8:29
Memorize Joshua 21:43–45

Joshua's Job

In the book of Joshua, we see God's people finally entering their land and managing to conquer it by God's power. They're subduing the earth and having dominion over it in a very real and obvious way—just like God told humanity to do in the beginning. And Joshua tells how they start filling the land God promised them—just like God told Adam to fill the earth. These are real signs of hope.

The book of Joshua is, of course, named after the leader who takes Moses' spot when that great leader dies. And as Joshua (one of the two faithful spies from Numbers) leads the people into the land, hope grows even higher.

When the book opens, we see God's charge to Joshua. God gives Joshua some amazing promises. Perhaps the most important promise was that God would be with him in the same way He was with Moses (Josh.1:5; cf. Deut. 34:10–12). God also gives Joshua some specific instructions. He was to be strong and courageous because he would lead the people to take possession of the land that God had promised to them (Josh. 1:6).

More importantly, Joshua was to obey. He was to do all that Moses had commanded Israel to do. He should not turn from the law in any way (1:7). Only by doing exactly what it says would he have success. He was to meditate on it day and night so that he would know it so well that he would obey "all that is written therein" (1:8). Through obedience, the nation would be carrying out the Creation Mandate in the way that God intended.

The rest of the world was not exercising good and wise dominion over the earth in a way that honored God. But if the nation of Israel lived in the Promised Land according to the law God had given Moses, then all the nations would be able to see what good and wise dominion under God looked like.

The book of Joshua shows us how these commands were carried out. It shows how the people sometimes failed to carry them out, and how they succeeded in carrying them out.

It also shows us how God is fulfilling the covenant promises that He made to Abraham.

When God first speaks to Joshua, He focuses on the land that He is giving to the sons of Israel (1:2–4). God describes to Joshua the borders of the land and the security that they will find there. As you read the first chapter of Joshua, observe how many references are made to the land and other landmarks such as rivers and the sea.

The following lesson is an example of what happens to Israel when they fail to carry out God's commands. Simply put, they don't have success. In fact, they are soundly defeated. But this lesson also shows what happens when they carry out the commands. They have success. And it's not just any type of success; it is great success that points directly to God's mighty works on their behalf to fulfill His promises to Israel's forefathers.

Group Punishment

Nobody likes group punishment. Nobody likes it when one kid gets in trouble, and the whole class is punished. But we have no problem with group punishment in sports. One player commits a penalty, and the whole team has to move the football back fifteen yards. What's the difference? Why do we accept it in one situation and not the other?

Well, in sports we understand (or at least we should) that we win as a team and we lose as a team. No team is an individual, and no individual is a team. We never say, "Player number seven for the Lions lost today, but the rest of the Lions won."

Being part of a group usually comes with responsibility. If you're part of a sports team, you know that there are rules. If you have bad grades, you might have to sit out until you bring them up. If you get in trouble—that is, big trouble—you might not get to be on the team.

The same is true on a national level. If the leaders of your country act foolishly in provoking a war, it is not only the leaders who suffer a counterattack, but the nation. If your nation's leaders are foolish and seek to build illegal weapons, it may not be just the leaders who come under sanctions, but the nation.

Walking around a city for seven days is not usually the best means of conquering a walled and heavily armed stronghold—unless the Lord of Hosts is on your side and tells you to do it.

Being part of Israel came with responsibility—the responsibility to keep Israel's part of the covenant with God. When God gave Moses His law, He told the children of Israel that they had to do what was written in the law. You obey—blessings. You disobey—curses.

Part of obeying was to follow what God's leaders said to do. The consequences for disobeying them were the same as the consequences for disobeying God.

There is at least one account in the book of Joshua where the nation of Israel experiences group punishment. But no one could say that it wasn't fair. Joshua had given them explicit instructions, but one man disobeyed. And it cost the lives of thirty-six men.

Victory at Jericho

God's plan to use Pharaoh to show His power worked very well. Even forty years after the Exodus, a prostitute in Jericho remembers those amazing displays of God's power. She and all Jericho are afraid of this strangely blessed nation

(Josh. 2:8–14). (And Rahab's fear of the Lord wins her a place in the line of future Israelite kings!)

When the people are faithful to the Lord, miracles happen. Jericho's walls come tumbling down without Israel shooting a single arrow. When the omnipotent God, who created the universe, is on your side, walls don't present much of a barrier.

In fact, it was a rather easy victory. The Israelites had easily defeated what many thought to be an impenetrable and undefeatable city.

Joshua's fame was heard throughout the land.

One Soldier, One Sin, One Defeated Army

The Israelites were feeling good about their victory. They felt so good that they decided they didn't need to send many men to attack Ai. About three thousand would do. There would be no reason to worry the rest of the fighting men or make the people travel up to Ai and camp out. They could all stay home.

The first casualty probably came as quite a shock to the Israelites.

The three thousand (or so) men marched out to Ai and the rout was on. One after the other began to fall, and they were in full retreat. But the retreating men were the Israelites—not the men of Ai.

About thirty-six men from Israel were killed. The rest of the fighting men returned home and the "hearts of the people melted, and became as water" (Josh. 7:5). In other words, the Israelites were terrified—they were scared to death.

Joshua was perplexed. Why did this happen? He fell before the Lord and asked Him, "Why did the Israelites turn their backs? Why did this happen, Lord, and what are you going to do about it?"

The Lord told Joshua to get up. Israel had sinned, and Joshua must deal with it immediately. And until it was taken care of, the Israelites would continue to turn their backs and run.

Joshua called for all the people to prepare themselves. The next day, they would figure out who had sinned. And that person would pay the price—he would burn with fire.

The next morning, one by one, each of the tribes came near, and the tribe of Judah was chosen. Then the family of the Zerahites was chosen, and then the family of Zabdi, and then Carmi, and finally, Achan was chosen.

Joshua asked him what he had done.

Achan said that he had seen some beautiful things and some valuable silver and gold. But he lingered too long. He coveted them and took them. He was supposed to destroy them or give them to God so that he wouldn't covet them. But he didn't destroy them, nor did he give them to God. Instead, he had hidden them in a covered hole that was in his tent.

Achan's words were true. The stolen goods were exactly where he said they were.

So, he came clean. He's in the clear. Right? Not exactly.

Remember, thirty-six people died, the fighting men were humiliated, and the entire nation was terrified. But there was something worse—he had sinned against God.

Although he admitted to stealing and even admitted to sinning against God, he would still have to face the consequences for his actions. And the consequences were severe—both for him and his family—death by stoning followed by burning with fire. The punishment was necessary because Israel's covenant with God had been violated. Justice must be served. Through the punishment God could renew His blessing on the nation according to His own faithfulness to the covenant.

When even one Israelite was unfaithful to the covenant, there were terrible consequences. Although Achan was only one man, his sin was against God. And because he was part of the covenant group of Israel, his sin made not only himself accursed, it also made the camp of Israel accursed (Josh. 6:18). When God isn't on your side, one soldier can beat your whole army.

In their experiences at Jericho and Ai, God was teaching Israel two lessons: (1) *I'm the one who wins your battles, so stay faithful to My covenant.* (2) *If you are unfaithful, you won't get to stay in your land.*

Staying Faithful

Israel had to learn the hard way that God meant what He had said. Disobey and there will be consequences. But Israel also learned from the experience at Ai that God is faithful and would give them the victory if they would be faithful to His covenant.

The rest of the book of Joshua is about the successes and failures of the children of Israel and their leader. (Yes, even Joshua makes mistakes. He makes a covenant with the Gibeonites without consulting the Lord. He was to defeat them, not make peace with them.) As you read through the book, you see victory after victory over king after king and over territory after territory. God is fulfilling His promises.

When you come to the end of the book, you see just how much God fulfilled. Joshua reminds the people,

> Ye know in all your hearts and in all your souls, that not one thing hath failed of all the good things which the Lord your God spake concerning you; all are come to pass unto you, and not one thing hath failed thereof. (Josh. 23:14)

"Not one thing hath failed." In other words, not one promise is unfulfilled. God has been faithful, and they know it in their hearts and in their souls.

Conclusion

The first generation of newly freed Israelites had seen God perform amazing miracles: ten plagues, the Exodus, the parting of the Red Sea, the provision of manna. And yet they complained, they had no faith, and they left their bones in the wilderness.

The second generation of Israelites watched God knock down the walls of Jericho and hand them a beautiful land on the Mediterranean Sea, the very land He had promised to Abraham. And yet their faithfulness to the covenant lasted only as long as the lives of their godly leaders.

If people who watched God act with their own eyes won't (and, as Joshua says, *can't*) remain faithful to Him, how deep is the problem of mankind? How deep does sin go in your own heart?

Would you have been more faithful than Israel under the same circumstances? Don't answer that question by thinking about your personal history; answer it based on what the Bible tells you is true. From what you know about the sinfulness of mankind, what would you have done?

Thinking It Through 4.2

1. The focus of the book of Joshua is God's fulfillment of which Abrahamic promise?

2. What would determine whether the people were successful or not?

3. What two lessons did God teach the Israelites in their experiences at Jericho and Ai?

4. By the end of the book of Joshua, how many of God's promises had He failed to fulfill?

5. Give one illustration of how personal sin brings consequences on others.

4.3 JOSHUA: THE ROCKS THAT WERE A WITNESS

Read Joshua 3–4
Memorize Joshua 4:21–22, 24

A Wall of Remembrance

The Vietnam Veterans Memorial in Washington, DC, honors the members of the US armed forces who fought, died, or went missing in action during the Vietnam War. The memorial consists of three individual memorials. The first is called *The Three Servicemen*, and it is a bronze statue of three men overlooking the wall. The second memorial honors the women who served, most of whom were nurses.

Probably the most emotional part of the memorial is the Memorial Wall, which is a stone wall etched with the names of more than fifty-eight thousand servicemen and women who were either killed in action or went missing in action. In fact, each name is listed in the order that the person was killed.

The wall is polished black granite, and when you stand in front of it, you can actually see your own reflection. Some say that this is to make the wall more personal and to symbolically bring the past and present together.

For some the wall is a painful reminder of the lives lost in one of America's most controversial wars. "Yet the Memorial itself is dedicated to honor the 'courage, sacrifice and devotion to duty and country' of all who answered the call to serve during the longest war in U.S. history."

For Americans, the wall is a monument that forces us to remember our past—to remember that our country is not perfect nor are its leaders, and to remember the men and women who gave their lives for our country.

In the Old Testament the Israelites also set up memorials. They too needed to remember their past. They too needed to remember the good and the bad.

Remember

After Moses died, Joshua gathered the people together and said, "Remember the word which Moses the servant of the Lord commanded you, saying, The Lord your God hath given you rest, and hath given you this land" (Josh. 1:13).

Remember. The first thing they are to do is to remember the promise that God gave to Moses.

Throughout Joshua's time as Israel's leader, he wanted the people to remember the promises that God had made to them. He wanted them to remember what God had done for them. He wanted them to remember that they had a covenant relationship with God. He also wanted the people to remember what they had promised God—"All that thou commandest us we will do" (Josh. 1:16). And he wanted them to remember those who hadn't obeyed God and had paid the penalty.

Twelve Stones of Remembrance

Growing up you've probably heard the story of the children of Israel crossing the Red Sea on dry ground. You probably remember how Moses lifted his staff and stretched out his hand and how the sea divided. It was a miracle how God delivered the Israelites and destroyed Pharaoh's army in one day.

But how much do you know about how the children of Israel crossed the Jordan River on dry ground? Many people don't even know about what happened at the Jordan River. And that is a shame, because it is the first place Joshua built a memorial for the Israelites to remember what God did for them.

When they came to the Jordan River, Joshua needed a way to get all the people across. God said He would provide a way that would show the Israelites and the surrounding nations that the living God was among them. They would also know that God would drive out the people from the land. They would soon have peace from their wanderings.

As the people packed up their tents and their belongings, the Jordan continued to flow. As they got ready to cross, the Jordan continued to flow. But as soon as the feet of the priests who were carrying the ark of the covenant touched the water, it stopped flowing. And in fact, the ground dried up before them. The people could now walk across the Jordan River on dry ground.

Joshua recognized the importance of what was happening. He ordered that one man from each tribe, twelve in all, pick up a huge stone from where the priests had stood. The men were to lay them down and make a memorial. Why? Joshua basically told them, "This will be a sign for you, so that in the future when your children ask their fathers, 'What do these stones mean?' you can tell them, 'Israel came over the Jordan on dry land'" (Josh 4:6, 22). In other words, "Create a memorial so you can teach your children what God has done here for you personally."

But not all the stone piles were for remembering good things. Some of the stone piles were to remember what happened when sin entered the camp.

A Pile of Stones

In the last lesson, you read about Achan and how he was stoned to death because of his sin against God. At the end of that episode, the Israelites "raised over [Achan] a great heap of stones" (Josh. 7:26), and those stones were still there when the book of Joshua was written. The stones weren't piled on him to make sure he was dead (clearly he was already dead); the stones were piled up to remember why Joshua called the place the Valley of Achor.

The word *Achor* means "trouble." And for generations to come, the Israelites remembered what had happened in that valley—Achan had sinned, and his sin caused trouble for both himself and the whole nation.

An Altar of Stones

When Israel had crossed the Jordan, they took time to memorialize the event by erecting stones. When they came to Gilgal, they made a permanent monument and paused to purify themselves before attacking Jericho. The permanent monument would help them remember that God's kindness was a result of His covenant relationship with them.

When they came to Mount Gerizim and Mount Ebal, everyone was there—men, women, children, and foreigners. They divided into two groups and stood around the ark. They were following the instructions that God had given Moses (Deut. 27:11–13). Half of the tribes (Simeon, Levi, Judah, Issachar, Joseph, and Benjamin) stood in front of Mount Gerizim and half (Reuben, Gad, Asher, Zebulun, Dan, and Naphtali) stood in front of Mount Ebal. The ark of the covenant was in the middle, between the two sides. Those who stood on Mount Gerizim recited the blessings that would come from obedience to God's law while those on Mount Ebal recited the covenant curses. This was a way of remembering what God had told them in the law.

As they did at Gilgal, they paused to offer burnt offerings and to listen to the words of the Book of the Law. Joshua read every word of the law to them, both blessings and cursings. Joshua followed the law and wrote the Word of God on the stones (Josh. 8:32; cf. Deut. 27:2–4, 8). The Israelites were not only going to hear the Word of God; they were also going to be able to read the Word of God.

Ai was not to be repeated. The Israelites would know the law of God and do it.

A Stone of Witness

This was not the only time Joshua wrote out the law on stones. At the end of his life, he gathered all the tribes together at Shechem. There, they presented themselves to God. Joshua rose and spoke to the people about how God had brought Abraham out of idolatry. He reminded them how Abraham's descendants had ended up in Egypt and how God had sent Moses and Aaron to deliver them. He recounted the various battles God had brought them through, from the time they had entered Canaan until then.

Joshua made one last plea to the people:

> Now therefore fear the Lord, and serve him in sincerity and in truth: and put away the gods which your fathers served on the other side of the flood [Euphrates], and in Egypt; and serve ye the Lord. And if it seem evil unto you to serve the Lord, choose you this day whom ye will serve; whether the gods which your fathers served that were on the other side of the flood, or the gods of the Amorites, in whose land ye dwell: but as for me and my house, we will serve the Lord. (Josh. 24:14–15)

The people answered resoundingly, "God forbid that we should forsake the Lord, to serve other gods" (24:16).

Joshua knew them well. They were sinners, and their hearts would lead them astray. So he bluntly told them, "Ye cannot serve the Lord: for he is an holy God" (24:19). They needed new hearts, and they needed a new covenant that would transform their hearts. Then he reminded them of the consequences of forsaking the Lord.

The people responded, "Nay; but we will serve the Lord" (24:21).

Joshua gave a few more instructions for them to put away the foreign gods and serve the Lord. Evidently, they weren't exactly getting the point—idolatry was not obedience. They must put away their gods and set their hearts on the Lord.

The people agreed, and then they made a covenant with Joshua to serve and obey the voice of the Lord.

Joshua took the covenant seriously, and he wanted to make sure that the people did too. Making a promise to God is something that should not be done lightly. So Joshua took a huge stone and placed it under a large tree. The stone was to be a witness to what they had promised that day.

Joshua proclaimed,

> Behold, this stone shall be a witness unto us; for it hath heard all the words of the Lord which he spake unto us: it shall be therefore a witness unto you, lest ye deny your God. (24:27)

In other words, if they disobeyed, the stone would be a witness against them. Every time they saw the stone, it should bring back to their memory the things they had promised God, and the things God had spoken to them. And they would stay faithful and obey.

Conclusion

Joshua used stones to help the children of Israel remember what God had done for them. Stones were also used to remember the punishments that ensued when they disobeyed God. And stones were used to help the people remember the Word of God. Every time they saw that altar, God's Word was placed before them. Finally, a stone was used as a witness against the people if they disobeyed and went after foreign gods.

Thinking It Through 4.3

1. After Moses died, what two things did Joshua tell the people they needed to remember?

2. True or False. Stones were used to remember both God's faithfulness and the nation's unfaithfulness.

3. Why did Joshua write out the words of God's law on the stones at Mounts Ebal and Gerizim?

4. Why did the Israelites pile stones on Achan?

5. What kinds of "stones of remembrance" can you set up to help you remember God's promises to you and your commitment to God?

4.4 HIS FAITHFUL LOVE ENDURES FOREVER

Read Psalm 118
Memorize Psalm 136:1–4

Every family has memories. Some are funny. Some are sad. Some are about the hard times and how God provided a way through. But one thing is certain, each family has its own common memories. Those common memories provide unity. They provide an awareness that you are part of a family. Those memories help make you and your family unique.

Think about the memories you have with your classmates. If you've grown up together, you probably have a lot of good (and some bad) memories. But they are all common memories to your class. Your field trips are unique to your class. The teachers you've had, and the things that have happened to you and your classmates make your class unique. Those common memories provide unity and make your class . . . well, your class.

Israel was no different. As a new nation, they shared common memories that made them unique. No other nation could say the things that Israel could say. Israel was God's chosen people. They had a covenant relationship with Him. They were the object of His steadfast and loyal love. They were the ones that God delivered from slavery. They were the ones who got a promised land. These events provided cohesion. These experiences gave them a national consciousness. They were Israel, and they were unique.

That is why Moses tells the children of Israel,

Remember the days of old, consider the years of many generations: ask thy father, and he will shew thee; thy elders, and they will tell thee. (Deut. 32:7)

What exactly were they to remember about the days of old?

The psalmist clarifies for us:

I will remember the works of the Lord: surely I will remember thy wonders of old. (Ps. 77:11)

"The works of the Lord." That is what they were to remember. God's works.

In fact, the entire book of Deuteronomy was about remembering what God had done for Israel. When Joshua led the children of Israel into Canaan, he too wanted them to remember what God had done. In the last lesson, you saw how Joshua set up twelve stones for remembrance. Twelve stones for the Israelites to remember what God had done for them to cross the Jordan River on dry ground.

In this lesson you will see that years later, Israel would look back and remember what God had done for them. Sadly, after Joshua passed away, Israel would not—for quite some time—remember what God had done for them. The parents wouldn't teach their children what God had done. Basically, they would forget to remember.

Why So Much Emphasis on Remembering?

The biblical emphasis on remembering is much more than merely saying, "Oh yeah, I remember when that happened." Remembering how God has dealt with the nation and with people in the past should shape and direct our present actions.

> "If one remembers in the biblical sense, the past is brought into the present with compelling power. Action in the present is conditioned by what is remembered."
>
> —Edward P. Blair

Songs

One of the best ways to remember something is to put words to a song. You can probably remember the words to many songs fairly easily. It's hard to remember the twelve tribes of Israel or the twelve disciples, but when you put their names in a musical tune, you can easily recall them.

That is exactly what the Israelites did with their history. They wrote their history in songs

Ways to Remember

God gave the people ways to help them remember Him and what He had done for them because of His covenant relationship with them.

Below are some of the feasts that God commanded Israel to practice. Each feast is a way of recognizing a specific aspect of God's saving work for the nation of Israel (Lev. 23; Num. 28–29; Deut. 16).

- **Sabbath** festivals occurred weekly (the Sabbath day), monthly (the new moon celebration), every seven years (the Sabbath year), and every fifty years (the year of jubilee). The Sabbath was a day of rest to remember God's blessing of the seventh day during the creation (Exod. 20:9–11). The new moon celebration included sacrifices, feasting, and rest from work. The Sabbath year allowed the land to rest and was a celebration like the Sabbath day. The Israelites were to release their slaves and forgive debts. The year of jubilee focused on God's owning the land.

- **Passover** celebrated God's grace and Israel's deliverance from Egypt. A lamb would be sacrificed to remember the blood that was put over the door frame. The Israelites ate bitter herbs to remember the bitterness of being slaves in Egypt (Exod. 12:8). Unleav-

ened bread reminded them that the Israelites did not have time to wait for the bread to rise before leaving (Exod. 12:39). And everyone would dress in travel clothes to represent the Israelite slaves who were eagerly waiting for God's deliverance (Exod. 12:11).

- **Pentecost**—also called the **Feast of Weeks**—was to remember when the children of Israel renewed the covenant, both before entering the land (Deut. 29) and after they had conquered the land (Josh. 24).

- At the **Festival of Trumpets**, the trumpets would blow to signal a call for repentance. This was to remind the people to call on the Lord just as their ancestors did in Egypt (Ps. 81:7).

- During the **Feast of Tabernacles**, the people made shelters of boughs and lived in these booths for seven days. This was to remind them of how their fathers had lived in booths as they wandered in the wilderness.

- The **Day of Atonement** was a feast involving atonement (removing sin and turning away God's wrath) for the entire nation. The feast also served as a call to restore the people to a holy condition.

---

that they called psalms. Psalm 136 is one such psalm. The words of the psalmist can explain the stones from Joshua's time. When the Israelites saw those stones, by quoting psalms like Psalm 136, they could easily remember what God had done for them.

Psalm 136 recounts what God has done for the nation of Israel. Its purpose is to help the people of Israel remember the mighty works God did for them. It begins with creation, goes through the Exodus, and ends with God's providing for each individual.

When you study a passage, one observation strategy is to look for things repeated. When you read Psalm 136, did you notice something unusual? The psalmist repeats a phrase in every verse. Over and over he states, "For his mercy endureth for ever." Another way of saying this is

God's steadfast love, His loyal kindness, endures forever.

Anytime you see something repeated, it is probably important. When you see something repeated in every verse, you *know* it's important. In this case, the repeated phrase is the theme of the psalm.

In this phrase, the word *mercy* comes from the word *ḥesed*. In the section on Isaac and Rebekah (Section 2.5) we discussed that *ḥesed* means more than mercy or kindness. It means a loyal kindness or a steadfast love that stems from a relationship. God is loyally kind to Israel because He has a covenant relationship with the nation.

Psalm 136 shows God's loyal kindness to the world (as Deity, Creator, and Provider), and in particular to Israel (as Deliverer and Protector).

Why is He doing what He is doing? Because He has a relationship with His creation and with His chosen people.

In fact, that little word *for* that is at the beginning of each phrase simply means "because." So after you read the first part of each verse, you can ask *why*, and the answer is always, *because His loyal kindness never ends.*

God Is Good (136:1)

The psalm opens with a call to give thanks. The call to give thanks is based on what God is like—He is good. Why is He good? Remember the answer? Because His loyal kindness never ends.

God Is Deity (136:2–3)

The call to give thanks is also based on who He is—He is the "God of gods" and "Lord of lords." Moses told the people, "Hear, O Israel: The Lord our God is one Lord" (Deut. 6:4). This meant that there was only one God, one Lord. There is no god besides Him. How should they respond to this fact? "Thou shalt love the Lord thy God with all thine heart, and with all thy soul, and with all thy might" (Deut. 6:5).

Israel needed to look around them at all these other nations that claimed to have their own god or lord and remember that their God is the God of those so-called gods and the Lord of those "lords."

Why should they give thanks to God? Because His loyal kindness never ends.

> "In view of what Yahweh has done for the nation, the worship of any other god or gods is ingratitude of the basest sort."
>
> —Edward P. Blair

God Is the Creator (136:4–9)

It is God who does great wonders. It is God alone who has the understanding to make the heavens. It is God who made the land, the great lights, the sun, the moon, and the stars. Israel must remember who their Creator is. Why? Because His loyal kindness never ends.

God Is Israel's Deliverer (136:10–16)

For the people of Israel, God is more than the Creator. He is the one who delivered them. No other nation can claim what they can claim.

The psalmist recounts these things for a reason: the people needed this reminder of God's deliverance. Moses had said, "And remember that thou wast a servant in the land of Egypt, and that the Lord thy God brought thee out thence through a mighty hand and by a stretched out arm: therefore the Lord thy God commanded thee to keep the sabbath day" (Deut. 5:15). The children of Israel needed to remember what it was like to be slaves so that they would be motivated to be generous and kind to their servants and to the poor and needy (Deut. 5:14).

The people needed to remember what it was like to face Pharaoh and his great army. Israel had no army. Their backs were up against the Red Sea. They were facing an overwhelming situation from which they could not escape. But God had a strong hand and a "stretched out arm." And God (not Israel) parted the sea. And God (not Israel) overthrew Pharaoh. The people needed to remember this so that they would have confidence in God even when situations seemed impossibly difficult.

He alone delivered them. Why? Because His loyal kindness never ends.

They also needed to remember the wilderness experience. God did not forsake them. They had to humbly depend on Him for their food and provisions. Why did God sustain them? I think you know the answer.

God Is Israel's Protector and Provider (136:17–22)

God also protected Israel during the conquest. Many kings, even great kings, were struck down and slain by God. What was the purpose of God's slaying these mighty kings? He was fulfilling His promise to give Israel the land "for an heritage" (136:21; cf. Deut. 4:38). To emphasize that God did this to give them the land, the psalmist repeats that the land is "an heritage unto Israel his servant" (136:22). (Did you remember that something repeated is important?)

God protected them and gave them a land. Why? Because His loyal kindness never ends.

God Is Israel's Rescuer (136:23–24)

When God looked down on Israel while they were in Egypt, He didn't see a thriving nation that was prosperous and self-sufficient (Ezek. 16:1–14). Rather, He saw a nation that was as an infant, naked and afraid, with no one to pity it. They were like an infant cast out into a field left to die. But God looked down on them and spread His garment over them and covered their nakedness. He bathed them and gave them clothes to wear. He fed them, and they grew up to be not only beautiful, but also royal.

It was that kind of "low estate" that the psalmist brings back to Israel's memory. He wants them to remember that God remembered them in their low estate. In the wilderness He didn't forget them—He rescued them from their enemies.

Why did God remember them, and why did He rescue them? Because His loyal kindness never ends.

God Is Israel's Provider and the God of Heaven (136:25–26)

Israel's God was different from the gods of the other nations. Each nation had its own god and proudly proclaimed its own god. But Israel could claim that its God was not only the "God of Israel," He was also "the God of the heavens." For He is the one who provides food to "all flesh." Therefore, all creation must give thanks to God the provider. Why? Because His loyal kindness never ends.

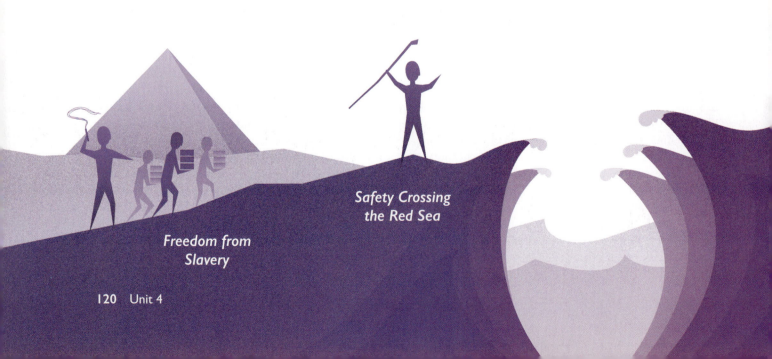

Freedom from Slavery

Safety Crossing the Red Sea

This Do in Remembrance of Me

God wanted the children of Israel to remember a central event in their history. That event was the Exodus. God wanted the Israelites to remember how He had delivered them from slavery when they could not deliver themselves. He wanted them to remember that He had remembered His promise to them and rescued them. He wanted them to remember the mighty works that He had done for them because of His relationship with them through the covenant.

As Christians, God wants us to remember a central event in our history as well. This event was Christ's "Exodus." It was His crucifixion. Before He was crucified, He sat down at the Passover meal and Last Supper. He broke bread, gave them juice, and said, "This do in remembrance of me" (1 Cor. 11:23–26).

As Christians, we do not participate in the Passover meal. We have Communion. And Paul tells us that as often as we have Communion, we are to remember the Lord's death and celebrate His resurrection. We are to remember the event that delivered us when we could not deliver ourselves. We are to remember the event (the Last Supper) where Christ established the New Covenant. God wants us to remember that He remembered His promise to all humanity to crush the head of the serpent (Gen. 3:15) and that He has rescued us from our enemy.

Why did He do that for us? Because His loyal kindness never ends.

Thinking It Through 4.4

1. What is the purpose of Psalm 136? What is the theme of Psalm 136?

2. True or False. Remembering God's dealings in the past should shape and direct our present actions.

3. Based on the different sections of verses in Psalm 136, how has God shown His steadfast love to Israel?

4. What was the central event for Israel to remember? What is the central event for New Testament Christians to remember?

5. How does Psalm 136 apply to the New Testament believer?

Provision in the Wilderness

Conquest of Enemies

Peace in the Promised Land

4.5 DEBORAH: A GODLY LEADER

Read Judges 4
Memorize Judges 2:10

As long as Joshua modeled deep faith in God (and picked other leaders who did the same), the whole nation saw success. But after that godly leader died, and when the godly leaders he'd chosen eventually died too, Israel started to slip.

The Decline

First, they failed to drive out the Canaanites from the Promised Land (Judg. 1). And God was not pleased. He basically said, "I won't break the covenant I made with you. But since you've disobeyed Me, I won't drive out the Canaanites. Instead, I'll leave them in your land as a trap for you—to see whether you will follow Me or not" (2:1–5). In fact, these traps were proof that God was keeping His covenant because part of the covenant was the promise that God's faithfulness to the covenant would lead to judgment for Israel's unfaithfulness to the covenant.

Judges shows that, far from remaining faithful, the second generation of Israelites apparently failed to teach their children about God as they had been commanded (Deut. 6:4–8) and as they had promised to Joshua. A whole generation grew up without knowing the Lord or what He had done for Israel in the Exodus (Judg. 2:10). So the grandchildren of the people who had watched God do amazing miracles turned away from Him and started worshiping Baal instead.

They simply had forgotten God. They didn't remember to remember what God had done for them.

It's no wonder that this provoked the Lord to righteous anger. And He started to deliver Israel over to their enemies, just as He'd promised He would do if they broke His covenant (Deut. 28:45–51).

Israel's enemies had little mercy on them, and mercy is what Israel began to cry out for. God heard them and pitied them, just as He had when they were slaves in Egypt.

Here Come the Judges

God's answer to the problem of Israel's enemies was to give Israel a series of "judges." That, of course, is where the book gets its name.

Now it may not be obvious how a judge could help if you're being crushed by a cruel oppressor. Can a judge hit enemies with his gavel or smother them with his big black robe? But we're not talking about the kind of judge who sits high on a court bench telling people what the punishment for their crimes will be (even though these judges did some of that). In the book of Judges, the judges were more like governors and sometimes military generals who could successfully call troops together and lead them to push out the other nations that were oppressing Israel.

Othniel was the first judge, and after God's Spirit came on him, he delivered Israel from the king of Mesopotamia. Then the people had rest in the land God had promised Abraham. But after Othniel died, a pattern developed: the people would sin, God would bring a foreign people to oppress them, and God would raise up a new judge and start all over again.

The next judge happened to be Ehud, who assassinated the oppressive king of Moab. After Ehud died, the pattern repeated itself. This time the oppressors were the Philistines, and the judge was a man named Shamgar, who killed six hundred Philistines with a cattle prod.

Baal

The way the Bible talks about Baal can be a little confusing—but that's only because the way his worshipers talked about him can be a little confusing. People in some Canaanite areas treated him as the top god. But it also appears that people in the ancient Near East worshiped different Baals, because God speaks many times in the Old Testament of "the Baals" and not just of "Baal."

Baal means simply "lord" or "master"— and can also refer to a "husband." Baal was the god of weather, who brought fertility (fruitfulness) to people's crops. He proved to be a continual temptation to the Israelites for hundreds of years.

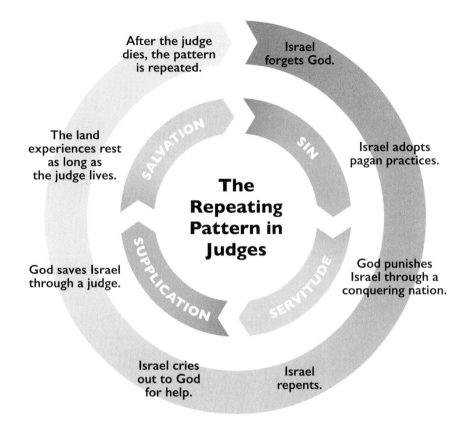

The Repeating Pattern in Judges

Israel forgets God.

Israel adopts pagan practices.

God punishes Israel through a conquering nation.

Israel repents.

Israel cries out to God for help.

God saves Israel through a judge.

The land experiences rest as long as the judge lives.

After the judge dies, the pattern is repeated.

SIN

SERVITUDE

SUPPLICATION

SALVATION

The Debut of Deborah

The fourth judge is a surprise because he's not a he. The fourth judge of Israel was a woman named Deborah, the wife of a man named Lappidoth.

Othniel

Each time Othniel is mentioned in Judges, the author notes that he is the son of Kenaz, thus emphasizing that he was a descendant of Esau. (See Gen. 36:11, 15, 42; note also Num. 32:12 and Josh. 14:6, 14, which reveal that Caleb was also a Kenizzite.) Othniel wasn't a native Israelite but was a proselyte, a convert. He was a former pagan who had been proselytized, or we could say, "Israelized." This was God's plan for Israel (Exod. 19:6; Deut. 4:1, 6–8). The nations were to see Israel and desire to have Israel's God. Sadly, later judges were Israelites who had been "Canaanized."

Everything Scripture says about Deborah is good. She spoke for the Lord as a prophetess, and her prophecies came true. She gave praise to God and not to herself when He delivered Israel. In fact, Deborah may have been the godliest of all the judges. She and Othniel are the only judges that the Bible doesn't say anything negative about—either directly or indirectly.

Deborah's judgeship is unusual, and not just because she is a woman. Several things stand out as different about her:

- She was the only judge actively serving the Lord before helping deliver Israel.
- God empowered other judges with His Spirit (Othniel, 3:10; Gideon, 6:34; Jephthah, 11:29; and Samson, 14:19 and 15:14), but there is no reference to God's Spirit coming on Deborah.
- Deborah does not actually deliver or "save" Israel. She calls upon Barak to do that. She doesn't assume that God will deliver Sisera into her hands, but she tells Barak, "This is the day in which the Lord hath delivered Sisera into thine hand" (4:14).

- She is also never called the deliverer of Israel, but rather, she is called "a mother in Israel" (5:7).
- When others recount the deeds of the judges, they list Barak's name and not hers (cf. Heb. 11:32).

These things make her judgeship unusual. But perhaps the most unusual thing about her judgeship was that she was performing the role that God had given to the priests and to the men who were to serve as judges in each town (Deut. 16:18; 17:8–10). The fact that Deborah is fulfilling this role shows that the priests and other leaders in Israel were not fulfilling their God-given roles. They were often ungodly. By the time of Samuel, the final judge, the priests didn't even recognize the voice of the Lord (1 Sam. 3:4–18).

> "The fact that the Israelites came to her instead of the priest reflects the failure of the established institution to maintain contact with God."
>
> —Daniel I. Block

Deborah Delivers the Message of God

When the story of Deborah opens, Israel had done evil in the sight of God. But they called to the Lord for help because Jabin, king of Canaan, and his commander, Sisera, had oppressed Israel for twenty years.

The people came to Deborah asking her for help. She in turn summoned Barak and told him that God had commanded for him to get ten thousand men and go to Mount Tabor to fight Sisera. She told Barak that God said He would deliver Sisera into his hands.

But Barak had a problem. A big problem! He was disobedient, and evidently, he also lacked faith in what God had said. For Barak says to Deborah, "If thou wilt go with me, then I will go" (4:8a).

"If . . ."

That is how he responds to God's command—"If."

His resolve not to obey is reinforced when he says, "If thou wilt not go with me, then I will not go" (4:8b).

You don't say "if" to God, and you don't say "I will not do it unless I get my way." Barak is showing a lack of both faith and discernment. He is acting like a spoiled child. Male leadership in Israel has taken a step backward. And as the book of Judges progresses, you will see it take leaps backward until eventually, there is no leader in Israel, and everyone does whatever he or she wants.

But God is not limited in who He can use. And in this case He uses the hesitant leader. But He also goes outside what is normal for Israel. He uses a godly woman to spur Barak to do His commands and another woman to finish the job.

Deborah says that she will go with him, but he will not receive the honor for the victory. Sisera will die at the hands of a woman.

Barak Goes Forth

Then Barak called for the men of Zebulun and Naphtali to meet him at Kedesh. After they met, Barak and his ten thousand men went up to Mount Tabor. When Sisera heard that Barak was at Tabor, he brought his army and nine hundred iron chariots and prepared to do battle.

Barak must have needed a push because Deborah proclaimed, "Up; for this is the day in which

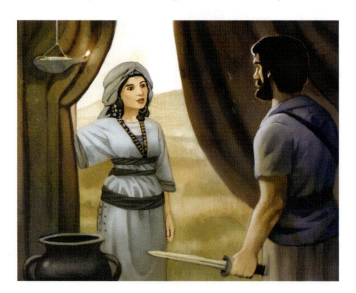

Deborah calls Barak to lead God's people.

the Lord hath delivered Sisera into thine hand: is not the Lord gone out before thee?" (4:14).

And to his credit, Barak arose and pursued Sisera—so much so that he routed Sisera's army.

Sisera's Final Hiding Place

Sisera had to flee for his life. He jumped out of his chariot, ran away, and hid in the tent of a woman named Jael.

Jael was kind to Sisera and gave him a place to lay down and rest. When he was thirsty, she gave him some milk to drink. But when he fell asleep, she took a hammer and a tent peg and drove it into his temple. And so he died.

Deborah's prophecy had come true. Sisera died at the hands of a woman and not at Barak's.

But the victory was not because of what Deborah had said, what Barak had or hadn't done, or even what Jael did. The victory was because God saw His people in need, and He delivered them. Yes, the people played a role, but it was God who deserved the praise.

The Point of the Deborah Story

To put it simply, most of the judges are not godly like Deborah. They aren't a permanent solution to Israel's problems since they obviously have horrendous problems of their own.

Israel doesn't immediately go from A-plus to F-minus. Othniel was a good judge. In fact, he was the model judge. He gets an A. Ehud was a cunning warrior. He effectively assassinated Israel's oppressor. But his deceptiveness does cast a bit of a shadow. We'll give him a B. The next major judge is Barak. He gets a C because Deborah should not have needed to step into the role that Israel's elders and priests should have been filling.

After Barak, the judges get noticeably worse and worse. Gideon did some good things—but then some very odd things (as we'll see). Jephthah

sacrificed his own daughter. And Samson couldn't keep his hands off Philistine women.

If Israel is getting a D-plus with Samson, the rest of the book brings them all the way down to an F-minus. By the end of Judges the writer makes it obvious that Israel has become as bad as Sodom and Gomorrah. Judges tells how Israel had actually become "Canaanized."

Deborah and the Big Story

When the story of Deborah and Barak opened, the first thing we saw was the Israelites doing evil in the sight of God. As a result, their enemies were persecuting them.

So why does God deliver them again? First, it's because they called out for help. He had not forgotten the promises He had made to them. Even when the leadership was not what it should have been, God still provided a godly leader to spur on a hesitant leader.

Second, these enemies of Israel were also God's enemies (Judg. 5:31). In the end, it was God who orchestrated the defeat of Sisera. As a result, the nation of Israel would go on.

But things were good for only forty years, and then the cycle starts all over. Israel does evil, they're oppressed by their enemies, they call on God for help, and He delivers them again . . . and again . . . and again . . .

Why is a depressing book like Judges even in the Bible? Is God, after all the trials in the wilderness, going to have to finally give up on His promises to Abraham? Is He going to have to find a new way to bless the whole world? A new way to crush the serpent's head?

We'll see that even at the lowest point in Scripture, the book of Judges gives us a hint that there's a way out of this mess. And it has something to do with a king.

Thinking It Through 4.5

1. What promise had the people made to Joshua but failed to keep, leading their children to be unfaithful during the time of the judges?

2. List the first four judges and the enemy that each defeated.

3. Summarize the repeated cycle recounted in Judges.

4. Why did God deliver the wicked people of Israel through Deborah?

5. What was wrong with Barak's response to Deborah?

4.6 GIDEON: A TURNING POINT IN JUDGES

Read Judges 6:1–8:3
Memorize Judges 8:34

The story of Gideon is a turning point in Judges. He starts out with at least a B-minus, and so does Israel—a solid passing grade. It's understandable that Gideon would ask for confirmation when the angel of the Lord stops by his house. He gets two confirmations—a miracle fire and a vanishing angel.

His grade goes up to an A when he obeys the Lord and pulls down his father's altar to Baal. But he goes back down to a B because, the Bible says, he was so afraid of people seeing him that he did it at night.

Gideon descends further, however—hovering perilously close to a C—when he asks God for yet another sign. But God is determined to deliver Israel from the Midianites, so He patiently gives Gideon a wet fleece just like he asks—and then a dry one for good measure, just in case.

Using a Fleece to Find Out God's Will?

A true story: A Christian guy couldn't decide whether or not to marry a particular girl. He said to God, "I'm going to put a towel out in front of my dormitory all night. If it's wet in the morning, I'll stay with the girl. If it's dry, I'll break up with her."

When he woke up the next day he was overjoyed: it had rained during the night! But when he ran out to get the towel, he couldn't find it! Then he spotted it. Someone had parked a car over the towel, leaving it dry.

The guy broke up with the girl. (She was probably lucky.)

The moral of the story: Gideon's use of a fleece is not a biblically approved method for determining God's will. Judges paints it as a way Gideon avoided obedience to God's already-stated command. God was merciful and played along, but you have God's Word to give you wisdom and don't need to try silly tricks to find out what He wants you to do.

But to Gideon's credit, that's the end of his requests for signs. Gideon becomes a man of action. Soon, as the Midianites gather for battle, some 32,000 Israelites join Gideon to do battle against their oppressors. Maybe Israel has found the leader it needs.

Whittling Down the Army

When you are outnumbered 135,000 to 32,000, classic military strategy is simple: Run! You can't win. Every Israelite would have to kill four men without getting killed himself. It would take a divine miracle.

So, naturally, God decides to make it easier on the Israelites. He manages to find a lot more Israelite soldiers who were in hiding! Now it won't be so hard, right?

Wrong. God takes the opposite plan: get rid of some men. If you're Gideon, you're thinking, "Lord? Are you sure this is the best plan? You just sent 22,000 of my men home. Now each of us will have to kill *fourteen* men!"

But apparently Gideon is not thinking that. At least he never says it. He somehow maintains his faith in the God of Abraham even as that God whittles down his army by 70 percent.

That 70 percent of the men go home because they're afraid anyway, so maybe it's a good thing. Maybe they would have done more harm than good, like starting a panic.

But God isn't done. And this part of the story requires you to think a little. From the very beginning, this textbook has been trying to show that the Bible is the story of what God is doing to redeem His fallen creation. Over and over, we've seen that God is the true hero of that story. People like Noah and Moses and Gideon are instruments in His hand, but it's His hand that carries the real power.

So what happens if an army of 32,000 takes down an army of 135,000? Almost overnight Israel gets some respect among the surrounding nations. But maybe Yahweh's role in the miracle gets left out.

But if a force of 10,000 soldiers routs an army almost fourteen times its size, then Yahweh starts to get some credit. Everyone knows that's not possible without the hand of God.

> "God's battles are not fought with human weapons nor for the sake of human glory. The honor of Yahweh's name is the primary concern."
>
> —Daniel I. Block

What, then, do some people think was God's reason for whittling the army down to 300 men? Was it because those men were particularly alert?

Water-Lappers vs. Water-Gulpers

God tells Gideon that 10,000 soldiers is still too many. He wants it to be obvious—for the whole world's benefit, including the Jews themselves—that He is more powerful than any army.

And that's why God sets up the water-lapping vs. water-gulping test. He tells Gideon to bring the men down to a spring and separate those who lap water from those who gulp it. It turns out that gulping is far more popular since 9,700 of the men do it. That leaves 300 men in Gideon's army.

But why did God use such a strange test to pick those three hundred? Many Bible scholars speculate that God chose these men because they were alert, keeping their heads up in case enemies arrived. Some scholars, on the other hand, think that God chose the weakest soldiers, the ones who needed the most water. Both positions have to make guesses about things the Bible doesn't explain.

And both have a tendency to miss the point. There's a third and better viewpoint that says God was being arbitrary. Random. All on purpose. God can save His people with many soldiers, God can save them with a few, and God can save them with a tiny number randomly selected by a test that has nothing to do with their battle-readiness.

FROM GIDEON'S ARMY TO GOD'S ARMY

Midianite Army 135,000

Gideon's Fearless Army 10,000

Gideon's Original Army 32,000

God's Army 300

22,000 WERE AFRAID AND GOT SENT HOME

9,700 KNELT TO DRINK AND GOT SENT HOME

300 WERE GOD'S ARMY

= 100

SO THAT **GOD** WOULD BE **GLORIFIED**

No matter what the nature of the water test is, the overall point is clear. And a later Israelite leader, Jonathan, puts that point very well: "There is no restraint to the Lord to save by many or by few" (1 Sam. 14:6). Whatever good Gideon is doing—and he did great good—it's because God's hand is on him. Judges says that "the Spirit of the Lord came upon Gideon" early in the story (6:34). We're watching a man who is God's tool to deliver His people.

> "We need not be anxious to count heads, when we are sure that we are doing His work, nor even be afraid of being in a minority."
>
> —Alexander Maclaren

God Wins

With 135,000 men, the Midianites had no logical reason to fear 300 men. In most battle situations, if an army of 300 attacked an army the size of the Midianites, the smaller army would be crushed. An army of 135,000 would laugh at the 300, and they certainly wouldn't fear them.

But that's not what happens when Gideon and his three hundred men blow their trumpets, crack their pitchers, and yell, "The sword of the Lord, and of Gideon." All of a sudden, the Midianites are killing each other. Yahweh *does* have power over human hearts.

The battle is won before Gideon and his men even have to pull their swords out of their sheaths. God has won a glorious victory! All the Israelite soldiers need to do is chase after the fleeing Midianites and pick up the spoils. As Gideon told his men, "The Lord hath delivered into your hand the host of Midian" (Judg. 7:15).

The Turning Point

It would be nice if the story just ended here. It would be nice if Judges just said that the land had peace for the last forty years of Gideon's life and left it at that. It's actually tempting to just ignore what comes next. But you wouldn't stop in the middle of a movie and feel satisfied. To really understand the story of Gideon you have to read the story till the very end.

You've already read the passage, but if you go through it and carefully observe the text, you will observe several things about Gideon—things that, sadly, bring Gideon down from an A to an F.

There's no doubt that Gideon's faith was praiseworthy when he led 300 men against 135,000. But all the details you observe were put there by the author to tell you something. Gideon didn't turn out to be the good and godly judge you might have expected. Soon after his great victory came a turning point in his life.

> "Gideon . . . represents the primary turning point from the 'better' judges to the 'weaker' ones."
>
> —J. Paul Tanner

And that turning point is a shame. He didn't have to respond in that way. Earlier in this book (Section 2.2 on Melchizedek), you read about Abraham's great victory over Chedorlaomer and his three allies. Do you remember how Abraham reacted? Well, he certainly didn't react the way Gideon did.

Before Gideon went into battle, he told the men to shout, "The sword of the Lord, and of Gideon" (7:18). Another way of saying that is, "For the Lord and for Gideon." It seems that from the beginning, Gideon wanted credit alongside God. And if that weren't enough, the Midianites flattered Gideon by telling him that he resembled a son of a king (8:18). The men of Israel also asked Gideon to be their king (8:22), and they gave Gideon, not God, credit for the victory.

Gideon's response was straightforward— neither he nor his sons would rule over them. Perhaps we're mistaken about Gideon wanting credit. Perhaps he is humble and doesn't want to be king.

But his actions betray him. He acts like a king and takes a treasure from the spoils of war for himself (8:24). He melts it down and turns it into an ephod. It's as if he is going to use it in some priestly manner. But regardless of his original intentions, the ephod ends up being a "snare" to him and his family (8:27).

By taking a treasure after the battle, Gideon differs from Abraham, because Abraham refused the spoils of war. In fact, Abraham tithed from what he had recovered and returned the spoils to the proper owners. Abraham, unlike Gideon, responded humbly and gave God the glory in both his words and his deeds.

Gideon's words at first were humble, but his deeds reflected his true attitude. Not only did Gideon take a treasure, he also took many wives and concubines—similar to what a king would do. Probably one of his more brazen actions was to name his son Abimelech, which means, "my father is king" (8:31). Abimelech would go on to be an arrogant and ruthless warrior who killed his rivals in order to be made king.

Descent

Unfortunately for Gideon and for Israel, that downward turning point in Gideon's life becomes a hinge point in the history of Israel as recorded in Judges. From this time on, the judges only get worse.

So the whole book of Judges keeps making this point over and over again: God's people are full of sin. They need someone to save them. The Jews in Gideon's time got someone—sort of. But he didn't turn out to be the king they needed.

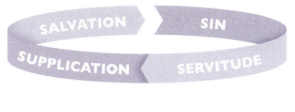

► ENTER GIDEON ◄

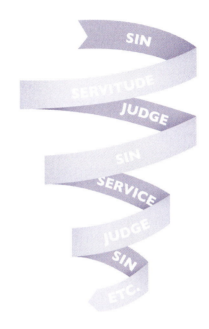

The people of Israel need a king. They need a king filled with God's Spirit at all times, not just during special battles. They need a king who will lead them to be faithful to the covenant they have with God.

As we read Judges, we're still looking for that king.

Thinking It Through 4.6

1. Describe the growing and the shrinking of Gideon's army.

2. Why did God change the size of Gideon's army?

3. List three ways that Gideon was exemplary in his behavior and then list three ways he did not please God.

4. True or False. Using a fleece is a biblically approved method for determining God's will.

5. Why do you suppose the writer of Judges devoted so much space to Gideon?

4.7 JEPHTHAH: THE JUDGE WHO VOWED RASHLY

Read Judges 11
Memorize Judges 10:13–14

Hopefully your parents don't let you watch just anything on TV. (Maybe they don't let you watch anything. Don't feel bad; you're not missing much.) And parents have good reasons for being careful about what they let their kids watch.

For one thing, even a lot of non-Christians admit that television tends to be a time-waster. It's just not a good way to spend a life—there are so many more profitable things to do than vegetate! And TV tends to make you expect to be entertained all the time. That's not spiritually healthy.

But one of the biggest reasons Christians don't watch certain shows is what are sometimes called "objectionable elements." Gory violence, harsh language, ugly immorality are things Christians just don't need to be entertained by because they offend a holy God.

Then why are all those things found in the book of Judges?

Jephthah the Man

Judges describes violence and immorality because it happens every day in this fallen world. But the Bible doesn't glorify these sins or make them seem appealing as movies so often do. The sins in Judges are sickening. They make you feel so sad—or at least they're supposed to.

One of the most surprising sins in the whole book occurs in the story of Jephthah. And to Bible readers who have been paying attention, it should be no surprise that sin has gotten this bad. Adam's fall has had huge effects on his descendants, and God's chosen people Israel are no exception.

The Bible gives us a little insight into Jephthah's background, and it isn't good. He was the son of a prostitute, and his half-brothers resented him so much that they kicked him out of the house because of who his mother was.

Obviously, his background was not his fault. But neither was his background an excuse to do wrong. Jephthah had an opportunity to do right—an opportunity to make a fresh start.

But instead he starts to attract a bunch of deadbeats (11:3). Different Bible translations use words such as *lawless*, *worthless men*, and *scoundrels* to describe the men that gathered around Jephthah. Obviously, Jephthah is no Deborah.

Jephthah the Judge

But this is the man God chose to be the deliverer of Israel when they cried out to Him this time. God looked beyond his background and gave him a great responsibility. Like with Gideon, the Spirit of the Lord came on Jephthah (11:29), and he became God's weapon to save the Israelites from their bondage to the Ammonites.

But it's right after God's Spirit comes on him that he commits the blunder that leads him to commit one of the worst sins in the book. We need to pay attention to exactly what he said on that occasion:

> Jephthah vowed a vow unto the Lord, and said, If thou shalt without fail deliver the children of Ammon into mine hands, then it shall be, that whatsoever cometh forth of the doors of my house to meet me, when I return in peace from the children of Ammon, shall surely be the Lord's, and I will offer it up for a burnt offering. (Judg. 11:30–31)

Sounds good, right? And sure enough, Jephthah's forces conquer Israel's enemies. But when Jephthah returns home triumphant, his vow hangs in the air. What (or who) will come out of his house to greet him?

It's almost the worst dilemma imaginable. He strides into his gate, proud of his victory. And the first living thing in the house to step out is not a goat or a sheep. It's his daughter—his only child. Jephthah is stricken with grief. He had promised God that he would kill his daughter.

But did he do it, or not?

Well, what do you think? She did go mourn for a time, but after that, this is what the Bible text says:

It came to pass at the end of two months, that she returned unto her father, who did with her according to his vow which he had vowed. (Judg. 11:39)

What does that sound like to you? Many Christians have tried to think of a way to read the verse so that Jephthah didn't really kill his own daughter. But what else could it mean that he "did with her according to his vow"? And what would make you want to say that he didn't do it?

The reason Christians don't want to think that Jephthah really and truly murdered his own daughter is probably simple: they think Jephthah is supposed to be a good guy (or at least they can't imagine anyone being this bad). And there's no denying that, while he was filled with God's Spirit, Jephthah did some real good (Hebrews 11:32 even implies that he exhibited admirable faith). But you have to remember some of the other negative elements Judges includes about Jephthah—like his fight with other Israelites (the Ephraimites). And most importantly, you have to put Jephthah's story in context: this is the book of Judges! The whole point is that Israel has gotten so bad—so much like the Canaanites—that even its best leaders do terribly sinful things.

Jephthah doesn't seem to be a very good leader if you compare him to the moral standards in the Mosaic law. And that's exactly the point. Every time the Israelites turned their back on God, they got worse—and they got a worse leader.

Jephthah's Line

Jephthah came from the line of Abraham, and his story has one big parallel to Abraham's. Abraham also put his special child on an altar to sacrifice him to God. In that story we read things that seem to be the beginnings of gory details: Abraham ties Isaac up and places him on the kindling. He raises the knife to sacrifice his son . . .

But we go no further. The angel of the Lord tells Abraham to stop. The Bible describes the scene only to prove that Abraham was really going to go through with it. No gore at all.

And in the story of Jephthah, we get none of those details. No knife, no screams, no blood. It's as if the scene is too horrible even to write about. The Bible just says he did it. That's all.

Daniel Block, who has studied Judges very carefully, points this out: "Whereas Abraham's sacrifice of his son assured him of a hope and a future, Jephthah's sacrifice of his daughter robbed him of both. The conquering hero is reduced to nothing."

And that's where the story stops, with the end of Jephthah's line. He judged Israel six years and died.

A Devotional Nugget

It's easy to start thinking that the purpose of Bible reading is to get a little nugget to chew on during the day—maybe a promise to treasure or a command to work on obeying.

And that works with some parts of the Bible. You get up early, you turn on your lamp at your desk, and you read God's holy Word. You want to get closer to God, the Author.

But what are you supposed to do with Jephthah? Where's the nugget? If there is one, it seems like it's either deeply hidden or has rotted away over the centuries.

No, there's something here for you, even in a depressing story like this one. The Bible, in this case, is like a doctor. If a doctor truly wants to help you, he can't bring only good news. The human race is deeply diseased, and sometimes watching it stumble is a necessary reminder: I've got the same disease unless God delivers me.

The people of Israel at this point in their history clearly need a better leader, someone who will lead them to be faithful to their covenant with God—if that's even possible. Here are two broad principles we can learn from Jephthah's story:

1. Even when God's people sin horribly, the Lord is merciful toward them and delivers them.
2. Not just a little mercy is needed for Adam's race, because *we need deliverance from something inside of us.*

Thinking It Through 4.7

1. Describe Jephthah's early life.

2. Read Judges 11:30–31. What was Jephthah's terrible vow, and why did he make it?

3. Use a concordance, Bible software, or a website to find five examples of how the term *burnt offering(s)* is used in the first six books of the Bible. According to these passages, what is a burnt offering?

4. Why don't people want to believe that Jephthah actually sacrificed his daughter as a burnt offering? Why should you understand that Jephthah actually did sacrifice his daughter?

5. Summarize two broad principles from Jephthah's story.

4.8 SAMSON: A MIRROR OF THE NATION

Read Judges 13–16
Memorize Judges 14:4

Deborah, Gideon, Jephthah—done. Last round: Samson. These are the four judges who get the most attention in the book named after their role in Israelite history. These are the judges God wanted us to know the most about.

> "Far from being solutions to the Canaanization of [Israel] . . . , Gideon, Jephthah, and Samson were themselves all parts of the problem. These are not noblemen; they are 'antiheroes.'"
>
> —Daniel I. Block

Samson gets a lot of space and has by far the most interesting and entertaining adventures! For that reason, Samson gets more publicity than any other judge. His biography features romance, fighting (which tended to have something to do with the romance), and amazing feats of strength. Samson was a colorful character.

So let's jump right in and try to learn just three things the Bible tells us through the story about Samson.

How God's Sovereignty Drives Samson's Story

Judges 13:1 says that the Israelites fell into sin again after Jephthah's death. God, therefore, let the nation fall into the hands of the Philistines. Only after forty years does God raise up Samson to deliver them.

But there's something missing from the pattern this time—did you notice it? The Israelites never cried out for help! God in His mercy reached down to save them even though they never asked.

And the story of Samson provides a fascinating look at the way our merciful God works. His plan to carry out His mercy is amazing, and you'll see it if we work backward through the story.

> "[In this case] the Israelites display little discomfort or evidence of even wanting to be delivered."
>
> —Daniel I. Block

We'll start not at the end of the story but just before that—at the last victory of Samson before he was seduced and betrayed by Delilah. Let's go step by step back in time from the point when he lies down, thirsty and just a bit tired, at a place called Lehi.

- Samson was dehydrated and fatigued because he had just gotten a major aerobic workout by killing a thousand Philistines (15:14*b*–18).
- Samson killed a thousand Philistines because they were trying to arrest him (15:14*a*).
- The Philistines came to arrest Samson because three thousand men of Judah handed him over to them (15:13).
- Judah handed him over because he tried to hide in Judah (15:8*b*–12).
- Samson hid in Judah because the Philistines were chasing him (15:8–9).
- The Philistines were chasing Samson because he killed a great number of their men (15:7–8*a*).
- Samson killed a great number of Philistine men because they burned his new wife (15:6).
- The Philistines burned Samson's wife because he burned their crops (15:3–5).
- Samson burned the crops because his father-in-law gave his wife to his best man (15:1–2).

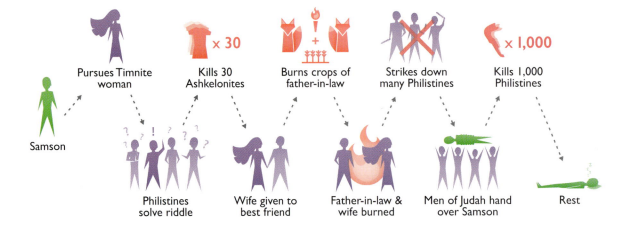

Samson → Pursues Timnite woman → Kills 30 Ashkelonites → Burns crops of father-in-law → Strikes down many Philistines → Kills 1,000 Philistines

Philistines solve riddle — Wife given to best friend — Father-in-law & wife burned — Men of Judah hand over Samson — Rest

- Samson's father-in-law gave his wife to his best man because Samson returned home (14:20).

- Samson returned home because the Ashkelonites were trying to get him (14:19*b*).

- The Ashkelonites were trying to get him because he killed thirty Ashkelonites (14:19*a*).

- Samson killed thirty Ashkelonites because the Philistines solved his riddle (14:18).

- The Philistines solved his riddle because they pressured his wife to tell them the answer (14:15*b*–18*b*).

- She was Samson's wife because he wanted her (14:1–3).

- Samson wanted a woman from Timnah because . . .

[list adapted from Daniel I. Block]

Because why? What was the first event that started this whole chain of events? Why did Samson want to marry a Timnite, a Philistine he was not supposed to marry?

The answer may surprise you, but it's very clear. There was definitely one person who toppled the first domino. Samson wanted the Timnite woman, and his parents didn't like the idea. But the text says,

His father and his mother knew not that it was of the Lord, that he sought an occasion against the Philistines. (Judg. 14:4)

So here's the last bullet point:

- Samson wanted a woman from Timnah because the Lord wanted to confront the Philistines who were oppressing Israel.

Yahweh started the chain. Yahweh set up every domino. As they all toppled, a lot of Philistines did too. God could have snapped His fingers or thought a thought, and those Philistines would have vanished. But He sent Samson instead.

Samson wanted a woman from Timnah—because the Lord wanted to confront the Philistines who were oppressing His people.

How Samson Mirrored Israel Itself

God was not sinning by using Samson in this way. Neither was He making Samson sin. God simply chose to use a man who lacked discernment to deliver His people. This is a God of amazing power who uses someone's life like a pen to write a story—instead of just doing everything Himself. And what was that story? What did the carefully planned actions of Samson picture?

In order to know that, we have to understand first that Samson was a Nazirite. The rules for Nazirites are laid out very clearly in Numbers 6, and the most famous of those rules is well-known because of the story of Samson: Nazirites were not supposed to cut their hair. They also weren't supposed to drink wine or ever touch any dead body.

The point of these special rules seems to be that these people were set apart, set apart even from a whole nation of people who were already set apart from other nations! Nazirites were people who gave themselves up totally to the service of God. All of Israel was supposed to be holy, but the Nazirites followed extra rules that weren't strictly necessary.

Samson is the only Bible character that we know for sure was a Nazirite (there are only a few others, such as Samuel, that we think probably were), and God is the one who made him one before he was ever born.

Why would God go to the trouble of making Samson a Nazirite when He knew that Samson would turn around and break every one of the Nazirite rules as well as most of the Ten Commandments?

"While he was used of God for deliverance, and while he even called upon God on occasion to help him . . . , his life was nevertheless one of continued unfaithfulness, just like that of the nation he judged."

—David M. Howard

Because that's exactly what Israel did. God set them apart from other nations and gave them special rules to distinguish them from people like the Canaanites. He gave them the job of representing Him to the nations. But they broke their vows to Him, loved foreign gods (like Samson loved Philistine women), and finally were blinded by their own sin, losing all their spiritual power. This kingdom of priests had become worse than its heathen neighbors.

SAMSON	◀ ▶	ISRAEL
Nazirite	SET APART	Chosen People
Foreign Women	TURNED AWAY	Foreign Gods
Philistines	OPPRESSION	Canaanites
Cries to God	SUPPLICATION	Cries to God

Even so, the story of Samson shows how God was being faithful to a faithless people. His promises to Abraham were that serious.

The Perfect Leader Israel Still Needs

But if God still intends to fulfill those promises to Abraham, something will have to change in Israel. They keep sinning themselves out of control of their land.

And the rest of Judges actually gets worse. Here's a brief run-down of the stories that finish out the book:

- A Levite (a member of the priestly tribe) sets up a weird and unauthorized priesthood in an Ephraimite's home (Judg. 17).

- A lawless bunch of Danites (members of an Israelite tribe) steal the priest (Judg. 18).

- Another Levite takes his adulterous concubine (sort of like a mistress) with him to the Benjamite city of Gibeah, where a group of homosexuals pound on the door and demand to "know" the visitor (Judg. 19).

- The rest of Israel finds out about their sin and wages a civil war on Benjamin, killing twenty-five thousand men (Judg. 20–21).

That's pretty much where the story ends, but throughout these passages, the author of Judges keeps repeating a telling phrase: "In those days there was no king in Israel, but every man did that which was right in his own eyes" (17:6; cf. 21:25). These are, in fact, the very last words in the book. Obviously, the author has a point to make.

> "The depravity of Israel makes God's faithfulness shine all the brighter."
>
> —Robert Bell

There were kings in Israel during the times of the judges, of course—they just weren't Israelite kings! They were Canaanites who were still ruling over land that God had given to *His* people. But there was no king gifted by God to lead God's people.

And what was the result? Well, look up at the third story listed above, the one about the Levite and the concubine. What do those men pounding on the door remind you of? It's unmistakable if you remember the story of Abraham's nephew Lot—these Israelite men are doing exactly what the men of Sodom did in Genesis 19. The next day, fire fell from heaven and killed the Sodomites. And now Israel has sunk to their level.

The judges God sent to fix Israel's problems were not the real solution. The Israelites need a king who will lead them to do what is right in *God's* eyes.

A King

You ought to feel a little depressed at this point in the Bible's story. God is still at work lovingly redeeming His fallen creation, but that Fall continues to cause a lot of pain for both God and man.

Our own world culture is full of the very same sins that fill the book of Judges: idolatry, heterosexual immorality, homosexual immorality, violence, deceit, strife, and murder. And your own heart may be drawn after any one of those sins or all of them.

But God wasn't done redeeming the world when the events in the book of Judges happened. And He still isn't done today.

> "The greatest threats to Israel's existence do not come from outside enemies who may occasionally oppress them. Israel's most serious enemy is within. She is a nation that appears determined to destroy herself. Only the gracious intervention of God prevents this from happening."
>
> —Daniel I. Block

There's hope even in the middle of a book like Judges. God clearly hasn't given up on this people He chose. No matter what they do—even sometimes when they are too blind to call out to Him—He faithfully saves them.

Yes, Yahweh is the one who gave them over to oppressors in the first place. God is too holy to let evil go by, but He also cares about His people too much to let them get away with sin.

Yet mercy always seems to win over judgment, and the four places in Judges that mention the absence of a king (17:6; 18:1; 19:1; 21:25) hint at more mercy to come. Abraham's seed are going to get their land. And kings will come from them—and lead them to be faithful to their covenant with God.

One of those kings will rise above all the others. One of those kings will step on the head of the serpent that is at the heart of Israel's deepest problems.

But who is that king? Every story points to Him.

Thinking It Through 4.8

1. Which four judges get the most coverage in the book of Judges? Of those four, who gets the most?

2. How is Samson a mirror or an illustration of the nation of Israel?

3. Explain why the last verse of Judges is a fitting description of the book.

4. Read Deuteronomy 28:15–44, a sampling of the covenant curses Moses gave Israel before they entered the Promised Land. Paraphrase two curses you see being fulfilled in the book of Judges.

5. What was the first event that started this whole chain of events in Samson's life?

UNIT 4 REVIEW

Scripture Memory

Deuteronomy 30:6	Judges 2:10
Joshua 21:43–45	Judges 8:34
Joshua 4:21–22, 24	Judges 10:13–14
Psalm 136:1–4	Judges 14:4

Understand the Story

1. True or False. God chose Israel because they were more willing to follow Him than any other nation.

2. Why did God punish the whole nation for Achan's sin?

3. Based on the theme throughout the book of Joshua, why do you think it is important to remember what the Lord has done?

4. Based on Psalm 136, why does God say He did all that He did for the nation of Israel?

5. Why wouldn't Barak get the glory for delivering Israel?

6. Why is Gideon's story a turning point in the book of Judges?

7. If Jephthah had known the law (Lev. 27), what could he have figured out? Why didn't Jephthah know the law? Whose fault was that?

8. The book of Judges repeats the same cycle over and over. What's missing from that cycle in the story of Samson?

Developing Observation Skills

9. Read the key verses from Moses' second sermon in Deuteronomy (5:29; 6:4–6; 7:17; 8:2, 5, 14, 17; 9:4–5; 10:12, 16; 11:13, 16, 18; 13:3; 15:7, 9–10; 17:17, 20; 26:16). What theme does Moses emphasize? What are his two major points about that theme?

10. Use an electronic Bible to search for the word *stone* or *stones* only in the book of Joshua. How do you know that one of the major themes of the book must relate to these stones?

11. Read Psalm 118:1–4. After reading the first four verses of the psalm, what do you think the main point of the psalm is? How do you know?

12. Read Judges 6:1–14 and identify each part of the cyclical pattern that shows up throughout the book of Judges.

13. Read Judges 11:39. When did Jephthah fulfill his vow? Why is this a very strong argument against the interpretation that Jephthah fulfilled his vow by sending his daughter off to be a virgin forever?

14. Identify the major conflict in Judges 13. How was that conflict resolved?

15. How are Joshua and the people of Israel fulfilling the Creation Mandate?

16. Why does God keep delivering His people over and over during the time of the judges?

17. How does Jephthah's sacrifice of his daughter compare to Abraham's sacrifice of Isaac?

18. How is Samson a mirror or an illustration of the nation of Israel?

Lessons for Life

19. Talk to a family member (or a church member) about what he or she remembers about the steadfast love of the Lord in the family's life (or in the church family's life). Write down some of the highlights.

20. The Israelites fell into a cycle of sinning, being judged for sinning, crying out for help, and being delivered. But then they just went back through that same cycle again. Identify where you are in that cycle. How many times have you gone through that cycle in your own life? Plan a way to escape that cycle through an accountability system that reminds you of God's Word, teaches you how to fight sin, and helps you depend on the Spirit through prayer.

UNIT 5

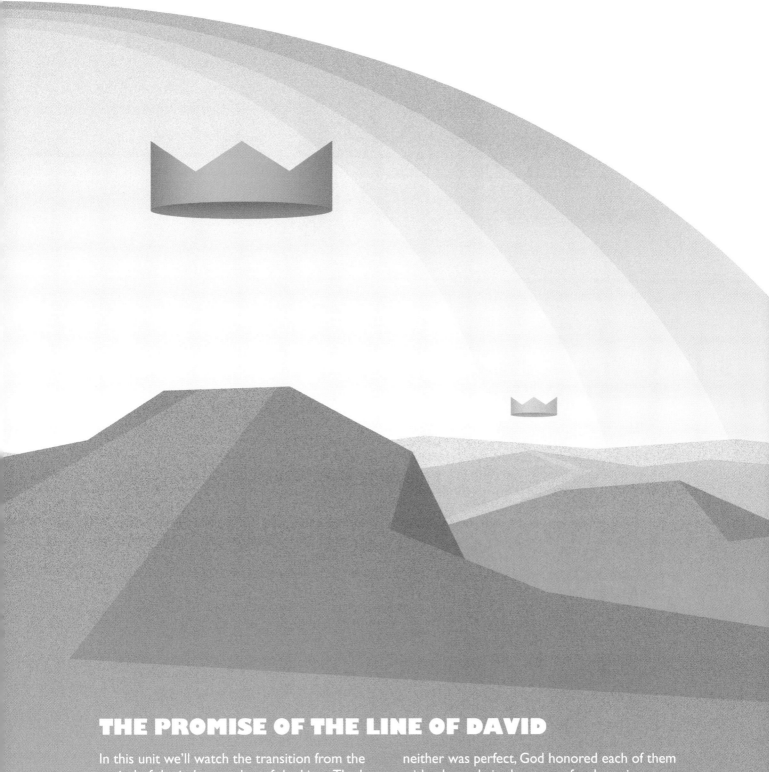

THE PROMISE OF THE LINE OF DAVID

In this unit we'll watch the transition from the period of the judges to that of the kings. The last judge, in fact, is the one who anoints the first two Israelite kings.

But two special women get to make their appearance first: Ruth and Hannah. Though

neither was perfect, God honored each of them with a key role in the story of redemption.

They are the first rays of lasting light since the death of Joshua to shine on the land God promised Abraham. There's a coming dawn that will shed its light not just on that land but also on everyone on the planet.

God promised that David's seed would sit on the throne forever.

5.1 RUTH: A GENTILE IN THE KING'S LINE

Read Ruth 1–4
Memorize Ruth 4:14

After reading a book like Judges, the book of Ruth is a big relief. It's just refreshing to meet two major characters who are worthy. Ruth and Boaz are honorable people who show that faith in Yahweh has not died out in Israel, even during the wicked time of the judges.

If Judges shows how bad Israel can get without a righteous king, the book of Ruth tells part of the story of how God is graciously beginning to give them one. Ruth is God's way to start fixing the huge no-king-in-Israel problem.

Ruth

But the first lines of the book don't seem very promising. Israel is experiencing a famine—which is exactly what God said would happen if the people broke His covenant (Lev. 26:19–20). And so one family decides to move out of the land God gave Israel and into the land of the Moabites. Israel is unraveling.

The father of the family dies in Moab, the two sons marry Moabite women, and then after about a decade the sons join their father in the grave.

Before her sons died, the Israelite widow Naomi was already in a weak position. This was a time and place in which widows were especially vulnerable. Now the household is a collection of three widows trying to scrape out a life together.

But there is good news from Naomi's hometown of Bethlehem. There is food there. Considering that she is a widow in a foreign land, she can see that her best option is to return home, and maybe there she can make a life for herself. She thinks it's best for her daughters-in-law to stay in Moab. They would have an easier time finding a new husband in their home country than they would as foreigners in Israel.

Naomi encourages and practically pleads with both of them to stay when she leaves. The scene is gut wrenching as you read their parting conversation. They hug and shed many tears. One daughter-in-law, understandably, stays in Moab. The other, inexplicably, goes on with Naomi.

Even in a story that has a lot of dialogue, we don't find the newly widowed Ruth saying very much. But what she does say is significant. She doesn't just tell her mother-in-law, "I have no better place to go!" She very specifically says that Naomi's people will become her people—*and Naomi's God will become her God* (1:15–18). There's a kindness and a loyalty in Ruth that are rare and memorable.

But that doesn't mean that life is going to be easy for these two poor widows. They will basically have to live off the kindness of others—during a time when Israel was not known for its kindness.

Boaz

Worthy woman, meet worthy man.

Israelites who had food were expected to share with those who didn't, but not simply by giving it to them. They were to leave the corners of their fields unharvested, so the poor could come along and glean some grain for themselves (Lev. 19:9–10).

Boaz did this, and the Bible introduces him as the kind of man who would do it on purpose—because he wanted to please the Lord. "The Lord," in fact, is the first thing out of Boaz's mouth in the book: "The Lord be with you!" (2:4).

When Boaz meets Ruth, we get some reminders that we're still in a not-so-nice period of Israel's history—and some hints that Boaz may have his eye on this young woman. He has to warn the young men not to touch her. He has to warn Ruth not to glean in anyone else's fields so that she won't be harmed. Boaz, like Ruth, shows a kindness that is uncommon and attractive.

Naomi

Naomi had been "bitter" when she came back to Israel. "The Almighty hath dealt very bitterly with me," she told old friends in Bethlehem. "I went out full, and the Lord hath brought me home again empty" (Ruth 1:20–21).

Empty? What about her faithful daughter-in-law? At that point, apparently, Naomi doesn't quite have the faith in Yahweh that her Moabite daughter-in-law does.

But all that changes when Ruth comes back from gleaning in Boaz's field. In the kindness of Boaz, Naomi immediately (and accurately) sees a divine hand. She starts saying something Ruth couldn't have understood: "Blessed be the Lord, whose kindness has not forsaken the living and the dead!"

She sounds like she's getting awfully excited over just getting some extra barley from a stranger. But that's just it. Boaz is *not* a stranger. Naomi knows something about him—he's a relative who can help them. And more than help them.

> "In the kindness of Boaz, Naomi perceives the kindness of Yahweh."
>
> —Barry Webb

Naomi quickly warns Ruth, just like Boaz did, not to glean in anyone else's field. She doesn't want Ruth to be hurt, she says. (Or does she have another motivation?)

Old Customs

There are a few well-known families in the modern world: think about political families like the Bush family, for example. But family name and identity were much more important in ancient times than they are today, and not just for famous people. That's in large part (as you learned in the Judah and Tamar story) because wealth was so hard to get. If you got it—or any of it—you didn't want it split up among distant relatives. You wanted your family to keep it. So customs developed to make this possible, and one of them was levirate marriage.

It is essential to know at least a little about customs like these if you want to understand the story of Ruth. The book itself explains one of those customs: the way people "signed" a contract by taking off their sandals (4:7). But the book never explains levirate marriage because the original readers of the book would have known it. God included it in His laws for Israel (Deut. 25:5–10). If a man died without children, his family line would die out too. The law actually said that the brother of the dead man should marry the widow, but it could be another close relative instead. This so-called kinsman-redeemer would, in effect, buy back the family inheritance so that it remained within the family. The first son of this union was supposed to carry on the dead brother's name. (If this all sounds weird to you, just remember that some of our laws and practices would seem weird to Ruth!) Boaz was a close relative of Ruth's dead husband, so she had a claim on him due to this principle.

Ruth's Loyal Kindness

Naomi instructs Ruth to boldly make her claim on Boaz and to do it in a dramatic way. He wakes up in the middle of the night at his threshing floor to find Ruth there at his feet! Startled, he asks who she is. Ruth tells him who she is, and then she tells him that he is "a near kinsman." She is, in essence, proposing to Boaz.

Boaz immediately says to Ruth, lying at his feet in the dark, "You have made this last kindness greater than the first."

To whom was she being kind? And what does he mean by *last* and *first* kindness?

Boaz's Loyal Kindness

The word for "kindness" that Naomi used is the Hebrew word *ḥesed* that you learned about in an earlier lesson. One of the meanings is "loyal kindness"—that is, kindness based on a relationship. God is being kind through Boaz. And Boaz shows kindness that is loyal to his family (both the living and the dead).

Here are some acts of kindness that Boaz does for Ruth:
- He allows Ruth to glean with his young women (2:8, 15).
- He offers Ruth protection (2:9*a*, 15, 16).
- He provides water (2:9*b*).
- He provides food (2:14).
- He has his servants drop grain on purpose so that she may pick it up (2:16).

Once again, *ḥesed* shows up. In this situation it means loyal kindness. Boaz is acknowledging that Ruth has been loyally kind. The first kindness was Ruth's leaving her homeland and going with Naomi. She was loyally kind to Naomi because Ruth, as her daughter-in-law, had a relationship with her.

Boaz explains that Ruth's second kindness is that she went after him and not a younger man. By doing this, Ruth was showing family loyalty and devotion to Naomi.

Now it's Boaz's turn to be bold, and without even reading the story you know what's going to happen. Ruth and Boaz get married. Happy endings weren't invented when movies came along. This one happened more than three thousand years ago.

God's Loyal Love

One great irony of the book of Ruth is that she, a Gentile, is quite obviously more faithful to Yahweh than the prominent Jewish leaders of her time. The judges Gideon, Jephthah, and Samson have little of the pure godliness of this Moabite woman.

God delights to lift lowly people up to heights of honor. All the same, God isn't giving Gentiles the favored place He already set aside for the Jews. Ruth is only one Gentile. As far as we know, all the other Moabites (including Orpah) died far from God. And His purpose in raising up Ruth was not primarily to provide a nice love story for people to enjoy. It was, as this section has already said, to provide a king.

And you don't have to wait to read more of the story to find out who that king is because he's literally the last word in the story—*and* the last word in the book. Right after the story comes a family tree, and on the top branch is *David*. The writer of Ruth makes it obvious that this story is mainly a prequel to the story of King David.

The whole story of Judges, really, points to David too. (Remember that the incidents in Ruth happened during the time period of the judges.) When will the Israelites get good leaders? When will they be able to stay in their land without feeling like they have to escape to Moab to live?

David is, at least for now, the best answer we have to those questions. The book of Ruth could be called "The Book of David's Great-Grandmother." Through the story of Ruth, God is putting on display His loyal love to the Jewish people. The covenant He made with Abraham is still guiding His actions hundreds of years later.

God's Sovereignty

It wasn't just an accident that Ruth ended up in Boaz's field, even though the writer seems to play with his readers a little by saying that Ruth *just happened* to wind up there (2:3). It wasn't an accident that Ruth had a rich, unmarried relative to redeem her—or that the other relative didn't want to. You get the feeling reading this story that it was all planned out in advance.

You could say that this planning all came from the mind of the writer. He made it all up. If you were talking about the human writer (he doesn't say who he is), you'd be wrong. But if you mean the divine writer, that's exactly what we've said He's been doing throughout this whole textbook! Every story we've read is part of God's "Plan A" to redeem His fallen creation. He somehow organized these details.

And His Plan A is taking more and more shape. Are you following it? God points ahead in every story, starting all the way back in Genesis 1–3. He points to an answer to the world's problems.

If you find that the loyalty, faithfulness, boldness, and integrity of Ruth and Boaz are difficult to live out consistently, you need God's Plan A to redeem you too.

Thinking It Through 5.1

1. In a few sentences, explain how Ruth became a believer in the true God through His providential working in her life.

2. List at least two of the acts of loyal kindness that Boaz showed Ruth. List at least two of the acts of loyal kindness that Ruth showed.

3. Explain the custom of the kinsman-redeemer.

4. What is the primary purpose of God's providential working throughout the book of Ruth?

5. What is guiding God's acts of providence throughout the book of Ruth?

5.2 HANNAH: MOTHER OF A KINGMAKER

Read I Samuel I
Memorize I Samuel 2:10

Polygamy only rarely gets talked about in the Western world. Some fundamentalist Mormon sects still practice it—illegally. But the Western world inherited its moral rules from Christianity, so polygamy is still assumed by most people to be wrong or weird—or at least inconvenient.

Polygamy was certainly inconvenient for everyone in the Bible who tried it because it wasn't the way God designed mankind to operate. God gave Adam only one wife. That's the model.

But Jacob himself was a notorious polygamist. God doesn't limit the blessed line of Abraham to those who are perfect, or it wouldn't include anyone.

The book of 1 Samuel opens with a polygamous marriage that was—surprise!—full of tension between two competing wives. The rules of their competition were simple: whoever has more kids wins. By these rules, Hannah was losing big. Her rival Penninah had multiple sons and daughters, but Hannah had a grand total of zero.

In the modern world, having children isn't that big a deal for most people. Some married couples want to have children, but they aren't able to for one reason or another. But some married couples, despite God's command to "fill the earth," decide not to have kids at all. In Hannah's day, a woman's worth was measured by the number of children she bore, especially the number of sons. This attitude was rooted in both a desire to fulfill the Creation Mandate by filling the earth and a desire to be the mother of the promised Seed who would redeem all mankind (Gen. 3:15; cf. 1 Tim. 2:15).

Hannah, therefore, appeared to be worthless.

Yahweh

God has a soft spot in His heart for "worthless" people because He knows there's no such thing. Every childless woman is made in God's image and therefore has amazing worth.

So Hannah goes to the right source for help with this terrible problem. She goes to the Lord. She promises Him that if He gives her a son, she will gratefully dedicate him to the Lord's service. She takes an additional vow: no razor will touch his head. She is going to make her son a Nazirite like Samson.

Hannah's Prayer

Generally speaking, the Bible doesn't encourage people to cut deals with God: "Hey, if you do this for me, I'll do that for you." You can't push God around like that.

But Hannah isn't trying to cut a deal, and we know that because when her miracle child does come, she willingly gives him up. She even bursts out in a joyful prayer which begins, "My heart rejoiceth in the Lord" (1 Sam. 2:1). You don't rejoice after giving away your only son unless the person to whom you gave him means even more to you than the child does.

That long prayer Hannah prays at this point in the story (2:1–10) is easy to pass over. It's beautiful, definitely. But if you've been reading the Bible for a while, it just sounds like a psalm of praise—something we have a lot of in Scripture already.

But pay even a little bit of close attention, and you'll notice something remarkable about this prayer. Hannah's story—and this prayer—stand at the very beginning of the book of Samuel for a reason (1 and 2 Samuel were originally one book).

The point of the prayer seems to be drawn first from Hannah's conflict with Penninah. God

Vows

The Bible doesn't command God's people to make vows to Him as Hannah did. All it says is that if you do voluntarily vow something, you'd better not be foolish enough to try to get out of paying up (Lev. 27:1–34). It's better not to even vow than to vow and not pay, Ecclesiastes says, because God takes "no pleasure in fools" (Eccles. 5:4)!

has a way of lifting up the low and putting down the mighty, Hannah says. People who are arrogant because they have children, because they have food, or because they have riches—these proud people had better be careful, or they may find themselves childless, famished, and penniless. But the God who brings salvation delights in "reversals"—He loves to lift up the childless, the famished, and the penniless. That's just what He's done for Hannah!

> "Every time God lifts you out of the miry bog and sets your feet upon a rock is a sample of the coming of the kingdom of God, a down payment of the full deliverance."
>
> **—Dale Ralph Davis**

But this beautiful prayer doesn't speak only of Hannah. It echoes far into the future: if you've ever read the prayer of a teenage mother named Mary (Luke 1:46–55), it almost seems as if Mary just transposed Hannah's prayer into a slightly different key.

Hannah speaks of how God breaks the bows of the mighty, how those who were full have had to hire themselves out for bread, how it's the Lord who brings people to the grave, brings them low, or makes them poor. But on the positive side, it's the Lord who gives strength to the stumbling, food to the hungry, children to the barren, and riches to the destitute. The Lord lifts people up.

The most remarkable words in the prayer come at the end, however:

> He will keep the feet of his saints,
> and the wicked shall be silent in darkness;
> for by strength shall no man prevail.
> The adversaries of the Lord shall be broken
> to pieces;
> out of heaven shall he thunder upon them:
> the Lord shall judge the ends of the earth;
> and he shall give strength unto his king,
> and exalt the horn of his anointed.
> (1 Sam. 2:9–10)

A king? What did a woman in a polygamous marriage in the time of the judges know about any king? There was no king in Israel! And God's anointed? Who is that?

In 1 Samuel 2:1–10 we go from a close-up view of God's plan to zooming way out. It's like we were seeing blocky pixels, but now an image is taking shape.

God gives Hannah the privilege of being the first person in recorded history to utter one of the special names of Jesus (see the last word in Hannah's prayer). That name is *Messiah*. You won't see *Messiah* in most English translations, and it's not that they're trying to hide something. It's just that they're giving the *meaning* of the name rather than the name itself. *Messiah* means "anointed one."

Hannah probably didn't have much of a theological education. Remember, this was during the terrible time of the judges. But somehow she knew that God was planning a kingly solution to Israel's problems. What she didn't know was that her miracle son was going to play an important role in that solution. Her son was going to be God's tool to anoint God's anointed king, the David mentioned at the end of Ruth.

Messiah and Christ

Hannah, at the end of her prayer in 1 Samuel 2, speaks of God's "anointed one." In the Hebrew language Hannah used, that word was *mashiach* (ma-SHEE-yak). In Greek, that same word is *christos*.

As we saw earlier with the word *Yahweh*, these Hebrew and Greek words can be brought into English in two different ways: translation and transliteration.

If you *translate* the meaning into English, both words just mean "anointed one," somebody set apart in a ceremony—an anointing with oil—to do some specific job.

If you *transliterate* the words, just turning the letters into similar English letters, you get *Messiah* and *Christ*. There is one Anointed One who stands above all others, and those are the names we tend to use for Him.

But Hannah can't be talking only about an earthly king. She seems to be talking both about David and somebody greater than David. That's because she talks about a day when the Lord will judge the whole earth and smash all His enemies to pieces. David (as we'll see) was a powerful king, but he never did that.

Hannah's prayer is something like a table of contents for the story of David—but also for a greater David who will one day do even more than he did.

Hints

Notice two other little hints in Hannah's prayer about the coming story of David.

One comes in 1 Samuel 2:3: "Talk no more so exceeding proudly," she says to arrogant people like Penninah. The phrase "exceeding proudly" is actually just the word *tall* twice: "Tall, tall!" Proud people stand up tall to their full height; they think of themselves highly. That's the idea.

The other hint about the story of David to come is in 2:9: "By strength shall no man prevail." In other words, you don't win battles just because you're strong—or tall. It's the Lord who wins battles.

Do either of these things Hannah prays remind you of the story of the shepherd boy, David? Are there any tall, proud people in his story?

Yes, and you'll see them soon. In fact, they're everywhere in the Bible. Hannah's prayer shows that those who try to take credit for their successes are going to get cut down a notch or two (or ten!).

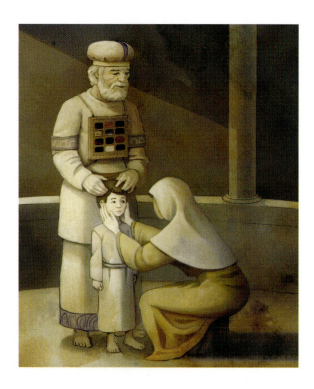

God can't let people take glory that belongs to Him because they will ruin their lives if they do that. He's the one who wins battles, and life goes so much more smoothly if you simply rest in that fact.

The Bible is not the story of how mankind works hard to become strong enough to fix its own problems; it is the story of what *God* is doing to powerfully redeem His fallen creation. God will send a great king who will destroy all His enemies. The book of Samuel is the story of how God raised up a lowly shepherd to become the first king in that greater King's line.

Thinking It Through 5.2

1. What was Hannah's vow? Why did she make this vow?

2. What evidence can you see that Hannah was *not* being selfish in her request for a child?

3. Read Hannah's prayer in 1 Samuel 2:1–10, and briefly list the kinds of people who experience reversals in it (for example, the mighty and the feeble in v. 4).

4. What in Hannah's prayer suggests that she's predicting the future? What phrase in 1 Samuel 2:10 shows that Hannah isn't talking only about David when she speaks about a king?

5. What does Hannah's prayer hint at about the coming story of David?

5.3 SAMUEL: REVERSALS

Read I Samuel 8
Memorize I Samuel 8:7, 19–20

Hot Dogs and Underdogs

This is how baseball works in the major leagues: when you win, you make money—from tickets, jerseys, even hot dogs. And that money helps you buy better players. And those players help you win more. So the cycle continues.

But when you lose, the cycle goes the other way. And that's what happened to one underdog team—the Oakland Athletics. The famous book *Moneyball* by Michael Lewis, however, describes what the A's general manager Billy Beane did to reverse the losing trend.

Basically, Beane figured out how to win games with the players he could afford. He didn't care what else they could do as long as they could get on base. He even took a washed-up catcher who couldn't throw and moved him to the first base position because the guy could hit.

The A's started winning. They had the longest major league winning streak in seventy years—twenty games in a row (that catcher-turned-first-baseman hit the homer that gave them their record-breaking victory!). All of a sudden the losers were beating the winners. A major reversal had taken place!

Reversals

Reversals happen, and sometimes they are astonishing. And we've already seen some pretty amazing reversals of fortune in the Bible:

- Adam and Eve, deserving death, receive the promise of a seed who will crush the serpent who deceived them.
- God lifted up Noah above the waves and put the whole world down below him.
- Abraham's wife Sarah, a woman far past childbearing age, had a miracle son.
- Joseph went from favored son to slave. Then, in an even more amazing reversal, he moved to second in the kingdom.
- The powerful nation of Egypt was cut down to its knees while its slaves, loaded with Egyptian gold, escaped.

Each one of these reversals is more amazing than what happened with Oakland A's. Old women just don't have babies. A big group of slaves just doesn't escape from the most powerful nation on earth.

The book of Samuel contains even more reversals: a powerful king replaced by a godly one, that godly king put out of his rule by a rebellious son. And we just studied the big reversal in Hannah's life. In fact, her prayer in 1 Samuel 2 is all about reversals. God seems to delight in putting down the high and mighty and raising up the lowly and weak.

So we shouldn't be surprised if the life of Samuel brings yet another reversal. When little Samuel enters the service of the high priest Eli, the Bible comments that the word of the Lord was "precious" in those days—it was rare (3:1). People weren't hearing from God like they used to back in the days of His prophet Moses.

> "When young Samuel is called to be a prophet, it is a sign that a major reversal is about to happen."
>
> —Stephen Dempster

But God is about to throw the situation into reverse! The tarnished high priest Eli—tarnished because his two wicked sons used their position for bribes and immorality—was about to be replaced by someone who would speak God's words openly and often to all Israel.

Eli's fall is Samuel's rise.

Samuel the Prophet

The first message Samuel received from God was a bad one: Eli's house will be judged because Eli hasn't stopped his sons from their wickedness. "Samuel grew," the Bible says, "and the Lord was with him, and did let none of his words fall to the ground" (1 Sam. 3:19). Nothing Samuel prophesied failed to happen. He spoke for God, and anyone watching and listening to him knew it. Samuel was the last judge.

Mercy and Grace

Samuel was a sign of God's grace, this section says. What's the difference between mercy and grace?

Imagine that your favorite painting set is stolen. You can't find it anywhere for months. And then you find out that the thief was your very own sister. And she's completely ruined the set!

Mercy is not giving the thief the bad consequences she deserves. Mercy means you forgive her and don't ask to be repaid.

Grace is giving the thief a good gift she does not deserve. Grace means you forgive her and generously buy her a painting set of her own.

Salvation from God is a matter of mercy because it means sinners don't get the bad consequences they deserve. But even more deeply, it's a matter of grace. In salvation God gives the generous gift of life to people who deserve only death.

But Samuel was different from the main judges we have studied. He was godly. He led the people into repentance for their sins (1 Sam. 7), and he maintained a godly testimony for his whole life (except in the reputation of his sons). Ungodly leaders such as Gideon, Jephthah, and Samson were a sign of God's judgment on Israel. This new godly leader is a sign of God's grace.

And just as Gideon was a transition in Israel's story—from more or less good judges to more or less bad ones—Samuel is a transition from the judges to the kings. He is an important figure, but since he's mainly a transition, the Bible doesn't give very much attention to his period of leadership.

After the chapter about his childhood with Eli (1 Sam. 3), he gets basically one chapter in which he's the leader of Israel (1 Sam. 7), and then the transition to a new kind of leader starts to happen. The people start demanding, basically, that Samuel be replaced (1 Sam. 8). They want a king.

Samuel's influence is far from over, but the transition to kingship has begun.

After making sure that this is OK with the Lord, Samuel goes and gets a king for the people (1 Sam. 9) and anoints him (1 Sam. 10). Then Samuel gives a farewell speech to the nation (1 Sam. 12).

It looks as though things may finally be coming together for Israel, and we'll take a look at this new king in the next section.

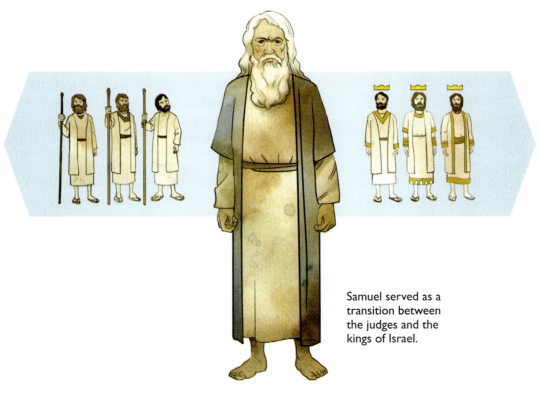

Samuel served as a transition between the judges and the kings of Israel.

Samuel's Farewell

But there's a major problem with this transition in Israel from judges to kings, and lots of readers of the Bible have noticed it. Samuel and, more importantly, his God are not happy about Israel's request for a king, and yet God still gives them one.

What's so wrong with having a king? And if God is so upset with Israel's request, why doesn't He just say no?

Judges pointed out several times that the lack of a king was a big reason for Israel's horrific sins in that book. And Moses said way back in the time of Deuteronomy that it was OK to have a king—he even set up some rules for Israelite kings. Most importantly, one of the promises of God to Abraham was that kings would come from him (Gen. 17:6).

> **"For Israel to entrust its future to a human deliverer instead of anchoring it in their relationship with the Lord was both wicked and futile."**
>
> **—Robert D. Bergen**

In order to answer these questions we'll need to take a look at Samuel's farewell to the people in 1 Samuel 12. It falls neatly into three paragraphs. In the first one (12:1–5), Samuel gets the people to agree that he has led them with integrity. In the second paragraph (12:6–18), Samuel does what this textbook is trying to do: he tells a story. He outlines very quickly the parts of Israel's story that got them into the mess they're currently in:

- The people were oppressed in Egypt.
- They cried out to God for deliverance.
- God brought them into the land of Canaan.
- They forgot God!
- God let them fall into the hands of their enemies.
- They repented and cried for deliverance.
- God sent judges to deliver them.

Yahweh vs. Dagon

The Bible is a big book, so this textbook is skipping over a lot of it. One of the parts you just skipped contains a great reversal story: Dagon and the ark of Yahweh.

In 1 Samuel 5:1–5, the ark of God has been captured by the Philistines, who have Israel under their thumb. But when the ark gets placed in the temple of Dagon, the Philistine god, Dagon falls down before the ark during the night.

Dagon's worshipers pick him back up, but the next night his fall knocks off his head and his hands. There is no question who is the most powerful God. Even though that God has let Dagon's people rule His people, Dagon is nothing. Yahweh is everything.

This whole pattern looks very familiar. Samuel is only putting into words what we saw clearly in the book of Judges.

But then the pattern changes. New threats come up in Samuel's time, like Nahash, king of the Ammonites. Instead of crying out to God for deliverance, the people have asked for a king. They want to be like all the other nations, they say.

We're getting close to our answer. It isn't wrong for Israel to have a king, or even (necessarily) to ask for one. But their motivation in this case is wrong. They don't seek the Lord for deliverance; they seek a human king like the kind everybody else has. A powerful king they can see with their eyes is more appealing to them than an omnipotent King they can't see.

> **"They want a king *instead of* God rather than a king *under* God."**
>
> **—Vaughan Roberts**

In essence, Israel does not want a king to lead them to obey God's law; Israel wants a king to protect them from the consequences of breaking God's law (1 Sam. 8:20).

The Israelites' demand for a king has gotten them in deep trouble. They're afraid, and they ask Samuel to pray for them. But Samuel brings comforting words: it pleased the Lord to choose Israel as a people for Himself. He won't forsake them.

Samuel's speech shows how the king can be part of God's plan for His covenant people. The people and their king must simply fear the Lord and faithfully serve Him. Obedience will bring blessing. But the last words of Samuel's speech are fearful: "If ye shall still do wickedly, ye shall be consumed, both ye and your king" (12:25).

We now know enough about the history of Israel to be nervous again. Israel's track record suggests strongly that Samuel's warning is exactly what will happen.

But we shouldn't be pessimistic—God has chosen these people, and kings were part of God's covenant with Abraham. Somehow this is all going to fulfill those good promises to Abraham, and even to Adam. This story has to have a happy ending because way back in the garden God said it would. The serpent will be crushed. The world will be fixed. Somehow!

Before that happens there are a few more interesting plot twists—a few more reversals. The books of Samuel contain some of the most interesting stories and characters in the Bible. Keep reading!

Thinking It Through 5.3

1. List three biblical people who experienced big reversals in the story of Scripture so far.

2. Why doesn't the Bible devote more chapters to talking about Samuel and the things he did for God?

3. How did Israel's praying change during the time of Samuel?

4. Someone might argue, "The Bible contradicts itself twice! God said in Deuteronomy that the Israelites could have a king, but when they ask for one He's angry! And then He turns around and gives them one anyway! God is being inconsistent." How would you respond to that?

5. Summarize both the comfort and the warning in Samuel's final speech to the nation. Why is the warning foreboding, and why is the comfort assuring?

5.4 SAUL: A KING AFTER ISRAEL'S OWN HEART

Read I Samuel 9–11
Memorize I Samuel 15:22

Let's Chew On It

For some, reading is a labor of love. Reading takes them to faraway places in a different time, and it introduces them to people they have never met. Reading is seen as an escape from the pressures of daily life.

But for others, reading is just labor. Some students hate reading. Their parents try to motivate them to do it through fear of being grounded for life, but the instant their parents give up, so do they. (Or maybe it happens a few instants *before* that.)

But some kids, in the middle of their forced reading labor, discover that they're actually enjoying it. Those kids, motivated by love for stories and characters and mysteries and beautiful language, are true readers.

It sometimes takes a true reader to catch certain details put there by the author. And even true readers will tell you that they don't always notice those things until the second read. (That's another mark of true readers: they'll read a great book more than once!)

True readers will also tell you that they don't stop thinking about the book when they put it down. They will continue to think about it and ponder what the author has written and why he or she wrote it that way. As the old saying goes, they will chew on it for a while.

A quote often attributed to Edmund Burke sums it up nicely, "Reading without reflecting is like eating without digesting." So let's chew on what you've just read.

Tall, Tall!

Did you catch a little detail at the beginning of the Saul story, a detail that was hinted at in Hannah's prayer?

How is Saul described? As very "tall"! Does that remind you of anything Hannah said? "Talk no more so exceeding proudly," she said to arrogant people (1 Sam. 2:3). And the underlying Hebrew for that phrase is "Don't talk very tall, tall!"

> "Saul is the only Israelite specifically noted in the Bible as being tall; elsewhere it was only Israel's enemies whose height was noted. Israel had asked for a king 'like all the other nations,' and the Lord was giving them the desires of their heart, even down to the physical details!"
>
> —Robert D. Bergen

This is a hint for good readers, but so far only a hint. Good readers develop a sense for when an author is hinting and when there's just a coincidence. It's not Saul's fault that he's tall. We'll have to keep our eyes out for more evidence from the author.

The stories about Saul that come next still leave us wondering where the writer of 1 Samuel is going. Saul doesn't seem like much of a godly leader to start with, but it's hard to be sure.

- Saul's father's donkeys get lost and Saul can't find them for three days. Not very encouraging (9:3–6).
- It's his servant who suggests talking to a prophet, and the servant offers to pay whatever that prophet charges (9:7–8).
- When Saul under the Spirit's influence begins to deliver prophetic messages, it's a shock to everyone who knows Saul that he would be acting like a prophet (10:9–13).
- Saul doesn't tell his uncle about what Samuel said to him (10:14–16).
- When Samuel finally proclaims Saul king—or tries—Saul is hiding (10:20–22).

Is Saul being humble or wimpy? Hard to say. He says his family is the least important of all the families that are from Benjamin—the smallest tribe of Israel (and his hometown of Gibeah was the city most like Sodom in the days of the judges). But it's hard to know his motivation for saying this when his father clearly had some wealth.

But when the Spirit of God "rushes" on him (10:10; 11:6)—like an adrenaline rush might hit you when you're in danger, only far more important and powerful—Saul becomes the leader Israel needs. He energetically leads the people into battle against some Ammonites who were terrorizing an Israelite city. He "exercises dominion" in a decisive way.

And when he wins, he gives the credit to God (11:13). A good reader comes away from these stories about Saul still wondering what to make of him—but pretty hopeful that he'll do well.

The Promise of the Line of Saul?

Those hopes don't last long. (Hopes in human heroes rarely do.) Saul has the look of a king. His height makes him seem like a natural leader. It's human nature, then as now, to "look up" to someone who's tall. But Saul is not the king Israel needs, only the king Israel wants.

The headings in this section of Samuel tell the story:
- Saul's Unlawful Sacrifice (1 Sam. 13)
- Saul's Rash Vow (1 Sam. 14)
- Saul's Rejection by the Lord (1 Sam. 15)

Saul's unlawful sacrifice was Israel at Sinai all over again. He couldn't trust God enough to let God's prophet perform a sacrifice as the Lord had commanded. While the man of God delayed (like Moses on the mountain), Saul took religious matters into his own hands and made the sacrifice himself (like Aaron with the golden calf).

Benjamin: The Smallest Tribe

Saul was not exaggerating when he called Benjamin "the smallest of the tribes of Israel." The tribe was small for a reason. It was notoriously wicked during the time of the judges and had suffered the consequences for its actions.

In the final chapters of Judges, the tribe of Benjamin was guilty of a heinous sexual crime. It was so wicked that the other tribes in Israel gathered together to fight against the people of Benjamin and punish them for their sins.

But the other tribes weren't innocent either. They were wicked in their own ways, so God used the tribe of Benjamin to punish them. In fact, on the first day of battle, twenty-two thousand men of Israel fell, and on the second day, eighteen thousand fell. Only after the tribes repented and then fasted and offered sacrifices did God allow them to successfully carry out the judgment on Benjamin.

The judgment was so severe that it almost annihilated the tribe of Benjamin. The other tribes felt sorry for them and helped them to rebuild and find wives.

So Benjamin was small because of its sin. And when Saul says that Benjamin was the smallest, everyone knew what he was talking about. It's hard to tell exactly what Saul meant about his own family, but it is understandable why he would be perplexed that a king would come from his tribe.

Did God Commit Genocide?

The number one evil most people can think of is probably genocide—trying to kill every member of a religious, racial, ethnic, or national group. Few would disagree that Adolf Hitler's Holocaust was one of the wickedest acts in the history of mankind. Nearly 70 percent of the Jews in Europe perished. The word *genocide* itself was invented in 1944 as the total number of Jews killed neared the final figure of six million.

So why was it OK for God to tell the Jews in 1 Samuel 15 to wipe out 100 percent of the Amalekites?

It's not wrong to ask this question as long as you keep a spirit submitted to God's rule—and as long as you look to the Bible for the answer.

In Exodus 17, the Amalekites attacked the weak and straggling Jewish nation not long after they escaped from Egypt. You might remember the story of Aaron and Hur holding up Moses' arms as Joshua led the people in battle against Amalek. That day, God promised to erase Amalek from the face of the earth.

In Deuteronomy 25:19, as the next generation stood on the border of the Promised Land, God reminded them that He still intended to destroy the Amalekites for their wickedness. Once the Israelites had rest from their other enemies, all Amalek would perish. So there's a history behind God's command to Saul to kill them all.

And there's another reason that goes all the way back nearly a thousand years before Saul to God's covenant with Abraham. The Lord told the father of the Jews that they would go into slavery for four hundred years and only then come out into the Promised Land. That's because, God said, "the iniquity of the Amorites is not yet full" (Gen. 15:16). This means God waited to put His people in their land until His mercy on the Canaanites had finally run out.

The final answer is that God is the Creator of the world and He has the right to do with His creation what He wills. Everyone in the world will die because of his sin; God is allowed to determine whether death comes at a time we would call "early" or "late."

A good study Bible will likely have an essay on this topic. The introduction to Joshua is often a good place to look for information about genocide.

God's response through Samuel is very swift: Saul will not last as Israel's king. "Your kingdom won't continue," Samuel told King Saul. "*The Lord hath sought him a man after his own heart*, and the Lord hath commanded him to be captain over his people, because thou hast not kept that which the Lord commanded thee" (1 Sam. 13:14). Saul is a king after Israel's own heart; God is looking for a man after His.

But Saul isn't deposed yet. He gets quite a few more opportunities to disobey the Lord. His rash vow recorded in 1 Samuel 14 very nearly results in the death of his own son (making Saul appear as bad as one of the judges—do you remember which one?). And in 1 Samuel 15, which you read for this section, Saul puts the final nail in the coffin of his own rule.

God's instructions couldn't have been easier to follow: every Amalekite—even every animal—must die. God remembered the many sins Amalek had committed against His chosen people. And He knew the danger of allowing His people to live near idol worshipers.

Saul and his armies failed to obey this simple command, and when Samuel confronted Saul about it, the king came up with a holy-sounding excuse: "The people spared the best of the sheep and of the oxen, to sacrifice unto the Lord thy God" (1 Sam. 15:15).

Samuel replies with memorable words: "Hath the Lord as great delight in burnt offerings and sacrifices, as in obeying the voice of the Lord? Behold, to obey is better than sacrifice, and to hearken than the fat of rams" (1 Sam. 15:22).

Boyfriends, Sundays, and Facebook

There's an obvious lesson here that we shouldn't skip over. You can come up with all sorts of explanations for why disobedience or half-obedience is better than trusting and obeying:

- "Andrew will probably come to God if I become his girlfriend!" But God said no (2 Cor. 6:14).
- "I'll be able to give more money to God if I can just work on Sundays!" But God said no (Heb. 10:25).
- "I can tell more people about God if I get a Facebook account!" But your parents (let's imagine) said no—which means God said no (Exod. 20:12; Eph. 6:1).

God knew best how to advance His kingdom in Saul's day. And the invention of the internet hasn't changed that. If you're one of God's children, you can trust that He has good intentions for you—you're part of the world that He wanted to bless through Abraham's seed! A two-year delay in getting on Facebook will not make you uncool for life. The character you develop by trusting Him (and your parents)—and the problems you avoid by waiting till you're older to get an account—make obedience totally worth it. Even if your parents turn out to be mistaken, obeying God means obeying them. And you will not regret it. (This doesn't mean that every thirteen-year-old who has a Facebook page is doing wrong; this is just a hypothetical example.)

Why Saul?

So Saul is out. At some point, David will be in. Why bother? Why did God pick Saul first? Why not just pick David?

God had a purpose: He was contrasting what He valued in a leader versus what the people valued in a leader.

Saul was what the people wanted—a tall, dashing, royal-looking king. And yet he was just like the people who demanded to have a king because he too tried to get out from under God's rule. That, of course, failed. And Saul's failure was God's way of rebuking the people for their request and pointing to what's *not* important in a king. As the story turns to David, even Samuel needs to learn this lesson. God says to him,

> Look not on his countenance, or on the height of his stature; . . . for the Lord seeth not as man seeth; for man looketh on the outward appearance, but the Lord looketh on the heart. (1 Sam. 16:7)

So mentioning Saul's height at the beginning of his story *was* a clue for good readers. Hannah criticized people who were tall, tall (that is proud) in their own estimation—because height and strength don't matter at all compared to the power of Yahweh (1 Sam. 2:3, 9).

What matters about someone is not his physical power or attractiveness (though that may be a comfort to you). What matters most about a person is whether, in his heart, he loves and trusts the only source of real strength in this universe. The best kind of king is the one with this kind of heart.

Thinking It Through 5.4

1. What did Saul do that made him appear humble or maybe wimpy? (1 Sam. 9–10)

2. What did Saul do that really convinced the people to make him king? (1 Sam. 11:14–15)

3. Describe briefly what Saul did to the Amalekites—and what he failed to do.

4. Why didn't God just pick David and skip over Saul?

5. Why won't Saul's kingdom continue? What kind of king was God looking for to replace Saul?

5.5 DAVID: PREPARATION OF A KING

Read I Samuel 16
Memorize I Samuel 17:46–47

God's ways are not our ways. His thoughts are higher than our thoughts. Even someone who has known God for decades may find himself surprised one day to find out (again) that God just doesn't think like we do.

At this point in the big story of the Bible, God knows the one He has chosen to be the next king of Israel, but instead of sending Samuel directly to the new king, He prepares one of those surprises.

Samuel is told to go to Bethlehem to see Jesse (whose grandmother, if you remember this important detail, was Ruth, the wife of Boaz). One of Jesse's sons was to be the new king.

When Samuel gets a good look at Eliab, Jesse's oldest son, his first thought is, "There he is— the next king of Israel. He's a fine specimen—tall, good-looking, kingly. The people will like him!"

That's when God says,

> Look not on his countenance, or on the height of his stature; . . . for the Lord seeth not as man seeth; for man looketh on the outward appearance, but the Lord looketh on the heart. (1 Sam. 16:7)

Here comes another surprise reversal in 1 Samuel. And it's like God puts a bunch of neon-yellow highlighter on His point by leading six more of Jesse's sons past Samuel: Nope. Nope. Nope. Nope. Nope. Nope.

Are there any sons left? Nobody, not even David's father, thought Samuel would anoint the youngest son. In fact, the word Jesse uses to describe him can mean "youngest" but most often means "smallest" (1 Sam. 16:11). David was not "tall, tall." (He was, however, good looking.)

This is a reversal that points back (again) to Hannah's prayer. The youngest and smallest, the least powerful—these are the ones God lifts up. The tall, tall—these are the ones God puts down.

What Was Saul's Problem?

In many translations, 1 Samuel 16:14 says that "an evil spirit from the Lord troubled [Saul]." An evil spirit from the Lord? What could that possibly mean?

The Hebrew word translated "evil" is a little broader than our English word *evil*. It can mean something like "misery" or "calamity." So some translations say that God sent Saul a "troubling" or "distressing" spirit. In other words, God didn't send a demon.

As Bible scholar Robert Bergen put it, "Saul's tortured state was not an accident of nature, nor was it essentially a medical condition. It was a supernatural assault by a being sent at the Lord's command, and it was brought on by Saul's disobedience."

Most importantly, the Bible says that God's Spirit rushed on David from that day on. Just one verse later, we find out that God's Spirit did the opposite with Saul. He departed from Israel's first king. A new era had begun—or at least its beginning had begun!

"Goliath's physical stature, armor, weaponry, and shield bearer must have made him appear invincible. However, the reader has just been warned against paying undue attention to outward appearances."

—Robert D. Bergen

Goliath

And now we come to one of the most famous stories in Scripture: David and Goliath.

Goliath is everything David isn't. He's massive. He's experienced, battle-hardened. He's tall, tall, *tall*! He has unbelievable metal armor (which probably no Israelites but Saul and his son have, since none of God's people even have swords at this time according to 1 Samuel 13:22). And then there's the most important difference between David and Goliath: they worship different gods.

We're going to do something special with this story. We're going to use it as a "test case" to see how well the story of Scripture is making sense to you up till this point. Read 1 Samuel 17 and then read the story here under "Slaying the Giants of Sin." Then answer questions 1 and 2 under "Thinking It Through 5.5a."

Slaying the Giants of Sin

It would be easy to tell the story of Goliath something like this. (Think hard as you read, because you're going to have to evaluate this in a minute.)

David was just a small shepherd boy visiting his older brothers in the army. But when David saw that all the other Israelite soldiers were too cowardly to fight the massive Philistine giant, Goliath, David stepped up and took on the cause!

David's bravery saved his whole country from defeat! He gathered five smooth stones into his pouch, but he needed only one of them to knock down the arrogant giant.

If you want to slay the giants of sin in your life, you'll need to be brave like David. And you'll need to use five smooth stones just like he did:
- Stone 1: Prayer
- Stone 2: Bible Reading
- Stone 3: Going to Church
- Stone 4: Doing Your Homework
- Stone 5: Not Dating an Unsaved Person

If you'll use these five smooth stones, the giants of sin in your life will come a-tumblin' down!

Now answer these two questions—then keep reading.

1. What do you think the biggest problem with this telling of the story of David is? (There are probably several right answers to this question.)

2. Knowing what you do about the story of Scripture, how would you connect the story of David and Goliath to the whole story of Creation, Fall, Redemption? What part does this small story play in that big story?

Evaluating the Story

Okay, how do you think you did answering those questions? Let's think them through a little. There are several problems with this way of telling the story. The biggest one is that the main character is missing! Hannah already told us that it's not by strength that a man prevails. And the Bible story in 1 Samuel 17 goes to great lengths to show how invincible Goliath was and how small David was. So if it wasn't David's strength that caused his victory, what was it? God! He was the main character, the hero. It was by God's might that David prevailed.

But David wasn't just any shepherd boy. He was the anointed king of God's people—even if they didn't know it yet. He was God's answer to the no-king problem we saw in Judges. He was God's answer to the bad-king problem we saw in 1 Samuel 10–15. By giving David such a prominent victory, God was lifting him up in the eyes of the people as a godly deliverer for them to follow. God (through David) cast Goliath to the ground and severed his head, just like He had done to Goliath's god, Dagon.

> "Saul (because he was very much like Israel) was the king Israel wanted. David (who was very much like the coming Messiah) is the king God had chosen. Saul is a symbol of rebuke to Israel. David is a symbol of hope."
>
> —**Bryan Smith**

David, of course, took no credit for his rapid victory. Even before he went into battle, he made it clear to everyone watching that the Lord was going to win—and *why* the Lord was going to win. Yahweh, David said, was going to show the whole earth something about Himself: that the Lord saves people without needing swords and spears. "The battle is the Lord's, and he will give you into our hands" (1 Sam. 17:47).

For God to win battles is exactly what Hannah prayed for decades before David's birth, and this is the big point not just of David's fight with Goliath but of the whole big story of which David is a part. God is giving strength to His king and exalting His anointed one (again, just as Hannah prayed).

Understanding the Story

So we don't have to make up clever things about the meaning of the five smooth stones (that's called "allegorizing" or "spiritualizing"). We don't have to make David the big hero or say that the really big point of the story is to be like him (that's called "moralizing"). We also don't have to pretend that Goliath represents the giants of sin.

No, the best way to understand the point of this story (or any other Bible story) is to do two simple things:

1. Make sure we understand where the little story fits in the big story of the Bible.

2. Pay close attention to the details of the story and try to figure out what those historical details tell us about God's work in people's lives in that context.

We don't have the space to look at all the details here, but let's think about this incident's place in the big story. The story of David and Goliath didn't come from nowhere. It's all part of what God is doing to save His chosen people.

What God is doing to save His chosen people didn't come from nowhere, either. It's all part of His plan to bless the whole world through Abraham.

That blessing, too, goes all the way back to the Garden of Eden, when God promised that the seed of the woman would crush the serpent's head.

If we fail to make connections like these, it's tempting to turn the story of David into something like one of Aesop's fables. There *are* lessons we can learn from David's life. It is, of course, essential to have deep faith like he did. And bravery is an important character quality. But we don't study David's life in order to figure out more effective ways to save ourselves from our sins. We study it because it shows us how God does that for us.

Bible Study Terms

Allegorize—to find in a Bible story hidden meaning that isn't really there

Spiritualize—to assign to the details of a Bible story spiritual meaning that God didn't put there

Moralize—to make it seem like you can be good without God

Literal—to give each word the same meaning that it would have in normal and ordinary use; to recognize figures of speech and try to understand what they are communicating

"David's reign is . . . a turning-point in the outworking of God's purposes of salvation."

—P. E. Satterthwaite

David wasn't a random brave shepherd. In his victory over the giant, God was giving strength to His king and exalting the horn of His anointed. David is the next part of God's plan to deliver Israel and bless the whole world.

The Giants of Sin

Sometimes our sins and temptations do seem like well-armored giants just daring us to oppose them. We might wish we could just throw a stone at our sins and kill them, but we can't. Modern Christians aren't a nation like Israel. So we don't physically fight God's enemies in order to advance God's kingdom.

And we know from other parts of the Bible that standing and fighting temptation like David fought Goliath isn't always the best option anyway. Sexual lust, for example, is a sin you will probably lose to if you stand and fight. Don't stand your ground and quote Bible verses; just flee the pornographic images you see. That's what the Bible says to do with that kind of sin (Gen. 39:11–12; 2 Tim. 2:22).

David's fight with Goliath is a mirror of a much more important fight that happened many years later. A King in David's line would hang dying on a cross. He would appear to have lost His fight.

But the truth was that He was triumphing over Satan just as David triumphed over Goliath. And just like the Israelite soldiers enjoyed the spoils after David's victory, so this King in David's line spread the spoils among His followers (Eph. 4:8–13).

David's victory over Goliath is not mainly a lesson in how to defeat sin; it's a picture of the knock-out blow God would later give to all sin through that King in David's line. Not by strength shall a man prevail. Deliverance comes from the Lord.

Thinking It Through 5.5b

3. Imagine you are teaching a Bible lesson to kids on the story of David and Goliath. These kids don't know the story of Scripture, so when they hear the story of David and Goliath, it sounds like a fable or a fairy tale to them. What memory verse(s) would you pick from 1 Samuel 17 that might help them get the real point of the story?

4. What's wrong with allegorizing, spiritualizing, or moralizing the stories in Scripture—like the David and Goliath story?

5. What event is the best New Testament comparison to the David and Goliath story?

5.6 DAVID: A KING AFTER GOD'S OWN HEART

Read 2 Samuel 6:1–11; I Chronicles 13
Memorize I Chronicles 15:13

Introduction

When David kills Goliath, Saul is still king. In fact, Saul will be king for quite some time to come. During this time, the relationship between Saul and David is tense. Saul wants nothing more than to kill David, and David wants nothing more than to leave Saul alone. On several occasions David goes out of his way not to harm Saul even when Saul is trying to kill him. It becomes a deadly game of hide-and-seek.

David thinks that it would be best for him to get far away from Saul and leave Israel for a while. He ends up going to Ziklag where Achish, the Philistine king of Gath, allows him to live among the Philistines and "help" them raid villages near Judah. (David actually helps the villages in Judah, but he makes it appear like he is helping the Philistines. In this way, he wins over the towns in Judah while making Achish think he is helping him.)

David's "success" impresses Achish. And when Achish decides to go to war against Israel, he tells David that he expects David and his

men to go along with him. Now David is in a predicament. Will he fight against the one who had given him a safe refuge from Saul? Or will he fight against Saul and go against his belief that he shouldn't harm God's anointed king?

But before David has to make a decision, it is made for him. The Philistine armies don't trust David. They are afraid that when they get into battle, David and his men will turn on them, and then they will be fighting both David and Saul. So Achish asks David to remain behind and return to his home at Ziklag.

David does as he was asked and returns to Ziklag, but when he arrives there, he finds that the Amalekites have invaded Ziklag and have captured all the women and children. David spends the next few days pursuing the Amalekites.

At the same time, Achish and his army are fighting against Saul. And the battle does not go well for Saul. When it is over, Saul and his sons, including Jonathan, are dead.

David can now ascend to his throne and be the king of Israel.

But most importantly, David is not responsible for Saul's death. When Saul was killed, David was away fighting the Amalekites. All Israel would know that David was innocent. He did not kill Saul to get the throne.

When David Became King

When David finally ascends to the throne, which God anointed him for as a youth, he moves his capital to what will become known as the City of David—Jerusalem. To this very day, Jerusalem is in many ways the most important and fought-over city in the world.

Scripture explains that David "grew great, [because] the Lord God of hosts was with him" (2 Sam. 5:10). The lowly shepherd boy who was now king knew this: "David perceived that the Lord had established him king over Israel, and that he had exalted his kingdom for his people Israel's sake" (2 Sam. 5:12).

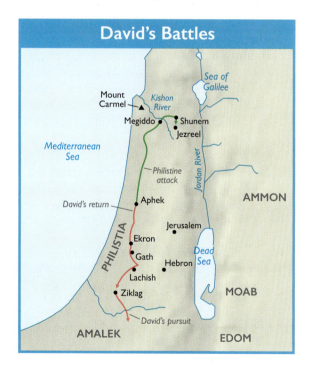

David's Battles

Sea of Galilee
Mount Carmel
Kishon River
Megiddo
Shunem
Jezreel
Mediterranean Sea
Jordan River
Philistine attack
David's return
Aphek
AMMON
Jerusalem
PHILISTIA
Ekron
Gath
Hebron
Dead Sea
Lachish
Ziklag
MOAB
David's pursuit
AMALEK
EDOM

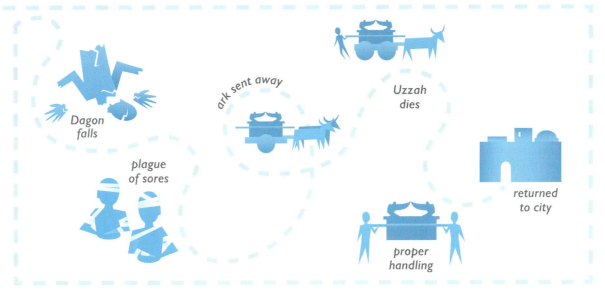

After being lost in battle, the ark traveled to several cities before its proper return to Jerusalem.

Tracking the Ark

David was indeed a king after God's own heart. His first act as the king of the united kingdom (both Judah and Israel) was to bring the ark of God back to Jerusalem. But why wasn't the ark with the king? Couldn't he have simply gotten it from Saul's palace? If not, where was it?

Tracking where the ark has been helps us understand why the ark wasn't with the king. Its location also shows us a difference between Saul and David.

When the children of Israel were in the wilderness, the ark of the covenant sat in the holy of holies in the tabernacle (Exod. 25:8–22). The Levites also carried the ark in front of them to find a resting place (Num. 10:33–35), to pass over the Jordan on dry ground (Josh. 3), and to accompany them into battle (Josh. 6).

In one such battle, the Israelites carried the ark of the covenant with them, but God did not fight for them. God was judging the wicked priests, the sons of Eli, and on that day, the Philistine overpowered the Israelites and took the ark.

But the ark didn't stay with the Philistines for long (1 Sam. 5). They had placed the ark in the temple of their god, Dagon. The next morning Dagon had fallen face-down to the ground. So they set Dagon back on his feet, but that didn't last long. The next morning they awoke to find Dagon face-down again, but this time his head and hands were broken off.

They immediately got rid of the ark and sent it to Gath where sores broke out on the men of the city. So the men of Gath sent it to Ekron, but the men there resisted and demanded that it go somewhere else.

As a result, the men of Ekron decided to put it on a cart and hitch two cows to the cart and let the cows take it wherever they wanted to take it. It ended up on Israel's border in Beth-shemesh where the people were glad to see it.

That is, they were glad to see it until the Lord killed more than fifty thousand of them in a great slaughter provoked by their looking into the ark. Messengers from Beth-shemesh went to Kiriath-jearim and asked the people there to come get the ark. From there, the Bible simply says that the ark remained at the house of Abinidab in Kiriath-jearim for twenty years (1 Sam. 7:2). Only once do we read where Saul requested the ark to be brought to him (1 Sam. 14:18), and the Israelites even acknowledged that they never sought after it in the days of Saul (1 Chron. 13:3).

Good Intentions, Wrong Way

Back to when David became king. He is now king of both Israel and Judah. And his first act is to bring the ark back. The ark of the covenant belongs in the tabernacle. The ark is God's chosen part of the tabernacle where He manifests His presence. It is essential that the ark be returned.

David is right to want to bring it back. He has good intentions. In fact, the Bible says that what David wants to do "was right in the eyes of all the people" (1 Chron. 13:4). All Israel has good intentions. David has a new cart made to carry the ark, and he has Uzzah and Ahio lead the ark. These two men are the brothers of Eleazar, who had been consecrated to guard the ark. Most likely, these men are Levites.

Everything is going well as they bring the ark back. David and all Israel are celebrating. Many people are singing and playing musical instruments. It seems that all is well. But it isn't.

As the oxen approach a threshing floor, they upset the ark on the cart. Uzzah reacts quickly and puts his hand on the ark to keep it from falling. God's anger burns against Uzzah, and He strikes him down. Uzzah dies, and the celebration abruptly ends.

David sees what has happened, and he responds with anger at God. And then he is afraid.

David had gotten caught up in the excitement of the moment. He thought he was doing the will of God by bringing the ark back. Everyone thought it was a good idea. In fact, David had even said that if "it be of the Lord our God," then let's do it (1 Chron. 13:2). But he never inquired of God. He never asked God how he should bring it back.

> "Doing what we believe to be God's will in a way that violates God's Word is wrong and displeases God."
>
> **—J. A. Thompson**

David had good intentions. But in his excitement, he neglected one thing that really mattered—giving respect to God's way of handling the ark.

Good Intentions, God's Way

David's fear is appropriate. He has just seen God strike down Uzzah for touching the ark. How he responds in fear will tell what he thinks of God's law.

His first response seems almost hopeless. He says, "How shall I bring the ark of God home to me?" (1 Chron. 13:12).

David decides to leave the ark at the house of Obed-edom until he can figure out how to bring the ark back to Jerusalem. It takes three months for him to figure it out. And during that time, he consults the law to see how he should proceed (1 Chron. 15:13).

The first thing David does is to prepare a place for the ark. He also prepares the Levites for their task. They are to consecrate themselves before they go get the ark. Once they get to the house of Obed-edom, they will carry the ark. There will be no cart and no oxen this time.

This time God is with them as they bring the ark back to Jerusalem. This time the celebration doesn't end prematurely. At the end of the day, they sacrifice seven bulls and seven rams to the Lord.

This time they did it God's way.

Similar Sins but Different Responses

David wasn't the only one who had good intentions but allowed the excitement of the moment to cloud his judgment. When Saul was king, Israel was getting ready for battle (1 Sam. 13). Samuel had said that after seven days he would come and sacrifice to the Lord before the Israelites went into battle. Seven days came and went, but Samuel had not arrived. Saul grew restless and decided that if he wanted God's blessing, he would offer the sacrifice before they went into battle.

Samuel arrived shortly thereafter and confronted Saul about what he had done. Saul said that he was concerned about the Philistines coming down on him before he had asked for God's favor.

Good intentions. Wrong way.

Samuel told Saul that his disobedience meant that his kingdom would end. There would be another to take his place. After Samuel rebuked Saul, you would think that Saul would listen and learn from his sinful mistake. It didn't take long for him to sin again with a similar mistake.

Later on, Samuel tells Saul to attack Amalek and destroy everything (1 Sam. 15). Everyone

SAUL	DAVID
SIN	SIN
REBUKE	REBUKE
LIE	LISTEN
SIN AGAIN	LEARN
CURSED	OBEY

must die, and every animal must be put to death. Saul partly obeys (which means he disobeys). He doesn't kill everyone, and he brings back many animals. When Samuel confronts him, Saul says that the animals are the best of the flock and are to be sacrificed. Once again, good intentions but the wrong way.

Samuel rebukes Saul and says, "Hath the Lord as great delight in burnt offerings and sacrifices, as in obeying the voice of the Lord? Behold, to obey is better than sacrifice, and to hearken than the fat of rams" (1 Sam. 15:22).

In other words, God doesn't want just your sacrifices, no matter how great they are. He wants you to listen to Him and obey Him. That is what He delights in—not sacrifices.

This time, Saul loses more of his kingdom; he loses God's favor when God regrets that He had made Saul king.

David was different. When he saw God's judgment on Uzzah, he at first responded with anger but then with fear. He didn't want anyone else to die, and his fear drove him to please God. Although fallen and sinful, David wanted what God wanted. He was a man after God's own heart. When the ark arrived in the city, David sang and danced with all his might. This was a king who followed the most important law: "Thou shalt love the Lord thy God with all thine heart, and with all thy soul, and with all thy might" (Deut. 6:5).

Thinking It Through 5.6

1. Why can't David ascend to the throne right away, even though he's already been anointed as king? How is David able to ascend to the throne?

2. Why did David grow in his greatness as a king?

3. What was one of David's first acts as king that proved that he was a king after God's own heart?

4. Even though David had good intentions, what did he neglect to do?

5. Compare and contrast the responses of Saul and David when they are confronted for their sins.

5.7 DAVID: COVENANT & FALL

Read 2 Samuel 11:1–12:14
Memorize 2 Samuel 7:16

God created Adam as a mirror to reflect God's glory. He also made him to have dominion over creation. After Adam failed to exercise dominion over the serpent, God promised that "the seed of the woman" would do it.

Centuries later, God narrowed that promise down to the line of Noah (by killing every other family line in existence). Centuries after that, God narrowed the promise down to Abraham—then to Isaac, then to Jacob, then to Judah. All these men in the line of the seed of the woman were remarkable in their own ways. Each of them had some kind of dominion over his land or his family.

But none of them was a king. That is, until God narrowed the line down to David. The king Hannah prayed for—God's anointed one—has now arrived on the scene.

And for the first time in its history, Israel has a king after *God's* own heart. They have had godly leaders before—like Moses and Deborah—but they've never had a godly king.

What role will David take in the one story the Bible is telling? Will he finally crush the head of the serpent?

David's Kingship

It takes David a good while to replace Saul, but during the wait he displays his godliness to the whole nation by refusing to kill Saul even in self-defense. Saul is the Lord's anointed, and David has deep respect for that fact.

Throughout David's long wait (which lasts from 1 Samuel 18 through 2 Samuel 3; something like seven to twelve years), God keeps exalting David more and more and putting down Saul lower and lower. More reversals!

During this time we also get to see in David a chivalry combined with faith in God that makes him one of the noblest characters in Scripture. And he has another important qualification Saul didn't have: he's from the tribe of Judah, the one that the patriarch Jacob predicted would rule over the other tribes.

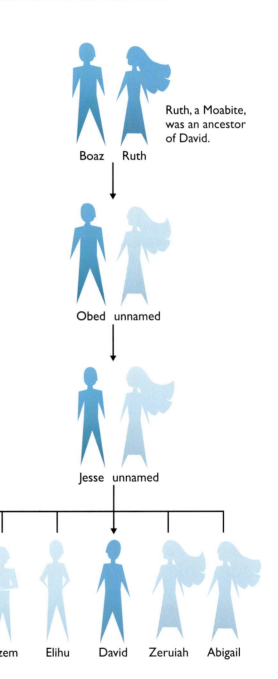

Boaz   Ruth

Ruth, a Moabite, was an ancestor of David.

Obed   unnamed

Jesse   unnamed

Eliab   Abinadab   Shimea   Nethanel   Raddai   Ozem   Elihu   David   Zeruiah   Abigail

The Davidic Covenant

As you read in the previous lesson, David's first act as king of Israel was to bring the ark of God back to Jerusalem. But bringing the ark into Jerusalem wasn't enough for David. As soon as the Lord had given him rest from all his enemies, he wanted to build a temple for the Lord too.

It was then that the Lord stepped in and informed David of his place in the one big story of Scripture. Second Samuel 7:1–17 is a key passage in the Bible, one that you should remember how to find. Most Bibles give it a heading that says something like "The Davidic Covenant." We've arrived at a new chapter—a major advance—in the story. Just as God made a covenant with Abraham and a covenant with his descendants (the one He made through Moses), God is now making special covenantal promises to King David.

Just like any important contract that benefits you (and this one does!), you need to note carefully what these promises are.

God first tells David that He is the one responsible for destroying David's enemies. Then He starts right into the promises:

1. I will make your name great.

2. I will choose a place for the people of Israel and plant them in it.

3. I will give you rest from all your enemies.

4. I will make your line into a dynasty (a line of kings).

All four of these promises have obvious links back to the promises God made to Abraham long ago.

- God promised to make Abraham's name great too.
- He promised Abraham's seed a land to live in.
- He promised Abraham that his seed would conquer all its enemies.
- He promised that kings would come from Abraham.

When December 25 comes around and you get every single Christmas present you asked for, it's not luck. It's not a coincidence. You might have made your wish list months before, but someone with the power to buy presents held on to it.

These promises are not coincidences either. David's story doesn't just come out of nowhere. It grows out of the other promises God has already made. Even if many Israelites didn't hold on to God's promises, God did. Often the hardest part of keeping your promises is just remembering what they were. God didn't forget a single detail.

"In the Davidic Covenant the promises made to Abraham become more focused."

—Paul R. Williamson

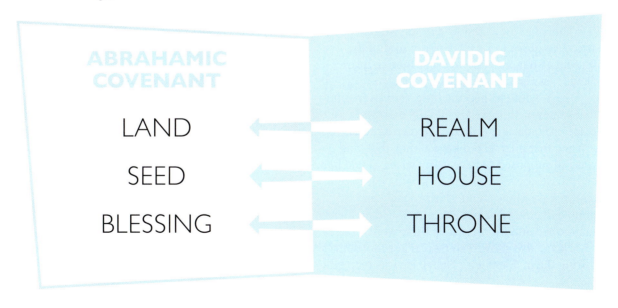

ABRAHAMIC COVENANT		DAVIDIC COVENANT
LAND	⬌	REALM
SEED	⬌	HOUSE
BLESSING	⬌	THRONE

God is very clearly narrowing some of His promises in the Abrahamic Covenant down to the line of one man—David.

But we can't stop here. There are two more special sets of promises that we'd better quote word-for-word:

5. "I will set up thy seed after thee . . . and I will establish his kingdom. He shall build an house for my name, and I will [e]stablish the throne of his kingdom for ever" (2 Sam. 7:12–13).

6. "Thine house [family dynasty] and thy kingdom shall be established for ever before thee: thy throne shall be established for ever" (2 Sam. 7:16).

We're learning something new about the seed. The seed of the woman who crushes the head of the serpent won't just be one of Abraham's descendants. He'll be a king—a king in the line of David, and he will build a house for the Lord. And that seed's throne will last forever.

God had told Abraham that in his seed all families of the earth would be blessed (Gen. 22:18). And God wanted Israel to be a kingdom of priests showing God to the world (Exod. 19:4–5). Now, apparently, the seed who will bless all the nations and show God to the world will be a king.

But what king could possibly sit on the throne forever? Every promise points to a coming seed who would redeem His people.

The Fallen Anointed One

The long line of the seed of the woman has stretched down to David. But the seed of the serpent also has a place in every human heart. David, very sadly, was no exception.

Even before he became king, there were hints that not everything in David's life met God's perfect standard of holiness. Deuteronomy 17:17 warned that if Israel did have a king, that king was not supposed to have many wives. David had eight wives, several concubines, and twenty-one children we know about. (He probably had double that number because only one daughter is mentioned and it's very likely there were more.)

David also showed some reckless foolishness during the incident with Nabal. He was rescued from committing vengeful murder only by the wisdom of Abigail, who later became one of his wives (1 Sam. 25:42).

In the Bible reading assignment for this section, you read about the very worst thing David ever did. Here was a man who had more wives than anyone could possibly love, and that wasn't enough. At the lowest point in his life, David decided that he needed someone else's wife too—Uriah's wife, Bathsheba.

There's no need to wallow in the details here. David is now an adulterer and a murderer. But there are two things you'll want to take note of in the story. One is David's response to his sin. The other is God's.

David's Response: Psalm 51

There are few more precious psalms than Psalm 51. It was written by David, the great king of Israel, after Nathan the prophet confronted him about his adultery and murder.

When most people get caught, they make excuses. David makes not one. He focuses like a laser beam on the real problem in himself. The effects of the Fall didn't skip him, Abraham's special kingly seed. When David prays to God, "In sin did my mother conceive me" (Ps. 51:5), he wasn't saying that his mother and father sinned in giving him life. No, David is talking about himself. He was born in sin, born a sinner.

But admitting that truth—and admitting that all his sins were, in the end, offenses against God (51:4)—was David's path to cleansing. "Create in me a clean heart, O God," he prayed (51:10).

Psalm 51 is a prayer you should come to know by heart—not by memorizing it for a verse test but by praying it for yourself. Even if your sin isn't as horrific as adultery and murder (or even if it is), you can and should pray what David did. God doesn't want you to pay Him back for your sin. You'd only sin again in the process. He wants you to have what David had, "a broken and a contrite heart" (51:17). In other words, your sin should make you feel wilted and sad like a popped balloon in the dirt.

But God won't leave you there. He wants to restore the joy of salvation to you (51:12). When you know down deep that you are delivered from and forgiven of your sin, joyful praise will fill your mouth like it did David's (51:15), and you'll rise up again.

Even after committing some of the worst sins in the book, David received precious divine forgiveness.

God's Response: Amnon and Absalom

But forgiveness doesn't erase all the negative consequences. After David's sin, his family is never the same. His son Amnon rapes Tamar, David's daughter (by a different wife). His son Absalom (Tamar's full brother) murders Amnon in revenge and then starts a rebellion that briefly exiles David from Jerusalem.

David keeps a godly and humble perspective throughout this time. He's still the honorable and kingly gentleman he used to be. But his former sins are now bearing bitter fruit.

David leads God's people to be faithful to the covenant, and he becomes the benchmark (the standard, the rule) for all later kings. Over and over throughout the course of history, the kings of Judah who come after David are all compared to him. Those who walk in the ways of David are considered good kings; those who don't, aren't.

Even so, at the end of David's life, there's a big footnote about his faithfulness. Yes, "David did that which was right in the eyes of the Lord, and turned not aside from any thing that he commanded him all the days of his life" (1 Kings 15:5). But there's a bloodstained asterisk: "[except] in the matter of Uriah the Hittite."

"While the [last chapters of] the book of Samuel celebrate David as a warrior and as king, his own personal flaws are only too evident. The last person on the list of his mighty men is named 'Uriah the Hittite' (2 Sam. 23:39). The hope for the future lies in a descendant of David."

—Stephen Dempster

So David was still not the ultimate solution to the world's problems. Sin infected this kingly seed too. The serpent's head was still not crushed. We're going to need the biggest reversal of all history to see that happen.

Thinking It Through 5.7

1. What are the promises that God repeated in His covenant with David? Be sure to include all six of them.

2. Explain four ways these promises connect back to the first covenant God made with Abraham.

3. How did David respond to his sin? How did God respond to David?

4. In the excursus on the book of Psalms (on the following pages), you should have read that "the first two psalms were probably placed at the beginning of the book to alert us to some of the main ideas found throughout the psalms." Summarize the main ideas from both of those psalms.

5. List and summarize the three works that the Holy Spirit does to make people wise. (See the excursus on Proverbs.)

The Psalms and the Story of Scripture

Students of the Bible have often wondered how books like Psalms fit into the story line of Scripture. From Genesis to 2 Kings we have the story from creation to the Babylonian exile. Books like Ezra, Nehemiah, and Esther tell us about history within and after the exile. The books of Chronicles summarize the whole story again from Adam until the return from exile. But Psalms, Proverbs, Ecclesiastes, and Song of Solomon are not continuing to tell the story. Instead these books call on us to think about the story and our relation to the story.

What Is the Book of Psalms?

Psalms are songs. The psalms were originally sung in worship to God. The Bible did not preserve for us the tunes that the Israelites used when they sang the psalms, but it did preserve the words. At a first reading, you might think that these psalms were just randomly written into a scroll in whatever order the scribe happened to copy them down. They certainly are not in chronological order. Psalm 3 says that it was written by David, but Psalm 90 was written by Moses. Psalm 89 was clearly written after David's death, but Psalm 101 was written by David.

But if you think about it, our hymnals typically do have some kind of order to them. It's not a chronological order but a topical order. If you look in a hymnal, hymns about worshiping God may appear toward the front, followed by hymns about Christ and His incarnation. And hymns about the Christian life may appear toward the back of the hymnal. There is some order to the hymns.

There is order to the book of Psalms as well. If you look carefully, you will see that Psalms is divided into five books. These book divisions and the divisions of the psalms themselves are not recent additions like chapters and verses in the rest of the Bible. These are old divisions that may reach all the way back to when the book of Psalms was put together. If you look at these different sections of Psalms, you'll notice that there are clusters of psalms about similar topics in these books. For instance, in Book 1 of the Psalms you'll read a lot of psalms about David seeking God's help against enemies who would do him harm. If you look at the end of Book 5, you'll read a lot of psalms that are praising God. So there is an order to the book of Psalms.

The first two psalms were probably placed at the beginning of the book to alert us to some of the main ideas found throughout the psalms. Psalm 1 contrasts the wicked man and the man who delights in the law of the Lord. As you read through the psalms, you'll read a lot about wicked men. They are often seeking to harm God's people. Often it appears that they are getting away with their evil deeds. The wicked seem to prosper, but the righteous suffer. In other words, many of the psalms are about being a follower of God in a world twisted by the Fall. Instead of telling us about how the Fall originally happened in history, the psalms give us songs to pray to God when we feel the effects of the Fall in our lives. And Psalm 1 tells us that we need to keep eternity in view: "The ungodly shall not stand in the judgment . . . , but the way of the ungodly shall perish" (Ps. 1:5–6).

A large part of the Pentateuch is taken up with the giving of God's law. God's law helps His people know how to live in His creation in a way that pleases Him. In this way, Psalm 1 is linking back to the story of creation. God's law isn't just written on the tablets of stone that Moses brought down from Sinai. God's law is written into the very creation itself (see "Proverbs and the Story of Scripture" on the following pages).

The person who delights in God's law and thinks about it and how it should affect his life is a blessed person. When a person lives according to God's law, he prospers because he is living in God's world God's way. This prospering doesn't mean that the righteous person is without troubles. Remember what was just said about the wicked and the way they treat God's people. But those troubles are not caused by living according to God's law. Those troubles are caused by the Fall.

Psalm 2 reveals that sinners are opposed not only to God's people. They are opposed to God Himself. Yet God scorns this opposition. He will enthrone His Anointed One ("Messiah" in Hebrew) on Zion, the Temple Mount in Jerusalem. From there He will rule over the "uttermost parts of the earth." Throughout the rest of the book, again and again, psalms remind readers of the rule of God and of His

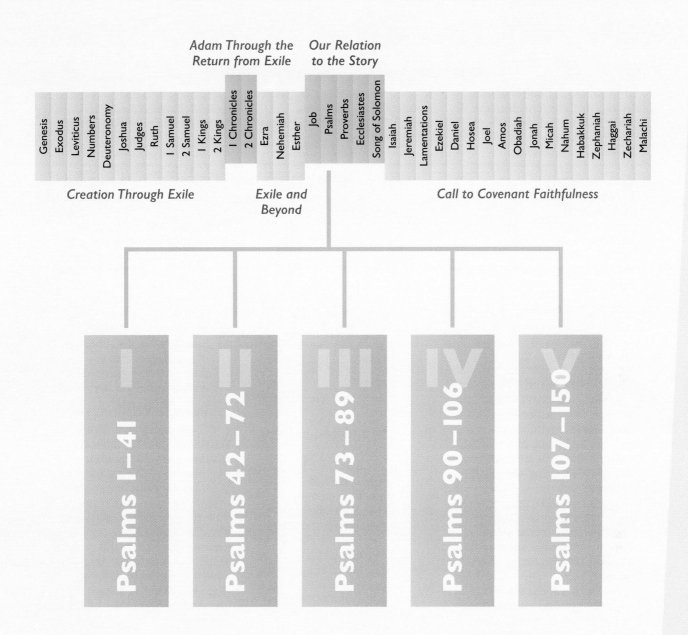

Adam Through the
Return from Exile

Our Relation
to the Story

Genesis | Exodus | Leviticus | Numbers | Deuteronomy | Joshua | Judges | Ruth | 1 Samuel | 2 Samuel | 1 Kings | 2 Kings | 1 Chronicles | 2 Chronicles | Ezra | Nehemiah | Esther | Job | Psalms | Proverbs | Ecclesiastes | Song of Solomon | Isaiah | Jeremiah | Lamentations | Ezekiel | Daniel | Hosea | Joel | Amos | Obadiah | Jonah | Micah | Nahum | Habakkuk | Zephaniah | Haggai | Zechariah | Malachi

Creation Through Exile

Exile and
Beyond

Call to Covenant Faithfulness

I Psalms 1–41

II Psalms 42–72

III Psalms 73–89

IV Psalms 90–106

V Psalms 107–150

Messiah. Psalm 72 says that He will bring justice to the righteous poor and will shatter their oppressors. Psalm 110 says that one day the Messiah will return to earth from reigning at the side of the Lord God and will judge wicked rulers in wrath. The ungodly, who seemed to prosper, will be scattered like chaff, and the righteous, who loved God's law, will receive justice.

The rule that God gave to mankind (Gen. 1:28; Ps. 8:4–6) will be restored from sin's corruption of it. The promises that God made in His covenants, and in the Davidic Covenant especially, will be fulfilled when a Davidic king rules over the world and sets all things right. The New Testament writers recognized that these psalms pointed forward to Jesus. When Herod and Pontius

Pilate crucified Jesus, they were the Gentiles raging and plotting against the Lord's Messiah (Acts 2:25–27). But God laughs at them from heaven because they were simply carrying out what He had "determined before to be done" (Acts 4:28). Jesus' ascension to heaven was in fulfillment of the Lord's command to the Messiah to sit enthroned in heaven until His enemies are made His footstool.

Proverbs and the Story of Scripture

Proverbs is a book of wisdom. In the Bible, wisdom is not the same as knowing a lot of facts. Wisdom is skill for living. For instance, a carpenter who can make beautiful furniture could be said to be wise in his craftsmanship (see Exod. 31:3). Proverbs is a book designed to make people wise for life. Much of its wisdom is found in short sayings that are easy to memorize.

Proverbs and Creation

Many people struggle to understand how this book of wisdom fits into the larger story Scripture is telling about God's work to redeem His fallen creation. Proverbs answers the question by connecting its wisdom to the very beginning of the story: creation. Proverbs says that "the Lord by wisdom hath founded the earth" (Prov. 3:19). In His wisdom, God designed the world with certain principles built into the way it operates. The rules that make life work aren't random; they are part of God's wisdom.

So it's no wonder that Proverbs urges all its readers to seek wisdom. Search for it as you would search for a million dollars in gold if you knew it was buried underneath your house! That's what Proverbs 2:4 says: Dig, dig!

If by wisdom God ordered the creation, then wisdom can be discovered by careful observation of the world. The wise man observes the diligence of the ant (Prov. 6:6), the seasons which bring snow or rain (Prov. 26:1), and how people behave in various situations (Prov. 26:16–21). But wisdom is not found merely through observation. The world is fallen and humans are fallen.

Fallen humans looking at a fallen world will likely reach wrong conclusions about the way the world is ordered.

> "The entire, complex fabric of the world, as it were, has been woven by Yahweh, so that to attain wisdom is truly to find the tree of life because it positions one to live according to the warp and woof of the world."
>
> —Craig Bartholomew

Proverbs and Redemption

People need God's work of redemption in order to be truly wise. The Holy Spirit does three different works to enable us to be wise. First, the Holy Spirit changes hearts so that people fear God. Second, the Holy Spirit gives us inspired wisdom in the Bible. Third, the Holy Spirit helps God's people make wise choices in their daily lives. Each of these works of the Spirit merits further explanation.

The Beginning of Wisdom

Proverbs opens with the instruction, "The fear of the Lord is the beginning of knowledge" (Prov. 1:7). A person who fears the Lord loves God so much that he desires above all things to please God and recoils from the thought of grieving God.

A person who observes the world in order to get life to work for his own benefit may learn a great deal, but he will not be wise. He may even figure out how to get his way in the short term, but he will not be wise. In fact, there will be much about the world that he will never understand because he will be living in opposition to the Creator who made the world to work the way it does.

But a person who fears the Lord studies the world to learn how God would have him live. This change of perspective makes a profound difference in his understanding of the world.

Inspired Wisdom

Our culture is a do-it-yourself culture. But biblical wisdom is never something that people get independently of others. Proverbs emphasizes that wise people learn from their parents and teachers. God also gave us the entire book of Proverbs as inspired and inerrant wisdom. If you want to know what it looks like to observe God's world and to discern the way God made it to work, look at Proverbs.

The individual proverbs are general statements about how the world normally works. For example, Proverbs 14:23 teaches, "In all labour there is profit: but the talk of the lips tendeth only to penury [poverty]." This proverb arises from the observation that work usually brings its reward. Hard workers earn wages. But people who spend their time talking instead of working end up poor.

The book of Proverbs also shows that just any observation will not do. The world needs to be observed through the lens of Scripture. Why is it true that "whoso mocketh the poor reproacheth his Maker: and he that is glad at calamities shall not be unpunished" (Prov. 17:5)? This observation uses the lens of Genesis 1:26, which teaches that all people are made in God's image. Thus when a poor person is mocked, God is mocked.

Other parts of Scripture can help us learn how to apply the general observations in Proverbs to specific situations. What does it look like to live Proverbs 14:21, which says, "He that despiseth his neighbour sinneth: but he that hath mercy on the poor, happy is he"? The Mosaic law applies the wisdom that God built into His world to Israel's specific situation. So God told the Israelites not to gather all the grain from their fields or all the grapes from their vineyards. Instead they should leave food behind for the poor (Lev. 19:9–10). We don't live in the same situation as Israel, but it is helpful to see how a general truth was applied to a specific situation.

Wisdom in Daily Life

Wisdom is not just about making wise observations and generalizations about how the world works. It is also about applying those observations to daily life. Think of an example from two common English proverbs:

"Many hands make light work."

"Too many cooks spoil the broth."

The first proverb instructs us that many people working together can make a difficult task easy. The second teaches that too many people working on the same task can damage the quality of the work. The wise person needs to know which proverb applies in which situations.

In the Bible one proverb recommends, "Answer not a fool according to his folly, lest thou also be like unto him" (Prov. 26:4). That's good advice—for some circumstances. But for others you need the very next proverb: "Answer a fool according to his folly, lest he be wise in his own conceit" (26:5). Sometimes you ignore a fool so you don't get trapped in a silly argument, and sometimes you answer him so he doesn't think he trapped you in his silly argument! Wisdom involves knowing which proverb applies to which situation.

The New Testament reveals that the Holy Spirit provides this wisdom to those who seek it from God. Paul prayed for believers that they "might be filled with the knowledge of his will in all wisdom and spiritual understanding," with the goal that they "might walk worthy of the Lord unto all pleasing (Col. 1:9–10). James tells his readers, "If any of you lack wisdom, let him ask of God, that giveth to all men liberally" (James 1:5).

When God created mankind He commissioned him to rule over the world. Wisdom is the ability to exercise this rule with God-honoring skill.

5.8 SOLOMON: WISDOM & FOOLISHNESS

Read | Kings 8:22–53
Memorize | Kings 8:60–61

As the life of David draws to a close, one reversal spills over from the book of Samuel into the book of Kings. Which son of David will inherit the throne—and, more importantly, the promises of the Davidic Covenant?

Once again God lifts up the low and puts down the mighty. The second-oldest son of David, the good-looking Adonijah, arrogantly tries to grab the leadership for himself, but God selects someone else. And just as He did with many others in the family line stretching back to Abraham, God chose the least likely candidate. He picked the youngest son of David, the one born to the wife he'd taken in adultery. This son's name is Solomon.

Solomon's Ascent

Before David dies, he has an opportunity to talk to his newly crowned son. Whatever Solomon already knew about God's covenant with his father, David at least made sure to mention the important point to his son on this occasion:

> Keep the charge of the Lord thy God, to walk in his ways, to keep his statutes, and his commandments, and his judgments, and his testimonies, as it is written in the law of Moses, that thou mayest prosper in all that thou doest . . . . that the Lord may continue his word which he spake concerning me, saying, If thy children take heed to their way, to walk before me in truth with all their heart and with all their soul, there shall not fail thee . . . a man on the throne of Israel. (1 Kings 2:3–4)

After David dies, the author gives us the best hope possible about Solomon by saying simply, "Solomon loved the Lord" (3:3). With his heart pointed in the right direction and following God's most important command (Deut. 6:5), Solomon has nowhere to go but up.

And up he goes. God invites him to wish for anything he desires, and he pleases the Lord he loves greatly by asking for wisdom to govern God's people well.

Solomon receives the wisdom he desires; that's the point of the story of the two prostitutes and the baby. But there is yet more glory and honor in store for the great King Solomon. He is to complete what David began and build a magnificent temple to Yahweh.

Solomon's Temple-Dedication Prayer

If you listen in at major political events like US presidential inaugurations, the talk is usually pretty predictable. If religion even shows up, it's pretty thin.

But Solomon's prayer during the ceremony to dedicate the new temple isn't just pomp and ceremony for its own sake. He is speaking to the God he loves, and he has deep concern for his people. When the glorious king steps up to deliver his grand dedication prayer, the people hush. He begins to pray.

Solomon has led the people to the greatest high point in their history. You might expect him to focus on thanking the Lord for His many blessings—riches, wisdom, honor, strength. But Solomon's prayer focuses on asking God to forgive Israel's future sins. And not just Israel's:

> Moreover concerning a stranger, that is not of thy people Israel, but cometh out of a far country for thy name's sake; (For they shall hear of thy great name, and of thy strong hand, and of thy stretched out arm;) when he shall come and pray toward this house; hear thou in heaven thy dwelling place, and do according to all that the stranger calleth to thee for: that all people of the earth may know thy name, to fear thee, as do thy people Israel; and that they may know that this house, which I have builded, is called by thy name. (1 Kings 8:41–43)

If you don't know the story of Scripture, this seems like just a nice prayer, kind of a generous way to think of others and not just your own country. But Solomon is descended from Abraham and enjoys the blessings God promised to him. (In fact,

King Solomon *is* one of the blessings God promised to Abraham.) And God said that He wanted to *bless the whole world* through Abraham's seed (Gen. 12:3). Solomon is also descended from people who were slaves in Egypt. And God told *them* He wanted Israel to be a kingdom of priests showing the world what God is like (Exod. 19:4–5).

Do you see some connections you wouldn't have seen before? Solomon wants this temple to help "all the people of the earth [to] know that the Lord is God, and that there is none else" (1 Kings 8:60). The temple is part of God's plan to fix the whole world, to redeem His fallen creation.

The highest creation of God—mankind—is fallen. Solomon's prayer says so: "There is no man that sinneth not" (8:46). The wise king Solomon knew what is in every person's heart.

Solomon demonstrates his commitment to the Lord at the temple dedication as he requests forgiveness for future sins.

Solomon's Fall

The wise King Solomon, then, must have known what was in his own heart. And yet he started off his leadership as well or better than David did.

Marrying Pharaoh's daughter was a mistake, of course. But marrying an Egyptian was not explicitly forbidden by God, just marrying Canaanites (Deut. 7:1–5). And Solomon's great-great-grandmother was a Gentile, after all. Plus, Solomon's wedding was a sort of triumph for God's chosen nation: the people who used to be slaves have now made a marriage alliance with the people who used to be their captors and tormentors.

The building of Solomon's temple was an even greater triumph. And the headings in your Bible are enough to tell you that Solomon only continues to rise after that:

- The Queen of Sheba Comes to Marvel at Solomon's Wisdom (10:1–13)
- Solomon Gains Great Wealth (10:14–29)

Finally! The people of Israel are happy and at rest, living in the land God promised Abraham (1 Kings 4:20–21). David had wanted to build a house for the Lord; now the Lord has built *David* a house, and David's son has built one for God—just like God promised in the Davidic Covenant. Israel has a beautiful temple and a godly king. They are doing just what they're supposed to, and God is blessing them for it. They are a nation of priests, showing the whole world what the one true God is like. That's why the Queen of Sheba—and many other kings and queens—are so attracted to them and their leader.

So the next Bible headings come as a terrible shock:

The world's greatest pleasures could not satisfy Solomon once his heart turned from the Lord.

- Solomon Turns Away from the Lord (11:1–8)
- The Lord Sends Enemies Against Solomon (11:9–43)

It makes you want to grab Solomon by the shoulders and shake him! "You have so much potential! You have divine wisdom! You're the heir not just to David's kingdom but to his covenant with Yahweh! And you're wasting it all!"

Of course, many people would gladly give up all those things to have what Solomon had—seven hundred beautiful wives and three hundred beautiful concubines. He had all the pleasures his world and his (God-given) wealth could give him. But as you can see in the Ketuvim section, those pleasures ultimately proved to be empty, like a juice box you've already drained the liquid out of. You can squeeze and squeeze, but for all you do, you'll get nothing.

Moses had warned centuries before that this would happen. In Deuteronomy 17 he said that the king of Israel should not marry many women, "that his heart turn not away" (Deut. 17:17). That, of course, is exactly what happened with Solomon. Nobody knows how many dozens of wives it took, but eventually they led him to worship their gods.

It didn't make any sense. In Solomon's day, you didn't worship the gods of nations you conquered; you worshiped the gods of the nations that conquered you, and that only because you had to. And yet here Solomon is choosing to worship wicked, false gods that, in addition to being wicked and false, have the major downside of not even existing.

Moses had also said that the king shouldn't multiply horses to himself (Deut. 17:16) nor should the king accumulate great amounts of silver and gold (17:17). Now look at Solomon. He had forty thousand stalls for his horses and chariots, and his horses came from Egypt (1 Kings 10:28–29). Although God told Solomon that He would make him wealthy, it seems that Solomon excessively increased his riches (1 Kings 10:14–29). So much so that he burdened the people under him (1 Kings 12:4).

> "Solomon worships the gods of people he has conquered and already controls. What could he possibly gain from such activity? The whole episode makes no sense, just as idolatry itself makes no sense."
>
> —Paul R. House

That last heading in the chapters on Solomon shows that God treated him the same way He treated his father David. Sin brought consequences. The Lord sent enemies against Solomon's peaceful land, and He even promised to split Solomon's precious kingdom.

Solomon's multiple marriages brought him nothing good in the end. The last words about Solomon's life show that even Solomon's marriage alliance with Egypt proved empty. Shishak, the Egyptian pharaoh, protected Solomon's enemy Jeroboam.

Thinking It Through 5.8

1. When Solomon comes to the throne, what indications do we have that he is headed in the right direction?

2. What did Solomon understand the main purpose of the new temple to be?

3. Read the last two verses of Solomon's grand prayer in 1 Kings 8. What does he say there that is sadly ironic considering what he did in the remainder of his life?

See the following pages to answer questions 4 and 5.

4. How would you explain that the books of Proverbs and Ecclesiastes don't contradict? What does Ecclesiastes identify as "the conclusion of the whole matter"?

5. Why is the Song of Songs in the Bible?

Ecclesiastes and the Story of Scripture

Ecclesiastes is an often-misunderstood book. In some ways it stands in contrast to the book of Proverbs. Proverbs is about discerning the order that God built into creation. The proverbs are general observations about the way the world normally works. But a fallen world doesn't always work normally. There are exceptions to proverbial generalizations. For instance, Proverbs teaches that the violence of the wicked destroys them, because they refuse to do what is just (Prov. 21:7). But in Ecclesiastes Solomon observes,

> There is a vanity which is done upon the earth; that there be just men, unto whom it happeneth according to the work of the wicked; again, there be wicked men, to whom it happeneth according to the work of the righteous:

I said that this also is vanity. (Eccles. 8:14)

Proverbs and Ecclesiastes are not in conflict or contradiction. Proverbs is looking at the way things generally are because of God's creational design (the wisdom He built into His creation). Ecclesiastes is looking at the exceptions to the norms that arise because of sin.

Vanity

Solomon opens the book with the assertion, "Vanity of vanities, saith the Preacher, vanity of vanities; all is vanity" (1:2). He concludes the same way, "Vanity of vanities, saith the preacher; all is vanity" (12:8). And throughout the book Solomon labels what he observes to be *vanity*.

What does it mean for something to be vanity? The Hebrew word Solomon uses means "vapor" or "breath." Everything in the world is like

a breath. Solomon says that pursuing earthly things is like trying to catch the wind (1:14). As one commentator observes, "You never catch it; but if you do catch it, you do not have anything anyway." If something is vanity it is unsubstantial: there is nothing there. Solomon also explains, "All the labour of man is for his mouth, and yet the appetite is not filled" (Eccles. 6:7). Vain things are unfulfilling. They do not satisfy. Or perhaps there is some satisfaction—but the satisfaction does not last; it is short-lived. It is like the vapor you see when breathing on a cold day. It appears for a moment and then vanishes.

When Solomon speaks of all being vanity, he means that everything is unsubstantial, unsatisfying, and short-lived (but *all* doesn't include God). Solomon says, "I have seen all the works that are done under the sun;

and, behold, all is vanity" (1:14). Throughout the book Solomon speaks of his perspective as being one that is "under the sun." It is all that is "under the sun" that is like a vapor.

From an "under the sun" point of view, a person does not know how he is related to God. No one knows by the things that happen to him whether God loves him or hates him. Bad things happen to the righteous and good things happen to the wicked (9:1). Even worse, in the end everyone meets the same fate: "All things come alike to all: there is one event [namely, death] to the righteous, and to the wicked" (9:2). Solomon calls this an "evil" (9:3). We might argue that the righteous dead are with God and the wicked dead are in hell, but Solomon is trying to make sense of life and how to live life "under the sun." Without looking beyond the sun, life is better than death. When one dies, his chance for accomplishing anything on earth, or even for knowing what is happening on earth, ends. The living at least know that they will die and can benefit from pondering this knowledge (9:4–6; cf. 7:1–4).

Enjoy Life

So how should a wise person live a life "under the sun" in light of the reality that "all is vanity"? How should a person live in the face of the universal reality of death? Solomon's answer throughout the book is enjoy life. He says that "there is nothing better for a man, than that he should eat and drink, and that he should make his soul enjoy good in his labour" (2:24). He counsels,

Go thy way, eat thy bread with joy, and drink thy wine with a merry heart. . . . Let thy garments be always white; and let thy head lack no ointment. Live joyfully with the wife whom thou lovest all the days of the life of thy vanity, which he hath given thee under the sun, all the days of thy vanity; for that is thy portion in this life. (9:7–9)

Solomon is not saying, "Eat, drink, and be merry, for tomorrow you shall die." There is a repeated idea in these passages that is important: "it was from the hand of God" (2:24); "this is the gift of God" (5:19); "which he hath given thee" (9:9). Solomon is saying that God's people should enjoy the good things of life as gifts from God. Do you have food and drink? Enjoy them. Do you have clean clothes and perfume? Enjoy them. Do you have a husband or a wife? Enjoy your life together. These are all gifts from God (9:7–9).

When a person looks for ultimate satisfaction in this "under the sun" life, he will find it to be like a vapor— unsubstantial, unsatisfying, and short-lived. But if a person receives the good things of life as gifts from God, then he can enjoy those things at present.

Fear the Lord

Wisdom, pleasure, hard work, wealth, honor—Solomon squeezed all the juice out of every one of those things, and all he was left with was a soggy juice box. The pleasure didn't last. But there is one enjoyment that can last forever: God Himself. And that is humanity's main purpose—to glorify God and enjoy him forever. All joys under the sun are to be used as ways to enjoy God.

Solomon identifies this way of life with "the fear of the Lord."

"Fading is the worldling's pleasure,
All his boasted pomp and show;
Solid joys and lasting treasure
None but Zion's children know."

—John Newton

If you make the fear of the Lord your starting point in all your joys, they can last—because they will just be different ways of enjoying and delighting in God. Every glass of orange juice will be a reason to say, "God gave me taste buds and citrus to remind me of the greater pleasures He can give me for all time!" Your hardest trial can be a reason to say, "God made my earthly hope fall through so that I would remember that He is the only permanent joy."

At the very end and climax of the book, this is what Solomon says, "Let us hear the conclusion of the whole matter: Fear God, and keep his commandments: for this is the whole duty of man" (12:13). If you fear the Lord, there will be lasting consequences— many of them good. That's the implication of the very last verse in Ecclesiastes: "For God shall bring every work into judgment, with every secret thing, whether it be good, or whether it be evil" (12:14). Here Solomon looks beyond the sun to the day when God sets all things right in this fallen world. And those who feared God and delighted in His goodness to them will, in fact, enjoy God forever.

Song of Songs and the Story of Scripture

The Song of Songs is a difficult book of the Bible. Major parts of the Bible's story line are never mentioned. Major religious themes make no appearance. There's no temple. No law, grace, sin, or prayer. If archaeologists discovered the Song of Solomon by itself on a dusty scroll they would have no idea that it was a religious book. And yet this book is part of the Bible. Thus interpreters have proposed different strategies for finding religious meaning in the Song of Songs.

Allegorizing and Spiritualizing

Christian interpreters from at least the third century AD interpreted the song as an allegory of Christ and His church. Augustine provides an example of this kind of interpretation. Commenting on Song of Songs 4:2, "Thy teeth are like a flock of sheep that are even shorn, which came up from the washing; whereof every one bear twins, and none is barren among them," he says,

I feel greater pleasure in contemplating holy men, when I view them as the teeth of the Church, tearing men away from their errors, and bringing them into the Church's body, with all their harshness softened down, just as if they had been torn off and masticated [chewed] by the teeth. It is with the greatest pleasure, too, that I recognize them under the figure of sheep that have been shorn, laying down the burdens of the world like fleeces,

and coming up from the washing, i.e., from baptism, and all bearing twins, i.e., the twin commandments of love, and none among them barren in that holy fruit.

But Puritan commentator James Durham offers this interpretation:

By teeth in the new man may be understood two things; 1. Faith; believing being often compared to eating, because it furthers the soul's nourishment, and is the means by which the soul lives on its spiritual food. . . .

Who is correct? Both Augustine and Durham see the act of eating as a significant part of the image (though the Song of Songs itself doesn't mention eating here at all, just teeth). For Augustine the eating represents incorporating people into the body of Christ, but for Durham the eating represents meditating on Christ.

Allegorical interpretation is subjective. As a result, different interpreters can reach very different conclusions about the meaning of text. Regrettably, this often loses the intention of the author.

Proper interpretation does not ignore figures of speech. For instance, the verse mentioned in the quotations from Augustine and Durham above is a complex simile: Teeth are like shorn sheep coming up from washing, each bearing twins, and none being barren. Proper interpretation interprets the simile in context. In this context, this verse comes as part of the man's description of the beauty of his wife. The

teeth are pictured as newly shorn sheep. Newly shorn sheep would be white (since the dirtied wool was freshly taken away). The husband is praising his bride for her white teeth. Furthermore, each one has a twin. No teeth are missing. The husband is simply praising his wife's beauty.

Lyrics of Love

But this still leaves us with the question, Why is this book in the Bible? This question is best answered after first figuring out what the book is. The Song of Songs is a collection of love poetry. It doesn't really tell a story. As one commentator observed, "lyric poems do not *tell* a story but *reflect upon* and *allude to* a story." For instance, Shakespeare's "Sonnet 29" isn't telling a story about losing a position at court or about a failed business venture. He is reflecting on a scenario similar to these. We don't know what that circumstance was, and figuring out what happened isn't necessary for understanding the poem. The gist of Shakespeare's poem—that faithful love is to be valued more than high position— is clear even without full understanding of the background.

Song of Songs is similar. Though the Song of Songs is written by Solomon (1:1), this does not mean that this is love poetry that Solomon wrote about a particular time in his life or to a particular woman. Solomon was a polygamist, but this book praises married, monogamous, and heterosexual love. The book speaks of one man with only one woman throughout. And the husband speaks of his wife in exclusive terms (e.g., "As the lily among thorns, so is my love among the daughters," 2:2). In fact, 8:11–12 may be a reference to Solomon's harem—a "vineyard" so vast that he had to hire people to take care of it. In contrast, the wife in these poems is able to take care of herself for her husband. If 8:11–12 is a reference to Solomon's many wives and concubines, the book may have been written by a repentant Solomon near the end of his life. The poems aren't telling the story of his love for a particular wife as much as they are describing the ideal love between a husband and a wife.

In the midst of the book, the man and woman celebrate the physical aspects of their love through metaphor-filled descriptions of each other's bodies. The metaphors serve as a veil to shield the intimacy of husband and wife from public view, since it is designed to be shared by them alone. And yet there is a purpose in observing the delight a husband and wife have in their spouse. After the Fall, nakedness became shameful. Adam and Eve's first response after they sinned was to cover themselves up. From the Pentateuch to the Prophets, Scripture is clear that to have one's nakedness exposed is shameful. Why? Because of sin, nakedness leaves one vulnerable to the abuse of others or is used to draw

others into shameful lust. But in the Song of Songs the husband and wife are again naked and not ashamed. The difference is marital love. The husband's delight is not self-focused but is bound up in hers. He doesn't take advantage of the vulnerability that nakedness brings to her. The Fall is reversed in this relationship because the husband expresses true love and selfless delight in his beloved.

Those who are unmarried should be particularly cautious when reading this book. Solomon realized this, and the woman offers a charge to the daughters of Jerusalem, who weren't yet married (2:7), to not stir up thoughts of love and intimacy until the time is right. It is possible to misuse

this book to stimulate lustful thoughts, but what could be more reprehensible than taking the very words that God has breathed out to instruct His people and instead use them to sin against Him? It's hard to think of anything that would be more akin to spitting in God's face.

The Song and the Story

Hopefully by now you can start to see how Song of Songs fits into the story of Scripture. Genesis 2 describes an unfallen world in which the husband and wife were naked and not ashamed. Genesis 3 reveals that marriage would be distorted by a power struggle between husband and wife. The Song of Songs presents a couple who demonstrated mutual love and once again were naked and not ashamed. Song of Songs displays God's redemptive work and the reversal of the Fall. Since the Fall affected marriage, it's appropriate for the Bible to present a picture of what a restored marriage ought to look like.

But there's more. Marriage pictures God's relationship with His people (Hosea 2; Jer. 2:1–3; Ezek. 16; Eph. 5:22–33). Once the book is understood in terms of the husband-wife relationship, application can be made to our relationship with God. We can see the ugliness of idolatry, which is adultery against the true God. We can see the beauty of love that is fully devoted to Him.

UNIT 5 REVIEW

Scripture Memory

Ruth 4:14	1 Samuel 17:46–47
1 Samuel 2:10	1 Chronicles 15:13
1 Samuel 8:7, 19–20	2 Samuel 7:16
1 Samuel 15:22	1 Kings 8:60–61

Understand the Story

1. Compare and contrast Ruth with what you know about most Israelites during the time of the judges.

2. True or False. The Bible is the story of how humans work hard to become strong enough to fix their own problems as they build up greater and greater moral character from within themselves, eventually bringing themselves to Jesus.

3. What made the Israelites' request for a king wrong?

4. Summarize at least three hints from Saul's life (up until the time Samuel publicly proclaims him as king) that should leave you wondering whether Saul is a good choice.

5. What is the main point of the David and Goliath story?

6. Why did God strike down Uzzah in holy anger?

7. What is the key chapter in the Bible that summarizes the Davidic Covenant?

8. What are some things in the Bible and in Solomon's own life that could have warned him about taking so many wives and concubines?

Developing Observation Skills

9. Whenever you read a narrative, you should observe its three basic parts: characters, plot (including conflict), and resolution. Based on 1 Samuel 1, who are the major characters, what is the primary conflict, and how is it resolved?

10. Being skillful at observing the text of Scripture includes paying attention to the little words that make key connections. The little word *for* in the middle of 1 Samuel 8:7 is an important word. The clause after that word explains God's instructions. What was God's explanation to Samuel?

11. One important observation skill to learn when studying narratives is characterization (see Exercise 5.4). How might Saul be displaying good character by what he says and does while he is looking for the lost donkeys? (1 Sam. 9:5) How might he be displaying questionable character? (1 Sam. 9:6–10)

12. Compare and contrast Saul and David. (1 Sam. 16:23) How does this distinction reinforce the role reversal spoken of by Hannah in 1 Samuel 2:1–10?

13. Being able to compare two different passages about the same event is an important observation skill. Summarize what David said and how the people responded. Then explain the timing of the events in 1 Chronicles in relation to 2 Samuel. (2 Sam. 6:1–2; 1 Chron. 13:2–4)

14. What keywords in 1 Kings 8:25 let you know that Solomon's prayer request is based on what he said in 1 Kings 8:22–24?

Connecting the Story to the Big Story

15. If Judges shows how bad Israel can get without a righteous king, what does the book of Ruth show?

16. Hannah's prayer is the first prediction that the promised Seed will be called by what name because of His kingly role?

17. How would you connect the story of David and Goliath to the whole story of Creation, Fall, Redemption?

18. How does the book of Proverbs fit into the larger story of Scripture?

Lessons for Life

19. Based on Israel's situations that you learned about in this unit, write a paragraph relating a similar experience of trust and obedience or of distrust and disobedience in your own life.

20. Choose a psalm from Psalms, a proverb from Proverbs, or a wise saying from the book of Ecclesiastes. Observe what it says, research what it means by using a commentary, and identify how you can act on it in your own life.

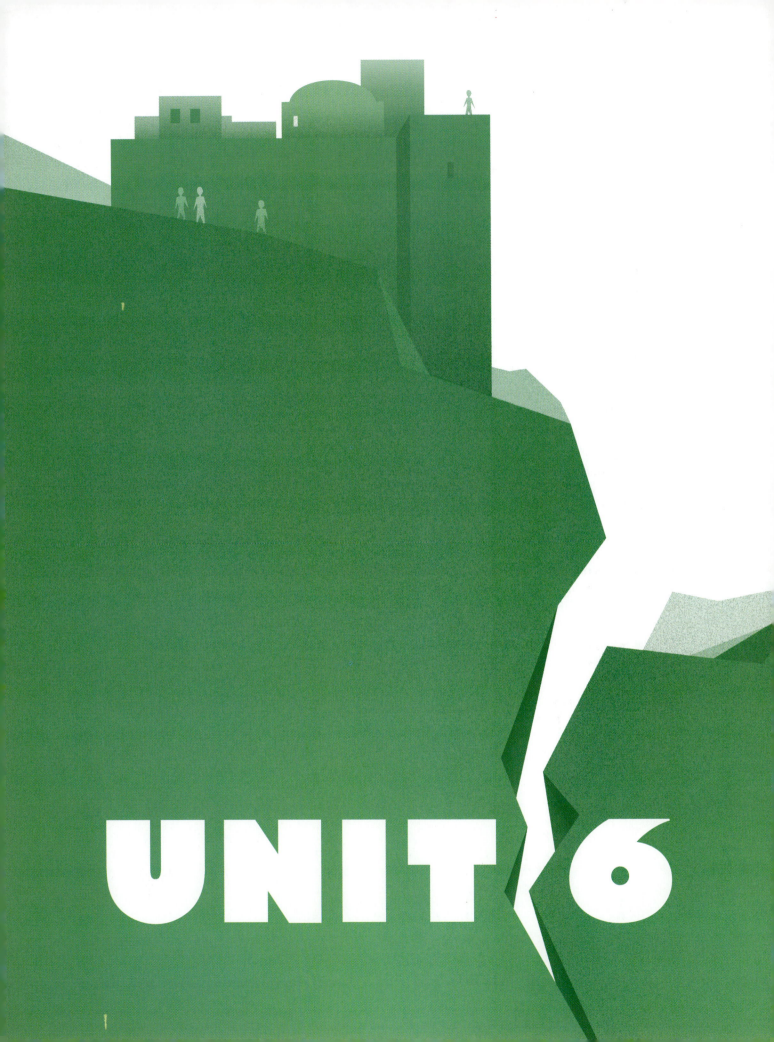

THE LINE OF DAVID: FAILURE & HOPE

This unit is about the failure of human kings. God promised Abraham that kings would come from him. God promised David that a king in his line would sit on the throne forever.

But He also promised the following about David's seed: "If he commit iniquity, I will chasten him with the rod of men" (2 Sam. 7:14). This is

exactly what happens, and Kings tells the story of the troubled Southern (Judah) and Northern (Israel) Kingdoms.

This unit is also about several prophets who urged God's people to turn from their sins and to God lest God's judgment fall on them.

The prophets saw future answers to Israel's problems, but they did not know the details.

6.1 JEROBOAM: THE TRENDSETTER

Read I Kings 12
Memorize I Kings 13:33–34

An exhaustive list is one that leaves nothing out. That's the purpose of the phone book, for example. Every person in town—from Aaron Abels to Zoey Zukowski—is supposed to make it in there.

Just imagine if your history textbook tried to be exhaustive. How many pages would it have if it recorded every person, every conversation, every marriage, every drawing, every journey, every meal, every game, and every decision that ever happened?

Only God has a book like that because only He has the time and ability to read it (let alone write it). Every other person who writes a history book has to pick and choose what to include. But those choices aren't random; every historian has reasons for putting in Aaron and leaving out Zoey—or vice versa.

The men who wrote the Bible, though inspired by God, were no different. The big story of the Bible includes some little stories and omits others for a reason—or reasons.

Now that you know more about the big story of Scripture (what God is doing to redeem His fallen creation), you have a better idea of why the little stories appear: they help the main plot along in some way. That's obvious with big names such as Abraham, Jacob, Moses, and David. But it's not so obvious as we get into the book of Kings. Why do we need to know about all the different kings that God's people had? Why not just hit the highlights?

The book of Kings is as long as it is because God's mercy lasted as long as it did. There's a tension in the book between two poles—like a rubber band being stretched between two fingers before it finally breaks. The tension is between God's promises to Abraham and David on one side and God's warnings to Israel in the Mosaic Covenant about the consequences of their sin on the other. God had told the people at the end of Deuteronomy that violating their covenant with Him would bring curses on them (Deut. 30). And He had warned David that his sons would need to stay faithful to the Lord as he had or face God's displeasure. If David's seed sinned, God promised He would "chasten him with the rod of men" (2 Sam 7:14).

Solomon's Folly

You read in the last unit that Solomon was led into idolatry by his many wives. And you read just now in 1 Kings 11 that God decided to impose some serious consequences for Solomon's sin.

But did you notice what the writer said about God's motivation for showing mercy even in that punishment? The writer of 1 Kings gives you a window into God's own heart and plans, including the reason God chose not to judge Solomon during his lifetime:

> I will not take the whole kingdom out of [Solomon's] hand: but I will make him prince all the days of his life for David my servant's sake, whom I chose, because he kept my commandments and my statutes: But I will take the kingdom out of his son's hand, and will give it unto [Jeroboam], even ten tribes. And unto his son will I give one tribe, **that David my servant may have a light alway[s] before me in Jerusalem, the city which I have chosen me to put my name there.**
> (1 Kings 11:34–36)

God judged Rehoboam and not Solomon out of love for Solomon's father David. And God kept David's descendants on the throne of one tribe, Judah, so that David's line would be like a lamp in Jerusalem shining all day, every day, year after year. And then there's this: God chose to bind up His own identity with one city out of all the cities in the whole world—Jerusalem.

Rehoboam's Folly

The Old Testament isn't a place where people tend to live happily ever after. Maddeningly, frustratingly, sadly, the stories just don't end that way.

When Solomon's reign ends, the people look to his son Rehoboam to carry on the dynasty. After they make him king, they go to him and plead for mercy. "Thy father made our yoke grievous: now therefore make thou the grievous service of thy father, and his heavy yoke which he put upon us, lighter, and we will serve thee" (1 Kings 12:4). In other words, "Your father was a hard master, and his taxes were too heavy to bear. Lighten up a little."

That sounds reasonable enough.

Rehoboam has an opportunity to win over the people. The elder advisors who served Solomon even tell him that if he lightens the Israelites' load, the people will love him forever. But Rehoboam consults his friends, and they tell him to be aggressive and show the Israelites who's boss. His young advisors say that he should tell the people that his little finger is thicker than his father's waist and that he will add to their burden and punish them severely. And that's what he tells them.

Rehoboam lacks discernment, and it backfires on him. Instead of loving him, the people leave him and cry out, "See to thine own house, David" (1 Kings 12:16). They want nothing more to do with the line of David. They will choose their own king.

Rehoboam isn't going to give up his kingdom without a fight, and he sends Adoram to force the northern tribes to work for him. But the Israelites stone him to death. The message is clear. They want no part of Rehoboam's forced labor or his kingdom.

As a result, Rehoboam flees south to avoid the rebellion.

Rehoboam's lack of discernment allows Jeroboam to ascend to the throne and rule over the ten northern tribes of Israel. His foolish choices split the kingdom. But the split had a deeper source—God's own plan. "This thing is from me," the Lord says quite clearly (1 Kings 12:24).

> "The Lord is ... the living God who controls history."
>
> —Iain Provan

David's lamp keeps on burning. God has shown mercy. Rehoboam could easily have lost his kingdom and his life, but he manages to hang on to a throne that is a lot less imposing than it used to be. A mere shadow. Most of his subjects have revolted against his rule. The "rod of men" is starting to chasten and discipline David's seed.

Jeroboam

The split between Judah (the Southern Kingdom)—the tribe that included Jerusalem—and Israel (the Northern Kingdom) had serious consequences. And Jeroboam, the new king of the northern tribes, knew that. If he let his subjects go worship in Jerusalem every year as God's law said they must, they might start feeling loyal to Rehoboam instead of to him.

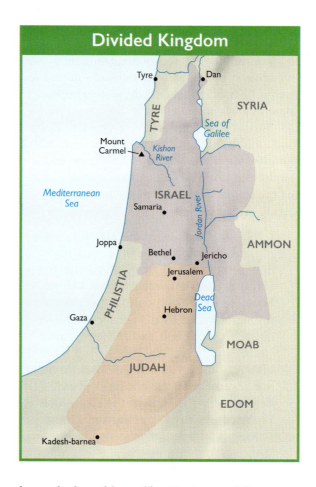

Divided Kingdom

Samaria and Israel

After God's people split into two kingdoms, Judah kept Jerusalem as its capital. The Northern Kingdom, often called Israel (as opposed to Judah), built the city of Samaria as its capital. Samaria is also, however, the name of the whole region where the city is located. It's like today when we speak of the New York metropolitan area as including many cities beyond the actual city of New York.

When the kingdom split, the tribe of Benjamin stayed loyal to Judah. That's how the twelve tribes are divided into ten and two.

Jeroboam's first recorded act as king was not what God desired—he turned to idolatry. Over and over again throughout Kings and Chronicles, the Bible comments about such and such king that "he departed not from the sins of Jeroboam the son of Nebat, who made Israel to sin." The book of Kings speaks of "the sins of Jeroboam" fourteen times. Five times it says an Israelite king walked "in the ways of Jeroboam." That makes a total of nineteen times.

Not a very nice legacy to hand down. How did he earn such a reputation? He decided that in order to keep Israel out of Judah and away from the influence of Rehoboam, he'd have to give them alternate places to worship. So he set up idols at two convenient places, the lush northern city of Dan and the strategic southern city of Bethel.

But he didn't even go as far as Solomon went. He didn't promote Baal or Molech or some obviously false god. He told the people of Israel exactly what Moses' brother Aaron told the people when

he made the golden calf at Sinai around five centuries before: "Behold thy gods, O Israel, which brought thee up out of the land of Egypt" (1 Kings 12:28). Israel had been down this road before; they knew this wasn't right even if it seemed close. Israel was now worshiping idols in direct disobedience to God's second commandment—just forty years after the death of David!

> "If Jeroboam is the arch villain [of 1 and 2 Kings], then David is the hero of the book. David is the standard for the evaluation of the kings of Judah, just as Jeroboam is the standard for Israel."
>
> —Robert Bell

Jeroboam made a fatal error. He didn't just disobey the God who promised to bless him for obedience. He tried to use God as a convenient way to control history. He failed to notice that, as author Iain Provan put it, "God cannot be captured in an image any more than be confined in a temple." God is not tamable! These powerless statues had nothing to do with the all-powerful Yahweh who really rescued Israel from slavery.

Jeroboam was already on his way down.

Simple Obedience

God really does know best. Sometimes it seems like a little compromise or a little fudging is not a big deal. If it takes one tiny white lie for you to get the job you've been praying for, then God will overlook it, won't He? If you just happen to see where your mom has hidden her internet passwords, it's not your fault that curiosity drives you to peek at them. Right?

A true story. A Christian school student— let's call her Gracie—went to a school that required her to never go to a movie theater. She couldn't watch even G movies there because of the other immoral films being shown in the same place. The rule was quite clear, and it was given to her by authorities God had told her in the Bible to obey. (And if that wasn't enough, her parents had the same rule because the school had it.)

Now it just so happened that she heard a believable rumor from the principal's daughter that the rule was going to be taken out of the student handbook the next year. It just hadn't been announced yet.

One day, she was talking with her non-Christian aunt about the new Pixar movie that had just come out. It was getting great reviews, and all the Christian websites were saying it was totally clean. Even the trailer on YouTube was awesome. Her aunt invited her to go with her to see it. Now she had a choice to make: "Do I embarrass myself by telling my aunt I'm not allowed to go to a totally clean, G-rated movie? Or do I just go along with her and see it since I know that the rule is about to be changed?"

She had only an eighth of a second to decide, but she didn't go the route of Jeroboam. She didn't bend the rules. She consciously prayed to God to honor her decision to obey, and she told her aunt she couldn't go and why. Her aunt's mouth dropped open. She couldn't believe there would be such a (to her) silly rule. But Gracie just trusted that God knew best. Obedience to Him was the safest road to take.

The bottom line. The Bible never says, "Don't watch movies in a theater," but it does tell children to obey their parents. Small disobediences twist your character, making it easier to commit big disobediences later. You don't want to go down that road. It isn't safe.

It would have been cool if her aunt had trusted Christ after that because of her decision. That didn't happen. But Gracie had a little sister—and another, and another. Her split-second decision to trust God was, thankfully, part of a long pattern that helped influence those siblings to trust that the Lord knows best.

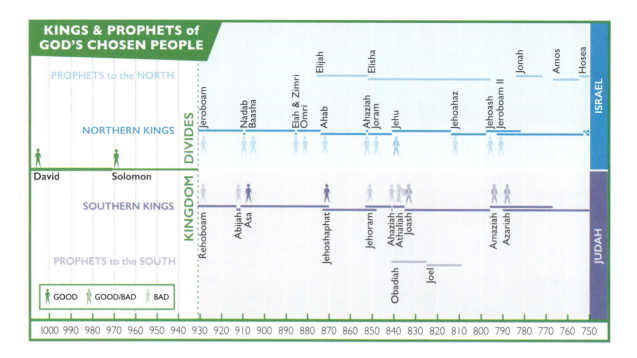

The Beginning of the End

The saddest truth of Jeroboam's story—and the reason it keeps getting mentioned throughout the book of Kings—is that the Northern Kingdom never did come to believe that the Lord knows best. Even though Jeroboam was a rod in God's hand for punishing the seed of David, Jeroboam still had a duty to point the people of Israel toward the one true God. That meant leading them to Jerusalem for feasts. But Jeroboam failed to trust God to keep his kingdom secure, and he led the whole nation astray as a result.

They never recovered from Jeroboam's sin. Over the coming centuries, Judah would have a few godly kings, but Israel would have zero. Not one of its other nineteen monarchs followed David's ways. They all imitated Jeroboam.

Thinking It Through 6.1

1. Describe the tension in the book of Kings. Why is there this tension?

2. Why didn't God judge Solomon in his own lifetime?

3. How did Rehoboam's lack of discernment threaten God's Davidic promises?

4. In five or six sentences describe how Jeroboam became king.

5. How often do the books of 1 and 2 Kings refer to Jeroboam as the pattern or the model that the Northern Kingdom followed?

6.2 ELIJAH: PROPHET OF THE LIVING GOD

Read I Kings 17–19
Memorize I Kings 18:21

Just because their first leader put them on a wicked, idolatrous path doesn't mean God gave up on the Northern Kingdom of Israel. They had a number of wicked kings and no small amount of turmoil. One king "reigned" for only seven days, and he ended that reign by burning himself to death (1 Kings 16:18).

By the end of 1 Kings 16, the story line has reached Israel's king Ahab. The Bible gives more space to him than it does to any other Northern king. And, no surprise, he was a really bad one. We'll focus on him in the next section.

But now, nine years into Ahab's reign and after about a century of disobedience, God sends the Northern Kingdom a notable messenger.

That messenger was Elijah. And here was his first message from the Lord: "No rain until I say so!" For a society that relied almost completely on farming, this was nothing less than a death sentence.

Starvation isn't something most of us ever think about. But here it is, staring God's people in the face. But the God who controls the rain controls the rest of His creation too, so Elijah, at least, has food to eat. Ravens bring it to him.

God's control, however, goes even further. When the brook Elijah is living by dries up, God commands not ravens but a person to feed Elijah.

> "When Yahweh sends Elijah out of the land, his word is silenced in Israel. To the famine of bread, Yahweh adds a famine of the word."
>
> —Peter Leithart

Provoking His People to Jealousy

The strange thing is that this person is not an Israelite. She's a Gentile widow living in the territory of Sidon, northwest of Ahab's kingdom (see map on page 193). It seems that since the Israelites have provoked their God to jealousy, God is going to provoke them to jealousy. Just as they have given their favor and love to other gods, Yahweh is going to send His favor and grace to other nations.

This is exactly what God said back in Deuteronomy that He would do:

> They have moved me to jealousy with that which is not God; they have provoked me to anger with their vanities: and I will move them to jealousy with those which are not a people; I will provoke them to anger with a foolish nation. (Deut. 32:21)

So Elijah crosses the border from Israel to Sidon, a center of Baal worship over which Yahweh—according to the thinking of most people in that day—has no power. But Sidon has been affected by the Lord's drought too. And the widow who is supposed to feed Elijah has only enough food left to feed herself and her son one last meal before they have to give up and die.

The test Elijah gives her is almost impossible. "Feed me," Elijah says, "before you feed your own son." But this Gentile has a faith unlike that of the faithless Israelites. She does it. And the Lord blesses her by providing food. Elijah stays in her home throughout the three-year drought. He is, in a sense, a life-giver to her—later on even bringing her son back from the dead—because he serves the God who lives.

Showdown

The famine God sent was something else He had said in Deuteronomy that He would do. If the nation of Israel failed to keep covenant with Him, their rain would turn to dust (Deut. 28:24).

After three years of judgment, would God's people be ready to repent, to turn to Him? Or would they continue to follow their evil king (Ahab) and worship his false god (Baal)?

Obadiah, King Ahab's steward, is one who does fear the Lord. He personally hides and feeds a hundred of God's prophets when Ahab's wife, Jezebel, tries to kill them. But Jezebel's actions show that Israel has not repented. Instead of returning to the one true and living God, they keep trying to get Baal to send rain.

So when Elijah finally leaves Gentile territory, it's time for a showdown—Yahweh vs. Baal. Which one truly lives?

There's hardly a more dramatic story anywhere in all the Old Testament. When Elijah asks, "How long halt ye between two opinions?" (1 Kings 18:21), what he's really saying is "Quit hobbling around going nowhere! If the Lord is God, follow Him! If Baal is, follow him!"

Halt!

Most modern readers of the King James Version probably assume that *halt* in "halt ye between two opinions" means "stop." English has changed significantly, however, in four hundred years. To be halt back then was to be "lame"—to lack the use of a leg or two. So to halt was to limp or hobble. That's the picture here: someone staggering around on crutches not really going anywhere.

Elijah's test is simple: whichever deity can send fire from heaven wins. He lets the 450 prophets of Baal go first. Hour after hour they go limping around the altar. "O Baal, hear us!" No answer.

Normally, sarcasm is not a godly virtue. But sometimes, even in the Bible, mocking is just what sin deserves. And Elijah dishes it out royally here: "Shout louder! He's probably busy thinking or using the restroom! Or maybe he's gone somewhere on a trip—or he's sleeping!"

The prophets of Baal even cut themselves in an effort to make Baal listen. Still nothing.

When Elijah's turn comes, he wants everyone to see and hear exactly what happens—

because, even in his prayer, Elijah has a message for the people. They are the people of the one God, the "Lord God of Abraham, Isaac, and of Israel" (18:36). And Elijah prays that God will turn their hearts back to Himself. This test wasn't a circus or an entertainment (although it surely was funny!). It was a merciful display of the one truth everyone there sorely needed to admit: the Lord is the one true and living God.

> "Idolatry corrupts and destroys lives, and Yahweh is too righteous to be so unconcerned that he does not discipline. The discipline is meant to lead to salvation."
>
> —Jim Hamilton

By the end of the story, of course, they've all admitted it. Like their forefathers who had seen the Red Sea crossing, they can't deny what their eyes have just seen. They all fall on their faces and acknowledge that "the Lord, he is the [true] God" (18:39). And they help Elijah kill every one of the false prophets that has been leading God's people into destruction. Then the rains come.

Elijah Flees

There's at least one person in this story, however, who can and does deny undeniable evidence. Despite hearing eyewitness testimony from her husband, Jezebel is so committed to Baal that nothing can shake her faith, not even fire from heaven.

Elijah sees Jezebel's unrepentant heart and her determination to kill him, and it breaks him. Spineless Ahab might just let Elijah go, but steely Jezebel wants blood. She won't give in to the one true living God. She swears by multiple gods that Elijah will be dead in a day (19:2). So on the heels of this stunning victory, Elijah, disappointed and broken, ends up fleeing for his life.

God deals gently with him, giving him food and letting him go all the way to Mount Sinai in the far south—as far away from Jezebel as possible. And instead of terrifying him back into his senses, God uses a "still small voice" (19:12).

> "It is in his disappointment, not in his terror, that we see Elijah as a 'man with a nature like ours' (James 5:17a)."
>
> —Ronald Barclay

Elijah thinks he's the only person left who follows the Lord even though he has to know that's not true. God corrects him gently but firmly, telling the prophet to go back up north: "I have left me seven thousand in Israel, all the knees which have not bowed unto Baal, and every mouth which hath not kissed him" (1 Kings 19:18).

The one true and living God has not allowed His people to slip completely through His fingers. He has kept seven thousand pure worshipers.

And Now Back to Our Story . . .

One reason Old Testament stories like this are in the Book is that it's good to let God's personality wash over you. To soak in it. You get to know someone by watching what he says and does. God is no different. Seeing His mighty

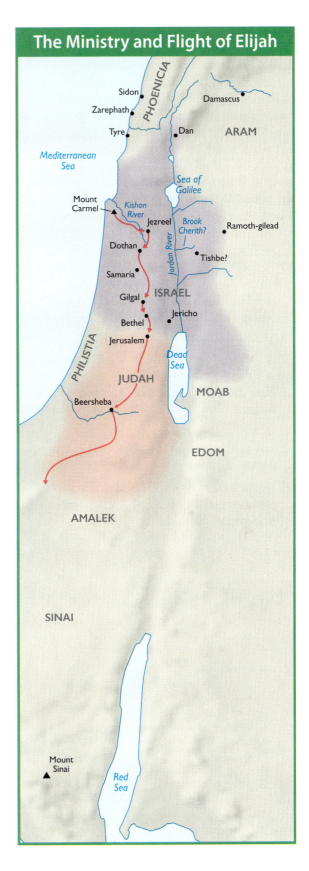

The Ministry and Flight of Elijah

power on display on Mount Carmel tells us something about Him. But so does hearing His "still small voice" on Mount Sinai.

Elijah's courage and faith are shown for you to imitate; just as his self-pity is on display for you to avoid. (And hopefully it's not necessary to say this, but please don't be like Jezebel!)

But this textbook is mainly about helping you see how stories like this fit in the one big story of Scripture. Where does Elijah fit? What's the point? There are several points:

- God's own people still need redemption because they're part of the fallen creation He's working to redeem. The seed of the serpent seems to be winning, especially in the Northern Kingdom, over the seed of the woman. But God has great patience with His fallen people.

- God is faithful to bring both covenant blessings and covenant curses. Israel would do well to pay attention to what the Lord promised and threatened back in Deuteronomy.

- God doesn't leave His people permanently without a word from Him. No other nation in the world heard direct messages from God. But Israel got blessed with both a prophet and a massive public demonstration of the power of Yahweh.

- All the same, part of God's judgment on Israel was His willingness to feed one Gentile widow while all of Israel suffered from His famine. God still intends to bless all nations, even if Israel is first in line.

Thinking It Through 6.2

1. How did God display His judgment on the nation? Why would this have been a severe judgment?

2. List at least two reasons God judged the nation of Israel.

3. List at least two reasons God sent Elijah to a widow in Sidon when the brook Cherith dried up.

4. Why did Elijah challenge the prophets of Baal on Mount Caramel? How did the people respond to the display of God's power over nature? How did Ahab and Jezebel respond?

5. When Elijah fled to Mount Sinai, he heard directly from God, who spoke in a "still, small voice." What hope did God assure Elijah with?

6.3 AHAB: ROTTEN TO THE CORE, BUT HUMBLE (ONCE)

Read | Kings 21
Memorize | Kings 21:29

One of the most memorably bad kings of Israel was Ahab. You just read several stories from his life, so you know why. He was as bad as the most corrupt politician you can imagine. The biblical text points out—several times—that he was worse than all who went before him. But there's also no denying that Ahab has an interesting personality that you can't help but laugh at sometimes.

God has chosen several incidents from Ahab's life to include in Scripture. Let's see how each of them fits into the big story of Creation, Fall, Redemption.

Ahab and Ben-hadad

Ahab isn't just any king of some random country. He is Israel's king. The leader of ten tribes of God's chosen people. In spite of his pattern of sin, God continues to give him mercy. As the huge army of Syria amasses on Ahab's doorstep, God sends a prophet to him to predict Israel's victory.

Ahab seems to have enough religious sense to know what to do. Just because he worshiped other gods didn't mean he knew nothing about Yahweh. Ahab asks the prophet who should lead the charge against the enemy, and Ahab doesn't seem to flinch when God chooses a small number of inexperienced servants as the advanced fighting force. God is using the same tactic he used with Gideon: the smaller and less imposing the army, the more glory goes to the Lord.

And that's exactly the point of this brief story. The prophet tells Ahab that the purpose of this divine intervention is that "thou [you singular, referring to King Ahab] shalt know that I am the Lord" (1 Kings 20:13). This victory will be a merciful message straight from God to the wicked king ruling over a portion of His chosen people.

At God's direction an inexperienced Israelite advance force is sent out and causes a panic in the massive Syrian army. And God gets great glory.

But God has more to teach His people through Ahab's fight with the Syrians. The following year, the Syrians give God an easy setup. Ben-hadad's advisors assure him that the reason they lost is obvious: they say the god of the Israelites is a god of the hills. If they fight Ahab's forces on the plains instead, they'll surely win. (That would be like your local high school football team saying they lost to the Green Bay Packers only because the NFL team had the home-field advantage.)

But the particular God being discussed happens to be a God of both the hills and the valleys—and of enemy war councils. So a prophet soon tells Ahab what his enemies have said as well as what God is going to do to reveal the truth. This time, however, there's a subtle shift in what the prophet says. The purpose of this divine intervention is that "ye [this time the word *you* is plural] shall know that I am the Lord" (20:28).

You and You

What's the difference between "I want you to wash the car" and "I want you to wash the car"? They look the same, but the same exact English word—*you*—can mean one person or a group of people. Context is the clue you need: if there's no one standing there but you, it's obvious what your mom means. But if she gestures to your siblings, too, then the *you* is plural. (Or in certain parts of the United States, she might say, "y'all" or "you guys," and that would make it clear.)

But over four hundred years ago, when the King James Version was translated, English still had two different words for singular *you* and plural *you*. Mothers in that day could say to one child, "I desire that *thou* shouldst wash the horse"—or they could say to all their children, "I desire that *ye* should wash the horse." *Thou* is singular. *Ye* is plural.

If you are reading a modern translation, and if for some reason you want to know whether the word *you* in a certain verse is singular or plural, you can check the King James.

The plural is used here because God wants the whole nation of Israel to see that He is God of hills, valleys, oceans, and any other geographical feature you can think of. God was going to use Ahab's victory to show the whole watching world that the Lord is God over the whole watching world!

That's why this little story of Ahab vs. Benhadad is in the big story of the Bible.

Ahab and Naboth

Ahab actually has nothing up his sleeve when he asks Naboth if he can buy his vineyard. He offers to pay for it, fair and square. But what Ahab doesn't appear to know or care about is that some families in his land still seek to follow God's laws. If you had been one of God's chosen people in Israel, you wouldn't have been allowed to sell the family land (Num. 36:7); God wanted that land to provide for generation after generation of your family. He didn't want the rich to gobble it up. So Naboth refuses Ahab's offer, and he gives the Lord's command as his reason.

Ahab is something of a wimp. When he doesn't get his way, he goes home and sulks. But Ahab married someone who knew how to get things done: a non-Jew—Jezebel, daughter of the king of the Baal-worshiping Sidonians (a city-state on the sea at the edge of Israelite territory).

Jezebel manages to get Ahab the vineyard by bribing some good-for-nothings to lie about Naboth. In the end, Naboth lies dead, and Ahab takes the vineyard.

The Lord doesn't hold only Jezebel responsible for this theft and murder even though she's the one who conceived it and had it carried out. Ahab, by passively allowing it to happen, also bears guilt.

So God's reaction as reported through His prophet Elijah is swift (1 Kings 21:21–24): Ahab will die, and so will Jezebel. And every male in Ahab's family!

Ahab's Humility?

There's no way you could have predicted what happens next. Ahab actually takes Elijah seriously! It's the last thing anyone would have expected: Ahab "rent his clothes, and put sackcloth upon his flesh, and fasted, and lay in sackcloth, and went softly" (1 Kings 21:27).

"Went softly" just means he went around meekly, dejectedly.

The Bible teaches that every person has a conscience, whether or not he is a believer in Yahweh (Rom. 2:14–15). The effects of sin are incredibly deep, reaching down to our innermost souls. But sin hasn't ruined everything. God made us in His image, and God's common grace can restrain even wicked people from always doing the worst possible things all the time. Even Hitler fed his dog.

> "The mercy of God cannot be explained. But it can be received. King Ahab received free grace because he was a needy sinner. . . . It was not too late for Ahab [to repent], and if it was not too late for him, it is never too late for anyone!"
>
> —**Phillip Graham Ryken**

Humility and repentance, even in one of the wickedest kings Israel ever had, were accepted by God. He promises to delay some of His judgment on Ahab's house. Apparently, God is so eager to show mercy and grace to His covenant people that He doesn't need much of a reason. Truly, the mercy of God reaches very, very deep. As deep as sin in the human heart.

Ahab and the False Prophets

So Ahab lives to fight another battle. And in 1 Kings 22, he even joins up with Jehoshaphat, king of Judah.

The battle this time is—again—with the Syrian king who should have been killed by Ahab three years before. It seems King Ben-hadad hasn't given up the cities he had promised to return to Israelite control. He's still holding on to Ramoth-gilead.

Jehoshaphat—a king who wants to please the Lord—can tell immediately that something is wrong with Ahab's prophets. All four hundred of them are telling Ahab to go for it: "Fight the battle!

Ahab will win!" They all agree. But Jehoshaphat wants one more prophet—one who will really speak for God.

> "God's inactivity is really patience in disguise."
>
> —Iain Provan

Ahab knows just who to call, but he doesn't want to. "I hate him," he explains helpfully. "He doth not prophesy good concerning me, but evil." Jehoshaphat basically replies, "Oh, don't say that!" (1 Kings 22:8). So the prophet comes. Micaiah is his name.

He opens with some of the most obvious sarcasm in the Bible. Paraphrasing again: "You'll totally own the Syrians, O king! The Lord will most definitely give you the victory!"

But perhaps Ahab picks up on the prophet's facial expression. Or perhaps he knows that his own four hundred prophets tell him only what he wants to hear. So he tells Micaiah, "Just go ahead and tell me the truth!"

He does, and the truth isn't very pretty. God's people will be scattered without a shepherd, Micaiah says. That means no Ahab.

Whether Ahab cared or not, he and his people were in a special covenant relationship with the God of the universe. And way back in Deuteronomy 28, in the list of curses God threatened if the Israelites violated the covenant, He promised something quite simple: "The Lord shall cause thee to be smitten before thine enemies" (Deut. 28:25). Ahab had led his people to worship idols. God's amazing mercy on him was running out. He was about to suffer a covenant curse.

Ahab Suffers the Curse

And so ends the life of one of Israel's most notorious kings. The only other important details are that (1) God's judgment did fall on Ahab's son, who reigned for just two years (1 Kings 22:51) and (2) the Bible makes a curious comment about Ahab's death. It says an enemy archer drew his bow "at a venture"—other translations say "at random"—and shot Ahab fatally through a chink in his armor (22:34). Ahab had disguised himself and tried to hide, but he couldn't escape God's judgment.

Over and over again, humans test God's limits—and then find that sin is far more dangerous and far more serious than they ever imagined. Ahab could turn his back on the Lord, worshiping idols and leading his people to do the same. Ahab could pretend he never saw God send fire from heaven. He could insist that Baal really was on vacation and just didn't want to bother with beating Yahweh in a competition.

But in the end Ahab couldn't avoid the truth. He couldn't erase the covenant. Its blessings came to him (despite his wickedness), and then later its curses fell on him too.

Like Ahab, nonbelievers are enjoying God's blessings. And like Ahab, they ignore and suppress the evidence all around them that the Creator reigns. If there's any more compelling evidence than fire falling from heaven, it's the fact that our amazing world exists at all. Judgment will fall on those who reject God, especially those who, like Ahab and like us, ought to know better.

Thinking It Through 6.3

1. What tactic did God use to win the first victory over the king of Syria? Why did God arrange it this way?

2. What did God prove in the second victory over the Syrians?

3. Why would God be merciful to deliver the sinful nation of Israel and its sinful leaders like Ahab? (1 Kings 20:13)

4. List at least three ways God was merciful to Ahab.

5. How do the stories of Ahab's various responses to the Lord show us both the greatness and limitations of God's mercy?

6.4 NAAMAN: MICROCOSM OF ELISHA'S MINISTRY AND GOD'S SALVATION

Read 2 Kings 5
Memorize 2 Kings 5:15b

Two lessons ago, you read about Elijah's fleeing from Jezebel. During his time on the run, Elijah finds a cave and lodges there. This is his own self-pity party. While he is sulking, the word of the Lord comes to him and asks him, "What doest thou here, Elijah?" (1 Kings 19:9).

Elijah replies that he has been very zealous for the Lord, but the children of Israel have forsaken the covenant and killed the prophets. He exclaims, "I, even I only, am left; and they seek my life, to take it away!" (19:10).

The Lord replies softly to Elijah that he is to go anoint Jehu king over Israel. And then he must go anoint Elisha as prophet in his place. Then the Lord assures him that there are in fact seven thousand people in Israel who have not bowed the knee to Baal.

Elijah is not the only one left. It's time he ends his pity-party.

When Elijah finds Elisha, the young prophet-to-be is plowing in the field with twelve pair of oxen. Elijah speaks no words. He simply walks by Elisha and throws his mantle (like a sleeveless coat or a cloak) on him.

It takes a minute for Elisha to figure out what is happening. When he does gather his thoughts, he runs after Elijah and asks if he can kiss his father and mother goodbye. Elijah responds, "Go back, again: for what have I done to thee?" (19:20). Elijah is basically saying, "I did not call you. God did. Now decide what you should do."

Elisha's actions reflect his decision. He goes back, sacrifices the oxen, and uses his plow and tools as firewood to cook the meat. He feeds his family and friends. And then he leaves them and the farm to follow after and minister to Elijah.

After Elisha's calling we hear nothing at all about him until Elijah is taken up into heaven. Just before that happens, Elisha asks Elijah for a "double portion" of the spirit that rests upon him. Elijah tells Elisha, "If thou see me when I am taken from thee, it shall be so unto thee" (2 Kings 2:10).

And it was so. Elisha saw Elijah being taken up into heaven by a whirlwind.

Elisha's ministry would now begin, and its impact would be greater than that of his teacher's. He would do greater miracles than his teacher, and he would do more of them. He would minister to kings, to widows, to Jews, and to Gentiles. Leaders would come from afar to seek his counsel (2 Kings 3:10–12).

This lesson tells about one such Gentile leader that Elisha ministers to. It represents in a small way Elisha's ministry, but more importantly, it represents what God is doing in the larger story of Scripture.

Microcosms

A microcosm is literally a "small world." (Did you notice the prefix *micro-*?) Elisha's ministry to Naaman is a microcosm—a small picture of a big reality—just as a model ship is sort of a microcosm of a big one. A city can be a microcosm of its whole country, reflecting the same issues the whole nation is facing.

And every little salvation in the Bible is a microcosm. It's a small picture of the big salvation coming to all the earth on the day when God will restore the world to the way it ought to be.

Likewise, every little judgment in the Bible is a microcosm of the big judgment coming one day, something the Bible calls "the Day of the Lord."

The story of Naaman's healing is a microcosm of both God's salvation (Naaman) and God's judgment (Gehazi). (It also shows the

Memory Tip

Do you ever have trouble remembering who came first—Elijah or Elisha? A little mnemonic (a memory device) will help you easily recall who came first. They came in alphabetical order—Elijah then Elisha.

availability of God's salvation to Gentiles and His judgment on His own people when they sin.) In this story, God heals an ugly disease and restores a man's skin to the smoothness of a baby's. In it, an enemy of God becomes a submissive servant of Yahweh.

And in it, God fulfills a little bit of the promise He made to David in 2 Samuel 7. Here's a reminder of what He said all those years before:

> I will appoint a place for my people Israel, and will plant them, that they may dwell in a place of their own, and move no more; neither shall the children of wickedness afflict them any more, as beforetime, and as since the time that I commanded judges to be over my people Israel, and have caused thee to rest from all thine enemies. (2 Sam. 7:10–11)

One key to understanding the Bible is seeing that God likes to illustrate the future with the present. He keeps giving little tastes of the big feast that will one day be ours. The Naaman story is one of those tastes because it shows one way God can keep the children of wickedness from afflicting His people: He can turn them into His people! What happened to Naaman is a microcosm of the huge salvation God will one day bring to Israel and the world, including the Gentile nations, just as God had promised when he told Abraham that He would bless all the nations of the world through him.

Reading Carefully

Where does the story of Naaman fit into the story of Kings? It fits in, obviously, sometime during the ministry of the prophet Elisha. It fits, sadly, in the middle of a long period of decline for the Northern Kingdom of Israel.

But God hasn't let that decline go on without any action to restrain it. Do you remember King Ahab's two victories over the Syrian king Ben-hadad, who was Naaman's "boss"? And do you remember the purpose of those victories?

Ben-hadad's men think they lost the first battle because Israel's God is a god of the hills (1 Kings 20:23). God brings Israel victory a second time because He wants the whole nation of Israel to see that He is God of hills, valleys, oceans, and any other geographical feature you

God Rules

There's one very interesting little note to make about an off-hand comment in the introduction to this story. Scripture says that Naaman the Syrian was high in his master's favor "because by him the Lord had given deliverance unto Syria" (2 Kings 5:1). The God of all hills, valleys, oceans, and everywhere doesn't give victory (or defeat) only to His people. If victories and defeats happen in other places, Yahweh is also the source. He hands victory to one side and defeat to the other for His own purposes. And this isn't the first indication in the book that God rules Syria as well as Israel. Back in 1 Kings 19, God called His own prophet Elijah to go anoint the next Syrian king! God is the great King of the book of Kings.

can think of. He actually uses Ahab's victory to show the whole watching world that the Lord is God over the whole watching world!

At least one Syrian gets the message that God sends through Ahab's victory over Ben-hadad. But it takes a little more convincing for him to fully believe it.

That Syrian is, of course, Naaman. And though his troops initially lose to Ahab, they later beat him. In fact, they kill him. And in all the mess of war, Naaman ends up with an Israelite slave girl who becomes a servant to his wife.

A Priestess to the Nation of Syria

This little slave girl is doing something her nation is supposed to do and yet isn't doing: she is being a "priestess" to the nations. She's showing what God was like to Syrian Gentiles—the very people who stole her from her home and forced her into servitude. Instead of becoming bitter and sullen, she expresses concern for her owner and master. She recommends that he go to Elisha the prophet.

Her little testimony is enough, and Naaman is desperate for help. So the Syrian king sends a message on Naaman's behalf to the king of Israel (Jehoram, Ahab's son). Jehoram is supposed to heal Naaman!

Healing Power

The Syrian king doesn't know that the Israelite king has no such ability and that no amount of money can buy the healing power that belongs to Yahweh alone.

Elisha knows, however. And he wants Naaman to know. In order to make the message clear, Elisha doesn't even go out to meet Naaman and his huge, impressive retinue of soldiers and servants, horses and chariots. Elisha simply sends a message: "Go dip in the Jordan seven times."

At first Naaman is angry. Livid. "Dip in the Jordan?! We've got our own rivers in Syria! Where's the guy's magic wand? If he were truly powerful, I'd be cured by now! We're outta here!"

A slave girl took up the call of God for one nation to represent God to other nations.

> "From Genesis 12:2–3 onward in the Old Testament, God desires to bless all nations through Israel. This ideal becomes a reality here due to the witness of the Israelite servant girl and the work of the Israelite prophet."
>
> **—Paul R. House**

But the great and powerful Naaman is either humble or desperate enough to listen—again—to his servants.

Depth of Mercy

God has stored up some mercy for Naaman, and it's waiting in the Jordan River. As Naaman comes up for the seventh time, it's not just his skin that's fixed. Something inside Naaman's very heart is mysteriously changed.

This Syrian general now gets it. He has understood the implications of his own amazing story. It's not enough for him to say, "Now I know that only the Lord God of Israel can truly heal." No, Naaman echoes Deuteronomy 6:4 ("The Lord our God, the Lord is one") and says quite clearly, "Now I know that only the Lord God of Israel truly exists."

Naaman has gone from a polytheistic idolater to a worshiper of the one true and living God in seven dips.

Naaman's request for clemency (2 Kings 5:18) for having to go into the house of an idol shows that he really and truly does understand and believe Yahweh's claim to uniqueness. Yahweh isn't a god among other gods. He's the only God.

Lessons Learned

So what does this story tell us? In light of all we've read about God's purposes on earth and in the disobedient nation of Israel, there are some obvious lessons:

- God is intent on blessing all nations, not just Israel. Many lepers lived in Israel in Naaman's day, but he, a Gentile, was the only one who got healed (Luke 4:27).

FAITH & HEALING

Gehazi's lack of faith led him to leprosy.

Naaman's healing led him to faith.

- It is a terrible shame to God's chosen people that while their own king wickedly follows idols in Dan and Bethel, a foreign dignitary confesses belief in Yahweh (Isa. 66:18).
- A faithful little Israelite slave girl did more to bless the nations than any of the great men in her native land. God uses the weak things of this world to shame the mighty (1 Cor. 1:27).

Gehazi

The little subplot of Gehazi follows the story of Naaman. In it, Gehazi gets the leprosy Naaman had—right after Naaman got the faith Gehazi had (or was supposed to have). Gehazi sees more value in Naaman's money than in faithfulness to the God who just miraculously healed a Gentile leper.

The healing Naaman experienced was a miracle, but one that didn't last forever. He still died.

The real miracle took place inside Naaman. He experienced a cleansing that water, no matter how holy, could ever produce. That cleansing is one every Jew and every Gentile still needs today.

Thinking It Through 6.4

1. What is a microcosm? How does the story of Naaman and Gehazi function as a microcosm?

2. List two ways God favored Naaman before he ever went to see Elisha. What covenant promise of God is the basis of His blessing on a Gentile?

3. What are some indications that Naaman's healing was internal as well as external?

4. Why would Naaman have been an unlikely candidate for God's salvation? (Matt. 19:23; 1 Cor. 1:27; Rom. 10:14; Deut. 7:6; Rom. 9:4)

5. Contrast Gehazi with Naaman.

6.5 ELISHA: THE MAN OF GOD

Read 2 Kings 6:24–7:20
Memorize 2 Kings 7:17

When Elisha came on the scene, the nation of Israel and its leaders were practicing idolatry. The leaders had caused the people to sin and would often provoke the anger of the Lord. The nation needed someone to stand against the wicked and to oppose their idolatry. They needed a man of God to carry on what Elijah was doing.

Man of God

The title "man of God" is used of prophets and leaders of Israel. Like Moses and Elijah, Elisha is called the man of God (others refer to him more than thirty times as the man of God in 2 Kings). The title shows that Elisha is God's servant, and as such he is part of a unique line of men who bring the word of God to the nation of Israel.

As you read in the last lesson, Elisha had asked Elijah for a double-portion of his spirit to come upon him. When Elisha saw Elijah taken up in a whirlwind, his request was granted—he would have a double portion. He would need that double portion as he confronted the wickedness of the people and their rulers. Thus, Elisha's role would be similar to Elijah's role—but his influence would be heightened.

What exactly was that role? Several themes are repeated throughout Elisha's ministry—themes similar to those emphasized throughout Elijah's ministry: the Lord God rules over the earth (2 Kings 3:17–20), controlling the nations and their kings (8:7–15). And the Lord God rules over nature, healing the lepers (5:1–14). But both the rulers and the people in the nations of Israel and Judah disobey and refuse to repent.

Perhaps the most daunting task of Elisha's ministry was to confront Israel's kings when they sinned against God. Elisha makes it clear that he wants nothing to do with the wicked king Joram, but he prophesies to him because of his respect for Jehoshaphat (3:13–19). Although the task was daunting, God's task for His prophets was for them to confront the constant sinning of the nations of Israel and Judah in order to call them back to covenant faithfulness. Despite the numerous miracles that Elisha performed, most of the people refused to repent—they refused to turn from their sin to God.

But Elisha dealt with more than kings and leaders. His ministry was also one of comfort to the hurting. Many of his miracles involved ordinary people who, for example, couldn't pay a debt (4:1–7) or whose son had died (4:18–37). In these accounts God shows His power over nature; He showed His power to deliver the weak and the helpless who put their faith in Him.

Not a King

Elisha was a man of God. And in some ways, he was like Joshua, the second leader of Israel. Both Joshua and Elisha succeeded a man of God (Moses and Elijah respectively), and both of their names deal with salvation. Elisha means "my God saves," and Joshua means "Yahweh saves."

> "[Elisha] is presented not as an alternative to the political and social structures of monarchy, but as a supplement, designed to influence those structures toward proper behavior."
>
> —Amy Balogh

But Elisha was different from Joshua. Elisha was not meant to be the political leader of Israel, nor was he meant to be like a king to them. His job was to remind the kings and leaders of Israel that God, and not Baal, ruled. He was also to confront the sins of the people and point them toward what God demanded for them to do in the covenant. Prophets called the nation to covenant faithfulness.

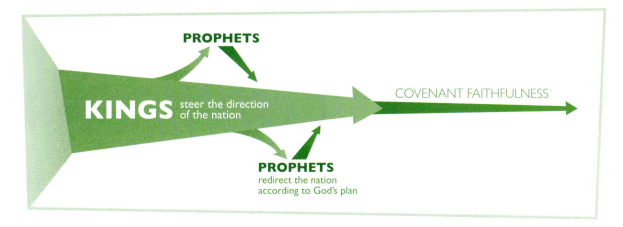

PROPHETS

KINGS steer the direction of the nation

COVENANT FAITHFULNESS

PROPHETS
redirect the nation
according to God's plan

A Bleak Situation

Sometimes Elisha's job was to give good news to the nation, but even that good news was often given alongside a message of judgment for others in the nation. As the story opens, Israel is once again in the middle of a conflict, and this time it is with Ben-hadad, the king of Syria. Ben-hadad has laid siege to Samaria, which is the capital of the Northern Kingdom of Israel.

Besieging a city is a long and complicated process, and it was preferred to a direct assault on a city. Directly attacking a city was a difficult military operation, especially if the city had good defenses with dedicated and experienced soldiers. Some armies could not afford to lose numerous soldiers assaulting a city. So instead of invading a city, the army would surround the city with the intent of conquering by attrition. Attrition is a military strategy in which an army attempts to break down the enemy by limiting one or more resources. In this case, Syria is seeking to wear down Samaria by limiting its food supply. No food or other goods can come into the city.

Evidently, the siege has been going on for quite some time, for when the narrative opens, we see Samaria in the middle of a great famine. It is so severe that disgusting things are considered valuable—a donkey's head sells for eighty pieces of silver and dove's dung for five pieces. Most likely the people are eating the donkey's head and using the dung for fuel for cooking.

The famine is actually worse than merely causing people to be desperate enough to eat a donkey's head. It is much worse.

A Powerless and Godless King

One day the king is walking along the wall and a woman cries out, "Help, my lord, O King" (2 Kings 6:26). The king sarcastically says, "If the Lord do not help thee, whence shall I help thee? Out of the barnfloor, or out of the winepress?" (6:27). In other words, "If God doesn't give you any food, where do you think I'm going to get it from?"

He asks, "What aileth thee?" (6:28).

But he is not prepared to hear her answer.

She says, "This woman said unto me, Give thy son, that we may eat him to day, and we will eat my son to morrow. So we boiled my son, and did eat him: and I said unto her on the next day, Give thy son, that we may eat him: and she hath hid her son" (6:28–29).

Cannibalism.

The city of Samaria in Israel, the chosen nation of God, is resorting to cannibalism.

Worse than that, the woman shows no remorse or regret for killing her son and eating him. She is upset only because she can't kill the other woman's son and eat him too.

She is right about one thing: she needs help. And so does Israel. Perhaps the king will turn to God and ask for help.

He does turn to God, but not for help. He turns to God to blame both Him and His prophet Elisha for the problems the nation is facing. In fact, the king determines to send a messenger to kill Elisha before the day is over.

Elisha Promises Food

When the messenger arrives at Elisha's house, he does not kill Elisha. Instead, he blames God for the disaster and asks why he should wait on the Lord any longer (6:33). His logic is absurd. God caused the disaster, but God can't stop the disaster? His words soon reveal his logic comes from his unbelief.

Elisha tells him, "Hear ye the word of the Lord; Thus saith the Lord, To morrow about this time shall a measure of fine flour be sold for a shekel [a small amount of money], and two measures of barley for a shekel, in the gate of Samaria" (7:1).

The royal officer responds, "Behold, if the Lord would make windows in heaven, might this thing be?" (7:2).

His use of the interjection *behold* is significant. It shows his resolve for his unbelief. He is basically saying, "Look! I don't believe a word you're saying, Elisha. Even God Himself couldn't make that happen."

Not only is he calling Elisha a liar, but he is dismissing what the Lord said through Elisha. And that dismissal brings a harsh rebuke. Elisha responds with his own "behold" to show the certainty of what God says: "Behold, thou shalt see it with thine eyes, but shalt not eat thereof" (7:2).

An Army on the Run

The army outside the gates of Samaria is a powerful army, but they are not invincible.

At the gate of the city sit four lepers. These men are outcasts and are not allowed to live in the city. They are forced to sit there and wait—wait until they die.

And it appears that they will die, but it will not be the way they thought it would be. Most likely they will die of starvation and not from their leprosy. And that doesn't sit too well with them.

So they concoct a plan: "If we stay here we die. If we go into the city we die. But if we go into the camp of the Syrians, perhaps they will let us live and give us food. If they don't, then we die there. So going into the camp is our only hope."

And off they go.

As the four lepers make their way to the camp, the Syrians hear a noise—a great noise

---

The Gate of the City

The gate of a city was much more than a place to enter or exit the city. It was often the center of city life. Men of God would deliver their messages at the gate (Neh. 8:1, 3; Jer. 17:19–20). Kings and elders would meet at the gate to administer justice (Josh. 20:4; 2 Sam. 19:8). Men would conduct business at the gate and use the elders at the gate for witnesses of the agreements made there (Ruth 4:1–12). People would buy and sell merchandise at the city (Neh. 13:15–22). Some gates were called by the name of the merchandise sold there (Sheep Gate in Neh. 3:1, 32; Fish Gate in 2 Chron. 33:14).

That is why Elisha tells the royal messenger that there will be food sold at the gate of the city. You can imagine the chaos that would ensue when the food is brought to the gate. After all, the people are starving, and they will be eager to buy food. That is why the king sends that same messenger to take charge of the gate lest chaos ensue.

---

that sounds like horses and chariots and a great army charging after them—and they flee. In fact, the army departs so quickly that they leave their tents and their horses, and they even leave a trail of clothes and equipment behind them all the way to the river.

A Promise of Life and Death Fulfilled

So when the lepers arrive at the campsite, there is no one there—just food, tents, goods, and horses. And it is all for the taking. And take they do! They begin to rob the tents and go and hide their newfound treasure. They gorge themselves on the food until they feel guilty about what they are doing.

Then the lepers begin to say to one another that this isn't right. They shouldn't be eating all this food while the city starves. So they decide to go and tell the people at the city gate what they have found.

You can imagine what the gatekeepers think of four outcast lepers standing at the gate telling

And the messenger that had talked to Elisha sees it all. He is at the gate attempting to keep order when the mob of starving people trample him to death while struggling to get to the food. He saw the food, but he did not eat it—just as Elisha had said.

The Certainty of God's Prophetic Word

At the end of 2 Kings 7, the author emphasizes that God's word is certain. Notice how the author reiterates the prophecy and says that it happened just as the man of God had spoken and "according to the word of the Lord" (7:16). In fact, he retells the confrontation between the royal servant and Elisha, and he specifically points out that it happened exactly as the prophet said it would.

In the end, God had mercy on a nation and judged an individual. In His mercy, God showed the nation that His word of promise—food in the midst of the siege—was certain. Even though their king and their leaders didn't turn to God for help, they could trust in God. They could trust His word that came through His prophet. God likewise shows the nation that His word of judgment—the royal servant would see but not eat—was certain.

God's faithfulness in keeping His word on such a small scale would show Israel that He is able to keep His word on a larger scale. What God had promised Abraham, He will do, and He will do it in a powerful way.

them about all the food and the army that had vanished. The gatekeepers don't believe them. And neither does the king. He figures it is some kind of trap. Once they leave the city to get the food, the enemy will come out of hiding and pounce on them.

But one servant believes them, and he suggests to the king to send a few men to check it out. If they go out and die, so what? They're going to die in the city anyway.

So the king lets a few men go out and see about the camp. And everything that the lepers have said is true. And so the fine flour is sold for a shekel and the two measures of barley are sold for a shekel at the gates of Samaria—just as Elisha has said.

Thinking It Through 6.5

1. What are two major themes of Elisha's ministry?

2. How are these two major themes related to Elisha's role in ministry?

3. Distinguish the role of the prophet from the role of the king.

4. Describe the conditions of Samaria under siege by Ben-hadad, king of Syria. How did the people respond to those conditions? Why was the response of the messenger to the king so absurd?

5. What did Elisha prophesy? How was it fulfilled?

6.6 OBADIAH, JOEL, AND ZEPHANIAH: THE DAY OF THE LORD

Read Obadiah 1:1–21
Memorize Joel 2:1–2

Introduction to the Prophets

The last seventeen books of the English Bible are called the Prophets. The Prophets are divided into the five books of the Major Prophets (Isaiah–Daniel) and the twelve Minor Prophets (Hosea–Malachi). Each of these prophets ministered during the time of the divided kingdom. They had to confront wicked kings and the evils that existed during this turbulent time in Israel's history. Some of them spoke about the Day of the Lord, and some of them never mentioned it.

Those who did speak about it used the phrase to refer both to God's immediate judgment on the nations and also to God's future judgment on the world. For us in the twenty-first century, some of those prophecies have already been fulfilled. There are numerous prophecies that have not been fulfilled and point to a time in the future when God will judge the nations and bless the world.

The Day of the Lord

In late 2016, months without rain and unseasonably warm temperatures left the southeastern United States in a precarious situation. The ground was parched. Leaves, both on and off the trees, were crisp and dry. A perfect recipe for a forest fire. Add a steady wind and you have the recipe for massive forest fires. And that is exactly what happened—the fires came.

Fires raged across multiple states and destroyed tens of thousands of acres. Thousands were evacuated from their homes—many of which were destroyed. The fires moved so quickly that one small town was almost completely lost. The fires were so large that cities hundreds of miles away were dealing with the ensuing thick smoke. In these faraway cities, visibility was limited to less than a thousand feet. And within the fire zone, the smoke was so thick that it blocked out the sun and made it appear to be late evening when it was in fact noon.

Only a few hundred miles east, other cities were recovering from a massive hurricane that brought intense rain and extensive flooding. It seemed as though things were bleak and dark for these states. The devastation was real. And it was massive. We don't know when natural disasters are a direct punishment from God, or when they have occurred simply because we live in a sin-cursed world. But these disasters pale in comparison to the judgment that God will bring upon the world in a time called "The Day of the Lord."

Forest fires and hurricanes pale in comparison to the judgment God will one day bring upon the world.

The Nature of the Day of the Lord

Many of the prophets use the phrase "Day of the Lord" to emphasize a unique time when God will intervene in human history in a climactic way.

The Day of the Lord has two parts to its nature (what it will be like). In one part, God will pour out His divine wrath to punish His enemies. The prophets speak of natural disasters (Joel 1:19–20), armies gathering against other armies (Isa. 13:4), and supernatural disasters (Joel 2:2–11). In the other part, God will pour out His blessings on His people—in particular, the nation of Israel. The Day of the Lord is a time of great judgment, but it is also a time of great blessing. The prophets speak of God's absolute sovereignty over the universe and His overpowering victories over His enemies.

The timing of the Day of the Lord is another important concept throughout the prophets. The prophets use the phrase with two timeframes in view: Sometimes the prophecy has near fulfillment—it specifies a time when God would soon execute His judgment, taking care of injustice and oppression. Other times the prophecy concerns far fulfillment—it refers to a future time when God will judge all the nations of the world and establish the Messianic Kingdom. The near fulfillment mainly provides an illustration of what God will one day finally and fully accomplish in the actual climactic Day of the Lord.

The Purpose of the Day of the Lord

The purpose of the Day of the Lord is to finally and fully restore God's creation. It is a time for God to judge sin, followed by His blessings. It is a time for God Himself to intervene in order to reestablish His rule on earth. The ultimate goal is to free God's people from the source of sin, from those who love to sin, and from the effects of sin on both humanity and the world.

Three prophets who spoke about the Day of the Lord are Obadiah, Joel, and Zephaniah.

Obadiah

The book of Obadiah is the shortest book in the Bible. We know little about the prophet Obadiah, who delivered the message. It is difficult to say exactly when he prophesied, but most likely it was during the reign of King Jehoram in Judah (848–841 BC).

During Jehoram's reign, the nation of Edom revolted against Judah. Edom was a descendant of Esau, and from the beginnings of the two nations (even the beginnings of their fathers) they did not have a good relationship.

Edom was able to convince other nations to help them attack Judah (2 Chron. 21:16–17). They partially destroyed Jerusalem and wreaked havoc among the people. It was a dark time for Judah, and it seemed that the wicked nations were prospering at Judah's expense. "Why, oh why is this happening?" they wondered.

Following Edom's rebellion, the Edomites grew proud and thought that the mountains surrounding them made them invincible. It seemed that both Israel and Judah would have to live in terror, knowing that a cruel and unmerciful enemy lived just outside their borders.

But God didn't wish for His people to live in fear. And He sent Obadiah with a message: judgment for God's enemies and salvation for His people. Obadiah's message was meant to encourage God's people that the Lord was going to step in and take care of Edom. The Day of the Lord would come upon Edom.

Obadiah said that Edom would be humbled and brought down to earth. Their homes nestled high in the mountains would provide no protection for them. Robbers would come in and steal everything, and what they did not steal, they would destroy. The nation would have no one to turn to for help because its friends would forsake it, and God would destroy even the wisest of its men.

When Edom had rebelled against Judah, the Edomites stood idly by and watched others loot and destroy Jerusalem. Even worse, Edom itself joined in, violently destroying the people of Jerusalem—people who were their brothers and sisters. God declared that, at the Day of the Lord, that same violence would come against Edom.

Many of the prophecies in Obadiah's message have been fulfilled. The Edomites saw their destruction in numerous battles that reached their climax when the Roman general Titus defeated them in AD 70.

But not all of Obadiah's prophecies were ful-filled. Obadiah says that the Day of the Lord will come upon "all heathen," but at that time, Israel will have a place of escape. The nation will be like a fire devouring all its enemies. And Israel will possess the land that God has promised. Those prophecies will be fulfilled when Christ returns to earth.

> "For the day of the Lord is
> near upon all the heathen:
> as thou hast done,
> it shall be done unto thee:
> thy reward shall return
> upon thine own head."
>
> **—Obadiah 1:15**

Joel

Joel is another prophet that we know little about, and most likely he prophesied a few years after Obadiah. Joash would have been king of Judah when Joel prophesied (835 BC).

Shortly before Joel began prophesying, a locust plague had devastated the land. The modern Western world knows very little about locust plagues. When locusts swarm, they can be so numerous that they turn the midday sky into night. It is not uncommon for a plague to cover more than a hundred thousand square miles with the locusts eating every plant in their path. The results are devastating. Food immediately becomes scarce. The death of the locusts brings disease in both humans and animals. And on top of all that, there is an awful stench left behind.

Joel starts his prophecy by talking about the recent locust plague that had come upon Judah. He describes the locusts as a nation without number and as having teeth like a lion. They have devoured everything in their path.

This is not the first time Israel has been through a locust plague. They know that the plague is a dark time (both literally and figura-tively), and they know that a darker time will follow—famine, sickness, and death.

Joel takes his cue from their knowledge and tells them that the Day of the Lord will be like that locust plague. And it will be on both God's enemies and His own people. He says that they should blow a trumpet and sound an alarm to warn the people of the impending danger:

Let all the inhabitants of the land tremble:

For the day of the Lord cometh,
    for it is nigh at hand;
A day of darkness and of gloominess,
    a day of clouds and of thick darkness,
as the morning spread upon the mountains:
    a great people and a strong;
there hath not been ever the like,
    neither shall be any more after it,
    even to the years of many
        generations. (Joel 2:1b–2)

Joel continues to describe how horrible this time will be. But there is hope. And in order to see this hope, Israel must return to the Lord with fasting and weeping (2:12). This includes everyone—the people, the elders, the children, the infants, and the bride and groom. Even the priests and the ministers must weep and repent. If they would do that, God would be gracious and merciful to them. Why? Because He is "of great kindness [*ḥesed*]" (2:13). In other words, He abounds in loving-kindness, or steadfast love, because He is the Lord their God and they are His people (2:17–18).

The hope that God gives is a hope of resto-ration—the restoration of His covenant blessing. God will restore what the locusts have devoured. They will have an abundance of food. More importantly, God will once again dwell with them. Why? Because God said, "I am the Lord your God, and none else: and my people shall never be ashamed" (2:27).

Joel's prophecy contains a promise of bless-ing. Joel prophesied that God would pour out His Holy Spirit with the result that "your sons and your daughters shall prophesy, your old men shall dream dreams, your young men shall see visions: And also upon the servants and upon the handmaids in those days will I pour out my spirit" (2:28–29).

The prophecy also includes a time of judgment for the nations. This future judgment will occur after the Second Coming of Christ (Matt. 25:31–46). During that time the nations will gather in a valley, and God will "sit to judge all the heathen" (Joel 3:12). It will be a dark time of judgment that will cause the heavens and the earth to shake.

But not all is dark and gloomy. God will provide for His people, and they shall have abundance of food and water to satisfy their needs. It will also be a time of peace, for God will have rid their land of their enemies. But most importantly, God will cleanse His people and forgive them for their sin (3:21).

Zephaniah

About two hundred years later (625 BC), God sent the prophet Zephaniah to preach a message of judgment. Josiah was king in Judah. He was a good king, but he was young. During his reign a spiritual revival began when Israel rediscovered the Law that they had neglected for years. God had sent Zephaniah to warn the people that they should turn from their sins to worship God.

Zephaniah preached that the coming destruction of Judah was an example of what the Day of the Lord would be like. The people of Judah would be taken captive, and many would die. Their land would be destroyed. But God would gather the nations together and visit them.

Zephaniah describes the Day of the Lord in vivid terms. He warns Judah that they must turn from worshiping Baal and turn to God.

> The great day of the Lord is near,
> it is near, and hasteth greatly,
> even the voice of the day of the Lord:
> the mighty man shall cry there bitterly.
> That day is a day of wrath,
> a day of trouble and distress,
> a day of wasteness and desolation,
> a day of darkness and gloominess,
> a day of clouds and thick darkness,
> A day of the trumpet and alarm

> against the fenced cities,
> and against the high towers.
> And I will bring distress upon men,
> that they shall walk like blind men,
> because they have sinned against the
> Lord. (Zeph. 1:14–17a)

These terrifying descriptions are why Zephaniah pleads with the people to seek the Lord before His fierce anger comes on them (2:1–3). It seems that the people are too far into idol worship to trust in the Lord and draw near to Him (3:1–7). Their punishment is certain.

It is not only Judah that will face the judgment of God, but all the nations of the earth will also face His judgment. This will be a time when God cleanses the nations so that they can call upon His name and serve Him (3:8–10).

Although the Day of the Lord will be a dark time of judgment, it will also be a time of restoration for Israel (3:11–13). This restoration will happen at the time of the future millennial kingdom. During this time, Israel will contain only meek and humble people who trust in God. God will have removed the proud and haughty.

It will also be a time of blessing for Israel (3:14–20). The Lord will have taken away their punishment and turned away their enemies. They will be in the land that God has promised them. Most importantly, He Himself will be with them, and they will have no reason to fear anyone or anything.

Conclusion

The Day of the Lord includes both judgment and blessing. The judgment will come upon both Israel and the nations of the world. The blessing will be a time when the Lord will establish His rule in the Messianic kingdom. As you progress through the rest of this textbook, the theme of the Day of the Lord will appear in many of the remaining Prophets. Each one of them highlights different aspects of the coming judgments and the coming blessings of the future kingdom.

The judgment in the Day of the Lord will far surpass the worst disasters known to the world today.

Current Events

God doesn't relate to New Testament believers today through the Mosaic Covenant curses and blessings. However, everyone lives in a fallen and broken world. Everyone depends on the promises of common grace that God gave through the Noahic Covenant—God will uphold and sustain the world until the end of the age. In the meantime, God demonstrates to all humankind that something is wrong with the world and needs to be made right. As you look around our world today, you will see many disasters occur each year. Tornadoes, hurricanes, earthquakes, tidal waves, forest fires, and flooding are a mere sample of these types of disasters. These all pale in comparison to what the judgment will be like in the Day of the Lord.

On the flip side, there are many blessings that we experience every day. Many of us have good food, clothing, shelter, and other comforts of life. But one day these things will also pale in comparison to what the Lord has planned for us in His Messianic kingdom and throughout our eternity with Him.

Thinking It Through 6.6

1. What does the phrase "the Day of the Lord" refer to?

2. What will the Day of the Lord be like? (There are two major parts.) When is the Day of the Lord?

3. What is God's ultimate purpose for the Day of the Lord?

4. After reading summaries about the Day of the Lord from Obadiah, Joel, and Zephaniah, you may have noticed that the Day of the Lord judgments come on Israel's enemy Edom, but the judgments also could come on both Israel and Judah. So what was the key for escaping God's judgments?

5. How does the Day of the Lord affect us as New Testament believers?

6.7 JOASH: GOOD UP TO A POINT

Read 2 Kings 11–12; 2 Chronicles 24:15–27
Memorize 2 Kings 11:17

If you were to look through some binoculars at two deer, one of them may edge off to the left and the other to the right. But you could still see both. As they move further apart, however, you can watch only one at a time. That's what it's like reading the book of Kings. Once the kingdom splits, the two come back into the same field of vision only a few times (like the times when Jehoshaphat makes an alliance with the Northern Kingdom). But mostly they run off in separate (though often similar) directions.

Which of those two kingdoms is, theologically speaking, more important? Both of them are full of people God chose to be His special possession forever. But only one of them contains Jerusalem, the city where God set His heart and His temple. And only one of them is ruled by a king from the line of David.

That's why 2 Kings 11 brings a serious problem. The Northern Kingdom of Israel and the Southern Kingdom of Judah have wandered back into a spot where we can see them both. And the sight isn't pretty. A granddaughter of the wicked Israelite king Omri is now the queen of Judah. When her son Ahaziah, the king, dies, she tries to kill the whole royal family and seize power.

We have to see this for what it is. Athaliah

is not just an individual queen trying to gain influence and authority. Depending on what translation you read, you may not have noticed that in 2 Kings 11:1 the keyword *seed* gets used. It's not a coincidence. Athaliah wants to destroy the royal seed. She's like Pharaoh, trying to kill off the line of promise by killing male Jewish babies. Only this time she has focused her wrath on the same narrow line on which God has focused His grace. She is trying to annihilate the line of David!

In fact, she succeeds in killing all of her own grandsons—except for one little guy named Joash. We are one murder away from the extinction of David's royal seed and the end of God's covenant promises. The seed of the serpent is coming as close as ever in history to crushing the seed of the woman. The "rod of men" that God promised to send against David's sinful seed has beaten David's line almost completely to death (2 Sam. 7:14).

But one tiny seed remains. Joash is in a safe place physically—the temple. And he's in an even safer place spiritually—the center of God's promise. God is acting to preserve His covenant with Joash's great-great-great-great-great-great-grandfather. David's line can't die out. God promised him a lamp that would never stop shining (2 Kings 8:19).

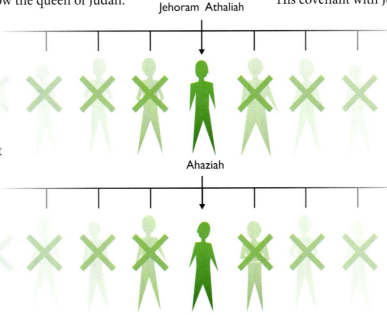

Jehoram Athaliah

Ahaziah

Joash

Shine, Joash, Shine

And in six years, shine he does. Led by the godly priest Jehoiada, people loyal to David's line are able to burn off the darkness in the land. They destroy Athaliah, the house of Baal, and Baal's high priest. They publicly reaffirm the covenant between the Lord and the people and between the people and the king.

Can we finally breathe a sigh of relief, sit back, and just enjoy reading about blessings for a change?

Not exactly. Joash, like Jehoshaphat, was a godly king overall—as long as Jehoiada was alive, at least. The 2 Kings summary of his life says so. But the stories God chooses to put in the Bible about Joash's kingship are not all flattering. He lets the temple go twenty-three years without being fixed, even though he did (rightly) provide money for the renovations. He gives up all his gold and the temple's gold to pay off Syria. Whenever a biblical king (even a godly one) has to do that, something is wrong. In the end Joash is murdered by his own servants at age forty-seven.

The End to Joash's Story

It seems that Joash is indeed a good and godly king—until the chief priest Jehoiada dies. Without that powerful, godly influence Joash begins to listen to people going in another direction. Soon he and other leaders in Judah abandon the house of the Lord and begin serving idols.

When God mercifully sends prophets—including Zechariah, the son of the priest who saved Joash's life and made him king—to warn Joash, Joash has Zechariah stoned. As he dies, he calls for the Lord to avenge his death.

And God does—using the Syrians, a favorite tool of His in those days. As the next-door neighbors of God's people, they have plenty of reasons to envy the Promised Land. They don't send very many men against Judah's large army, but that's totally irrelevant. God can use a small army to accomplish His purpose, and that's what He did in judgment of Joash (2 Chron. 24:23–24).

As a further indignity to Joash, his own servants plotted his murder specifically because he had no mercy on the son of his former father-figure, Jehoiada (24:25).

Idolatry Then and Now

It's probably hard to identify with Joash's turn to idolatry. What in the world was so attractive about Baal and Asherah?

But there are some applications we should make to ourselves. Just like Rehoboam, Joash wanted to please certain people, but they led him astray (24:17). Does that ever happen to you? It's not always obvious. People don't usually whip out hard drugs and wave them in front of your face when they first meet you. Instead they build a friendship; they put you in situations where it's awkward and embarrassing to be the righteous one and easy to fudge a little. If that hasn't happened to you, it probably will.

Here's another parallel to think about. The Bible says that covetousness is idolatry. When you daydream about that new smartphone or bike or car or video game or TV—or even a leather-bound Bible!—that you really-really-really want, God ceases to be the ultimate desire of your heart. The line between a legitimate desire for something you need (sometimes you need a new Bible or bike) and covetousness is not always easy to see, and the people who make TV commercials are certainly not trying to help you tell the difference between the two! Covetousness is something the Bible specifically warns us to be on guard against (Luke 12:15; Col. 3:5), and that has to be true especially today when we have so many things available and so much extra money to buy it with. Life is a lot more than stuff. Leather-bound Bibles, no matter how beautiful and useful, don't belong on God's throne.

> "The love of money leads to idolatry; because, when led astray through money, men name as gods those who are not gods."
>
> —The Testament of Judah

We're making a connection here that Scripture doesn't mention; the Bible doesn't say Joash was guilty of covetousness, just idolatry. It's just that today covetousness is one of the major forms idolatry takes, whereas in his day it took the form of actually offering sacrifices to a physical idol. If it doesn't make sense to you that someone would do that, just remember that it probably wouldn't make sense to them that you sacrifice all your allowance money for another video game.

Due North

If you are in the wilderness and your compass is off even by two degrees, you might be a mile out of your way after an hour of walking. But after a week? After a lifetime? If God is not due north in your heart, you could soon be a thousand miles down the broad road to destruction. Putting something else on God's throne inevitably messes up your world.

But let's stop and consider again where we are in the story. What hope is there that you or your classmates or the people in your family or church will truly love God with all their hearts? What hope is there if even people like Solomon, with all his wisdom, failed miserably? What chance do you have when Joash, who heard directly from a messenger of God, ultimately proved to be a spiritual failure despite all God's mercy?

We will cover three more kings later in the book. Two were good kings, and one was bad. But all three of them were guilty of sin. Their overall trajectory is still down. When a satellite starts to experience a "decaying orbit," it may stay up for a long time. But eventually it will fall into the atmosphere and burn.

There's got to be a better solution to the world's problems than these good-but-fallen kings. Even when truly godly kings arise—like David—the sin in their hearts leads them into damaging failures. And there's no guarantee that the next king will be godly. Only once in the whole history of Judah does a very good king ever follow a very good king.

What will God do to fix this problem? Abraham's great nation—and the whole world God wants to bless through it—simply needs a much better King.

Thinking It Through 6.7

1. What did Athaliah almost completely wipe out? If she had succeeded, what would it have meant?

2. Describe the way Joash finally became king.

3. Was Joash a good king or a bad king? Explain your answer.

4. What makes Joash's murder of Zechariah so shameful, proving how far from the Lord he had wandered?

5. What prompted Joash's idolatry? (2 Chron. 24:17)

6.8 AMOS: SEEK GOOD AND NOT EVIL

Read Amos 5:1–17
Memorize Amos 4:12

Willing and Obedient

In the eighth century BC, Amos prophesied to the nation of Israel. During this time, God also sent Hosea to the nation of Israel, and He sent Micah and Isaiah to the nation of Judah.

Amos preached against sin and prophesied that God would send judgment on the Northern Kingdom of Israel, the Southern Kingdom of Judah, and the surrounding nations. The theme of Amos's message was God's faithfulness to His covenant and law and His holding Israel responsible for failing to keep their obligations to both the covenant and the law.

The book of Amos was named for the prophet who bore its message (1:1). Amos made his living as a shepherd (1:1; cf. 7:14–15) and as a grower of figs (7:14) near Tekoa, a small town in Judah about ten miles south of Jerusalem. He traveled and prophesied to Bethel, a settlement in Israel that was about twenty-five miles north of Tekoa. His name means "burden bearer," and it was suitable since as a southerner, he had the difficult burden of bearing the news of the coming judgment to the Northern Kingdom of Israel.

Amos received his calling to be a prophet while he was a shepherd (1:1; 7:15). He was not educated in the prophet schools of the day (7:14–15), but he was willing to do what God needed him to do. This shows that God was not simply looking for an individual who had all the educational qualifications to be a prophet; He was looking for an individual who would be obedient to Him regardless of his qualifications.

A Political and Religious Mess

During the eighth century, Israel was sinning against God in every aspect of life. The Israelites had corrupt values. Their attitudes were prideful. Their leaders were violent thieves (Amos 3:10). Many lived in luxury while they oppressed the poor (4:1; 5:11; cf. 3:15). Some made mockery of the courts and perverted justice by condemning the innocent and letting the guilty go free (5:7, 10, 12).

For these Israelites, religion was only a formality to impress others. They had no problem violating their obligations to the covenant. They misused the sacrificial system and made a show out of offering a sacrifice (4:4–5).

In essence they were saying, "Who cares how much I sinned? Don't focus on that! Just look at all the sacrifices that I give. Aren't they wonderful?"

In other words, they felt they could do anything—no matter how wicked, as long as they were going through religious motions. They thought their sacrifices and religious practices provided them a way out of punishment. God, however, found every aspect of their worship to be intolerable.

The Lord said, "I hate, I despise your feast days, and I will not smell in your solemn assemblies" (5:21). His hatred shows that He detested Israel's religious practices. But even more, He abhorred and rejected them too. God wanted nothing to do with Israel's religious feasts (5:21–22).

God refused to accept their sacrifices (5:22) and commanded that their songs, called "noise," be taken away from Him. He wouldn't even listen to the melody of their instruments (5:23).

Why would God refuse all these things? Because the people were actually carrying miniature graven images on their person when they worshiped (5:26). They had replaced God with handmade images; yet, they were still pretending to worship Him.

But Israel was at ease. They were complacent and felt secure in their wealth and in being chosen by God. Judgment was far from their minds. God, however, saw the nation as a basket of summer fruit ripe for judgment (8:1–14).

Circling His Prey

Amos delivers his message at Bethel, which in Hebrew means "House of God." But the Israelites have profaned God's house, and Amos was sent to warn them that judgment would happen even at the "House of God."

Amos doesn't immediately begin his message by telling those in Israel that God would judge them. Instead, he sets them up. His method

Does God Do Evil?

In chapter 3, Amos asks a series of rhetorical questions. A rhetorical question is a question to which no answer is expected. Amos is doing this for effect. And one question in particular should have a strong effect on the listeners.

That particular question is sometimes misunderstood: Amos asks, "Shall there be evil in a city, and the Lord hath not done it?" (3:6). Our modern-day understanding of evil makes it sound like God is doing something sinful or wicked.

The Hebrew word used here for "evil" does not mean something wicked or sinful in this verse. Rather, *evil* is referring to calamities or disasters. Amos is basically saying "Does a catastrophe come to a city, unless the Lord has caused it?" In other words, does something like a flood, tornado, or some other disaster come to a city unless the Lord does it?

Amos asked this question because it is difficult to answer. It seems that Israel believed that the Lord would never bring or allow a disaster for His own chosen people. They thought they were immune from such happenings.

So if they answered "Yes," then they were admitting that God could do that to His own people.

But if they answered "No," then they were saying that some other deity did it.

Admit you're wrong or be an idolater? It's better to admit you're wrong.

Amos wanted them to agree and answer "Yes"—disaster does come from the Lord. In this way, Israel would understand that the oppression of the surrounding nations was ultimately coming from the Lord. He allowed it to happen, and He brought it on them.

So God was not committing a sin or doing evil deeds; He was bringing disaster upon a city. Israel had sinned, and the emphasis was that God—only God—would be the one to bring disasters and calamities on them.

---

is like that of a bird of prey that circles its target and then swoops down to make the kill.

Amos begins circling his prey by prophesying against Israel's longtime and hostile enemies the Syrians (1:3–5) and the Philistines (1:6–8). He has won the people's sympathy and their agreement. You can imagine the Israelites who heard him. "Yes! Let God judge those wicked enemies of ours!"

Amos tightens his circle by narrowing down his message and prophesies judgment on Israel's former ally and partner Tyre (1:9–10). Once again they agree, "Yes! Let God judge those wicked ones who turned on us!"

Amos continues to tighten the circle when he announces

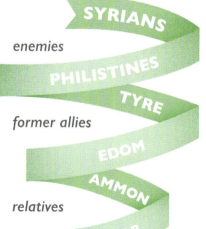

AMOS'S APPROACH

SYRIANS
enemies

PHILISTINES

TYRE
former allies

EDOM

AMMON
relatives

MOAB

JUDAH

brothers

ISRAEL

judgment on Israel's blood relatives Edom (1:11–12), Ammon (1:12–15), and Moab (2:1–3). You can imagine that the Israelites would also agree that their relatives were wicked and deserved judgment.

Amos is now in a tight spiral and hits closer to home with his next prophecy. He denounces Israel's brothers, the nation of Judah (2:4–5). The Israelite audience must have been captivated at this point.

And then he swoops down to make the kill. He focuses directly on Israel.

With the seven other nations, Amos lists only one sin, but with Israel, he rattles off numerous sins that they have committed. They are perverting justice by selling righteous people for silver (2:6). They mistreat the poor and ignore those who have been mistreated. They are sexually promiscuous and blaspheme God's holy name. They indulge in drunken feasts in the "house of their god" (2:8). Some scholars believe the phrase "their god" actually refers to God. If so, their hearts were even more calloused than those of idolaters.

Amos reveals that God's judgment will be impartial, and thus, it will fall on Israel.

The Day of the Lord: Not Just for Gentiles

This comes as a surprise to Israel. The Israelites, in their sinful condition, are actually looking forward to the day when God's judgment would come on others—non-Israelites. Amos responds that Israel, however, misunderstands the Day of the Lord: God's judgment will pour down upon all sinners—Israel included!

That's why Amos exclaims, "Woe unto you that desire the day of the Lord!" (5:18). It will not be a time of light, but rather, it will be full of darkness (defeat and disasters) for both the nations and Israel (5:20).

And no one will be able to escape. The fastest runners will have no time to retreat; the strongest men will lose their strength; the mighty men will be unable to save even themselves; the archers will not be able to stand their ground; the swiftest of soldiers will be too slow to escape; not even the cavalry will be able to outrun the judgment; and the courageous men will flee away naked (2:14–16).

Even if one tries to escape, he will run into a far worse danger. Amos says that the Day of the Lord will be "as if a man did flee from a lion, and a bear met him; or went into the house, and leaned his hand on the wall, and a serpent bit him" (5:19). Israel and all sinners will find that the Day of the Lord will be a time of certain judgment, and all hopes of escaping from God's wrath will be darkened.

From the very beginning of chapter 9 of the book of Amos, you can see the certainty of the judgment. There is no escape. The wrath of God will be poured out on sinners and on the nation of Israel. It will be a horrible time. Notice what God will do:

> I saw the Lord standing upon the altar:
> and he said,
> Smite the lintel of the door, that the posts
>   may shake:
>   and cut them in the head, all of them;
> and I will slay the last of them with the sword:
>   he that fleeth of them shall not flee away,
>   and he that escapeth of them shall not
>   be delivered.
> Though they dig into hell,
>   thence shall mine hand take them;
> though they climb up to heaven,
>   thence will I bring them down:
> And though they hide themselves in the
>   top of Carmel,
>   I will search and take them out thence;
> and though they be hid from my
>   sight in the bottom of the sea,
>   thence will I command the serpent,
>   and he shall bite them:
> And though they go into captivity
>   before their enemies,

thence will I command the sword,
and it shall slay them:
and I will set mine eyes upon them for
evil, and not for good. (Amos 9:1–4)

The God of Mercy

After reading that, it seems hopeless. But there is one thing we must always remember—God is a God of mercy. And when it comes to Israel, God is a God who has loyal and steadfast kindness for His people because of His relationship with them based on the promises He made to their forefathers. God always provides a way of redemption and restoration.

If you continue reading in chapter 9, you will see God's promise of restoration. Even though the Israelites have sinned and are going to be judged, God will restore them to a proper standing with Him. It is He, the Lord, who will raise up the children of Israel and bring them back to the Promised Land.

God promises that He will reestablish the house of David (9:11), and Israel will once again possess the land (9:12). This directly fulfills the promises that God made to Abraham and to David.

When God restores them, He says that a reaper will begin to harvest the crops, but the crops will be so abundant that the reaper will not be able to finish in time for the ground to be plowed for the next year's crop (9:13). The same is said for those treading the grapes—they will not be able to finish even when it's time to plant the next year's crop.

The hunger and thirst that Israel will have suffered during the judgments will become a thing of the past. Everything and everybody will be restored. Israel will not only be in the Promised Land, but they will also rebuild the ruined cities that their enemies had torn down. They will plant vineyards and gardens, and they will enjoy abundant crops.

And God makes one final promise. He will plant them back in the Promised Land, and there they will remain. The concept of planting implies that they will be placed permanently in "their land" (9:15). It will forever be "their land," and they will not have to worry about being removed.

The Lord does not leave Israel with a negative, hopeless prophecy of doom. Rather, He repeats the promises that He gave to their forefathers. In the closing verses of Amos, the Lord states that the Israelites are His people (9:14), and He concludes the book with the phrase: "the Lord thy God" (9:15).

> "And I will plant them upon their land, and they shall no more be pulled up out of their land which I have given them, saith the Lord thy God"
>
> **—Amos 9:15**

Once again, God can say to Israel, "[I] will be your God, and ye shall be my people" (Lev. 26:12).

Thinking it Through 6.8

1. Describe the social and political injustice in the nation of Israel. Describe the religious corruption of the nation of Israel.

2. Who brought the disaster that had come down on God's people?

3. Describe Amos's method of revealing to Israel God's judgment on the nations.

4. Why was Israel surprised that the Day of the Lord was not something they should be looking forward to?

5. Describe God's promises of restoration. (Amos 9:11–15)

UNIT 6 REVIEW

Scripture Memory

1 Kings 13:33–34	2 Kings 7:17
1 Kings 18:21	Joel 2:1–2
1 Kings 21:29	2 Kings 11:17
2 Kings 5:15*b*	Amos 4:12

Understand the Story

1. Rehoboam received conflicting advice from two sets of advisors. What did Rehoboam lack that caused him to make a bad choice, splitting the kingdom in two?

2. In the story of Elijah, when did God send rain back to the nation of Israel? Why is the timing important?

3. If Ahab had a conscience and even repented in sackcloth and ashes, why is he still considered a bad king? Did God not really forgive him?

4. Elisha didn't go out to meet Naaman and told him he must dip in the Jordan River seven times. What message did Elisha want to make clear to Naaman through this method?

5. What did God do to prove to Samaria, the rebellious capital of the Northern Kingdom, that His word is certain and His deliverance is powerful?

6. Describe the near fulfillments of the Day of the Lord in each of the three prophets: Obadiah, Joel, and Zephaniah.

7. How did God judge Joash for his idolatry?

8. Compare and contrast Israel's view of the Day of the Lord with Amos's description.

Developing Observation Skills

9. One of the skills you learned in this unit was to use cross-references. Read God's commands in Exodus 20:13, 15, and 17 and compare them to Ahab and Jezebel's actions in 1 Kings 21. Then compare God's commands to Israel's common practices (Isa. 5:8; Jer. 22:13; Mic. 2:1–2; Hab. 2:9).

10. How would you connect the truths outlined in 1 Samuel 2:1–10 with the story of Naaman and Gehazi?

11. One important observation skill is to compare and contrast characters in a story. Compare and contrast Naaman and Gehazi.

12. Being able to understand figures of speech is an important skill. What do the comparisons to the eagle and to the stars communicate about Edom's wrong view of itself? (Obad. 1:4)

13. Understanding the elements of a plot line is an important skill for reading narratives. Identify the inciting incident (the incident that sets the events of the plot in motion) in the narrative of 1 Kings 11.

14. Understanding the poetic structure of certain passages will help you better understand the emphasis of an author's argument. Identify the chiasm (the parallel lines that are in the mirror image of each other) in Amos 5:14–15.

Connecting the Story to the Big Story

15. What did God promise He would do if David's seed sinned? (2 Sam. 7:14) How did God fulfill this promise after the death of Solomon and during the reign of Rehoboam?

16. Connect the story of Elijah to the big story of Scripture. (Provide at least two major points.)

17. Differentiate the far fulfillments of the Day of the Lord from the near fulfillments in each of the three prophets: Obadiah, Joel, and Zephaniah.

18. What key promises does Amos 9:11–15 predict that God will one day fulfill?

Lessons for Life

19. Many of the stories in this unit illustrate the consequences of disobedience versus obedience. What should this teach you about the character of God and His dealings with people?

20. Many of the stories in this unit showcase various responses (good and bad) to God's mercy and judgment. How should you respond to God's mercy and judgment in your life?

UNIT 7

THE LINE OF DAVID: DOOMED TO FAILURE?

Israel and Judah continue to enjoy their sins more than they enjoy pleasing God. God is patient and continues to send His prophets to warn the people of certain judgment. But God's patience wears out. Israel goes into captivity first, and Judah soon follows. But there is hope. God has promised that a servant will arise from the nation and restore the people of God to their land. But before that happens, Israel and Judah must endure their punishment.

God allowed His covenant people to be deported.

7.1 ISAIAH: HOPE IN THE MIDST OF JUDGMENT

Read Isaiah 6
Memorize Isaiah 1:18

Every good story has a crisis, and every good story gives you hope that the crisis will be overcome. When the White Witch kills Aslan in the Chronicles of Narnia, you have hope that the lion will somehow come back to life and save the four Pevensie children. And when Eustace is changed into a dragon, you feel at first that he got what he deserved, but then as he realizes how bad he was, you feel sorry for him and have hope that he can be "undragoned."

People prefer stories where hope is realized. When the planet is about to be taken over by aliens, you hope for your favorite superhero to save the day. When the team is on the verge of losing, you hope for someone to step up and make a play. No one likes a story without hope. And no one likes a hopeless situation.

At this time in Israel's history, the nation is divided. Both the Northern Kingdom of Israel and the Southern Kingdom of Judah struggle politically, and both are declining spiritually. The Northern Kingdom has fallen into the hands of the Assyrian Empire (we'll deal with Israel's fall in more detail in Section 7.3), and it looks like the Southern Kingdom will soon follow. It was to the people of Judah in the South that Isaiah rose

to deliver a message of hope. But in order to realize that hope, Judah has to repent and change.

Isaiah and His Message

Isaiah grew up during a prosperous time in Judah's history. He and his wife had two sons named Shear-jashub (Isa. 7:3) and Maher-shalal-hash-baz (8:3). The sons were born during Isaiah's ministry and their names actually have symbolic meanings that Isaiah used in his messages. Shear-jashub means "a remnant will return," and Maher-shalal-hash-baz means "quick to plunder, swift to spoil." The first name was a promise that the judgment would not destroy all of God's people, and the second was a prophecy that Syria and Israel would be invaded by an Assyrian army (8:4).

Isaiah's ministry extended through the reigns of Uzziah, Jotham, Ahaz, and Hezekiah. King Uzziah's reign had provided a kingdom where people were able to be rich, safe, and successful (2:7). But this success and safety led the people to believe in their own ability to provide these things. They began to think they didn't need God. Instead of worshiping God and thanking Him for what they had, they exalted themselves and forgot God.

As a result, God sends Isaiah to remind the people that it is God and not any person that gave them these things (2:22). The essence of Isaiah's message is simple: "You have sinned and broken the covenant by worshiping idols, being unjust, and not being sincere when worshiping God at the temple." Isaiah tells them they must repent, and if they don't, then God will judge them. The judgment will be severe and many will die, but God will one day restore them as a nation.

But before Isaiah delivers this message, he has to realize that he too has sin in his life. His realization comes when he has the awesome experience of seeing the Lord in a unique way. He sees the Lord seated on His throne, and angels are calling out to one another saying, "Holy, holy, holy is the Lord of hosts; the whole earth is full of his glory" (6:3). When Isaiah sees and hears these things, he realizes how sinful he is, and he confesses his sins and the sins of the people of Judah (6:5). An angel tells Isaiah that his iniquity has been taken away (6:7). With his sins forgiven, Isaiah is ready to serve God.

God warns Isaiah that the people will not listen to him when he prophesies. As a result of their hard hearts, God will punish and destroy them—but not entirely. The nation will be like a tree that has been cut down and only the stump remains. But that stump will produce sprouts, and the nation will survive (6:13).

Guilty as Charged

Isaiah has brought the people to a courtroom, but not to just any courtroom. It is God's courtroom where He is the judge (3:13). The people of Judah are accused of breaking the covenant that they and God had agreed to keep.

Isaiah stands up as the prosecuting attorney and wastes no time. He calls on the heavens and the earth to be his first two witnesses against Judah. These two witnesses were there from the beginning. They had seen and witnessed the agreement that God and His people originally made (Deut. 4:25–26; 30:19; 31:28), and it is these two witnesses that have seen the sins of the people through the years.

The people of Judah don't stand a chance. They are guilty as charged, and they know this to be true. They are in big trouble and are already

suffering for doing wrong. This breaks Isaiah's heart.

Like a parent speaking to his child, Isaiah asks them why they continue to disobey when they know they are going to be punished (Isa. 1:5). He speaks plainly and basically says, "Stop doing wrong and learn to do right, because you will not escape God's judgment!" (1:16–17). God does not want it to end in judgment. He is merciful, and before the sentencing begins, He offers them one more opportunity to repent and turn from their sins:

> Come now, and let us reason together, saith the Lord: though your sins be as scarlet, they shall be as white as snow; though they be red like crimson, they shall be as wool. If ye be willing and obedient, ye shall eat the good of the land: But if ye refuse and rebel, ye shall be devoured with the sword: for the mouth of the Lord hath spoken it. (1:18–20)

This is their opportunity to escape judgment. The door is open. All they have to do is go through it. They can repent, and they will no longer have to suffer God's punishment. But they are unreasonable and refuse to obey. In essence, they shut the door in God's face. At this point, their fate is sealed. They are guilty as charged, and God will judge them.

But exactly what was Judah guilty of doing? They had committed many sins, but the worst sins were ignoring God and worshiping other gods. God considered Judah to be His children that He had brought up. These children were rebellious, and even worse, they no longer knew Him as their parent. Isaiah said that even a dumb ox knows who its owner is, and a donkey is smart enough to know where its master lives (1:3).

But not Judah.

What a comparison! An ox is a stubborn creature that wants its own way, and a donkey is too stupid to do what it is told. But both of them know who feeds them and who their owner is. The people of Judah chose to be like both animals, but they were worse because they chose not to remember who fed them and who their owner was.

Isaiah said that not only had they forgotten who God was, but they had also abandoned

Him. To make matters worse, they were now "gone away backward" from God (1:4). In other words, they had turned their backs on God while He was talking to them.

Imagine your mom or dad catching you doing something and calling you into your bedroom for a talk. As they start talking, you stand up and turn your back to them; you pick up your iPod, put your headphones on, and ignore them while they talk to you. How do you think that would work out for you?

How do you think it worked out for Judah?

The people thought they could ignore what God told them to do as long as they were going to the temple and sacrificing animals to God. They figured that sacrificing gave them the right to do whatever they wanted to do. A sacrifice was like a magic word to them.

Have you ever had someone be unkind to you and then say "Sorry!"? And five minutes later they are doing the same mean things again and they say "Sorry!" To them, sorry is a magic word that excuses their actions.

How do you think God felt when Judah did that to Him? Their idea of saying sorry was to offer sacrifices, and then sin some more, and then offer more sacrifices. How do you think God would feel if you did that to Him?

Just Like Sheep

But we have to admit that is exactly what we often do to God. We often go our own way and then ask God to forgive us. Sometimes we are sincere. But sometimes we're not so sincere and ask for forgiveness with no intention of changing how we act. You would think we would know better, but as Isaiah says, "All we like sheep have gone astray; we have turned every one to his own way" (53:6). We are no different from sheep. At least being called a sheep is better than being called an ox or a donkey, but a sheep can be so

A Child to Save the Children

Isaiah tells about a special child that will be born who will do wonderful things for the people of Judah and Israel. Isaiah tells the people that this child will be accompanied by a unique sign (7:14). A virgin will give birth to a son who will be called Immanuel (in Hebrew the word means "God is with us"). His name is significant. After Adam and Eve sinned in the garden, God cast them out from the garden and from His presence. When Israel became a nation, God temporarily dwelt with His people in the tabernacle and then later in the temple. This child brings God's presence with Him because He is God with us.

This child will shatter the nations that are hostile to the land of Judah. But there's more. Isaiah says the child will be called "Wonderful, Counselor, The mighty God, The everlasting Father, The Prince of Peace" (Isa. 9:6). This child will fulfill the promises that God made to David in 2 Samuel 7. He is to be the Messianic King, and His kingdom will be known for its endless peace, its principles of justice and righteousness, and its unending rule upon the throne of David. Matthew makes it clear that Mary would have a baby who would fulfill exactly what the prophet Isaiah had said (Matt. 1:22–23).

focused on eating that it will wander into danger without knowing it. It will find itself lost and have no idea where the shepherd is.

When that happens, the sheep cannot save itself. A shepherd must come find the sheep and rescue it. That is exactly what would happen to the people of Judah. They would go their own way and find themselves scattered across foreign lands, and they would not be able to save themselves. So God promised Judah that He would send a Servant to restore them to their land. There is hope, and this called for a time of celebration. Isaiah proclaimed:

Sing [for joy], O heavens; and be joyful,
　O earth;
　　and break forth into singing, O mountains:
for the Lord hath comforted his people,
　and will have mercy upon his
　　afflicted. (49:13)

Isaiah says a lot about this Servant, and in the next lesson we will read more about Him. The Servant will be a special and unique Servant of God who is essential to bringing a future restoration for both God's people and the nations of the world. That means God will bring back the people of Judah and Israel to their homes in Israel.

They will no longer suffer persecution from their enemies. Most importantly, the restoration means they will have a good relationship with God.

Conclusion

Isaiah's message is one of judgment and hope. The people of Judah had sinned against God, and they were found guilty in God's court of law. They were to be punished for their sins. But there was hope. God gave them an opportunity to do right, and they chose not to do it. As a consequence, God would judge them.

Isaiah also told them that although God would severely punish them, He would provide a Servant who would deliver them from captivity, and even more importantly, the Servant would deliver them from their sin. God gave them hope even while they were being punished.

Do you think you would have been better than the people of Judah if you faced similar circumstances? Think about what you know about the sinfulness of humanity and answer the question, "What would you have done?"

Thinking It Through 7.1

1. Summarize Isaiah's message to the prosperous people who exalted themselves and forgot God. How do the names of Isaiah's two sons relate to the messages he gave during his ministry?

2. Describe Isaiah's call into the ministry. What did God promise would be the results of his ministry?

3. If the people were sacrificing to God to take care of their sin just as the law prescribed, then why was God angry with them? What opportunity did He provide for escaping judgment and meeting His expectations?

4. Summarize how Isaiah's prophecy about a child relates to the fulfillment of the Davidic Covenant.

5. What do we need as sheep who wander and go our own way?

Hosea: Redeeming Love for the Faithful

Hosea was a prophet who lived during the reigns of Uzziah and Jeroboam II. Hosea had a unique ministry because God commanded him to marry a harlot. Hosea was to use his marriage to portray the relationship that Israel had with God. Gomer was unfaithful to Hosea and had broken their marriage covenant. This pictured what Israel had done. Like Gomer was to Hosea, Israel was unfaithful to God and had broken its covenant with Him.

Israel was unfaithful because it had committed spiritual adultery—the people served other gods. In addition, the Israelite leaders did not put their trust in God. They displayed their lack of trust by seeking help from other nations instead of from God.

Hosea calls out to the sons of Israel and tells them God has a case against them. They are unfaithful and lack *hesed*—kindness. But what's worse is that there is no "knowledge of God in the land" (4:1). They don't know what God loves and what He hates, and it shows in their sinful actions. Worse than that, they don't know God personally. They cannot say what God desires for them to say: "Thou art my God" (2:23).

Hosea shows their ignorance of God by listing out their sins. They are guilty of swearing, lying, murdering, stealing, and adultery. They are violent: when one person kills another, someone else retaliates with more killing (4:2).

This lack of knowledge has consequences. God says, "My people are destroyed for lack of knowledge" (4:6). The destruction will come as God's judgment on them. Their lack of knowledge

about God is because they have "forgotten the law of [their] God" (4:6). Instead they worship idols—idols of wood. They offer sacrifices to their gods, and even present their daughters and brides as temple prostitutes.

> "Turn thou to thy God: Keep [steadfast love] and judgment, and wait on thy God continually."
>
> —Hosea 12:6

God tells them that they are not loyal to Him. They did try to reform themselves, but their loyalty (*hesed*) to God is like a morning cloud that disappears when the sun comes out (6:4). They think they can appease God with sacrifices, but He desires mercy (*hesed*—steadfast love) and not sacrifice and the knowledge of God rather than burnt offerings (6:6). In other words, He wants them to have steadfast love for Him like He has for them. He wants them to turn to Him, to know Him, to have a relationship with Him, to have steadfast love, and to practice justice (cf. 12:6).

In chapter 10 Hosea describes Israel as fertile farmland that produces much fruit. But the fruit is only that of idolatry. God tells them it is time for a change: "Sow to yourselves in righteousness, reap in mercy [*hesed*]; break up your fallow ground" (10:12).

When God says He wants them to "reap in mercy," it means He wants them to have the same kind of steadfast love for Him that He has for them. God loves them and wants their love in return.

The people need spiritual healing, and the answer is to turn from idolatry and seek righteousness. They have been destroyed for lack of knowledge, and God says, "It is time to seek the Lord, till he come and rain righteousness upon you" (10:12).

Because of their wickedness, God will send them into exile. He will judge them. Yet He gives them hope.

In the beginning of Hosea's message, God promises Israel that there will be a time of restoration. He will cleanse the nation, He said:

> And I will betroth thee unto me for ever; yea, I will betroth thee unto me in righteousness, and in judgment, and in lovingkindness, and in mercies. I will even betroth thee unto me in faithfulness: and thou shalt know the Lord. (2:19–20)

God will bring Israel back to Himself because of His lovingkindness (*hesed*)—because of His promises and relationship with Abraham. And He wants Israel to love Him in the same way. He says to them, "Turn thou to thy God: keep [steadfast love] and judgment, and wait on thy God continually" (12:6). Even though the people of Israel forgot God and did not know Him, He looked after them; He was the tree that gave them fruit (14:8).

7.2 ISAIAH: THE SHEEP & THE SERVANT

Read Isaiah 55
Memorize Isaiah 55:6–7

The Servant

A college athlete commits a horrible crime, the jury finds him guilty, but the judge sets him free because the athlete plays for the college from which the judge graduated. Another person takes a stand against immoral conduct but loses his business and home because the judicial system calls him "intolerant."

It seems that every week we hear of someone getting away with something or of someone being punished for doing right. Justice has flipped on its head—right is wrong and wrong is right. The world needs someone to return things to the way they should be.

Isaiah writes about a coming special and unique Servant of God. This Servant will be the one who sets things right. He will be the one to restore both God's people and the nations of the world. For the people of Israel, that means God will bring them back to their homes in Israel. They will live without fear of their enemies, but most importantly, the restoration means they will have a good relationship with God.

In several passages in the latter part of Isaiah, Isaiah tells the entire story of the Servant's life in what are called the Servant Songs. The Servant is the answer to the problems of both Judah and Israel.

The Servant is a man who will be called from His mother's womb to be a prophet (49:2, 5). God says, "Behold my servant, whom I uphold" (42:1). In other words, God says, "He is mine. There is no power that can overcome Him!"

He is more than powerful; He is God's chosen. Not even the most honorable, noble, and faithful person can fulfill this position. The Servant's tasks are unique and require a special person—one chosen by God.

God delights in Him. This indicates that the Servant has a close relationship with God.

God will put His Spirit upon Him, and He will be a humble and non-aggressive Servant (42:1–3). The Servant will establish justice on the earth (42:1), and God will empower the Servant to have a righteous rule (42:5–7).

But the Servant will suffer, and His suffering will be **vicarious**. Vicarious means that the Servant's death is on behalf of sinners—His death takes the place of those who deserve to die.

> Vicarious death describes someone's death that takes the place of others who deserve to die.

People will not believe the Servant (53:1), and they will despise Him (53:3) and be cruel to Him (50:6). But He will never open His mouth to protest what they do to Him (53:7). He will be condemned as a criminal, and they will treat Him like a wicked man even though He is innocent. He will give up His life voluntarily and accept the punishment meant for others (53:4–6). His death will please God (53:10). He will be buried with the rich (53:9), but He will live again, for "he shall prolong his days" (53:10). His **sacrificial** death will justify many (53:11).

> Sacrificial describes something of value offered to God.

The Servant's death benefits not only Judah and Israel, but it also benefits many nations (52:15) and establishes justice throughout the earth (42:4). The Servant is doing exactly what God intended for Abraham and his descendants to do—mediate a blessing to the nations. They would be a blessing by being a kingdom of priests to the world (Exod. 19:6). In other words, they had the responsibility of representing God to the world so that the world could know God and come to worship Him. It is the fulfillment of the Servant's death that allows us as Gentiles to have our sins forgiven.

The Line of David: Doomed to Failure?   227

Servant Song	Summary	Description of the Servant
42:1–7	Humble Savior	The Servant has a humble ministry, but He will be the one to bring salvation and establish order throughout the earth.
49:1–9	Human Prophet	The Servant is a prophet called from His mother's womb. The Servant will bring Jacob (Israel) back to God. He will also be a light unto the nations. Thus, the Servant accomplishes the goal of Israel's being a kingdom of priests, which points the world to God (for a description of a kingdom of priests, see both Section 3.4 and Handout 3.4).
50:4–9	Suffering Servant	The Servant becomes a sufferer. He meets disbelief and becomes subject to humiliation and abuse.
52:13–53:12	Sacrifice for Sinners	The Servant is condemned as a criminal and treated like a wicked man when He dies (53:8–9). The Servant voluntarily accepts the punishment for the sins of others and gives up His life (53:4–7). The Servant's death pleases God (53:10), and the Servant is buried with the rich (53:9). But God prolongs His days [i.e., He is resurrected] (53:10), and He receives a portion with the great (53:12). His sacrifice justifies many (53:11), and He makes intercession for the transgressors (53:12).

You have probably figured out by now that this Servant is someone very special. In Acts 8:32–34, the Ethiopian eunuch also knew that the Servant was someone special, but he couldn't quite figure out exactly who He was. When the Ethiopian met Philip, he asked him if the Servant was Isaiah or someone else. Acts tells us that Philip told the eunuch the good news that the Servant is none other than Jesus Christ, the Son of God. There is hope!

Destined to be Cyrus

Part of God's punishment for His people was their captivity in Babylon. But God promised them He would bring them back to the land of Israel, and He told them exactly which king would allow them to return. What is amazing about this is that the king had not yet been born. In fact, the prophecy was made more than a hundred years before this king was born, but God called him by name: Cyrus (Isa. 44:28). Cyrus was destined to be named Cyrus even though he did not know God. This is significant because God was going to use someone who did not know Him or have a relationship with Him. God spoke about Cyrus:

For Jacob my servant's sake,
    and Israel mine elect,
I have even called thee by thy name:
    I have surnamed thee, though
        thou hast not known me.
I am the Lord, and there is none else,
    There is no God beside me:

I girded thee, though thou hast
    not known me:
That they may know from the rising of
    the sun,
    and from the west, That there is
        none beside me.
I am the Lord, and there is none
    else. (Isa. 45:4–6)

God also said this about Cyrus:

He is my shepherd, and shall perform all
    of my pleasure: even saying to Jerusalem,
    Thou shall be built; and to the temple,
    Thy foundation shall be laid. (Isa. 44:28)

Ezra records when this happened (Ezra 1:1–4). Josephus, a first-century Jewish historian, said, "When Cyrus read this, and admired the divine power, an earnest desire and ambition seized upon him to fulfill what was so written."

Righteous Living

The Servant will restore Israel, Judah, and all the nations to a right relationship with God. But until that happens, people must live righteously (do what is right) and be genuine in their worship of God. That sounds easy enough, but it isn't—at least when you try to do it in your own strength. You have to learn that if you are going to consistently do what it right, you have to depend on God to help you. And that is exactly what the Israelites had to learn, but there was one thing they needed to learn first.

Being born as an Israelite had its privileges. Israelites had the opportunity to hear firsthand and obey the Word of God. They had the temple in which to worship the true God, and they had the blessings of God. But being born an Israelite did not automatically make anyone a servant of God. Every Israelite needed God's help and His power to live righteously.

The same is true today. Let's say that both your parents are Christians. When you were born, you were not born a Christian. Even if you have faithfully attended every church service, you are not a Christian unless you are saved. Being born into a Christian home does not make you a Christian any more than putting a bunch of metal and tires in a garage makes a car. You need something outside to change you on the inside.

God made it clear that foreigners and outcasts who worshiped Him and loved Him were His servants (Isa. 56:1–8). Being a servant of God does not depend on who your parents are. Your love for God, your repentant heart, and the way you worship Him reveal if you are a true servant.

The Israelites had to learn how to live righteously. What exactly does that mean and how do you "live righteously"? Living righteously means doing what is right. Israel's leaders, for example, did not live righteously. They had no problem lying. They made sure their friends didn't get into trouble when they broke the law, and the leaders had no problem killing innocent people who got in their way. When they sacrificed to God, they used animals that were unacceptable to God. They didn't even worship God the way He had told them to.

Living righteously means you tell the truth. It means you obey God's commands and take your punishment no matter who you are or who you know. It means you value human life and don't kill innocent people. Most importantly, it means that you worship God the way He wants you to and that you do it with a sincere and repentant heart. Isaiah sums it up nicely:

> Keep ye judgment, and do justice: for my salvation is near to come, and my righteousness to be revealed. Blessed is the man that doeth this, and the son of man that layeth hold on it; that keepeth the sabbath from polluting it, and keepeth his hand from doing any evil. (56:1–2)

You do not have to try to do right by yourself. There is hope for living righteously. God will help you obey Him if you seek Him with all your heart.

Isaiah's messages about the Servant gave Israel an assured hope. Although they would be punished, God would give them a humble Servant who would bring justice for all. The Servant would do more than give them peace on earth. He would deliver them from their sins and give them peace with God.

Isaiah also told his audience to live righteously while they waited to be delivered from their captivity and restored to their lands. They could not do this in their own strength—they would need God's help to do right.

Thinking It Through 7.2

1. Describe what the Servant would be like, what the Servant would do, and how the Servant would be treated.

2. Identify who the Servant is, and explain how you know.

3. Read Isaiah 53:1–12. What report about the Servant of God would be so hard to believe?

4. What does it mean to live righteously? Does God expect His people to live righteously, or can they live however they want since they are God's people?

5. The book lists several ways of living righteously. What are several ways that you live righteously? Why can't you take the credit when you do what is right?

7.3 HEZEKIAH: JUDAH IN DECLINE AS ISRAEL FALLS

Read 2 Kings 19
Memorize 2 Kings 17:22–23

Finally Banished!

Judah had several very good kings, but Israel had only one partially good king (Jehu; 2 Kings 10:28–31). And then God's mercy gave way to judgment. The covenant curses God promised way back in the time of Moses were fulfilled. The Northern Kingdom of Israel was taken away from its land. "The Lord," Scripture says, "was very angry with Israel, and removed them out of his sight" (2 Kings 17:18). None of the kings feared the Lord enough to stand against the sinful trend set by Jeroboam (they continued turning away from Yahweh and worshiping idols). The kings and their people served other gods, even burning their sons and daughters as a way to appease the gods. The people God had delivered from slavery ended up making themselves slaves to something worse than any Egyptian pharaoh.

In 722 BC, God decided to use the king of Assyria to inflict the covenant punishments on His people. After a three-year siege, Samaria was conquered and the people of Israel were deported to other lands.

These ten northern tribes were essentially lost to history. No one today knows for sure which Jews are descendants of Issachar, which descended from Zebulun, which came from Gad, Asher, Dan, Naphtali, Reuben, Simeon, Manasseh, and Ephraim.

God Remains Faithful

Second Kings 17 does include one interesting story that points to God's faithfulness despite Israel's sin. The geographical area God chose for Israel didn't drop out of His vision once the people who belonged there were forced out. There remained something holy about the Promised Land itself. We know that is true because Scripture tells us God did something unique in history when non-Jews moved into what had been the Northern Kingdom. When the Babylonians and others who resettled there did not worship Yahweh, He sent lions to kill some of them. There was something special about that

land, the Promised Land. It was still connected to God even if, for the time being, it was no longer connected to His people.

This is a hint that God's plans for that land did not end in 722 BC.

Hezekiah and the Rabshakeh

Meanwhile in Judah, the line of David is continuing. And it actually reaches its height in Hezekiah, whose twenty-nine-year reign began just seven years after the Northern Kingdom was conquered. The author of Kings comments that this Davidic king "trusted in the Lord God of Israel; so that after him was none like him among all the kings of Judah, nor any that were before him" (2 Kings 18:5).

This trust in the Lord gets tested—and displayed—in dramatic fashion in the story that follows. The introduction of Hezekiah at the beginning of 2 Kings 18 speaks about him in glowing terms. But for all that, he still responds faithlessly to the first challenge that comes his way. He acts without discernment (see Section 3.7 for a detailed explanation of discernment). He gives away the very gold of the temple to keep the king of Assyria off his back (18:16).

It didn't work. Hezekiah was going to have to trust something other than gold to save him. The very same army that just took away the Northern tribes is now knocking at his door.

The one standing on the doorstep is the Rabshakeh. Like Goliath before him, the Rabshakeh makes a huge, huge mistake. He doesn't just boast to Hezekiah about having a bigger army (though he does do that). He doesn't just say that Israel's allies are weak (though he does do that). He practically guarantees his own defeat when he challenges the people of Judah not to trust in the Lord their God. And he doesn't stop. He keeps saying it. He couldn't be more direct either:

> Neither let Hezekiah make you trust in the Lord, saying, The Lord will surely deliver us, and this city shall not be delivered into the hand of the king of Assyria. . . . Hath

any of the gods of the nations delivered at all his land out of the hand of the king of Assyria? Where are the gods of Hamath, and of Arpad? where are the gods of Sepharvaim, Hena, and Ivah? Have they delivered Samaria out of mine hand? Who are they among all the gods of the countries, that have delivered their country out of mine hand, that the Lord should deliver Jerusalem out of mine hand? (2 Kings 18:30, 33–35)

When you see a major character in a story keep saying things like this, it's probably because the author is trying to tell you something. He's often saying, "This is the major topic of my story!" The nations around Israel challenged and tempted God's people not to trust in the Lord. Where would their trust lie?

The Rabshakeh's words are no empty threat. The Assyrian army has proven over and over that it can smash anyone it wants to. They've just done it to the five nations the Rabshakeh lists off—and one he doesn't: the Northern Kingdom of Israel, God's own people. From an earthly perspective, it looks like Judah is about to become the next victim. Hezekiah has no

good reason to trust in the Lord—from a human point of view.

But God sends some heavenly perspective Hezekiah's way to help him make the most important decision of his career as king. The prophet Isaiah (who wrote the huge book of Isaiah in the Old Testament) soon comes with a message from God: pray and the Lord may retaliate against Assyria for its mocking.

Hezekiah follows Isaiah's advice and not the Rabshakeh's. Despite the earthly odds, Hezekiah immediately runs to the Lord. His faith has led him to have good discernment. And Hezekiah doesn't miss the point of his own story. He makes it clear in his prayer what the issue is: ungodly nations mock Yahweh and worship gods that are not gods. They need to know that there is, always has been, and always will be only one true and living God (2 Kings 19:19). Hezekiah uses the classic argument that appears over and over in the Bible and seems to persuade God to act: "Act on behalf of your name and reputation, Lord!"

God Is in Control

And act God does. In the most massive and direct display of His power over armies in all of Scripture, the Lord slays 185,000 Assyrians in one night. He spares Sennacherib, the Assyrian king, only to allow him to be murdered by his own sons. The place of his murder? It was no accident. It was "in the house of Nisroch his god" (2 Kings 19:37). Yahweh, not Nisroch or the gods of Hamath or Arpad or Sepharvaim, truly rules the universe.

The message Isaiah gives Hezekiah in 2 Kings 19:21–34 makes this even clearer. It's a poem that imagines Assyria's boasts and God's response. Assyria says, "I'm so powerful I dried up the Nile with my foot, like stomping all the water out of a puddle!" And the Lord replies,

> Hast thou not heard long ago how I have done it, and of ancient times that I have formed it? now have I brought it to pass, that thou shouldest be to lay waste fenced cities into ruinous heaps. (19:25)

The Assyrians have left us graphic pictures of what they did to the people they conquered. This is from the Lachish Relief in the British Museum. Hezekiah didn't need pictures like this; he would have heard about it from eyewitnesses.

Assyria can't boast that it defeated other nations any more than an axe can boast that it chopped down a big tree (Isa. 10:15). People chop down trees using axes as tools. Yahweh chops down nations using Assyrians as axes.

But not this one nation, not Judah. At the end of this story, the tree stands firm and the axe lies broken to pieces on the ground.

Hezekiah's End

Remember that most of the events in Hezekiah's life are not recorded in the Bible. We have no idea what his tax policies were or what construction works he completed (except the amazing tunnel mentioned in the information box). We don't know anything about his relationship with his wife (or wives?), or what his hobbies were. We know only what the authors of various Bible books (under the inspiration of the Holy Spirit) thought was important enough to tell us.

So the story of Hezekiah's illness and recovery is there for a reason: it shows that Hezekiah trusted in the Lord not just for national emergencies but for personal ones. As you read, you're supposed to wonder how full of faith Hezekiah is if he would ask for such a thing. God, however, gives it to him—along with fifteen more years of life.

> "Even a king who has done what is good survives now only because of grace."
>
> —Iain Provan

Hezekiah's Tunnel

A little comment at the end of the Hezekiah story in 2 Kings mentions something the king built: "He made a pool, and a conduit, and brought water into the city" (2 Kings 20:20). Hezekiah's tunnel, cut through solid rock, still brings water into the city to this day. It is a marvel of ancient engineering. Even the tourists who now wade through it can see how the chisel marks from the workers change directions in the middle of the tunnel—this is where the two sets of diggers met.

But how did they manage to meet in the middle about 150 feet underground without passing each other? Did they listen for hammering up on the surface? Did they follow a natural fissure in the rock? It's unclear, but we do know that the two teams of chiselers put an inscription in the rock: it sits in a Middle Eastern museum even now. The inscription shows how well aware these ancient people were of their depth underground.

Hezekiah's tunnel was not rediscovered until 1838, when it was found by American Bible scholar Edward Robinson.

The inscription found in Hezekiah's tunnel tells of the construction of the temple.

Hezekiah's tunnel brought water safely into the ancient city of Jerusalem, making it much less vulnerable during a siege.

The story of the visit of the envoys from Babylon is there for a reason too. Sadly, it's not a good one. Despite Hezekiah's faithfulness to the Lord, he acts without discernment. Judah is still like a plane that's out of control, slowly losing altitude, spinning in a downward spiral toward a crash.

The Babylonian emissaries Hezekiah shows all his treasures to don't seem to be a threat. Babylonians were some of the people that the king of Assyria resettled in Samaria at the beginning of Hezekiah's reign. At this point in time, Babylon isn't a world power. But the God who planned Assyria's triumphs before that nation ever existed knows what Babylon will one day become—Judah's captor.

Hezekiah is godly and trusts the Lord, but his reaction to this news still isn't a good sign. He thinks, "Ah well, at least it won't happen till after I'm dead."

Hezekiah's Example

This textbook has worked hard to make the point that the primary reason for Hezekiah's appearance in the larger story is not to provide a good example. It's to demonstrate the continuing plan of God in Israel's history.

But just because Hezekiah's example isn't the main thing doesn't mean you should ignore it. Hezekiah's faith was monumental, especially in the one big crisis that could easily have cost him his kingdom—and his life. The Bible is saying, in part, "Be like Hezekiah. Obviously, don't imitate his sins. Don't lack discernment. But imitate his faith."

Does God promise to deliver you from all troubles? Not in this life. But the kind of person who immediately rushes to God when he's in need, the kind of person who argues in prayer that God's reputation is at stake—that's the kind of person you ought, by God's grace, to be. There is comfort and life in making God your rock and your place of refuge.

Thinking It Through 7.3

1. Why did the Northern Kingdom fall to Assyria in 722 BC?

2. What hint in Scripture reveals that God still recognizes the land of Israel to be the special possession of His people even after He has exiled them?

3. Why did the Lord destroy the Assyrian army when it threatened Hezekiah and Jerusalem even though He had just used the very same army to judge the Northern Kingdom?

4. How did God work out His continuing plan for the nation through Hezekiah's life?

5. If the primary purpose of Hezekiah's story is not his good or bad example for how we should live morally, then why would his story be included in the Bible? Why shouldn't you ignore the values that Hezekiah exemplifies even though that's not the primary purpose of the story?

7.4 MICAH: "WHO IS A GOD LIKE UNTO THEE?"

Read Micah 1–2
Memorize Micah 6:8; 7:18

A courtroom is a solemn place. Depending on the type of court, the decisions can be as simple as handling a speeding ticket or as complex as deciding whether a criminal lives or dies.

Each person in a courtroom has a job to do. And each job must be done with the greatest respect for the law, for the members of the court, and for the parties represented.

It is not a time for joking. When you enter a courtroom, it is a serious matter. You are entering a place where justice must be meted out with great care.

In this lesson, Micah tells the people of Judah that God has a court case against them. God will summons an audience to witness as He presents His case against His people. They will be found guilty, and they will face judgment.

In God's court, He is the one testifying, the one judging, and the one executing the sentence. It is a serious matter to be summonsed to God's court.

Micah: Who Is Like Yahweh?

Micah prophesies to the Southern Kingdom of Judea in the days of Jotham, Ahaz, and Hezekiah—kings of Judah during the eighth century BC (cf. Jer. 26:18). He prophesies at the same time as both Hosea in the North and Isaiah in the South. Micah emphasizes social injustices and religious corruption, which demand judgment. He uses courtroom terminology to indict the people for their sins (Mic.1:2; 6:1–2). His messages reveal God's unwavering condemnation of sin and God's steadfast commitment to the covenant He made with the people of Israel.

Micah's prophecy focuses on God's uniqueness and His faithfulness to His covenant. God will hold Israel responsible for sinning and violating its part of the covenant. Micah presents God as the sovereign Judge who will punish those who are disloyal to the covenant. But Micah also presents God as a merciful God who will preserve a righteous remnant.

Micah delivers three messages to Judah. Each of these messages begins with the command "Hear." Each of his messages has a different theme that highlights the seriousness of the sins of God's people.

The First Message

In Micah's first message, he begins the legal court case against Israel and Judah. He summons the peoples of the earth to listen to the testimony of God. The Lord is leaving His holy temple and coming down to earth to judge. When He comes, the mountains will melt under Him, and the valleys will be split. He comes because of the sins of His people and in particular, the sins of Samaria (the capital of the Northern Kingdom) and of Jerusalem (the capital of the Southern Kingdom).

> "Hearken, O earth,
> and all that therein is:
> And let the Lord God
> be witness against you."
>
> —Micah 1:2

Destruction will come down not only on Samaria and Jerusalem, but on all the peoples of the earth. God is calling all people to account for their actions, because He is more than just Israel's God—He is the God of all nations.

The Lord has much against His people. They have turned from Him and turned to worshiping idols (1:7).

Micah cries out, "Woe to them that devise iniquity" (2:1). These people are so greedy they lie in bed planning how to get other people's money and possessions. They see land and houses they like, and then they steal them from the owners (2:2). The more stuff they take, the more stuff they want to take!

But it won't last long. God will bring judgment on them. When they lose their land and their possessions, the people they exploited will make fun of them by singing songs about the rich losing their land.

The wealthy made land and possessions their gods. Now God will take it all away, and they will have no god to worship.

But they don't believe it, and they basically tell their prophets, "Don't say such things! God won't do that to us." They think God's patience with them will last forever. The people think they can do whatever they want for as long as they want.

They are wrong.

The Lord is taking notice of what they are doing, and He lists off several specific sins. They sit by the road and when innocent people walk by, they attack them and steal their robes. Worse than that, they kick women out of their houses. Most likely these are widows. They kick the widows, along with their children, onto the street. In essence, they are cowardly thieves who prey on the helpless—the very people God commands the Israelites to protect and help.

But justice is coming. As the wicked have evicted the helpless from their houses, so God will evict them from the land.

As sure as justice is coming, so is salvation. Micah abruptly changes topics from judgment to salvation. God promises that a remnant will return and be saved. God, the Great Shepherd, will gather together the remnant like sheep into a fold. Although they return as a remnant, their numbers will increase, and they will once again become a great people (2:12–13).

The Second Message

The second message is similar to the first message. There will be a time of judgment followed by a time of salvation and restoration for the nation of Israel.

Once again Micah commands his audience to hear what he has to say. But this time his audience is made up of the leaders of Israel and Judah.

Instead of being examples to the people and correcting the people when they do wrong, the leaders are corrupt. Micah asks them a rhetorical question: "Is it not for you to know judgment?" (3:1). In other words, "Shouldn't you know what justice is?" Of course they should know, and they did know what it was. But they hated good and loved evil. They looked the other way or winked at the evils that people were doing.

The leaders were cruel to their people. Instead of gently shepherding them, they treated the people like rough animals. Instead of protecting and providing for the people, the leaders took advantage of the people—they would use them for anything they could get out of them.

Surely somebody would stand up against these leaders. Surely that somebody would be one of the prophets. But the prophets weren't any different. They too were as corrupt as the leaders.

The prophets were supposed to be the ones called by God to be His spokesmen. They were the ones who should stand up against injustice and call the people back to God.

But these prophets were not of God. They were counterfeits. Instead of calling people back to God, they led them astray. They were sweet and kind to those who fed them, but the false prophets declared holy war on those who would not serve them. These prophets were exactly like those enemies of Christ that Paul would one day encounter in Philippi, "whose end is destruction, whose God is their belly, and whose glory is in their shame, who mind earthly things" (Phil. 3:19).

In turn God will declare holy war on them. At one time these prophets were called "seers." But these seers will not be able to see because God will take away their ability to "see" (to prophesy). The sun will go down on them, and it will become dark for them. God will withhold His word from them (make it dark), and they will have nothing to prophesy (because they cannot see). They will be ashamed and embarrassed because God will not answer them when they cry out to Him.

> ## "Is not the Lord among us? [No] evil can come upon us."
>
> **—Wicked judges, priests, and prophets in Judah**

Now Micah turns his attention to the leaders of Judah. They too despise justice, call wrong right, and pervert all that is right. The judges accept bribes. The priests make themselves rich by charging extra to teach. And the prophets tell fortunes for money. In their wickedness, all these people still think God is with them and won't punish them.

God says that because of the wickedness of these leaders, destruction will come on them. Jerusalem will become ruins, and the temple will be devastated. Jeremiah recalls these two verses only a century later (Jer. 26:18) when God has executed judgment on the nation. In the book of Lamentations, Jeremiah records the fulfillment of the prophecy and how terrible it was.

Little Among the Thousands

In the middle of Micah's second message, he delivers a powerful promise for a little city in Judah:

> But thou, Beth-lehem Ephratah, though thou be little among the thousands of Judah, yet out of thee shall he come forth unto me that is to be ruler in Israel; whose goings forth have been from of old, from everlasting. (5:2)

Bethlehem was a small and unimportant town. Yes, it was the town where Ruth and Boaz started their family, and it was the birthplace of David. But other than that, it was a relatively insignificant little town in Judah.

But out of the town a ruler would one day come. That ruler would be someone special. He would not pervert justice, and He could not be bought. He would declare what is righteous and what is not. He would be a real ruler.

Although this ruler would be born in Bethlehem, His origins are from long ago and even from eternity! This could mean only one thing—the Messiah would come from Bethlehem.

He would be more than a ruler. He would also be a shepherd who would "stand and feed" the people (Mic. 5:4).

Matthew says, "And thou Bethlehem, in the land of Juda, art not the least among the princes of Juda: for out of thee shall come a Governor, that shall rule my people Israel" (Matt. 2:6). Another way of saying "rule" is that He will shepherd His people.

In His providence, God would use a small and insignificant town to be the birthplace of the Messiah—the promised Shepherd of His people. No longer would the small town be insignificant. It would be a place of honor.

After so much prophecy of destruction, Micah concludes his second message with hope. This hope will be realized in the millennial reign of Christ.

God's temple will be rebuilt. People will come from many nations to be taught in "the house of the God of Jacob" (4:2). God's law will go throughout the land, and the Lord (as opposed to crooked judges) will be the judge. He will settle disputes between nations, and there will be no need for armies. The people of each nation "shall beat their swords into plowshares, and their spears into pruning hooks: nation shall not lift up a sword against nation, neither shall they learn war any more" (4:3).

Micah goes on to say that each man shall sit under his own vine and fig tree. This is Micah's way of saying that the time will be prosperous. They will have plenty to eat. And they will not have to fear someone coming to steal their food or attack them. God has spoken, and it shall come to pass.

God's judgment will be severe, but He promises that a remnant shall return. Once again God gives hope in the midst of judgment. He will deliver them in the time of their distress, and He will turn their hopeless situation into victory.

The Third Message

Micah's third message focuses on Judah, and in this message God brings Judah into His courtroom. Micah summons the people to hear what the Lord says:

> Arise, contend thou before the mountains, and let the hills hear thy voice.
> Hear ye, O mountains, the Lord's controversy, and ye strong foundations of the earth: for the Lord hath a controversy with his people, and he will plead with Israel. (6:1–2)

The mountains and the hills are the Lord's witnesses. God's people have sinned, and He has a case against them.

The Lord asks, "O my people, what have I done unto thee? and wherein have I wearied thee? testify against me" (6:3). What He has done for them is deliver them from slavery and save them from wicked kings.

HEAR! HEAR! HEAR!

1	**2**	**3**
All people	Leaders of Israel	Judah
Judgment is coming.	Where is justice?	God must judge.
But God will save a remnant.	But God will establish His kingdom.	But God is steadfast in love.

But what do they do in return? They try to bargain with God (6:6–7). Notice that each time, they try to offer more to God. They think the more they sacrifice the more they can sin.

They think, "Perhaps I can come and *bow* before God and that will please Him. If that doesn't please Him, maybe I can offer some *sacrifices*. I'll even bring a one-year calf. That should please Him. Maybe the Lord will overlook my sin if I sacrifice *thousands* of rams and give Him *ten thousand* rivers of oil. That should please Him. If worst comes to worst, then I'll sacrifice my *firstborn* for my sin. That should please God."

But God does not want their firstborns, nor does He want their other offerings. He has told them what He wants and what He requires of them.

He hath shewed thee, O man, what is good;
　and what doth the Lord require of thee,
But to do justly, and to love mercy [*ḥesed*],
　and to walk humbly with thy God? (6:8)

Did you observe that carefully? He wants them to show Him the loving-kindness and steadfast love that He gives to them. Remember, it works both ways. God gives them steadfast love, and they in return give it back. That is a relationship—the type of relationship that God wants with His people.

He doesn't want to judge them and destroy their cities. He will do it, but He doesn't delight in it.

He delights in His people loving Him the same way He loves them.

> Who is a God like unto thee, that pardoneth iniquity,
>   and passeth by the transgression
>   of the remnant of his heritage?
> he retaineth not his anger for ever,
>   because he delighteth in mercy [*hesed*].
> He will turn again, he will have compassion upon us;
>   he will subdue our iniquities;
> and thou wilt cast all their sins
>   into the depths of the sea.

> Thou wilt perform the truth to Jacob,
>   and the mercy [*hesed*] to Abraham,
> which thou hast sworn unto our fathers
>   from the days of old. (7:18–20)

Why does God not retain His anger forever? Because of His steadfast love.

Why will God have compassion on His people? Because of His steadfast love.

Why will He cast their sins into the sea (which He will destroy at the end of time)? Because of His steadfast love.

He swore to Israel's fathers and made a covenant with them. He will keep His promise. Why? Because of His steadfast and faithful love.

Thinking It Through 7.4

1. What do Micah's oracles reveal about God? (Provide at least two major points.)

2. From Micah's first message (which was to the general public), summarize the charges against the people. Then describe God's corresponding punishment for their crimes.

3. From Micah's second message (which was specifically to the leaders), summarize the charges against the rulers and prophets. Then describe God's corresponding punishment for their crimes.

4. From Micah's third message (which was specifically to the Southern Kingdom), summarize the charges against the people of Judah. Then describe God's corresponding punishment for their crimes.

5. What were God's expectations for His people?

6. What was Micah's message of hope for God's people?

7.5 MANASSEH: JUDAH NEARING THE END

Read 2 Kings 21:1–18
Memorize 2 Kings 21:9

Not all Christians are Christians.

That sounds odd, but it is true. Not everyone who calls himself a Christian is a true believer in Christ (Titus 1:16).

If you ask many modern-day Christians what they've been saved from, they can't tell you. It seems they haven't committed any serious sins, so they don't need any saving! If you ask them if they've ever repented of their sins, they look at you blankly. For some people, Christianity is cultural, not personal. It's something they inherited from their surroundings. They "got saved" once (or twice!) at the church they say they go to, but they can't remember the name of their pastor or their church.

Other modern-day Christians know the gospel well. They know what every term means, and they know what to do at every part of every church service. Yet they live in a way that doesn't reflect Christian values at all. They sin over and over again, and it doesn't bother them. When they get caught, they "repent." And then go back to doing the same sin again.

The Israelites weren't much different from modern-day Christians. The Israelites loved to call themselves Israelites, but many did not worship the true God. In fact, many worshiped idols and didn't even follow the laws God had given to Moses.

If you're starting to feel weighed down by the dreary, depressing tale told in 1 and 2 Kings, that's a good thing. Just don't waste your depression. When even the stories about the good kings end badly, don't ignore the sad feeling you get. Don't skip over to the Psalms for a pick-me-up. Let yourself feel the weight for a little while. That weight is something many Christians need to feel. Because the sin that weighs down the stories of Gideon, Samson, David, Hezekiah, and every other major person in the Bible (except one!) is the same sin that you yourself have in your heart.

When reading about sin isn't depressing to you, you have a problem. When reading about sin is actually entertaining, you have an even bigger problem. God can forgive and solve both prob-lems, and these often depressing stories in the Old Testament are tools for addressing problems. They are meant to communicate the weight of sin.

> "Were it not said in clear terms, that divine wrath, and vengeance, and eternal death, lay upon us, we should be less sensible of our wretchedness without the mercy of God, and less disposed to value the blessing of deliverance."
>
> —John Calvin

Manasseh

Hardly any stories in the Bible are as depressing as the record of the life of King Manasseh. The reason is that there are few more depressing lines in Scripture than the end of 2 Kings 21:9: "Manasseh seduced [the people of Judah] to do more evil than did the nations whom the Lord destroyed before the children of Israel."

God wiped out whole Canaanite nations for those sins, and now the Israelites aren't just equally bad. They're worse. The people who were supposed to be a kingdom of priests, a holy nation, and God's treasured possession are dirtier than the people they conquered centuries before.

King Manasseh burned his own child as a burnt offering to an idol. He put idols in the very temple of God. And he led others into sin. It was like he spread idolatrous garbage all over the whole beautiful land God had chosen for His people. Beyond that, he filled Jerusalem up to the brim with innocent blood (21:16).

King Manasseh failed to realize that Yahweh records every drop of innocent blood. And that count was started in Judah long before Manasseh was born. The one true and living God records every knee bowed to an idol, even every sinful desire of every sinful heart.

With Manasseh, the iniquity of the Israelites becomes full.

God's incredible mercy—displayed over many centuries to a disobedient and obstinate people (Isa. 65:2)—is about to be replaced with His incredible wrath.

Infinite Wrath

The Bible says about Manasseh, "He filled Jerusalem with innocent blood; which the Lord would not pardon" (2 Kings 24:4). Forgiveness is not a given.

> "Where God in His holiness confronts His image-bearers in their rebellion, there must be wrath."
>
> **—Don Carson**

All the same, even people who love God and believe the Bible are sometimes tempted to wonder why He gets so angry, especially in Old Testament narratives. Read again what God says about His precious possession, Israel:

> Behold, I am bringing such evil upon Jerusalem and Judah, that whosoever heareth of it, both his ears shall tingle. . . . I will wipe Jerusalem as a man wipeth a dish, wiping it, and turning it upside down. And I will forsake the remnant of mine inheritance, and deliver them into the hand of their enemies; and they shall become a prey and a spoil to all their enemies; Because they have done that which was evil in my sight, and have provoked me to anger, since the day their fathers came forth out of Egypt, even unto this day. (2 Kings 21:12–15)

You may be thinking, "Why so harsh?" But notice four quick things:

1. The Lord says they provoked Him to anger from the Exodus till the reign of Manasseh. That's a lot of patience! If God's anger is like water being heated, He must have been watching that pot intently for a long time—because it took eight hundred years for it to finally boil over.

2. The Jews of Manasseh's day had been given incredible gifts. Their nation had seen miracle after miracle over hundreds of years. They heard directly from Yahweh through faithful prophets such as Micah and Isaiah. Most of all, they had God's very words in written form. They were more responsible for their wickedness than the ignorant Canaanites, who had none of those things.

3. The God of the Old Testament is the same as the God of the New Testament. Even "gentle Jesus, meek and mild" took a whip and angrily drove the money-changers out of the temple (John 2:15; cf. John 5:22–23).

4. The great American theologian Jonathan Edwards pointed out that God, as an infinite Being, is worthy of infinite glory. Therefore, a sin against an infinite Being is worthy of infinite punishment. That's at least one reason why the lake of fire lasts forever. And it makes God's centuries-long patience with Israel that much more amazing.

Slapping your sister is bad, worthy of some punishment from your parents. But slapping your mother—that's worse and worthy of a greater punishment. Now go slap the president of the United States. What will your punishment be? The higher the person you sin against, the more serious the punishment.

But typically a person doesn't wake up one day and out of the blue commit a great sin against God. Normally, it takes time. One sin is overlooked and then another and then another, and then the great sin is committed.

The people of Israel were like that. They began to slowly turn from God. At first it may have been something small that seemed unimportant. Then it no longer bothered their consciences, so they did something slightly worse. And they kept doing it until it no longer bothered them. And slowly, the nation turned from God and went its own way.

In the case of Israel, the people, who had been rescued from slavery, stiffened their necks and savagely bit the divine hand that gave them all their good gifts. They slapped the God of the universe in the face over and over.

God's punishments are not harsh; they're deserved.

Creator and Redeemer

In the United Kingdom, every public school has religious education classes. "RE," they call it. Many or most RE teachers are not Christians, and Christianity isn't the only religion taught in RE. But on occasion, a genuine Christian becomes an RE teacher.

One of these Christians was having a difficult time teaching her students about the seriousness of sin. The young boys in her class were pretty rough. And bored. Desperate to find some way to connect with them, she had them make their own little world out of plaster of Paris. They created animals, a little town, a lake, and trees.

Don, a biblical scholar, tells what that teacher did next:

She had the boys make up the "backstory" behind each little creature and begin to weave the accounts together. Eventually she asked them to pool ideas for some rules or laws that they thought they should impose to preserve some order. The boys came up with quite a number, including a prohibition against going too close to the edge of the "world" lest they fall off and break, and a prohibition against going into the lake, where of course they would dissolve. These and other "laws" were grouped together to see if they could be boiled down for simplicity. The boys decided that the one law "Do what I tell you" was the most comprehensive.

The next day, the teacher came into class and asked them to imagine that one of the little creatures the boys had created stood up and said to his maker, rather defiantly, "Leave me alone. This is my world, not yours. I'll do what I want. I certainly do not want you telling me what to do. Get out of here and leave me alone!" How, then, should the boys respond?

There was a moment of stunned silence, and then one of the boys volunteered, "I'd break his [little] legs!"

You would feel anger and indignation if your creation rebelled against you, and you would feel it because you're made in the image of God, who feels it intensely when His creatures defy Him. It's wrong for anyone, let alone God's treasured possession, to rebel against his own Creator. The laws this Creator made were intended to keep us from harming ourselves, and yet we humans keep on breaking them.

Manasseh broke them. Israel broke them. We break them every day of our lives. It's a wonder, a mercy of God, that He doesn't break all our legs.

Too Little Too Late

In 2 Chronicles 33:10–20, we find out something the author of Kings chose not to tell us. At the end of his life, Manasseh did repent. This is an interesting fact. God's mercy is great. But the wheels of justice had already begun to grind, and Manasseh's repentance—though a very good thing—could not stop the downward spiral Judah was in.

Thinking It Through 7.5

1. List three of the ways Manasseh "did much evil in the sight of the Lord" (2 Kings 21:6–9).

2. When is God's incredible mercy replaced with His incredible wrath? Why should this cause you to be responsive to God? (Prov. 1:22–33; 2 Cor. 6:2)

3. Give three reasons why God's judgment on Israel shouldn't be considered harsh.

4. What was the intention of God's laws for His creation? So how should the Creator feel when we break His laws?

5. Was Manasseh a good king or a bad king? Defend your answer.

7.6 THE NINEVITES: A STORY OF COMPASSION AND CONDEMNATION

Read Nahum 1
Memorize Nahum 1:3, 7

Nineveh

The story of the Old Testament is mainly about God's relationship with His people. On occasion, the Scripture tells us about His dealings with other nations.

Jonah was a prophet who lived during the reign of Jeroboam II of Israel (2 Kings 14:23–25). Jonah had no problem prophesying to Israel, God's people. In fact, God used Jonah to prophesy the expansion of Israel's northern border, and the prophecy came true (2 Kings 14:25).

But when it came to prophesying to Nineveh, one of Israel's hated enemies, Jonah wanted no part of it. So he went to the local port, found a ship that was going far away from Nineveh, paid the fare, and sailed to Tarshish—in the opposite direction of Nineveh.

He went to Tarshish for the sole purpose of getting away "from the presence of the Lord" (Jon. 1:3).

That didn't exactly work out too well for him. God sent a great wind and a great storm that almost destroyed the ship. You can imagine how afraid the sailors were. They were doing everything they could to save the ship. Each of them was praying to his own god. They were lightening the ship by throwing things overboard. They were afraid for their lives.

But Jonah wasn't. He was sound asleep in the bottom of the ship. After the captain woke Jonah up, the men cast lots to figure out whose fault this was. And the lot fell on Jonah.

Jonah confessed and asked the men to throw him overboard. That way God would save them and their ship. They were hesitant to do it, but they did throw him overboard.

While all this was going on, God had prepared a great fish to swallow Jonah. And so it happened.

After Jonah's sincere prayer of thanksgiving and plea for help, God commanded the fish and it vomited Jonah onto the dry land.

Jonah ended up going to Nineveh and preaching a short message. In the end he got mad because the people repented and God didn't destroy Israel's enemies.

That's the story in a nutshell.

More Than a Fish Tale

Most likely you have heard the story of Jonah multiple times. And most likely whoever was telling the story focused on the same things we did here: Jonah ran from God, got on board a ship, was thrown overboard, was swallowed by a huge fish, and then was vomited out onto dry land. He finally submitted to God and went to preach God's judgment and then got mad when the Ninevites repented and God showed them mercy.

But the book of Jonah is more than that. It is a story about a great and powerful God who had compassion on a nation other than Israel.

As you read the book of Jonah, observe all the things the author says about God. He speaks. He is powerful: He controls the wind at sea (1:4) and the scorching east wind from the desert (4:8). He controls the storm (1:4), He calms the sea (1:15), He is the Creator (1:9), and He can do as He pleases (1:14), appointing both a great fish (1:17) and a small worm (4:7) to do His bidding. He alone gives salvation (2:9), and He is gracious, compassionate, slow to anger, and abundant in loving-kindness (4:2, 11).

A Compassionate God

Reread that sentence: He alone gives salvation, and He is gracious, compassionate, slow to anger, and abundant in loving-kindness.

When Jonah went to Nineveh he had just experienced the loving-kindness of the Lord, but Jonah was not so interested in showing loving-kindness to Nineveh.

His message was short and simple (only five words in Hebrew!): "Yet forty days, and Nineveh shall be overthrown" (3:4). That's it. That's all of Jonah's message that we have.

God Repented?

Three times in the book of Jonah, God is said to "repent" (3:9, 10; 4:2), and in two of those times, He is said to have repented of "evil."

Does God repent? And what does it mean that God repented of evil?

As time goes by, words change meaning. At one point in time, a computer was an employee who manually added numbers all day long. Now a computer is an electronic device.

The same thing has happened to the seventeenth-century word *repent*. But today it doesn't mean exactly the same as what it once meant. A word in modern English that better reflects the Hebrew is *relent*. The word *relent* carries the meaning of changing what you are going to do because of compassion or forgiveness.

The same is true with the word *evil*. In our time it means mainly "something that is wicked or sinful." At times it does mean that in the KJV, but at times it also means "a calamity or disaster." If an earthquake or some other type of disaster hit, people would say, "A great evil hit the city."

So when you see in the Bible that God repented of the evil that He was going to do, it does not mean God is sorry for doing wrong. Rather, it means God relented of the calamity He was going to do.

In the case of Nineveh, that calamity was God's judging the city for its sin.

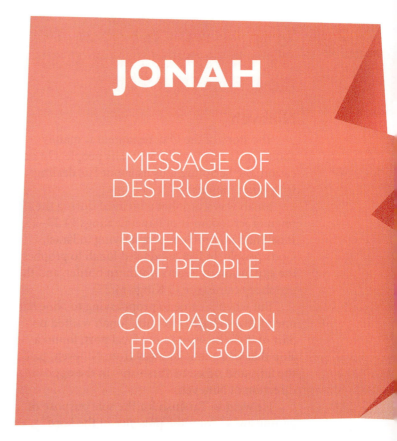

JONAH

MESSAGE OF DESTRUCTION

REPENTANCE OF PEOPLE

COMPASSION FROM GOD

told the fish to spit him out in the middle of the sea, but God allowed Jonah to land (albeit in a rather nasty condition) on dry ground.

And now the people of Nineveh have cried out, and God is once again compassionate.

A Pouting Prophet

At the end of the book, Jonah is not happy about God's compassion for the Ninevites. He tells God he fled because he knew God would relent if the people repented.

So Jonah goes up on a hill to sit and hopefully watch Nineveh's destruction. He sits on a hill in the middle of the desert, and as it becomes hot, he makes a little hut where he can hide in the shade. God in His compassion appoints a plant to grow and shade Jonah.

Jonah is pretty happy about the plant. That is, until the next day when God appoints a worm to eat it. Jonah is so upset and miserable that he throws a tantrum—a pity party. God asks Jonah about the plant, "Doest thou well to be angry for the gourd?" And Jonah replies, "I do well to be angry, even unto death" (4:9).

But it was effective. Everyone, from the least to the greatest, believed God. The king even made a decree that all the people must cry out to God and turn from their evil ways.

God heard their cries and saw they had turned from their evil. He decided He would not destroy the people since they had stopped doing evil and had turned to Him.

This is not the first time in the book that God has been compassionate. When the sailors cried out to Him, He was compassionate toward them and calmed the sea. When Jonah cried out from the belly of the fish, God was compassionate toward him and commanded the fish to vomit him out onto dry ground. He could have

NAHUM

MESSAGE OF DESTRUCTION

REPENTANCE REJECTED BY PEOPLE

JUDGMENT FROM GOD

Let's step back and get the big picture.

Jonah was sitting on a hill under a plant hoping God would destroy a city and kill thousands of people. It didn't bother him at all to know they would die. But then his beloved plant dies causing him to be hot. Suddenly he has pity and feels sorry for the plant that died and wishes he could die too. This is when God rebukes Jonah:

> Thou hast had pity on the gourd, for the which thou hast not laboured, neither madest it grow; which came up in a night, and perished in a night: And should not I spare Nineveh, that great city, wherein are more than sixscore thousand persons that cannot discern between their right hand and their left hand; and also much cattle? (Jon. 4:10–11)

Jonah has more compassion for a plant than he does for people. God is not like Jonah but has compassion on them. Not only that, He also has compassion because of the cattle.

God's compassion is not limited to His own people. He desires that all people, regardless of nationality, should repent. Jonah's ministry to the Ninevites shows that this is true. When the people of Nineveh repented, God had compassion on them and did not destroy them.

The Other Half of the Story

God's compassion, however, has a limit. In Jonah's prayer he says God is both compassionate and slow to anger (4:2). He does not say God has no anger; he says God is slow to anger.

When Jonah preached to the Ninevites, they repented. Evidently it was a true repentance because God decided not to destroy them. But as the generations passed, Nineveh forgot about the compassion and mercy God had shown them.

It only took about 130 years before Nineveh returned to its wickedness with a vengeance. It seems Nineveh was worse than before Jonah preached to the city. When Nahum comes on the scene, he describes how cruel and wicked the nation has become. The Ninevites plot against God (Nah. 1:9, 11), practice idolatry (1:14), are wicked and vile (1:14), shed blood, lie, plunder (3:1), enslave nations (3:4), think they are better than others (3:8), and are extremely cruel (3:19).

They appear to be taking advantage of God's long-suffering. Not only have they forgotten God's mercy, they have forgotten His anger against sin—and sinners.

> "Because God sometimes delays His judgment, people often think of Him as passive, somewhat like an old grandfather who lets the grandchildren get away with almost anything."
>
> —Robert D. Bell

Perhaps Nahum's message is one to warn them of God's judgment, but it seems that this time there is no call to repentance. God's patience with them has ended.

Even though Nineveh is not God's chosen people, He deals with the nation similarly to how He deals with Israel. He gave them an opportunity to repent when He sent Jonah. They repented and He did not destroy them. When they eventually return to their wicked ways and turn from God, He brings justice. But this time, the punishment will be swift and final.

> "The curses called down on Israel's enemies do not reflect a low view of them as people, but a high view of the importance of right and wrong."
>
> —David W. Baker

Nahum does more than highlight the sins of Nineveh. He reminds them and us about God's power. Nahum shows that God has the power over the winds and is greater than the clouds (1:3). He controls the sea and the rivers and can make them dry up whenever He chooses (1:4). And He can make them overflow their banks and flood the surrounding areas (1:8). He has the power to shake the earth and stir up volcanoes when necessary (1:5–6). But He is also good and will protect those who seek refuge in Him (1:7).

The judgments in Nahum's message are harsh and severe, but the Ninevites get what they deserve. In fact, archaeological finds show that the Ninevites were cruel people who boasted about torturing their enemies. Their cruelty was so severe that Nahum said Nineveh's enemies would "clap their hands" when they heard that God had destroyed the nation (3:19).

A book like Nahum can sound discouraging. But it is discouraging only if you are a Ninevite or live like one. For the entire nation of Israel, this was a message of hope. Nineveh was an enemy of Israel and a cruel oppressor to God's people. God had seen Israel's plight, and He was going to handle the wicked nation of Nineveh.

The Big Story

In the big story, the books of Jonah and Nahum are important because they show that God has compassion both for His people and for other nations. This is part of what God promised Abraham. He and his descendants would be a blessing to the world. Jonah was that blessing to Nineveh. He represented God and called for Nineveh to repent.

It is also important to note that God did not withhold judgment because of who the Ninevites were. He withheld judgment because they repented when they heard Jonah's message. Likewise when Nineveh returned to wickedness, God didn't punish the Ninevites because they were not His chosen people. He punished them because they had turned from Him and back to their wicked ways.

The fact that God's compassion extends beyond Israel's borders is what gave us a Savior who would die for our sins. In Christ "there is no difference between the Jew and the Greek: for the same Lord over all is rich unto all that call upon him" (Rom. 10:12). As Christians we thank God that He sent someone to tell us we need to repent so that we do not have to face the terrible judgment of the Lord.

Thinking It Through 7.6

1. What is the book of Jonah primarily about?

2. What makes Jonah's lack of compassion for Nineveh so unjust? (James 2:13)

3. True or False. The messages of Jonah and Nahum prove to us that God is compassionate and never gets angry because He's a God of love.

4. How is the message of the book of Nahum a message of hope?

5. How does God's compassion for Nineveh foreshadow God's compassion for Gentiles?

The Last Best Hope

Josiah is the last bright spot in the long history of Judah's kings. As is often the case, the headings in your Bible can give you the story quickly:

- Josiah Reigns in Judah
- Josiah Repairs the Temple
- Josiah Listens to the Book of the Law
- Josiah Reforms the Nation
- Josiah Restores the Passover

But as usual with even the good kings of Judah, the final note is still bad:

- Josiah Dies in Battle

The bad note isn't very bad—the Bible doesn't describe any specific sin of Josiah that caused his death. And the good notes are really good. If there's one big way you should be like Josiah, it shouts at you from the most dramatic story of his life: he fears the Lord and believes His Word. Can you imagine your own country being one in which the Bible was literally forgotten and then rediscovered? Josiah lived in a world like that, and he had exactly the right response to the Scriptures' rediscovery. He was afraid—and then he took steps to obey! The fear of the Lord is the beginning of wisdom.

Here's another way you should ask God to give you grace to be like Josiah: he followed the Lord with all his heart and all his soul. This was the most important law God gave, way back in Deuteronomy: "Love the Lord thy God with all thine heart" (Deut. 6:5).

And the Jews of this era all follow their leader. That's something that can be said for them. When they have bad leaders, they follow along in the evil, but at least when they get good leaders, they follow along in the good. So 2 Kings 23:3 notes that the people of Judah joined Josiah in his faithfulness to the covenant.

One sign of how wicked Judah has become under Manasseh is how much work Josiah has to do to root out idol worship. It takes several paragraphs to enumerate all the steps he takes, but he finally completes the task.

Too Far Gone

However, it's all too late. Before Josiah gets to put his major reforms in place, God has already told him nothing will change the future. Josiah will not personally see it happen, but the people of Israel have been too wicked—judgment is inevitable.

> "Even though they have the temple in their midst, the people [of Judah] turn to other gods."
>
> —**Vaughan Roberts**

David's seed has sinned, leading God to punish Judah's kings with the "rod of men"—just like He promised David in the Davidic Covenant. But Judah has now broken and rebroken its covenant with God so many times that God has decided to enforce the full Mosaic Covenant curses, just as He did with the Northern Kingdom.

That's what God means when He says, "I will bring evil upon this place, and upon the inhabitants thereof, even all the words of the book which the king of Judah hath read" (2 Kings 22:16). God was going to bring the very punishments promised in Deuteronomy that caused Josiah to fear. Why? Listen to God, the prosecutor, as He spells out Judah's crimes:

> They have forsaken me, and have burned incense unto other gods, that they might provoke me to anger with all the works of their hands; therefore my wrath shall be kindled against this place, and shall not be quenched. (2 Kings 22:17)

God recognizes that Josiah responded with humility and sorrow to the words of Deuteronomy. So the consequences of the curses won't come in his days.

But they *will* come.

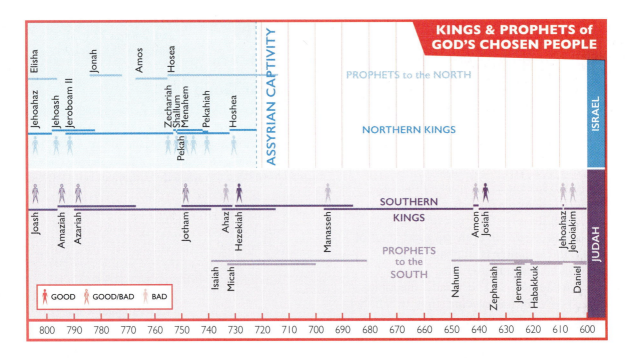

KINGS & PROPHETS of GOD'S CHOSEN PEOPLE

ISRAEL

PROPHETS to the NORTH

NORTHERN KINGS

ASSYRIAN CAPTIVITY

Elisha · Jonah · Amos · Hosea

Jehoahaz · Jehoash · Jeroboam II · Zechariah · Shallum · Menahem · Pekah · Pekahiah · Hoshea

JUDAH

SOUTHERN KINGS

PROPHETS to the SOUTH

Joash · Amaziah · Azariah · Jotham · Ahaz · Hezekiah · Manasseh · Amon · Josiah · Jehoahaz · Jehoiakim

Isaiah · Micah · Nahum · Zephaniah · Jeremiah · Habakkuk · Daniel

GOOD   GOOD/BAD   BAD

800 790 780 770 760 750 740 730 720 710 700 690 680 670 660 650 640 630 620 610 600

Life Support

Judah will exist for another twenty-two years, but during part of that time it will be on life support.

Here's how it plays out. Jehoahaz, Josiah's son, reigns for just three months. But he's evil. Jehoiakim, another of Josiah's sons, reigns for a bit longer, eleven years. And he's evil too. Then comes the beginning of the end. Nebuchadnezzar, king of Babylon, defeats Judah and forces God's people to pay tribute to him for three years. (Remember, it was to the Babylonian men that Hezekiah had shown all the nation's treasures several decades before this.)

"After Josiah's death, Jerusalem races to its doom, like a fanatic who has lost his way."

—Stephen Dempster

The full covenant curses have not come yet. But dark clouds are gathering on the horizon, and when King Jehoiakim rebels against Nebuchadnezzar, God sends other nations against

Judah. Then Jehoiachin (not to be confused with Jehoiakim, his father) reigns for three months.

And then Nebuchadnezzar comes back—and along with him comes the real end of Judah. Along with him come the curses God promised His people long ago. Along with him come siege and exile.

All the glories of Jerusalem are stolen away. The treasures of the temple and of the palace. The high officials. The mighty men. All the artisans and craftspeople like carpenters and blacksmiths. Gone. Only the poorest residents of the land are allowed to stay.

Nebuchadnezzar makes Zedekiah king in place of Jehoiachin, who is taken away with the exiles, and all the new king has to do is keep doing as he's told. But he doesn't. He rebels against Nebuchadnezzar, gets his eyes put out for his trouble, and brings even greater judgment on the nation. Now Nebuchadnezzar has the whole city of Jerusalem destroyed. The palace, all the houses, the temple—the temple! The temple, the glory of Solomon who built it, the dwelling place of the most high God, is looted and smashed! Even Jerusalem's walls aren't allowed to remain standing. They're all crushed and scattered, just like the people.

You should know the Author of this story well enough to recognize His hand in this. Zedekiah rebelled because God wanted Nebuchadnezzar to take even greater vengeance on God's people.

The same is true of the story of Gedaliah, the governor Nebuchadnezzar put over the few stragglers who managed to remain in Judah. Gedaliah actually gives the people good advice: just obey the king, and you'll be fine! But God's judgment for Judah's sin includes letting them commit even more sin. Ishmael, a member of David's royal family, assassinates Gedaliah, and all the remaining Jews in Judah flee to Egypt for fear of Nebuchadnezzar. To Egypt! It's what you call poetic justice. Out of Egypt they were rescued; back to Egypt they have come.

Cursed

This was the curse. God had warned the people that He would bring a foreign nation against them for their sins (Deut. 28:49). He warned them that they would be besieged (28:52). He even said He would send them back to Egypt (28:68).

If they had just read the covenant curses that so scared Josiah, they would have seen that all this was coming. Even the most chilling statements among the long list of covenant curses in Deuteronomy 28 seem to be coming true:

> It shall come to pass, that as the Lord rejoiced over you to do you good, and to multiply you; so the Lord will rejoice over you to destroy you, and to bring you to nought; and ye shall be plucked from off the land whither thou goest to possess it. (Deut. 28:63)

The book that began with the passing of the torch of the faithful David to the glorious and wise Solomon ends describing a time when not one descendant of Abraham remains in the land God promised to him. The covenant curses are complete.

The Peace of the City

The two key tasks God gave Israel are things they apparently can no longer do. They can't have dominion over their land, and they can't be much of a blessing to other nations. God's efforts to restore the world to the way it ought to be seem like they've been futile. Will He have to start all over again? Find a new "Abraham"?

Or is the story just over?

You can tell by the number of pages left in this textbook (and in the Bible!) that the answer is no. Though they are God's treasured possession, the people of Israel are now captives outside their land. But God's mercy follows them to their new faraway home.

"The house of David is still intact. The line of Judah still survives and the seed of Abraham can bring blessing to the world."

—Stephen Dempster

God even tells the people, through the prophet Jeremiah, that they should work and pray for the health and peace of the city of Babylon! If Babylon prospers, so will the Jews (Jer. 29:7). Abraham's family can and must still be a blessing to the nations.

And the book ends on a positive note, a small step forward. Jehoiachin, the last living member of David's line of kings, finds favor in the eyes of the king of Babylon. Jehoiachin is released from prison and given new clothes and a seat of honor for the rest of his life.

A Perfect King

But the book of Kings leaves us longing for a perfect king. If only God's people could have a king who always obeyed the Lord—then they would get rest. Where is a king who can say, "I do always those things that please [the Father]" (John 8:29)? Where is that King?

Thinking It Through 7.7

1. When Josiah heard the rediscovered Scriptures, what response (his first response) led him to make good reforms in the nation?

2. Why was God going to bring all the punishments promised in the book of Deuteronomy despite Josiah's reforms?

3. Describe the downward spiral of Judah's leadership after Josiah dies. (List Israel's next six leaders, what each did, and what happened to each of them.)

4. Explain the irony of the Jews fleeing to Egypt after the assassination of Gedaliah.

5. Explain how the final verses of 2 Kings (25:27–30) provide a glimmer of hope that God will continue to unfold His redemptive plan through His people, Israel.

7.8 HABAKKUK: FROM FRUSTRATION TO FAITH

Read Habakkuk 1:12–2:20
Memorize Habakkuk 2:4

Violence. Wickedness. Riots. Injustice.

Turn on the news and that's what you'll see. Pull up a news site and the page will be filled with stories and videos about sit-ins, riots, mob beatings, and all sorts of corrupt behavior.

Even worse, it seems that the judicial system is failing us—right is called wrong, and wrong is called right. Those who stand against wickedness are fined or jailed and called haters, while those who promote wickedness are praised as heroes by the media. Sometimes you want to ask why: "Why is this happening to us?"

In the Old Testament, the prophet Habakkuk did just that. He asked God why.

Habakkuk was a prophet in Judah during the reign of Jehoiakim (around 605 BC). That's really all we know about him. He may have been a priest, but we don't know for sure.

But what we do know is that Habakkuk was tired of all the wickedness around him. And he was confused about why God was not punishing the wicked. These weren't just any wicked people. They were the people of Judah.

A Unique Book

Habakkuk's book is unique in several ways. First, he never actually addresses the people of Judah. Other prophets typically record their messages, but Habakkuk doesn't. Rather, he talks about Judah. Second, Habakkuk asks God questions. He is never rude or hateful. He asks God some tough questions, but he is respectful. Third, he closes his book with a prayer for mercy and a personal testimony.

When you look at Habakkuk's book from beginning to end, you should see the development of two major themes: doubting and trusting God. At first Habakkuk doubts God because God is not intervening, and when He does, He uses a wicked nation to do His bidding. Habakkuk cannot understand why God does this. But he is wise enough to fear God and listen to what He has to say. He moves from doubting God to trusting Him.

The First Question and Answer
Question (1:2–4)

If you were to skim through the introductions of the other prophets, you would find a prophet speaking out against the people, issuing judgments against Israel's enemies, talking about God's call on their lives, or proclaiming God's love for His unfaithful people.

But when you got to Habakkuk, you would be surprised to find the prophet complaining to God about God. Habakkuk is upset that God is not listening to his cries for help. Habakkuk says that even when he points out the violence, God does not save His people.

He wants to know why God makes him see all this sin and wickedness, yet does nothing. The people ignore the law. There is no justice. The righteous are surrounded by wicked people who have abandoned God's just laws. It blows his mind that God does nothing to stop what is going on.

God had given Israel laws designed to keep order and justice. Habakkuk wants to know why God is not doing something about those who have perverted justice.

Habakkuk knows that God is a just God. He knows that God will not allow wickedness and injustice to prevail. He knows that God can restore righteousness and lawfulness to His people. Habakkuk wants to know how long he will have to wait for God to set things right again.

Answer (1:5–11)

And God answers him. But it isn't the answer Habakkuk expects, and it isn't an answer Habakkuk likes.

God tells him that He is not idle. God says He is going to "work a work" that His people won't believe even though He tells them about it. God is raising up the Chaldeans, an ethnic group from southern Babylonia, to come punish the people of Judah for their wickedness.

But these Chaldeans are not righteous people; rather, they are fierce and wicked people who are dreaded and feared by all others. They come in swiftly and take what is not theirs. They

have no one to answer to. They worship only one thing—their own strength.

Judah loves violence. So do the Chaldeans.

Judah loves wickedness. So do the Chaldeans.

Judah loves ignoring the law. So do the Chaldeans.

And when the Chaldeans come in, they will subject Judah to violence, wickedness, and

The Just Shall Live by Faith

In His answer to Habakkuk, God states that there are two types of people—the proud and the just. The proud person trusts in himself, and his soul is not upright. He is a crooked individual. The other type is the just person. He lives by his faith.

In the midst of certain destruction, God tells Habakkuk that the proud will be destroyed, but the just person will live because of his faith. Living by faith is the center of Habakkuk's message, and it is the center of both the Old and New Testaments (the New Testament quotes Habakkuk 2:4 three times: Romans 1:17, Galatians 3:11, and Hebrews 10:38).

But what does it mean to live by faith?

"The true believer, declared righteous by God, will persevere in faith as the pattern of his life."

—John MacArthur

In one sense it refers to the act of faith that a person has toward God. But it goes beyond simply believing and trusting God. A person who trusts God will have his life transformed. Faith is not something that you have at the altar and then you're done. Faith transforms your lifestyle.

Proud people look to themselves, but just people look to God in faith. Evidence of their faith is in their faithfulness toward God and toward each other. They are just in their relationships with both God and others. By having faithfulness they will escape the judgment because God rewards all people for their own righteousness and faithfulness to Him (1 Sam. 26:23).

lawlessness in a way that Judah has never seen. Judah will get a taste of its own medicine.

> "Habakkuk reminds us that God is at work. He is the Lord of the universe who works to accomplish his purpose in his world and in our lives."
>
> —Kenneth L. Barker

God is right. Who will believe that He is going to use such a wicked nation to punish His people for their sins?

The Second Question
Question (1:12–2:1)

Now, Habakkuk is even more confused. It's not uncommon for God to use other nations to do His bidding. God is sovereign over both His people and the rest of the nations. That God is using another nation to punish Judah is not what confuses or bothers Habakkuk. What confuses and bothers Habakkuk is that this nation, the Chaldeans, is a wicked and godless nation.

Habakkuk praises God and calls Him the Holy One who is from everlasting. In other words, God has always been holy. Habakkuk wants to know how God, as the Holy One who has always been, could send someone so wicked to judge and correct Judah. Is God overlooking the sins of the Chaldeans? Why is God being silent when the really wicked devour the not as wicked?

Habakkuk says, "We shall not die" (1:12), so he knows that a remnant will survive. But he also knows that the Chaldeans aren't concerned about punishing Judah; the Chaldeans are the type of people who would completely destroy Judah and let no one escape. He cannot understand how God is going to keep the Chaldeans from wiping out Judah.

Habakkuk then prepares himself for God's answer. He knows that God will answer, and he knows that when God does answer him, he will learn how he should respond.

Answer (2:2–20)

And again, God answers Habakkuk.

Although God will use the Chaldeans to judge Judah, He will not overlook the wickedness of the Chaldeans. They too will be judged for their sins.

In the same way that the Chaldeans plundered others, others will plunder the Chaldeans (2:6b–8).

In the same way that they exploited others, others will exploit them (2:9–11).

In the same way that they were violent, others will be violent to them (2:12–14, 17).

And then in an artistic taunt, the idol makers are mocked for trusting in their own handiwork to deliver them. They carve a piece of wood or stone, overlay it with gold, and think it will save them.

> Woe unto him that saith to the wood, Awake;
>   to the dumb stone, Arise, it shall teach!
> Behold, it is laid over with gold and silver,
>   and there is no breath at all in the midst
>   of it.
> But the Lord is in his holy temple:
>   let all the earth keep silence before him.
>   (Hab. 2:19–20)

When all is said and done, the Chaldeans will get what they deserve, and they will be silent before the God of Heaven. Both Judah and the Chaldeans will know that God alone is sovereign, and He is to be obeyed.

A Prayer (3:2–15)

Petition for God's Mercy (3:2)

Habakkuk has heard God's answer, and now he replies. This time Habakkuk doesn't ask God another question. Instead he responds with a petition and praises God for who He is and what He has done.

Habakkuk tells the Lord that he has heard Him and knows His works. They have caused him to fear, to be in awe of what God has done. And Habakkuk wishes to see those works in his own lifetime. He wishes to see God work now as He did in the past. He wishes to see God deliver His people from the Chaldeans in the same way He delivered them from Egypt.

Then he utters perhaps the greatest and yet most humble plea to God: "In wrath remember mercy" (3:2).

"In wrath remember mercy."

—Habakkuk

In his questions, Habakkuk had asked God why He was taking so long to punish Judah for its sins. He was praying for God to pour out His wrath on Judah. Now it seems he understands that the wrath will be devastating. Judah will suffer for its sins. And Habakkuk knows that God's wrath will be severe. And so he prays that when God pours out His wrath, He will "remember mercy."

Praise of God's Power (3:3–15)

God hears Habakkuk's prayer and answers him with a theophany (thee-AH-fuh-nee). In the Old Testament, a theophany is a visible appearance of God in which He shows His great power and glory.

Habakkuk sees God coming from the desert in the south—Teman. As He approaches, His glory and splendor light up the heavens and the earth. He is accompanied by two great judgments. Pestilence goes before Him and plague follows behind Him, each wreaking its own destruction.

His look startles the nations. As He approaches, the mountains fall before Him and the hills collapse.

He subdues the forces of nature to bring deliverance and salvation to His people. In vivid terms, the prophet tells how God will strike the head of the house of evil and destroy it.

Now Habakkuk has the answers to his questions. God is coming in judgment and will judge both Judah and the Chaldeans for their wickedness. He is not silently sitting by while evil prospers. God is coming in wrath, but He will provide salvation for His people.

A Testimony

All of this makes Habakkuk's heart tremble (3:16). His lips quiver, and he has no strength in his bones. His legs tremble where he stands.

This is the proper response. Isaiah had trembled and feared God when he had his vision of God (Isa. 6). Habakkuk's response is also one of fear and reverence.

Habakkuk's first question had been essentially, "How long, O Lord, until You do something about the wickedness in Judah?

Now Habakkuk says, "That I might rest in the day of trouble" (3:16). He realizes that he can quietly wait for God's judgment to come, because he knows that God will judge righteously and in His wrath remember mercy. He has come from impatience to quietly resting in what God will do.

There are several important truths we can learn from Habakkuk. First, we must trust God. Habakkuk is similar to Job because both had to learn to be patient and trust God. At first, Habakkuk seems to doubt God, and he questions God's justice. But as Habakkuk listens to God's answers, he realizes that God is sovereign, and His justice is beyond comprehension. So God can be trusted.

Second, God can use whoever He wants to carry out His judgment. In the big story, we learn that God is not limited in who He will use to carry out His judgments. God is not limited to using the righteous to punish the wicked. Sometimes God chooses to use very wicked people to do His bidding. This shows us that God is sovereign over all nations and can use them whenever He needs them.

Finally, no one will escape God's judgment. Just because God used the Chaldeans to punish Judah does not mean that the Chaldeans will escape punishment. They too will be punished for their wickedness.

Although the wicked may prosper now, we can wait quietly, for none will escape the hand of the righteous Judge.

Thinking It Through 7.8

1. Identify two things that make the book of Habakkuk unique.

2. What two contrasting themes are developed throughout the book of Habakkuk? And what brings about Habakkuk's change from one theme to the other?

3. What was Habakkuk's first question and what was God's answer?

4. What was Habakkuk's second question and what was God's answer?

5. What was Habakkuk's final plea to God in the last chapter of the book? What was God's response?

UNIT 7 REVIEW

Scripture Memory

Isaiah 1:18	2 Kings 21:9
Isaiah 55:6–7	Nahum 1:3, 7
2 Kings 17:22–23	2 Kings 22:17
Micah 6:8; 7:18	Habakkuk 2:4

Understand the Story

1. In the opening chapter of Isaiah, why did God say His people were dumber than an ox or a donkey?

2. What great king did Isaiah prophesy who would shepherd the children of Israel back into their land to rebuild Jerusalem and the temple? Why is this surprising?

3. What was the Rabshakeh's big mistake that guaranteed his defeat?

4. How does Micah's prophecy about Bethlehem fit into his second message?

5. There are different levels of greatness. Think of a king, who is greater than a servant. How would your punishment be different if you sinned against the king versus the servant? How does this principle apply to Israel's treatment of God?

6. What was God trying to teach Jonah by growing the gourd to give him shade and then appointing a worm to eat the plant and ruin Jonah's shade? (cf. Rom. 9:15)

7. What are two key tasks God gave Israel that they apparently could no longer do when they went into captivity?

8. What does the book of Habakkuk mean when it says, "The just shall live by his faith" (2:4)?

Developing Observation Skills

9. The theme of a verse or passage of Scripture can be identified by the repeated words or concepts. After reading Isaiah 1:16–19, explain the theme, and explain how you concluded it is the theme.

10. Identify the comparison made in Isaiah 55:10–11. (You don't have to interpret what the comparison means.)

11. The book of Micah is structured as if the people are in God's courtroom. God summonses His witnesses, presents the case against His people, and pronounces their guilt and judgment. From Micah 1:2–7, identify which verses describe God's coming as judge and the summonsing of witnesses, which verses describe the charges against God's people, and which verses describe the sentence of judgment.

12. Read 2 Kings 21:11–12. What particular words introduce and point back to the reason for God's actions? (You don't have to explain the reason—only identify the words that introduce the explanation given in the text.)

13. The book of Nahum announces God's judgment against His enemies. How does the prophet describe this Judge? (Nah. 1:2–3)

14. Habakkuk 2:6–20 is made up of a series of "woes" against the ungodly. God will certainly punish all those who are lifted up in pride (Hab. 2:4a; cf. 1 Sam. 2:1–20). In Habakkuk 2:4, what word introduces an important contrast? Describe that contrast.

Connecting the Story to the Big Story

15. How does Hosea's marriage to Gomer picture Israel's relationship to God? What does Hosea call the nation to do?

16. How did God work out His continuing plan for the nation through Hezekiah's life?

17. After reading about all the discouraging things that the wicked kings do, what should the book of Kings leave us longing for?

18. How does the book of Habakkuk assure us that God is not sitting idly by when the wicked seem to prosper and they persecute God's people?

Lessons for Life

19. Read Isaiah 1:10–18. How can you identify hypocritical worship and false repentance in your own life? How can you demonstrate genuine repentance in your own life?

20. Based on your answer to question 8, identify an area in your life where you know you need to live out your faith in the midst of your own corrupt culture. After identifying that area in your life, how can you use God's Word to help you in that area?

UNIT 8

GOD'S PEOPLE PROTECTED
AND RESTORED TO THE LAND

What will happen to Israel now that God has expelled them from their land? What will they do as captives in Babylon, and what will God do to keep His plan going? How will they ever posses their land?

How can God stay faithful to His promises to Abraham and David?

As the people slowly return to rebuild the temple and the walls, the prophets give them hope that God will fulfill His promises to Abraham and David. God's people will remain scattered for some time, but God will not eliminate them.

God has made a way for them to return.

Nehemiah led the reconstruction
of the wall of Jerusalem.

8.1 JEREMIAH: THE PROMISE OF A NEW COVENANT

Read Jeremiah 31
Memorize Jeremiah 31:33–34

Jeremiah was a prophet during the reigns of the last five kings of Judah (Josiah, Jehoahaz, Jehoiakim, Jehoiachin, and Zedekiah). He most likely prophesied at the same time as Habakkuk, Daniel, and Ezekiel—around 628–585 BC.

To say that he was unpopular is probably an understatement. His messages were not well-received by the people. His hometown of Anathoth plotted against his life. He endured persecution during his ministry; he was imprisoned, thrown into a cistern to die, and had his book cut to pieces and burned. All this and he mentions only two converts—Baruch and Ebed-melech.

Popularity was not his specialty, but faithfulness and obedience were. Jeremiah lived righteously and stood for what was right even in the middle of persecution. And by God's standard, he was an obedient servant who carried the message of God to His people despite all those negative things done against him. Jeremiah's obedience resulted in his penning the longest book in the Old Testament. Many scholars consider it to be one of the greatest prophetic books of the Old Testament.

Jeremiah's Delivery

Jeremiah was unusual among the prophets because of the way he delivered his messages. Instead of merely telling the people what would happen, Jeremiah acted out some of his messages so that the people could see what was going to happen. This would help the people understand and remember what Jeremiah preached.

For example, Jeremiah told the people of Jerusalem that God was going to judge them and put them under bondage to other nations. In order to help the people understand the bondage, Jeremiah put a yoke (a device to help control two animals) around his neck and on his shoulders. As he walked around with this yoke on his neck, he told the people that they too, like him, would one day have similar yokes around their necks. They would have understood what he meant because there were oxen walking the streets of Jerusalem with yokes around their necks while being controlled by someone else.

Israel's Situation

Jeremiah prophesied during a transitional period in Israel's history. He began to prophesy during the reign of the faithful Josiah. Josiah's death marked the beginning of the end for Judah. Within twenty years of his death, the nation had declined into wickedness in every aspect of life.

During this time, the Davidic dynasty was falling apart, and exile to Babylon was soon to happen. With each king that came to the throne, the nation slid further into sin. After Josiah's death, his son Jehoahaz became king. But he was a wicked king (Jer. 22:13–17; cf. 2 Kings 23:32), and his reign was cut short when he was imprisoned by Pharaoh in Egypt (2 Kings 23:33). Pharaoh then made Jehoiakim king.

Jehoiakim was a wicked king in God's sight (2 Kings 23:37). He was the king who burned a scroll containing Jeremiah's prophecy. A court official would read the scroll aloud to the king, and then the king would cut off what had been read and throw it into his fireplace. God commanded Jeremiah to write another scroll, and this time the prophecy contained a judgment against Jehoiakim: "He shall have none to sit upon the

throne of David: and his dead body shall be cast out in the day to the heat, and in the night to the frost" (Jer. 36:30). In other words, Jehoiakim's dynasty would end. His son Jehoiachin did rule, but his reign lasted only three months and ten days because "he did that which was evil in the sight of the Lord" (2 Chron. 36:9).

The last king, Zedekiah, became king after the people were led away into captivity. He too was evil. He tried to rebel against Babylon, but the Babylonians easily conquered him. As a punishment, the Babylonians slaughtered his sons in front of him and then gouged out his eyes.

And thus ended the Southern Kingdom of Judah.

The Message: Amend Your Ways

In the midst of this wickedness, Jeremiah stood at the gate of the temple and proclaimed the word of God to the people. His message from God was simple: "Amend your ways and your doings, and I will cause you to dwell in this place" (7:3). They needed to turn from doing wrong and turn to God.

Stop sinning and God would let them stay in the land He had promised them. Keep sinning and God would remove them from the land.

It seems the people of Judah thought they were safe because the temple of God was in Jerusalem (the capital of Judah). They thought God would surely not allow the enemy to come near the house that bore His name.

But God told them differently. He told them to go look at Shiloh, where He first made His name dwell. The city of Shiloh was where Joshua had had his headquarters (Josh. 18:1, 9). The tabernacle and the ark of the covenant had been located there (Josh. 18:1; 1 Sam. 4:4). It was the place where God had made Himself known to the children of Israel. After Joshua died, the city began to decline spiritually, and eventually, God rejected the priests who served in Shiloh (1 Sam. 1:3; 2:34–35). Even worse, God rejected Shiloh and removed His name from dwelling there (Ps. 78:60). And if the people of Judah did not turn from their sin, God would reject them as He did Shiloh.

No Prayers Allowed

God spoke to them, but they did not hear Him. He called out to them, but they did not answer Him (7:13). Because they had ignored Him, God said He would cast them out of His sight.

And then the unthinkable happened. God told Jeremiah not to pray for them because He would not hear him (7:16). He wouldn't hear them because He had taken away His steadfast love from them (16:5).

Why would God say such a thing? Because the people had turned from Him to their idols. They chose to give offerings to their gods instead of to God.

God had pleaded with them to obey His voice and to walk in the way of His commandments (7:23). Obedience was part of the covenant God had made with them. But they would not obey, and they would not listen. Because of the stubbornness of their evil hearts they "went backward, and not forward" (7:24).

The Real Problem

Their hearts—that's the problem. That's why they consistently broke the covenant.

Jeremiah shows us that Israel had a long history of not keeping the covenant. They repeatedly "backslid" away from God. In other words,

---

THE KETUVIM

Lamentations and the Story of Scripture

Introduction

The book of Lamentations is a lament over Jerusalem's destruction. A lament is basically a poem written for a funeral of a loved one. Most likely, Jeremiah was the author, and he was weeping and lamenting the people being taken away into captivity.

There are five poems in Lamentations—each one is a chapter. Four of these poems are acrostics. In an acrostic poem the first letter of each line spells a name or message or follows the letters in the alphabet. In this case, four of the poems follow the letters of the Hebrew alphabet.

Here's an English example:

Almighty God,
Blessed is Your name.
Creator of heaven and earth,
Deliver Your people.

Acrostics are not easy to write, and it takes time to think about what you are going to write. Using an acrostic shows that Jeremiah truly cared about what he was writing about. He took the time, even when he was mourning, to write poetry about his sadness.

Basis for God's Judgment

The book is more than a lament. Jeremiah also intended for it to express to the people of God that captivity and destruction were the appropriate responses to the way they were living. They had pushed God time and time again, and now He had to deal righteously with them. In other words, they were in captivity because of their sin and God's righteous response to their sin. Jeremiah is also telling them that they should respond to the chastisement with repentance.

God is patient and compassionate, not willing that any should perish (2 Pet 3:9; 1 Tim 2:4); but when all warnings are ignored, nothing remains but His judgment. We should never presume upon God's mercy and compassion. The Book of Lamentations contains the implied warning that sometimes it is too late to weep and repent; nonetheless, God is always faithful (3:23).
—F. B. Huey

The theme of Lamentations is not just despair for the people of God; it is also about hope in the midst of destruction. While everything was falling apart, Jeremiah could look back on what God had done for His people and exclaim, "I have hope" (3:21). The source of his hope is the steadfast love of God. He knew that God would show mercy in His wrath.

God's Steadfast Love

Judah's punishment would be severe. God would harshly punish them for their sins, but He would not destroy them completely, because He is loyal to the promises He made to Abraham, Isaac,

they abandoned God by turning their backs on Him and by turning toward sin (2:13).

They didn't think about God, consider doing His laws, or focus any attention on Him (18:15). Basically, they forgot about God (2:32). As a result they became ignorant of what He wanted them to do, and they did not know Him personally.

Why did they not think about God? Why did they forget Him?

They had evil hearts.

Why did they not obey God?

They had evil hearts.

The Solution

Obeying God's law was difficult for His people. There were a lot of laws to obey, and it was hard to know all of them and remember what to do. But that was not the real reason it was difficult. The real reason was an internal issue.

Jeremiah points out that Judah had tried to obey, but each time, the people fell back into idolatry and other wickedness. They didn't have the desire to obey. And they didn't have the faithful love for God that He wanted them to have.

Yes, the Mosaic Covenant was hard to obey, and yes, their hearts were evil and so they

and Jacob. He has a relationship with His people, and He wants them to desire a relationship with Him. When Jeremiah says that God's mercies are new every morning, he is saying that God's kindness to His people will never end. His faithfulness to His promises is great.

Jeremiah knew that God would bring suffering on His people for their sins, but Jeremiah also knew that God would have compassion on them. He says,

> For the Lord will not cast off for ever: But though he cause grief, yet will he have compassion according to the multitude of his mercies [steadfast love]. For he doth not afflict willingly nor grieve the children of men. (3:31–33)

God will not abandon His people forever. He doesn't enjoy causing sorrow or pain, and in the end He will show steadfast love to His people.

"It is of the Lord's mercies [steadfast love] that we are not consumed, because his compassions fail not. They are new every morning: great is thy faithfulness."

—Lamentations 3:22–23

Application

God is a merciful God, and He is loyally kind to His people. But don't mistake His mercy for leniency. It may seem like God is ignoring your sins, and then you get caught. Punishment follows, but you don't actually change. You go back to sinning and think that if you get caught again you can just endure the same punishment. "It'll be OK," you say. But Proverbs tells us, "He, that being often reproved hardeneth his neck, shall suddenly be destroyed, and that without remedy" (Prov. 29:1). A person who refuses to change even after

being caught will eventually go too far, and then there is no way to fix it. It's the Old Testament's way of saying you reap what you sow (Gal. 6:7).

In the case of Judah, the people of God had sinned. In fact, they had sinned over and over until God said enough is enough. When they reached that point, they could not turn back God's wrath. They were in trouble—deep trouble! And they reaped God's wrath.

But throughout the book of Lamentations we see that even in the middle of judgment, there is hope. God has not forgotten His promises to Abraham, and a remnant will survive His judgment. This shows that God still wants to have a relationship with His people even after they sin greatly.

The book of Lamentations also shows us that when we have sinned against God, we should confess our sins and ask Him to have mercy on us. Confession and repentance is the way to restore our broken relationship with God.

couldn't obey it. But the law couldn't fix the internal issues. It could only tell you what you ought to do. It was powerless to change a person to enable him to do what he ought. Something else was needed that could change the internal motivations and abilities.

So God promises them that a change will happen. And He will be the one who makes the change. If you read Jeremiah 31:31–34 you will see God's many "I wills." God describes His role and the parts of the New Covenant.

> ### *Heart*
>
> In Section 4.1, you read about the heart. You read how in the Old Testament, the heart represents everything about an individual. You also read that God desires His people to have a special kind of heart that would cause them to fear Him and keep all His commandments (Deut. 5:29). Early in Deuteronomy, God tells the people, "Thou shalt love the Lord thy God with all thine heart, and with all thy soul, and with all thy might" (6:5). Humanly speaking, this is impossible to do twenty-four hours a day, seven days a week.
>
> In the book of Jeremiah, God's people are showing how impossible it is to love and obey God without failing Him. Jeremiah repeatedly mentions how evil Judah's heart was.
>
> "O Jerusalem, wash thine heart from wickedness, that thou mayest be saved" (4:14).
>
> "This people hath a revolting and a rebellious heart; they are revolted and gone" (5:23).
>
> "But they hearkened not, nor inclined their ear, but walked in the counsels and in the imagination of their evil heart, and went backward, and not forward" (7:24).
>
> Jeremiah describes how wicked their hearts had become: "The heart is deceitful above all things, and desperately wicked: who can know it?" (17:9). In other words, the heart is sick. It is incurable. There is nothing they can do to change their hearts. They need new hearts.

- "I will make a new covenant" (31:31). God will make a New Covenant with them. Not like the one He had made with them on Mount Sinai (the Mosaic Covenant)—the one they repeatedly broke and the one that couldn't fix them on the inside. This will be a new and better covenant (31:31–32).

- "I will put my law in their inward parts" (31:33). The New Covenant will be better than the Old Covenant because it will be an internal covenant. God will put the law on each person's heart (31:33). And Ezekiel says this heart will be a new one that God will give them, and it will cause them to do right (Ezek. 36:26–27).

- "[I] will be their God, and they shall be my people" (31:33). It is better because it will reconcile God's people to Himself and it will be personal. They have rejected Him, but God will reestablish His close relationship with His people. And this New Covenant relationship will be personal. God says, "For they shall all know me" (31:34). Since God's law is written in their hearts, they will have no need for a teacher. All people, from the least to the greatest, will know the Lord and will know what God expects them to do—all because God will write the law on their hearts.

- "I will forgive their iniquity, and I will remember their sin no more" (31:34). It is better because God will bring forgiveness.

After God says He will do all these things, He tells His people they will be a nation for as long as the sun gives light by day and the moon and stars give light by night.

New Covenant

The book of Hebrews reveals that Jesus is the one who sets the New Covenant in motion and makes it happen. Jesus' blood was shed for the forgiveness of sins, and it is His blood that establishes the New Covenant (Matt. 26:28). Each time we celebrate communion and drink the

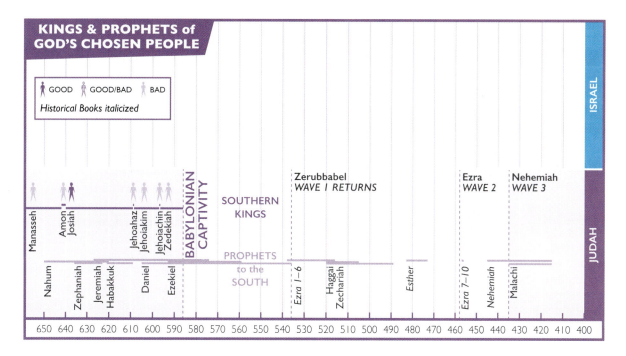

KINGS & PROPHETS of GOD'S CHOSEN PEOPLE

GOOD   GOOD/BAD   BAD

Historical Books italicized

ISRAEL

JUDAH

BABYLONIAN CAPTIVITY

SOUTHERN KINGS

PROPHETS to the SOUTH

Zerubbabel
WAVE I RETURNS

Ezra
WAVE 2

Nehemiah
WAVE 3

Manasseh
Amon
Josiah
Jehoahaz
Jehoiakim
Jehoiachin
Zedekiah

Nahum
Zephaniah
Jeremiah
Habakkuk
Daniel
Ezekiel
Ezra 1–6
Haggai
Zechariah
Esther
Ezra 7–10
Nehemiah
Malachi

650 640 630 620 610 600 590 580 570 560 550 540 530 520 510 500 490 480 470 460 450 440 430 420 410 400

fruit of the vine, we are celebrating the inauguration of the New Covenant (1 Cor. 11:25).

The New Covenant is an important part of God's plan for the nation of Israel and for the church. The New Covenant will ultimately fulfill the blessing to the world that God promised Abraham. You probably remember that God promised Abraham land, seed, and blessing. Part of that blessing is being a blessing to all the world. If you are a believer, you are part of the church and get to partake of some of the blessings of the New Covenant. You have a new heart and a new spirit (His Spirit), for example.

In the final days, Christ will completely fulfill the New Covenant. He will give the children of Israel a new heart and a new spirit (His Spirit). They will be obedient and walk in His ways. They will know God personally, and He will forgive their sin and remember it no more.

Think about that—He will remember their sin no more.

Have you ever done something wrong, I mean really wrong? You seek forgiveness and repent, but it's still in the back of your mind. You start thinking about what you did, and start to feel worthless even though you've confessed and repented. The devil likes for us to wallow in our past sins, but God doesn't. He doesn't dwell on our sins after we have confessed and repented of them. He remembers them no more.

Thinking It Through 8.1

1. How does Israel know that the New Covenant will be fulfilled?

2. What was the Mosaic Covenant unable to do?

3. What are the parts of the New Covenant?

4. What is so significant about God's writing His law on their hearts?

5. How does the New Covenant help fulfill the Abrahamic Covenant?

6. In Lamentations, what is the basis for God's judgment on His people?

8.2 EZEKIEL: RESTORATION OF GOD'S GLORY

Read Ezekiel 36:16–38
Memorize Ezekiel 36:26–27

The Watchman

Ezekiel was God's prophet to Israel for twenty-two years (592–570 BC). God addresses Ezekiel many times, but Ezekiel's name is mentioned only twice in the entire book (1:3; 24:24). God normally refers to him as "son of man." The title emphasizes that Ezekiel is merely a human, and as such, he is weak. In contrast, God is referred to more than two hundred times as "the Lord God" which emphasizes that God is powerful and sovereign. Ezekiel's title is also meant to remind him that Israel's only hope is God.

Ezekiel lived during the time of two other prophets—Daniel and Jeremiah. When God's people were taken into captivity, Daniel was taken to be with the leaders in Babylon. Ezekiel was taken to Babylon with the exiled Jews. And Jeremiah remained at home in Palestine. God provided His message to the leaders and people in exile, and He provided His message to the people who remained at home.

> "Son of man, I have made thee a watchman unto the house of Israel: therefore hear the word at my mouth, and give them warning from me."
>
> **—Ezekiel 3:17**

Ezekiel's main responsibility was to be a watchman for Israel. During Old Testament times, a watchman had the job of being a lookout for the city. The watchman was normally stationed at the highest point, usually a tower, along the walls of the city. His job was to watch for any danger outside the city walls. If an enemy or a fire or some other disaster was coming, it was the responsibility of the watchman to sound the alarm and let everyone know of the danger.

If he warned the people but they refused to listen, then the watchman was innocent when the danger came on them. But if he didn't warn the people of the coming danger, then the watchman was responsible for anything that happened to the city. It was a very important job.

God appointed Ezekiel as a different kind of watchman for Israel (3:17–27). He didn't have to climb a tower to see the danger and warn the people; rather, Ezekiel was a spiritual watchman, and his job was to warn the wicked to stop sinning and the righteous not to sin. His job wouldn't be easy. In fact, the people would bind him and keep him from going out to warn others.

Acting Out the Coming Siege

Ezekiel, like Jeremiah, often acted out his prophecies. At the end of Ezekiel 3, God closes Ezekiel's mouth and will not allow him to speak to the people until He tells Ezekiel exactly what to say. The spoken word is a powerful tool for communicating a message, but sometimes God chooses to use something visual. This time God tells Ezekiel to act out his prophecy.

In Ezekiel 4:1–8, God commands Ezekiel to act out a siege on Jerusalem. Ezekiel takes a soft brick and draws a map of Jerusalem on it. It would be clear to anyone watching that the brick is the city of Jerusalem. Then he creates a little siege ramp, sets up little camps all around the "city," and makes battering rams to attack the city. Then he uses an iron skillet as a siege wall to ensure that no one escapes from the city during the siege.

Although it may have looked like Ezekiel was playing with miniature soldiers, his whole act showed the people that Jerusalem would be sieged. They were not invincible. Jerusalem would fall. The iron skillet most likely illustrates that no one will escape the coming judgment.

God commands Ezekiel to lay on his left side for 390 days and face the north, which represents Israel. Then he is to lay on his right side for 40

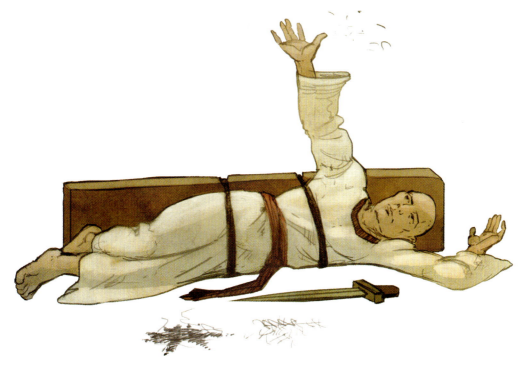

days facing south, which represents Judah. For all this time, he is to be bound by ropes so that he cannot move.

Ezekiel is making the point that the city of Jerusalem will come under siege. Just as Ezekiel cannot move around while he is on his side, so also Israel will not be free to move around when the siege starts. No one will escape God's judgment. Also, Israel's sin (390 days) is much worse that Judah's sin (40 days). They will have little to eat and drink during this time. And God will hold both Israel and Judah responsible for their sins.

The Shaved Head and Beard

While he is lying on his side, Ezekiel will eat defiled bread and drink only small amounts of water. He will also shave his head and beard. It was a disgrace for a priest to shave his head and beard, and that is exactly what God wants Ezekiel to represent to the people. They are a disgrace just like Ezekiel is.

As a priest, Ezekiel is supposed to represent God. He represents God's name and reputation. But he has to represent God in the way God wants him to look, act, and talk. With a shaved head and face he is a disgrace. He can't properly represent God. Israel is just like Ezekiel. They were supposed to be priests to the nations. They were supposed to represent God in the way God wanted them to. They were supposed to look, act, and talk a certain way. But in their sin, they

are a disgrace. And as a result, they can't represent God to the nations. So God has to send judgment to make them do what they should be doing.

After Ezekiel shaves his head, God commands him to take the hair and divide it into three piles. He burns the first pile of hair. Then he chops the second pile of hair into tiny pieces with a sword. Finally, he takes the third pile and throws it into the wind. He then finds any remaining hairs and puts them in the folds of his garment.

Can you imagine the people watching him shave his head and do these things to his hair? What does this all mean?

The hair that was removed from Ezekiel's head represents the Jews being removed from their land. One-third would die by fire in the siege, one-third would be killed by the sword, and one-third would be scattered around the world. But some would remain. There would be a remnant, and there was hope for the future.

This is exactly what God had said would happen to them back in Leviticus. God had told them that if they did not obey Him, He would strike them down in front of their enemies (Lev. 26:17), and He would bring a sword down on them (26:25). He would also scatter them among the nations (26:33). But He would remember His covenant with them and provide for those who turn to Him (26:39–46).

But why was God going to judge His people so severely? Because they had a problem—a big problem.

Heart Surgery

The problem with the people of Israel is difficult to see. Their laws are good—perfect, in fact, because they were written by God Himself (Ps. 19:7; Rom. 7:12). Their land is good; God gave it to them. Their heritage is good; it's full of God's miracles and God's mercy.

Their problem is not just difficult to see—actually, no one can see it. The problem is their hearts. They love sin. It's that simple.

The solution is simple too: God will have to give them new hearts. When it comes to good—when it comes to God—their hearts are as hard and unaffected as stones. God will have to perform a "rockectomy" and put new hearts in place of their old hearts.

This is exactly what God says through Ezekiel:

A new heart also will I give you, and a new spirit will I put within you: and I will take away the stony heart out of your flesh, and I will give you an heart of flesh. And I will put my spirit within you, and cause you to walk in my statutes, and ye shall keep my judgments, and do them. And ye shall dwell in the land that I gave to your fathers; and ye shall be my people, and I will be your God. (Ezek. 36:26–28)

There once was a young hiker, Aron Ralston, who had to amputate his own arm because he was pinned by a bolder in a remote canyon. He made headlines around the world and his story was turned into a movie, because everyone recognizes how incredibly difficult it would be to do such a thing.

But the kind of self-surgery necessary to change your heart? No one—not a Jew and not a Gentile—could do something like this. It takes a divine act of extreme power—and extreme grace—to accomplish this hardest of all operations. But that's exactly what God promises to do.

Notice what God said: "I will put my spirit within you" (Ezek. 36:27). The change comes because God's Spirit will cause the people to obey His laws. Before they had a new heart, they were careless and didn't really care about doing what God wanted them to do. Now with God's Spirit in them, they will be careful to observe and obey all God's rules.

Glory of the Lord

When God called Ezekiel, He gave him a vision of His glory. Ezekiel describes the glory of God in wonderful and magnificent terms. When you read Ezekiel's descriptions of what he saw, it is almost as if he is searching for words to describe what he saw. This vision of God's glory is similar to what Moses saw. It is also similar to what the people of Israel saw at the dedication of the temple when Solomon prayed.

While some details are similar between accounts, the descriptions of those details are vastly different. Why are they so different? The answer is a question: Who can ever describe the glory of God? We cannot understand or even describe God's glory, but He is giving us a hint of what it's like.

Ezekiel's vision is important to both his ministry and to God's purposes for Israel and Judah. When Ezekiel saw God's glory, he realized the greatness of God. This vision is what kept Ezekiel going. It is what helped him during the difficult times.

God's glory is also the reason behind the judgments God brought on Israel and Judah. God is a righteous and holy God. As such, He cannot tolerate sin and disobedience among His people. In order to cleanse His people, He must judge them. This judgment would include the destruction of the temple, and so God would have to remove His glory from the temple. God would no longer dwell with His people.

But this would not be permanent. God's glory would return after He had cleansed the people through judgment. Israel's new heart will one day allow them to follow God faithfully, and as a result God will dwell with them and reveal His glory to them forever.

The Restored Land

When they receive their new hearts and new spirits and are obeying God's laws, they will then be put back in the land God promised to their forefathers. The land will produce much fruit, and the people will not have to worry about famine. God is not doing this because they are a great and holy people. In fact they should be ashamed of their wicked ways. He is doing this for His name's sake. He is the one who promised Abraham, Isaac, and Jacob that they would have a land. And God is going to deliver on His promises.

And when God proves Himself holy by delivering on His promises, the nations will know that He is the Lord (36:25). The nations will see Israel return to its land, and they will see the land being marvelously restored from a ruined and desolate condition to a place like the Garden of Eden (36:35–38). And then the nations will know that the Lord is the one who rebuilt the ruined places and restored the desolate land. And they will all know that He alone is Lord.

The New Covenant

Ezekiel's prophecy of Israel's restoration is part of the New Covenant. In the New Covenant, God will give His people a new heart. In the lesson on Jeremiah, you read about this new heart. Do you remember that one key to understanding a passage is to look for things that are repeated? So if you see a word or phrase repeated over and over in a passage it's probably important. Well the same holds true for something repeated by multiple people in different books. Beginning in Deuteronomy, Moses talked to the people about their hearts. Jeremiah pointed out how wicked the heart was and the need for a new heart. Ezekiel also talks about a new heart. Things repeated need to be heeded.

When you see a word, phrase, or concept repeated throughout Scripture, you should pay close attention to what is being said. In this case, Israel, Judah, and even you need a new heart.

Thinking It Through 8.2

1. What is Israel's problem and what is the solution for restoring Israel?

2. What is significant about God's putting His Spirit in the people?

3. Why is God restoring Israel?

4. Why does God have to judge His people?

5. How did Ezekiel's disgrace as a priest (shaving his beard) reflect Israel's relationship with the world?

The Theme of Dominion

The book of Daniel, which picks up the story after Kings, says a lot about dominion, a special biblical theme.

What is a theme? Think of an analogy to music: John Williams is probably the best-known film-score composer of all time. And the *Star Wars* scores are definitely his most famous work.

In his *Star Wars* scores, Williams used a technique he borrowed from opera called "leitmotif." Whenever a certain character is being featured on screen, his "leitmotif" or "theme" will play on the soundtrack (e.g., Luke's theme, Leia's theme, or Anakin's theme). Darth Vader's theme—also called the Imperial March—is particularly grand and chilling (like Gustav Holst's "Mars, Bringer of War," from which Williams borrowed). But Darth Vader's theme isn't played the same way every time. As Vader lies dying in his son's arms, his theme melody is played softly on a harp.

The Bible isn't a movie; it's not a made-up story. But it is, among many other things, a work of art. It too has leitmotifs, themes that arise again and again. Think of sin, salvation, judgment, mercy, faith, sacrifice, temple, or even water.

And dominion. The theme of dominion got its start when God gave dominion to mankind in Genesis 1:26–28. There, the dominion theme is played in bright and upbeat music, promising a glorious future.

Adam's dominion over the earth was deeply damaged by the Fall, but it didn't disappear. Many years later, God gave His people dominion over the land of Canaan. They were supposed to make something of their land and rule it for God's glory. You can imagine the theme music being hopeful again—but with some darkness on the edges because of the Israelites' failures on their way into the land.

God's Dominion in Daniel 1–6

God couldn't have given dominion to humans if He didn't have it Himself. You can't make someone else king unless you have the authority to do so. God has all authority. So even when Adam messed up his dominion, the Lord remained firmly on His throne.

Now that we've reached the time of Daniel, however, it may appear that Yahweh has lost His supreme position; after all, His people are all scattered out of their land. His plan seems to have hit a brick wall of hard Jewish hearts. But the Lord doesn't want anyone to suffer these misunderstandings. He still rules, even if His people are temporarily undergoing terrible judgment. All the powerful kings named in the book of Daniel are forced in various ways to recognize this fact.

Daniel, carried off from Judah as a young man, lived through the kingships of at least six monarchs. Nebuchadnezzar, Belshazzar, and Darius are the most significant, and they're the ones named in the book of Daniel. In each of their three administrations, Daniel is a high official and a trusted leader. But each of these kings starts his rule having a serious disagreement with Daniel—although they don't know it. Nebuchadnezzar, Belshazzar, and Darius all assume that the title of "supreme world ruler" belongs to them; Daniel knows it belongs to Yahweh alone.

Nebuchadnezzar

Nebuchadnezzar's name, like many ancient names, was a way of honoring his gods. But through three major incidents in his life, which are recorded in Daniel, God compels Nebuchadnezzar to honor the one and only true God.

The first story is about Nebuchadnezzar's dream, the one no one could interpret (because he wouldn't tell anyone what it was!). Daniel, by the power and knowledge of God, discerned what the king had dreamed and told him what it meant. And don't miss the point of the dream: there will be many world kingdoms (represented in the dream by the statue made of gold, silver, iron, and clay), but one day "the God of heaven [will] set up a kingdom, which shall never be destroyed . . . and it shall stand for ever" (Dan. 2:44). God's kingdom was represented as the stone that crushed the statue. Daniel also says that Nebuchadnezzar has power only because this God of heaven has given it to him (2:37–38).

At the end of story number one, Nebuchadnezzar falls to the ground and manages to get his theology close to the whole truth: "Your God is a God of gods, and a Lord of kings, and a revealer of secrets" (2:47). But he's not ready to say, yet, that the Lord is the only God there is.

That becomes clear in story number two, which tells how Nebuchadnezzar sets up a ninety-foot statue of himself for everyone to worship! Clearly, he didn't get the point of his own dream! When he tries to get Daniel's three friends, worshipers of the true God, to worship his idol, there's another showdown between supreme world rulers. And Yahweh wins. Nebuchadnezzar can't even singe a hair on the three Jewish heads— and someone divine is spotted protecting them.

This time King Nebuchadnezzar makes a proclamation to his massive kingdom, letting everyone know that the one he calls the "Most High God" rules forever. But he still doesn't quite get it. He still thinks that he can take credit for his successes.

So God makes the lesson unmistakable in story three. He sends another dream, which (as Daniel explains) means that "the most High ruleth in the kingdom of men, and giveth it to whomsoever he will, and setteth up over it the [humblest] of men" (Dan. 4:17). And here comes the unmistakable part: after

Nebuchadnezzar praises himself for his successes, the Lord forces Nebuchadnezzar down to his knees and makes him eat grass. Hannah was right: God delights to put down the mighty and lift up the humble (1 Sam. 2:6–7). Few people have ever gone from as high to as humble as Nebuchadnezzar did.

Surprisingly, Nebuchadnezzar doesn't respond in anger. He finally gets the point. And it is from the lips of this pagan king that we hear one of the best statements of God's sovereignty in all of Scripture. He spits the grass out of his mouth and says,

> All the inhabitants of the earth are reputed as nothing: and [Yahweh] doeth according to his will in the army of heaven, and among the inhabitants of the earth: and none can stay his hand, or say unto him, What doest thou? (Dan. 4:35)

This is precious, precious truth. And as far as we know, no other king on earth at that time was willing to admit it. Only this one. Why did God work so steadily on him alone? Perhaps because he was the king ruling over God's exiled people. Or perhaps it's because he is so great (he is called the head of gold in another dream in Daniel 2:38) that he is the one who learns the lesson of humility.

God does give rulership to humans, but these people have to remember where their power comes from.

Belshazzar and Darius

When it's their turn to rule, Belshazzar and Darius have to learn the same lesson Nebuchadnezzar did. For Belshazzar, that lesson comes as a shock all in one night—at the end of which he lies dead.

Darius gets a better chance to learn. And he learns in an experience very similar to Nebuchadnezzar's. He sets up a new law to make himself not just the supreme ruler, but the one being that all people are supposed to pray to! This, of course, is treading on God's territory. Only He can really hear and answer prayer. So the story of Daniel and the lion's den is a way of showing us how Darius had to come to the same conclusion Nebuchadnezzar did. This is what Darius says after Daniel survives his night with the man-eating beasts:

> I make a decree, That in every dominion of my kingdom men tremble and fear before the God of Daniel: for he is the living God, and stedfast for ever, and his kingdom that which shall not be destroyed, and his dominion shall be even unto the end. He delivereth and rescueth, and he worketh signs and wonders in heaven and in earth, who hath delivered Daniel from the power of the lions. (Dan. 6:26–27)

One by one, the major world rulers of Daniel's day come to recognize that there's one Major World Ruler over all major world rulers. People have dominion, yes. But God has dominion over all dominion.

God's Dominion in Daniel 7–12

The second half of Daniel doesn't contain stories but a series of visions about the future—plus one long prayer for the Jewish people (Dan. 9).

The theme of dominion does not drop away in this section of the book but instead finds its glorious fulfillment. Throughout history humanity has rebelled against God's dominion and tried to make its own rules work (remember Psalm 2). In Daniel 7 these human kingdoms in rebellion against God are pictured as monstrous beasts. Man was to rule the beasts; instead he has become like them.

Seventy Years, Seventy Weeks

During the first year of Darius's reign, Daniel realizes something important. Jeremiah had predicted that Judah's captivity would last precisely seventy years (Dan. 9:2; cf. Jer. 25:12). This leads Daniel to pray in repentance for Israel's sins, and then to pray that God would not leave Jerusalem desolate. Daniel wants God to bring the people back to their home.

God actually sends the angel Gabriel to reply to Daniel because, as the angel says, Daniel is "greatly beloved" (Dan. 9:23). And Gabriel's reply includes some peeks into the future. Jerusalem will indeed be rebuilt, and after sixty-nine weeks of years an anointed one (a *mashiyach—Messiah*) will come.

This passage in Daniel 9 gets a little complicated; the seventy weeks Gabriel speaks of are sets of seven years each, and if this is true then Daniel could figure out when the Messiah would come.

Restoring the world means putting God and humanity back in their proper places—both should be rulers. But people have to rule under God's greater rule. The rest of the vision shows God's plan for restoring the world. Daniel sees the Ancient of Days—God Himself—sitting on His amazing throne made of a flame of fire. Then someone like a son of man approaches the Ancient of Days. This person is human—his appearance is as a son of man. But He is also God. It is only God who comes with clouds of heaven elsewhere in the Bible (Exod. 19:9; 34:5; Isa. 19:1; Ezek. 1:4; cf. Matt. 17:5).

What does this person, who is both God and man, receive? Dominion.

> And there was given him dominion, and glory, and a kingdom, that all people, nations, and languages, should serve him: his dominion is an everlasting dominion, which shall not pass away, and his kingdom that which shall not be destroyed. (Dan. 7:14)

When this dream is interpreted for Daniel by an angel, he finds out that the Son of Man will also give dominion to His people. They will rule with Him.

The whole story of the Bible up to this point has been the story of what God is doing to restore His dominion—and humanity's dominion—to the way He created it to be.

Thinking It Through 8.3

1. How do God's dealings with Nebuchadnezzar show God's dominion?

2. In your own words describe what Nebuchadnezzar said after God restored his sanity to him. (Dan. 4:34–35)

3. True or False. Humans have no place in ruling creation; only God does. Explain your answer.

4. Why was it important for Darius to see God deliver Daniel from the lions' den?

5. For what purpose does the Son of Man receive dominion?

8.4 EZRA: RETURN OF THE EXILES

Read Ezra 9:1–10:19
Memorize Ezra 7:10

Back in Section 1.2 you read about the great fictional detective Sherlock Holmes, who mentioned the obvious things that nobody observes. Along this same line, he once commented to his assistant, Watson, "You see, but you do not observe." The pattern of splashed mud on a man's pant cuff, the number of steps in the stairs leading up to 221B Baker Street (Holmes's residence), or the curious absence of a door knocker—anybody can see these things, but very few people observe them.

Similarly the careful Bible reader will spot details, clues left in Scripture by the writers. For example, what do you make of the following two paragraphs? The first one is the very last paragraph in 2 Chronicles:

Now in the first year of Cyrus king of Persia, that the word of the Lord spoken by the mouth of Jeremiah might be accomplished, the Lord stirred up the spirit of Cyrus king of Persia, that he made a proclamation throughout all his kingdom, and put it also in writing, saying, Thus saith Cyrus king of Persia, All the kingdoms of the earth hath the Lord God of heaven given me; and he hath charged me to build him an house in Jerusalem, which is in Judah. Who is there among you of all his people? The Lord his God be with him, and let him go up. (2 Chron. 36:22–23)

And this is the first paragraph in the very next book of the Bible, Ezra:

Now in the first year of Cyrus king of Persia, that the word of the Lord by the mouth of Jeremiah might be fulfilled, the Lord stirred up the spirit of Cyrus king of Persia, that he made a proclamation throughout all his kingdom, and put it also in writing, saying, Thus saith Cyrus king of Persia, The Lord God of heaven hath given me all the kingdoms of the earth; and he hath charged me to build him an house at Jerusalem, which is in Judah. Who is there among you of all his people? his God be with him, and let him go up to Jerusalem, which is in Judah, and build the house of the Lord God of Israel, (he is the God,) which is in Jerusalem. (Ezra 1:1–3)

You see, but do you observe? Obviously, you're supposed to notice a connection between the two books, like stitches holding two pieces of cloth together.

You have to remember that these books, Chronicles and Ezra, were written in a time before the invention of the technology we call the book. Before the book, it was pretty much impossible to have a table of contents for the Bible. How do you give page numbers to unconnected scrolls?

So "stitches" like the ones you just read were a way of letting readers know what order the books were supposed to come in. Someone wanted Chronicles-Ezra-Nehemiah to be viewed as one continuous story.

And the story is remarkable. Cyrus says something unexpected for a pagan king—just like the three major rulers in Daniel: Cyrus says that his rule is something he received from the Lord. This doesn't mean that Cyrus necessarily worships Yahweh. More than likely there are plenty of other gods in his collection, and he seems to think that Yahweh is just the God in Jerusalem (check out different translations of Ezra 1:3*c*). But still, Yahweh's hand is very clear in Cyrus's pronouncement.

Return in Three Waves

How else could you explain that, after seventy years, the Jews are being sent back to the land God promised their forefather Abraham? They got themselves kicked out of their land by sinning worse than the Canaanites who lived there before them (2 Kings 21:9). And now God—through Cyrus—is mercifully sending them back.

It's important to understand right away that the return of the Jews happens in three waves.

WAVE 1	WAVE 2	WAVE 3
536 BC	458 BC (78 years later)	445 BC (13 years later)
Zerubbabel leads 49,897 Jews back to Jerusalem.	Ezra leads about 1,800 Jewish men (and their families) back.	Nehemiah leads an unspecified number of Jews back.

The first six of Ezra's ten chapters are actually all about that first wave. Its leader, Zerubbabel, was the grandson of King Jehoiachin, and he led the people back with Cyrus's blessing to rebuild the temple. The lists of families and the many numbers at the beginning of Ezra are an annoyance to modern readers—we want action. But these lists are important because they demonstrate that God's people had not totally disintegrated during the captivity. Many Jewish people kept their family trees, at least, and remembered who they were. That's hard to do, especially over a period of many decades as a minority in someone else's country.

Some things even changed for the better during the seventy years. Some of the Jews clearly took Jeremiah's advice and worked for the peace and prosperity of Babylon because prosperity has now come their way too. Of the almost fifty thousand people who come back to Jerusalem in the first wave, close to ten thousand are servants, though it's unclear if these are Jews or not. Only prosperous people have servants.

After Zerubbabel's grand return, however, the rebuilding of the temple doesn't get completed for twenty years. Certain people in the land oppose it, and the work is not finished until God's prophets (Haggai and Zechariah) insist that the Jews build anyway. (God even forces their enemies to pay for the work!) When the new temple is dedicated in 516 BC, it doesn't match the glory of Solomon's temple—the old people who had seen the first temple know that much. But at least it's there.

Ezra Appears on the Scene

Six more decades pass and God wants more of His people back in their land. So He raises up a "scribe" (basically a scholar in Jewish law) named Ezra to lead more Jews back. Also a priest, Ezra is one of the rare people in Scripture about whom the Bible says nothing negative.

Ezra surely sinned like the rest of us, but the Bible says he had set "his heart to seek [or "study"] the law of the Lord, and to do it, and to teach in Israel statutes and judgments" (Ezra 7:10). This would make an excellent example for any young man or woman preparing to serve God as a teacher of the Bible. A man who gets up and preaches God's Word in a church, a woman who teaches orphans in a mission school, or anyone who teaches God's Word to others has to do heart preparation and intellectual preparation. Knowing God's Word takes hard work.

> "Ezra had prepared his heart to seek the law of the Lord."
>
> **—Ezra 7:10**

Ezra's studies and his heart make him a reliable theological voice. Even his gut instincts are right. He just knows—even without a particular Bible verse commanding him—that asking the king for soldiers to protect the Jews from robbers on their way to Jerusalem would be wrong. The Old Testament stories Ezra had read show that bringing soldiers would rob God of an opportunity to show His power—and His love for His people. So Ezra fasts and prays earnestly, and God protects the Jewish travelers.

After Ezra arrives safely in Jerusalem, the first thing he does is lead the people in making sacrifices and offerings to the Lord. Things are looking up.

Treachery

But not for long. Treachery is coming. A modern story may help you feel the force of the ancient one.

The Christian movie *The Time Changer* features a Bible professor from the 1800s who time-travels into our day. When the professor, Russell Carlisle, arrives in the twenty-first century, he soon finds other Christians he can fellowship with. He attends their church happily, and when the Bible study group he winds up in plans a movie night, he tags along.

The camera shows him sitting in his bucket seat with his popcorn. His first movie! Then the scene cuts to the empty lobby. You can see the doors to the room where the movie is playing. You can hear the dialogue muffled by the walls. And then Russell suddenly bursts through the doors with a terrible look on his face. He shouts, "Stop this movie! You must stop this movie! The man on the screen just blasphemed the name of the Lord!"

Other people roll their eyes; all the other Christians just stay inside the movie theater. But Russell Carlisle experienced something that seems to be getting rarer in modern America: he was appalled. He didn't just agree to disagree with the sin he saw; it deeply bothered and offended him. Hearing the Lord's name taken in vain stirred up righteous anger in his heart.

This is the same character quality we can see in Ezra. It seems the people of Judah in his day were blaspheming the Lord in a different way. The local Jewish officials tell Ezra soon after he arrives,

> The people of Israel, and the priests, and the Levites, have not separated themselves from the people of the lands, doing according to their abominations, even of the Canaanites, the Hittites, the Perizzites, the Jebusites, the Ammonites, the Moabites, the Egyptians, and the Amorites. For they have taken of their daughters for themselves, and for their sons: so that the holy seed have mingled themselves with the people of those lands. (Ezra 9:1–2)

Ezra, like Russell Carlisle, is appalled. Totally amazed and ashamed. Stirred with righteous anger. These returned exiles have betrayed the Lord!

We live in a world where sin is normal—and that in itself is nothing strange. People have always been sinners. But there is something different about our modern world: sin is on display in ways your great-grandparents could never have imagined. Even the smallest kid can watch and listen to sexual or violent acts that people a hundred years ago would have had to work very hard to see. Most modern Christians don't get appalled by sin—like Ezra was—very often. The sad fact is that they actually tend to take it as a badge of honor that they're not easily offended. But sometimes that's a mark of shame. Open sin ought to offend us.

The Jewish returnees in Ezra's day have started into one of the very sins that got them kicked out of the land in the first place: they've married pagans who will tempt them to worship other gods. So Ezra takes immediate action. Jewish men must divorce their non-Jewish wives, he insists. And the people do it.

Finished?

The book of Ezra demonstrates to everyone that God's promises through Jeremiah (Jer. 29) came true. The people were in exile for seventy years, but just as Jeremiah prophesied, they're back.

Right after God (through Jeremiah) made that promise, He promised something else even more important:

> Ye shall seek me, and find me, when ye shall search for me with all your heart. (Jer. 29:13)

This has happened too. Ezra has led the people to seek the Lord—but what will happen when he's gone? Does Israel's history give any indication that they will start to seek the Lord with all their hearts like Ezra did?

No. In order for that to happen, we need an Ezra who can take Manassehs and turn them into Ezras! We need a priest better even than Ezra.

Thinking It Through 8.4

1. How does God "stitch" the books of Chronicles and Ezra together?

2. What was the purpose of the first return under Zerubbabel? Was it successful? Why or why not?

3. What was Ezra's concern about having soldiers go along to protect the returning captives on their trip?

4. Compare Ezra's reaction and modern society's reactions to sin.

5. What is significant about Ezra preparing his heart?

8.5 ZECHARIAH: JUDGMENT & RESTORATION

Read Zechariah 1
Memorize Zechariah 1:3; Haggai 1:5

In the previous lesson, you read that the temple rebuilding didn't always go smoothly. Certain people in the land opposed it, and the work wasn't finished until God's prophets insisted that the Jews build anyway.

One of those prophets was Zechariah. His name means "Jehovah has remembered." He began ministering in 520 BC, the second year of King Darius's reign, and he worked during the same time as Haggai. The first wave of Jews returned to the land around 536 BC. So Zechariah started his ministry about sixteen years after Zerubbabel led the people back to Jerusalem to rebuild the temple.

God sent Zechariah to motivate the people to finish the job. God did not allow them to return to the land just so they could be back home. No, He wanted them to finish the temple. Zechariah and Haggai worked together to encourage the people to finish the job (Ezra 5:1–2).

> "Zechariah's first task was to support Haggai in encouraging the completion of the temple."
>
> —Joyce G. Baldwin

Zechariah's Message

When Zechariah arrived on the scene, Israel's neighbors were undermining the rebuilding work at the temple. The people were discouraged and somewhat afraid of those opposing the work. Zechariah's message addresses those issues and gives the people hope.

His message focuses on God's preserving the remnant of His people from their persecutors. God will judge Israel's oppressors and destroy them. He promises a Messiah who will provide restoration for His people and the Gentiles. The Messiah will establish the promised kingdom and rule over the nations. Zechariah's message reveals God's unwavering condemnation of sin and His steadfast commitment to the covenant He made with His servant David.

Israel isn't an innocent bystander in all of this. The people of Israel need cleansing and restoration. God is a sovereign God, and He demands justice. As a result, God will judge both Israel and the surrounding nations. But God is a gracious God, and He will not completely destroy either of them. He will provide cleansing for both Israel and the nations.

Zechariah begins his message by reminding his listeners of the judgments that fell on their forefathers (1:2). Their forefathers did not pay attention to God's warnings, and He judged them for their disobedience (1:4–6). They called out to God in the judgment, but God in His anger did not hear them (7:12–13). He scattered them and placed them under heathen rule (7:14). As a result, they came to their senses and repented.

A Message of Repentance

God had dealt harshly with Israel's forefathers, but He did not want to deal with this generation in the same manner. So the Lord says, "Turn to Me" (1:3).

Turn. From what?

"From your evil ways, and from your evil doings" (1:4).

Repentance is more than admitting you are wrong. It is also turning from your sin and turning to God. It means that you stop doing wrong and start doing right. It means separating yourself from what is sinful and clinging to what is righteous.

That is what Zechariah is telling the people. He is reminding them that they must repent. They must turn from evil and to God lest they provoke His anger against them like their forefathers did.

And they must turn so that God can return to them (1:3). When God turned from their forefathers, they were taken into captivity. Judgment came on them, and they suffered greatly. When God returns to them, judgment will cease and they will prosper again.

God's Judgment

God's judgment falls on more than just Israel; it also falls on the nations that surround Israel (9:1–7). Unlike Israel, the surrounding nations were living peacefully. But they were not as safe as they thought they were. Their peace would soon end, and they would face the judgment of God. God had summoned these nations and used them to execute His judgment on the nation of Israel. But these nations abused their privileges and were exceedingly cruel to Israel (1:15). Israel was the apple of God's eye, and Babylon had mistreated them (2:7–9). As a result, God would punish the nations (1:18–21; 11:1–3), and He would end His warnings (6:8). God would even use His people to carry out some of His judgments (9:13).

The Need for Cleansing

Although God's judgment of Israel's forefathers was severe, His purpose was not to annihilate them. God must judge Israel in order to cleanse and purify the nation. Israel was full of sin and uncleanness (13:1; cf. 3:4, 9; 5:8). In addition,

the people would pierce the Messiah whom God would send (12:10). The nation needed cleansing.

Perhaps the most vivid example of the need for cleansing is in Zechariah's fourth vision. In this vision, Zechariah sees Joshua the high priest (not the same Joshua that led the children of Israel into the Promised Land) standing before God in filthy garments (3:1–10). These garments aren't just dirty. They're covered in dung. They are absolutely disgusting.

But these are garments that the high priest, the one who represents the people before God, wears. His filthy clothes represent his sinfulness and Israel's sinfulness. So if the high priest—who is supposed to stand before God as the most clean individual—is defiled with garments covered in dung, then imagine how much more defiled are the sinful people he represents!

Standing beside the high priest is none other than the accuser—Satan. And he stands there accusing the high priest before God. "If the high priest is defiled," Satan accuses, "then he cannot represent the people before God." If there is no high priest, then the people are in big trouble. What will God say or do about this problem?

Imputation

Imputation means "to charge to one's account." A good example in the Bible of imputation is Onesimus, who became a believer under Paul's ministry. Onesimus was a slave who had run away from his master, Philemon. To help make amends for Onesimus's running away, Paul instructed Philemon that if Onesimus had wronged Philemon or owed him anything, "Put that on mine account" (Philem. 1:18). In other words, "Impute that to me. I'll pay it. Onesimus will owe nothing."

In the case of Onesimus, the debt was removed because Paul had Philemon impute (place) that debt on him. In a similar way, our sins were imputed on Christ (placed on His account). This is called *atonement*, and it happened at the cross.

In exchange for the believer's sins, Christ imputes His righteousness to us (places it on the believer's account). This is called *justification*, and it happens when a person repents of his or her sins and turns to God (salvation).

Imputation is what is going on here in Zechariah. The Lord is putting new clothes on the high priest. He is imputing His righteousness onto the high priest.

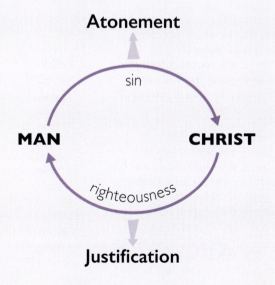

Instead of rebuking the high priest, God rebukes Satan! And He exposes Satan's evil plan against Jerusalem. Why didn't God rebuke the high priest? Because God had chosen Jerusalem, and He has a relationship with Israel and Judah through the covenants (1:17; 2:12). God is being loyally faithful to His people.

The high priest was like a charred stick that was pulled from a fire. He had been rescued from judgment, but like the stick, he was filthy and defiled by the sins of Israel. But God has compassion on His people. He is going to rescue them too.

God looks at the high priest in his filthy garments and has compassion on him. He tells those standing by Him to remove those filthy garments—this symbolizes God's gracious forgiveness of the sin of both the high priest and the people. In the place of filthy garments, the high priest receives clean garments—this symbolizes the restoration of the people before God through righteousness provided by the Lord. The priest is justified before God. God forgives his sin and imputes the righteousness of Christ on him.

When the Lord imputes His righteousness onto the high priest, the high priest is restored to fellowship with God. But the restoration comes

EXCURSUS

Haggai: Consider Your Ways

Imagine it is late summer, 520 BC. It's a special day in Jerusalem. There will be special sacrifices at the temple and the trumpeters will be playing. It's the first day of the month—the new moon festival—when families gather to eat festival meals (1 Sam. 20:18). But most importantly, it's a day appointed for God to remember His people and for them to acknowledge Him as their King (Num. 10:10; 28:11–15).

And so Haggai goes to the temple for the new moon festivities. But there is a problem. There is no temple.

When the people returned to Jerusalem, they had enthusiastically begun to rebuild the temple. But then they met opposition, and it became more and more difficult to work on the temple.

Slowly the people began to focus on their homes and not the temple. Eventually, they completely ignored building the temple. But they haven't ignored their own homes. Their homes are luxurious. The walls of their houses are overlaid with paneling—a great extravagance in this day.

This has gone on for fifteen years. In the people's minds, it just isn't the right time to rebuild the temple—too much opposition, and they have houses they need to take care of. Their priorities are out of order.

This People

And so God calls them "*This people.*"

Not "*My people,*" but "*This people.*"

They are no longer considered God's people! And so Haggai warns them twice, "Consider your ways" (1:5, 7).

Haggai's warning suggests a major overhaul for God's people:

The Hebrew says literally, "Set your heart upon your ways." In the Old Testament, the "heart" refers to the entire inner man, including the mind, emotions, and will. The word "ways" refers to the customs and habits of life. Haggai was calling for a change in thinking, feeling, and doing. The problem was serious, and the solution had to be pervasive.

—Michael P. V. Barrett

And the people of God respond. They consider their ways, and they turn from their sin and turn to God (1:12–15). They also fear the Lord and show reverence to Him (1:12) because He is now with them (1:13). Finally, they obey and immediately return to rebuilding the temple.

Unlike other prophets, Haggai's first message obtains the desired results. The repentance of the people most likely explains why his ministry is so brief. There is little else for Haggai to warn them about.

Take Courage

But he does have several other messages. In his second message (2:1–9), Haggai tells the people that they can take courage, because they are doing the right thing. God says that His Spirit is abiding with them in their midst (2:5). One day this temple will be filled with His glory.

In his third message, Haggai continues to encourage the people (2:10–19). He tells them they are doing right, and he reminds them of the consequences of doing wrong. They need to remember why their circumstances are so

with a warning. The high priest and the people must walk in God's ways and serve Him. This is outward evidence of internal repentance. As long as they walk in God's ways, they will have complete and free access to God's presence.

In other words, the high priest and the people must repent of their sins. They must turn from their sin and turn to God by obeying Him.

The Promised King

After telling the story about exchanging the high priest's filthy garments for clean ones, Zechariah tells about a man whom God calls His Servant, the Branch (3:8). The Branch is the one who will bring ultimate cleansing and restoration to Israel.

The Servant is more than a servant—He is a descendant of David. He has the right to rule, and therefore, He will be a king. Zechariah speaks of this King who is coming to be with God's people. This King is just and comes with salvation. And He will make a triumphal entry into Jerusalem on a donkey (9:9–10).

But someone will betray the King for thirty pieces of silver (11:12–13). The King, who is like a shepherd to His people, will be struck, and as a result His people will scatter like wandering sheep (13:7). Someone will pierce the King's side,

> "If people are not right with God, their society will be warped and ineffective, and their religion will reflect their character, not change it. The springs of life need to be clean if the outflow is to be clean."
>
> —J. Alec Motyer

difficult. They had been disobedient, and they suffered for it.

In his final message, Haggai speaks about a future time when all the kingdoms of the earth will fail (2:20–23). But God will raise up a new leader ("my servant") for His people. This leader will come through the line of David, and a kingdom will be set up that will not fail.

Holy and Unholy; Clean and Unclean

In Haggai's third message, he asks the priests two questions (2:11–13). In the first question, he asks, "If a priest carries holy meat in the fold of his garment and touches something that is not holy (such as bread, food, or oil), does it make that which is not holy, holy?"

The answer is no.

He asks a second question: "What if someone who has touched a dead body (and is, therefore, unclean) touches the bread or the food or even the meat the priest is carrying? Will what he touches be unclean?"

The answer is yes. Whatever an unclean person touches becomes unclean.

So touching something holy doesn't make you holy, but touching something unclean can make you unclean. Think of a healthy person and a sick person. You can't catch health, but you can catch sickness.

Defiled people spread their defilement to everything they touch. It affects their lives and the lives around them. It affects their work, and it affects their worship. Most importantly, it affects their fellowship with God. God demands cleanness, holiness, and purity in the lives of His children. Haggai is telling them to straighten up and do right because it affects everything they do.

Restoration of the Temple

The main problem that Haggai addressed was Israel's priorities. The people needed to put God first. In this case it meant rebuilding the temple. Yes, they faced opposition and difficulties. But these troubles should not have deterred them from doing what was right.

Rebuilding the temple was their way of contributing to the work of God's kingdom. In modern society we too face problems and opposition. But the work of God's kingdom should not stop or be limited because of those difficulties. The proper perspective is to make God and the work of His kingdom your most important priority in life.

and the people will mourn for Him whom they have pierced (12:10).

Does this sound familiar? Do you know of someone who had all these things happen to Him? You should. All of Scripture has been pointing to Him. Sometimes it is not obvious. But here in Zechariah it is clear that the prophet is speaking about the Messiah who was betrayed, crucified, pierced in His side, and slain.

But the story does not end there. The Messiah will one day return to cleanse the sins of the people. He will descend and stand on the Mount of Olives (14:4ff), and it will split into two halves forming a valley in between the two sides. The wicked will try to escape through this new valley, but they won't be able to. It will be a unique day (the Day of the Lord) that marks the start of a new kingdom.

The Messiah will set up His kingdom on the earth (14:9) and the curse will be removed. Jerusalem will once again dwell in safety (14:10). It will be a prosperous time for the nation. But most importantly, it will be a time when the holiness of God is made known to all people. This is the fulfilling of the New Covenant.

That time is still to come. And the coming kingdom is something all God's people can get excited about.

Thinking It Through 8.5

1. What did God intend to accomplish by judging Israel?

2. What is imputation? When was our sin imputed to Christ? When is His righteousness imputed to us?

3. What was the purpose of Zechariah's ministry?

4. Describe repentance.

5. What is the significance of the high priest having soiled garments?

6. What does Haggai mean when he tells the people to consider their ways—what all is involved in "consider your ways"?

8.6 ESTHER: WHY GOD'S SILENCE IS NOT ABSENCE

Read See Exercise 8.6.
Memorize Esther 4:14

Of the seven books in C. S. Lewis's Chronicles of Narnia series, *The Horse and His Boy* might be the most exciting. The horse is a talking Narnian horse named Bree. And his boy, Shasta, is a slave. Both are slaves, in fact, and stuck in the land of Calormen, where they don't belong. Through an amazing run of good luck, they escape back to their homelands together—along with two other escapees, a horse and her girl (Hwin and Aravis).

But these four met in the first place only because of remarkably bad luck. Lions chased them until they ran into each other! And later in the story, after an exhausting journey through the desert, Shasta, Bree, Aravis, and Hwin were chased by yet another lion just as they were about to reach safety!

Shortly after that chase, Shasta does succeed in his quest—but then he gets stranded alone! He stumbles through a dense fog, hungry and thirsty and tired and feeling awfully sorry for himself—until he runs into a person, a Thing, a Large Voice. . . . It's hard to tell what it is in all the fog.

Shasta starts a conversation with the Thing, and soon he's complaining about how unlucky he is.

"I do not call you unfortunate," said the Large Voice.

"Don't you think it was bad luck to meet so many lions?" said Shasta.

"There was only one lion," said the Voice.

"What on earth do you mean? I've just told you there were at least two the first night, and—"

"There was only one: but he was swift of foot."

"How do you know?"

"I was the lion."

If you've read any of the Narnia stories, you know that Shasta was speaking to Aslan, the Great Lion, the Son of the Emperor-over-the-Sea. Aslan in the Narnia stories represents Jesus Christ in our world. Aslan explains to Shasta that he has been laying out Shasta's path the whole time—in fact, for his entire life.

Aslan chased the four escapees because He wanted them to get together. Aslan chased them again to inspire fear and speed. Aslan was even the one who had saved Shasta's life as a baby.

C. S. Lewis's story points in a memorable way to what Christians call the sovereignty and providence of God. As even Nebuchadnezzar recognized (Dan. 4:35), God rules this world and no one can keep Him from accomplishing everything He purposes to do.

Shasta learned in his conversation with Aslan that God's silence is not absence. Someone Shasta had never met and had barely heard of was determining the path of Shasta's whole life.

A Bible Book That Doesn't Mention God

There's one book of the Bible that is very much like Shasta's story. God, however, never appears in a fog to tell the characters that He's been arranging things.

In fact, He never appears at all.

And yet He appears in every line.

How can that be? It's only His name that is never mentioned. It doesn't even show up once. But you can't miss Him because He's clearly running the whole show.

That book is the story of a Jewish orphan living in exile in Persia and being raised by her (much older) cousin. Her name comes from the name of the beautiful tree we call the myrtle. In Hebrew, that's Hadassah, but it's actually her Persian name that you know her by—Esther.

The events in Esther take place after those in Ezra 6 and before the ones in Ezra 7. It shows what happens when the seed of the serpent attacks the seed of the woman at a weak moment. It shows God's protection of the Jews even while they were in exile for their sins.

Esther's Story

The King's Banquet

At the beginning of Esther's story, King Ahasuerus had been displaying his riches for the last six months to princes, army officers, and nobles throughout the provinces he ruled, from India to Ethiopia. And he was concluding this great display of wealth by giving a banquet that would last for seven days.

During the feast, he summoned his queen, Vashti, to come display her beauty before his guests. But she refused to do so.

The king became very angry when he heard she would not obey his command. In his wrath, he asked the wise men what the law said he must do to her. They recommended that she no longer be allowed in the presence of the king and that her royal position be given to another.

And he did to her as the law required.

Favor in the King's Eyes

The search began immediately for Vashti's successor. Many girls were brought to the palace, and among them was the young Jewish girl named Esther.

Esther was a fair and beautiful girl. But even with her beauty, she had to go through the beautification treatments—an entire year of treatments—"six months with oil of myrrh, and six months with sweet odours" (2:12).

When Esther was finally presented to the king, she found favor with him, and he loved her more than all his other wives. He loved her so much that he made her queen in the place of Vashti.

Before Esther was taken to the palace, she had been brought up by her cousin Mordecai. He had taken her as his own daughter after her parents had died. When all of this began, he told her not to tell anyone that she was a Jew, and she obeyed.

Haman's Plot Against the Jews

A certain man named Haman was given great status and authority under the king, and all the king's servants would bow when Haman came through the gate. That is, all but one would bow.

Mordecai refused to bow to Haman even though the king had commanded that all bow before Haman. Mordecai's refusal to bow made Haman extremely angry—so angry that he wanted to kill not only Mordecai, but also every Jew because Mordecai was a Jew.

So Haman went and told the king that there was a people in the land who refused to obey the king. Haman convinced the king to sign a decree

to destroy all the Jews throughout the kingdom. The killing of the Jews would happen on the thirteenth day of the twelfth month.

Such a Time as This

As soon as Mordecai heard the king's decree, he tore his clothes and mourned. Esther heard that Mordecai was in mourning and sent a servant to find out the reason. Mordecai told the servant about the king's decree and how his people, the Jews, were in grave danger.

When the servant told Esther, she at first responded that there was little she could do, because she was afraid the king would kill her if she entered the throne room uninvited.

But Mordecai warned Esther that as a Jew she would not be safe either. And he asked her, "Who knoweth whether thou art come to the kingdom for such a time as this?" (4:13–14).

Esther was not safe being quiet. And if she didn't speak up, then a deliverer would come from somewhere else. Maybe she was put in the kingdom for this reason—to deliver her people.

The First Banquet

Esther understood what Mordecai was saying. She was in just as much danger remaining silent as she was speaking out to the king.

So she determined to go into the throne-room and approach the king. When she did go,

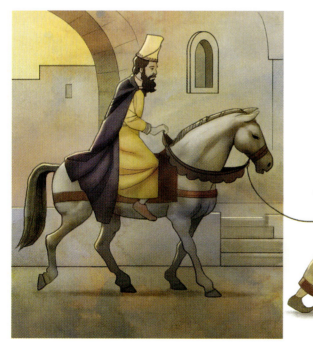

the king graciously extended the golden scepter and was more than willing to grant any request of hers.

Her request was for the king to come to a banquet for him and Haman. The two came to the banquet, but Esther did not tell the king about Haman's plot. Instead, she requested that they both attend another banquet on the next day.

Haman's Hatred for Mordecai

After Haman left the banquet, he was feeling mighty pleased with himself. Not many people got a personal invitation to a banquet prepared by the queen for just the king and that person.

As Haman passed Mordecai at the gate, Mordecai didn't tremble in his presence or stand up to greet him. This made Haman furious. He was so angry that he went home and plotted Mordecai's death. In fact, he even had gallows built on which he would have Mordecai hanged. He was personally going to see that Mordecai would die. All he needed was the king's approval.

The King's Sleepless Night

During that same night, the king couldn't sleep. So he had one of his servants come and read from the official historical records of his kingdom. The servant read an account of a plot against the king's life. He read about how Mordecai had overheard two assassins talking and had reported them to the queen.

The king then asked what had been done to reward Mordecai for doing this. The servant said that nothing had been done.

At this exact moment, Haman was standing outside the king's room and was going to request the king's permission to hang Mordecai. The king had Haman come in and asked him, "What shall be done unto the man whom the king delighteth to honour?" (6:6).

Haman could not believe what he was hearing. "To whom would the king delight to do honour more than to myself?" (6:6).

Thinking he was the one to be honored, Haman gave the king a long list of things that should be done to one as great as this. The honored man should wear the king's royal robes and crown, ride the king's horse, and let one of the noblest princes lead the honored man around the city while he shouts, "This is what happens to those whom the king wishes to honor" (6:9).

And so it would be done. Except it would be Haman leading Mordecai through the streets. So it was probably not the best time for Haman to ask the king about hanging Mordecai.

Esther's Plea

Haman was devastated at having to lead the man he hated through the streets like that. But as he was recounting to his wife and friends what had happened, the king's servants arrived to take Haman to the banquet Esther had prepared for him and the king.

After the king and Haman finished their drinks, the king asked Esther what her petition was. She basically replied, "If I have found favor in your sight, O king, and if it pleases you, spare my life and my people—this is my request and my desire: For my people and I have been sold to those who will kill and annihilate us. If we were to be sold as slaves, I could hold my tongue because that would not have been worth troubling you" (7:3–4).

The king was furious. Who would dare do this to his queen and her people? Esther revealed that it was Haman.

The king grew even more furious and had to leave the room. Immediately, Haman fell on the couch where Esther was reclining to beg for his life. But when the king returned, he thought he saw Haman assaulting the queen. The servants at once covered Haman's face and carried him out. This signaled Haman's doom.

Haman's Doom and Mordecai's Promotion

As the servants were carrying Haman out of the palace, one of the king's servants notified him that Haman had set up a gallows and was going to hang Mordecai on it. And the king said bluntly, "Hang him thereon" (7:9). After they hung Haman, Esther set Mordecai over the house of Haman (8:2).

A Day of Protection for the Jews

But there was still one problem. The king had signed into law that the Jews were to be destroyed in the twelfth month. He could not change the law, but he could give the Jews permission to defend themselves. And that is what he did.

On the day that the destruction was to be carried out, the Jews armed themselves. Many men who hated the Jews died trying to kill them, but the Jews were not destroyed.

Instead of a day of mourning for a nation destroyed by Haman's evil plot, the day turned into a day of rejoicing for the Jews who were delivered from their enemies.

God's Sovereignty

God's behind-the-scenes involvement throughout the story points to the major theme of the book of Esther: God's silence is not absence. God may look like He's nowhere to be found, but the truth is that He is in every line of Esther's story—and in every line of ours.

Feast of Purim

The Feast of Purim is a celebration that happens on the fourteenth and fifteenth days of the twelfth month. It is called Purim after the name *Pur*—which refers to the lots that Haman cast to determine what day (thirteenth) and month (twelfth) to destroy the Jews. In modern times, it would be similar to rolling dice to determine when something should happen (3:7; cf. 9:24–26).

The commemoration actually begins on the thirteenth day. But that day is a day of fasting, and the book of Esther is read aloud. The celebration begins the next morning (fourteenth day) and continues until the end of the fifteenth day. These two days are observed because of the length of time it took the different provinces to kill the enemies of the Jews.

The Feast of Purim is a celebration of salvation and deliverance from Israel's enemies.

Just tick off the places where impossible things (seeming coincidences) happen:

- Vashti is dethroned just in time to make way for Esther to be there when Haman's plot unfolds.

- Esther is chosen to be queen out of hundreds of women in the harem.

- Mordecai hears about a top-secret conspiracy to kill the king.

- When Haman casts lots to determine the timing of his attack on the Jews, the lots point to a date nearly a year away, allowing plenty of time for the Jews to prepare.

- One night when King Ahasuerus can't sleep, of all the royal annals that could be read to him, the story of Mordecai is chosen.

- Haman arrives just as the king is looking for ways to honor Mordecai.

- Even the odd way the king asks Haman a question is providential: "What shall be done for the man whom the king delights to honor?" That wording makes it possible for Haman to believe he is the one to be honored, setting up his own humiliation.

Make no mistake: God is in these lines. He may be silent, but He's certainly not absent. God artfully, carefully, and even (sometimes) humorously orchestrated the whole thing.

Your Story

The story of Esther is still going on—and you're in it if you're a Christian. The people God rescued from wicked Haman were the people through whom He promised to bless the world. Their survival means your blessing.

God has never promised that He will save the lives of everyone who believes in Him every time they are threatened. There is no guarantee that you will be delivered from your enemies the way the Jews in Persia were delivered from theirs. Many around the world who identify themselves as Christians are killed for their faith (an average of nearly 160,000 every year). But God is just as much in control of your story as He was of Esther's—and God's ultimate purposes for you are good, just like they were for her. The Bible points to a God who rules (who really rules!) this world. His plans will work.

Thinking It Through 8.6

1. What is unique about the book of Esther (and the Song of Solomon) compared to other books of the Bible?

2. List four examples of how God was silent but not absent in the story of Esther.

3. How did Haman and Mordecai have their fortunes reversed?

4. How were the Jewish people's fortunes reversed?

5. Explain how God's providence applies to both good and bad things that happen in our lives.

8.7 NEHEMIAH: OVERCOMING OPPOSITION

Read Nehemiah 9
Memorize Nehemiah 8:8

The story of Nehemiah starts out well. Nehemiah, the king's cupbearer (a very high position in Persia), asks about things in Jerusalem and what he finds out saddens him deeply. Its all-important walls and gates are broken down and burned. That's not the good part, of course. It's what comes next. Not only does Nehemiah pray in humility and repentance for his people's sins, but he shows that he knows God's Word. He appeals to God to remember His covenant and to call the people of Israel back to their land. He quotes God's covenant promises in Deuteronomy. He knows how to get a hearing with the Almighty King of Kings.

He also knows how to get a hearing with his own king—mainly by going to the Great King first. Nehemiah's silent prayer to God results in his getting the wisdom he needs during the scary moments after King Artaxerxes asks him why he is so sad. (People who looked sad in front of the king sometimes got their heads chopped off to cheer them up!) Nehemiah answers wisely, and soon he's off to inspect Jerusalem—with significant support from a Persian king who's been drafted to fulfill God's purposes.

Nehemiah wastes no time. Immediately he gets involved in rebuilding the city walls—with the help of a whole chapter full of Jewish families (Neh. 3). The work is immense, but so is the motivation of the people (Neh. 4:6).

When opposition comes, Nehemiah turns reflexively and automatically to God. There are many "silent prayers" from Nehemiah to God stuck into different places in his book. These prayers give the book the feel of an autobiography or a journal. For example, Nehemiah prays to God about the opposition he is facing from Sanballat and Tobiah:

> Hear, O our God; for we are despised: and turn their reproach upon their own head, and give them for a prey in the land of captivity: And cover not their iniquity, and let not their sin be blotted out from before thee: for they have provoked thee to anger before the builders. (Neh. 4:4–5)

Nehemiah the Leader

Nehemiah is truly an inspiring leader (he was also the governor of Judah). He sets about his work boldly, but not arrogantly or tyrannically. He's bold because he knows the good hand of his God is on him. Even more importantly, he knows that what he is doing is consistent with what God said in His covenant with Israel. Only God's words could give someone the confidence—and right—to say as Nehemiah did, "Our God shall fight for us" (Neh. 4:20). This is the kind of faith God delights to reward.

A Time of Remembrance

Although the book of Nehemiah is not located near the end of the Old Testament, the events in Nehemiah actually occur at the end of the Old Testament timeline. Of course, the men and women of Israel living in this time don't know that they're the final paragraph in a big chapter of Abraham's story, but they are.

It is interesting to see what they did when they finished their job.

Throughout this textbook, the authors have pointed out several times when God's people were commanded to remember the things God did for them. Joshua set up stones of remembrance to help the people remember how God had delivered them across the Jordan. There were stones piled high over those who disobeyed God, which reminded the people of what happens to those who rebel.

We looked at an entire psalm (Ps. 136) where the psalmist recalled all the wonderful acts God had done for His creation and His people. We looked at those who forgot to remember God and what He had done for them, and we saw how they and their children were punished because they strayed from God's ways.

In the story of Nehemiah, when the people finished building the walls around Jerusalem they came together to confess their sins, remember what God had done for them, and make an agreement that from that day forward they would walk according to the law God had given to Moses (Neh. 10:28–29).

After confessing their sins, they began to recount what God had done for them (9:5–37). In a similar fashion to Psalm 136, they recounted that God had created the world and was responsible for the life it contained (Neh. 9:5–6). They spoke of how God had chosen Abraham, made a covenant with him, and kept His promises (9:7–8). They recounted how God had delivered them from the bondage of Egypt, led them through the wilderness, given His law to them, and provided bread from heaven when they needed it most (9:9–15).

In His great compassion, God never forsook His people even when they would not listen and forsook Him.

They recounted how their fathers had rejected God and did not remember the wonders He had done for them (9:16–17). In their willingness to forget, they made an idol and worshiped it, but God was compassionate and did not forsake them in the wilderness.

He provided for them, gave them a land, and made their sons and daughters as numerous as the stars of heaven (9:21–23).

They recounted how God would graciously provide for them and give them victory after victory, but their forefathers would rebel and even kill the prophets God would send to warn them and help them turn back to Him.

As a result, God delivered His people into the hands of their enemies. But God would always hear their cries and provide deliverance. Each time He would admonish them to obey His laws and walk in His statutes. And each time, they would not listen but would sin against Him. And the cycle would continue (sin, judgment, deliverance).

Why would God allow the cycle to continue? Why didn't He just kill them all and start over with another group of people?

> For [His] great mercies' sake [He] didst not utterly consume them, nor forsake them; for [He is] a gracious and merciful God. (9:31)

He did not destroy them, because He is merciful. Then they called God one who "keepest covenant and mercy [*ḥesed*]" (9:32). There is the *ḥesed* of God again. God is merciful and faithful to His people because of the promises He made to Abraham their father.

In closing their song of praise, the people acknowledged that their difficult times were due to God punishing them for their sins. They also admitted that God was just in what He did to them (9:33).

And after this song of praise, they made an agreement in writing that they would obey God's laws and walk in His statutes.

And yet there's another angle to Nehemiah's faith. It didn't make him take foolish risks. His workers had their trowels in one hand and their swords in the other. They were ready to work, ready to fight.

It's somewhat like a sentence in that classic story of the Old West, *True Grit*, written by Charles Portis and then made into more than one film. Fourteen-year-old Mattie Ross comments in the story, "The author of all things watches over me. And I have a fine horse."

Did you catch what she's implying? We can, like Mattie and like Nehemiah, have total confidence that we are in the hands of the God who planned the end from the beginning (Isa. 46:9–11). And yet we can and should be glad for the swords and horses—and chemotherapy and police officers and security systems—that God planned to use to keep us safe. We trust God to fight for us, and yet we still strap on our swords. Nehemiah was a good leader in part because he understood this.

He also wisely saw through the deceit of his enemies, answering them boldly and forcefully (Neh. 6:3, 8, 11). The wall was finished in an amazingly short fifty-two days (6:15).

Covenant Faithfulness

Totally godless leaders can build walls in fifty-two days. They can say, "God bless America." They can inspire others with talk of God's care for the nation. But Nehemiah's religion wasn't a show. It went deep, giving him the strength to stand up against opposition and do the hard things to lead others in the right way.

Nehemiah stood strong, stopping the rich Jews from oppressing and even enslaving the poorer ones (5:1–13). And he didn't demand the taxes that he had a right to collect as governor; he was generous to the people of Judah (5:14–19).

He supported Ezra and other religious leaders as they read God's law to the people (8:9), confessed Israel's sins (9:3), and led the people to promise to be faithful to the covenant (10:1).

The End

Now, Nehemiah, please end your book right there. Don't add anything else. We like this part.

The people are finally (finally!) going to do right and be blessed. They admit their sin, and they recognize their continuing place in God's plan. They have promised—in writing—to abide by God's law. So please, Nehemiah, and all you ancient Israelites, just let us say, "They lived happily ever after and they stopped sinning pretty much from then on. The end."

But read Nehemiah 13, which is where the Old Testament narrative comes to a close, and you will know what happens. Nehemiah goes back to Persia, to King Artaxerxes, and nine or so years later when he returns to Jerusalem, the Jews there have married foreign women, and they're buying and selling on the Sabbath day. These are the very sins they promised—in writing—not to commit. In fact, these two sins are the very first ones on their list (Neh. 10:30–31*a*). Nehemiah himself reminds them as he pulls out the hair of the offenders (a helpful way to reinforce one's point) that marrying foreign women caused even Solomon to sin.

> "Remember me,
> O my God,
> for good."
>
> **—Nehemiah**

The people are no different than those who lived during the time of the judges. Like them, the people in Nehemiah's day have fallen into a dangerous cycle of forgetting what God said to do, disobeying, being confronted about their sins, repenting, and then back to forgetting about God and disobedience. What hope do the Jews in Jerusalem have of staying true to the Lord?

Redemption

The book of Nehemiah ends with the people, even the priests, acting treacherously against the Lord.

The Jews were rescued from slavery to Egypt and (much later) Persia; how can they be rescued from slavery to their sins?

If godly leaders like Ezra and Nehemiah couldn't fix them, no mere human can. So again we ask what hope the Jews have of ever making themselves stay true to the Lord.

None. That's the answer. That's the final conclusion the story of the Bible forces you to come to after two thousand years of Israelite history. From the time of Abraham to the time of Nehemiah, God's people have had the same sin problem the rest of the world has. The Jews had God's Word, at least, to let them know they were wrong. They had God's prophets and God's miracles to push them, for brief periods, in the right direction. None of the Gentile nations had these things.

But even with all these advantages, Israel failed. They were sent into exile, and when they came back, they failed again. They can't make themselves stay true.

It's a good thing, then, that people aren't the heroes of the Bible's story. Only God can step in and fix this problem.

Thinking It Through 8.7

1. Why was Nehemiah very sad at the opening of the book—and how did he respond?

2. Mattie Ross said, "The author of all things watches over me. And I have a fine horse." What spiritual truth does her comment illustrate? How did Nehemiah apply this same truth?

3. The Israelites were led by judges such as Samson, Gideon, and Jephthah because they didn't deserve better leaders. Why then do you think God gave them such good leaders, Ezra and Nehemiah, at the end of the Old Testament story? (Speculation is allowed!)

4. How are the people in Nehemiah's day like the people in the time of the judges?

5. Why is it good to stop and remember what God has done for you?

8.8 MALACHI: GOD'S MESSENGER

Read Malachi 1:1–5; 3:13–4:6
Memorize Malachi 3:7

Theme

Malachi—that's all we know about him personally—his name, which means "my messenger." We do know that he is the last prophet named in the Old Testament and that the next named prophet is John the Baptist in the New Testament. We also know that Malachi prophesied after the temple was finished. That means he prophesied when there were no kings in Israel. He most likely lived at the same time as Nehemiah (around 435 BC).

During this time, the priests are corrupt (Mal. 1:6–2:9; Neh. 13:7–9). They also have failed to teach the people the ways of God, and as a result, people work on the Sabbath and violate God's laws (Mal. 2:8–9; Neh. 13:15–22). The priests have also married foreign women, and their children can't even speak Hebrew—the language of the Jews (Mal. 2:11–15; Neh. 13:23–27). The people also fail to give their tithes to the Lord (Mal. 3:8–10; Neh. 13:5, 10). Israel is not a godly nation.

Throughout Israel's history, God tells His people many times that He will honor the covenants He made with Abraham, Isaac, and Jacob. But because the Israelites are going through difficult times, they think God has forgotten about them. It seems that some think God might not be powerful enough to deliver blessings to His people. Worse, some think that those who do evil are good in God's sight and that He even delights in evildoers. They even ask, "Where is the God of judgment [or justice]?" (2:17).

But Malachi tells them that God has not forgotten about them. And as the Lord of Hosts, He has the power and authority to bless them as He wishes.

Even when Israel was unfaithful, God still honored His commitment to His people because of His steadfast and loyal love for them—His *ḥesed*. By now you should know that loyal love is supposed to work both ways. They ought to be as loyal to God as He is to them.

Yahweh of Hosts

Malachi uses the title "Lord of Hosts" twenty-four times in his book. Considering that there are only fifty-five verses in Malachi, that means the title occurs on average almost every other verse.

The title is made of two parts. The first is the name Lord, which is really the covenant name Yahweh (see box on page 72). Yahweh is the personal name that God used with Israel (Lord is actually a title we use in place of God's personal name). God told Moses to use His personal name when the children of Israel asked who had sent him: "I AM hath sent me unto you" (Exod. 3:14). Yahweh is God's covenant name with Israel.

The second part of the name, "of Hosts," refers to those armies (both in heaven and on earth) that are at His bidding to do His will. When you combine the two names (Yahweh of Hosts), it means that God is the Almighty Warrior who fights against evil forces for His people, Israel.

"This lofty title [Yahweh of Hosts] identifies God as the commander in chief with all power and authority and with all resources at His disposal to accomplish His purpose."

—Michael P. V. Barrett

Israel may think that God was unable to bless them, but they are wrong. Malachi uses God's covenant name to show them that Yahweh of Hosts is more than capable of blessing them whenever He sees fit.

But Israel is not carrying out its end of the deal. They are not loving God loyally. Instead they are violating the covenant of their fathers (2:10). They are profaning it by despising God's name (1:6), offering unacceptable sacrifices (1:13), and practicing sorcery and adultery (3:5).

This is the situation that God sends Malachi to prophesy against.

And Malachi does not beat around the bush. He immediately calls them out for dishonoring God. Speaking through Malachi, God says, "A son honoureth his father, and a servant his master:

Accuse, Oppose, Refute

Imagine your mom saying this to you while you remain silent the entire time: "You have disobeyed me with your actions. But you say, 'How have I disobeyed you?' Because you have not done your homework, and your phone logs say that you have texted more than a hundred times this evening, when I told you not to text before you did your homework."

Notice what your mom did. She accused you of disobeying, and then she asked the question you were thinking. And then she told you what you did wrong.

This is one way that Malachi delivers God's message. He accuses them of some sin, and then he asks a question from their point of view—that is, from a point of view that opposes what he has accused them of. Then he offers a rebuttal where he shows them why he has accused them.

For example, Malachi, speaking the words of God, accuses them: "O priests, that despise my name" (Mal. 1:6).

He then asks an opposing question: "Wherein have we despised thy name?" (1:6).

Now for the rebuttal: "Ye offer polluted bread upon mine altar" (1:7).

This style of accusing, offering opposition, and refuting them is seen throughout Malachi (1:7; 1:12–14; 2:17; 3:8; 3:13–14). It is a powerful way of grabbing the audience's attention and showing them what they are doing wrong.

if then I be a father, where is mine honour? and if I be a master, where is my fear?" (Mal. 1:6). Sons and servants know how to treat those who rule over them, but Israel doesn't know how to treat God.

In the box "Accuse, Oppose, Refute" you can see Malachi's style of arguing with the people. In Malachi 1:6–7 the Lord accuses His people of despising His name. In English the word *despise* can mean "to treat something as worthless." In modern English we sometimes express this concept with the idiom "to make light of." You may have heard an adult say to you when you were in trouble, "Don't make light of the situation." In other words, "This is serious, and you need to take it seriously."

The Israelites have some major problems. They are giving sick and lame sacrifices to the Lord. They are treating His name as worthless. They are making light of His name.

The Lord asks them what would happen if they gave the same animals to their governor. Would it make the governor happy? The answer is obviously no (1:8–9).

Why are they making light of God's name? Because they don't fear Him. A person who sacrifices a sick or blemished animal is cursed (1:14). He should know better—even the heathen fear and dread God (1:14). But Israel isn't fearing God. And God has given His people a covenant with its blessings and cursings so that they would fear Him and be afraid before His name.

> "Fearing God is knowing God and living with constant awareness of Him. It includes awe, worship, respect, and the dread of displeasing the Lord."
>
> —**Michael P. V. Barrett**

Remember, this type of fear is not one where you cower uncontrollably in terror. This is supposed to be a fear where you do right because of the awe and respect you have for God.

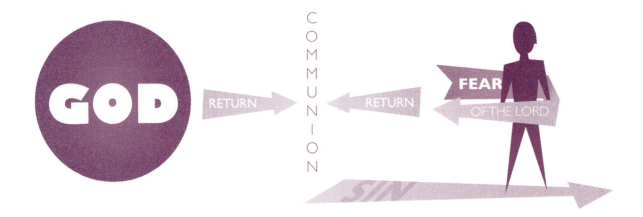

But for the one who doesn't have any respect for God—the one who makes light of God's name—there is a fear of terror, and those people will face the judgment of God (3:5).

The Solution

The solution to Israel's problem is simple. God tells them, "Return unto me, and I will return unto you" (3:7).

This statement has two parts. First, returning to God means they simply need to stop doing wrong and start doing right (for example, stop robbing God by not giving Him tithes and start giving Him tithes). God has left them, not because He doesn't care about them, but because they are doing wrong.

The second part of this statement gives Israel hope. If they will turn from their sin and return to God, He will return to them. And when He does, blessings such as protection and provisions (food) will follow.

Fear God

In returning to God, they would show that they fear Him and think highly of His name—they don't take His name lightly. And that is what happens. Those who fear the Lord get together, and God hears them (3:16–18). God promises that He will spare them and that they will not face the same judgment as the wicked.

Messianic References

Israel knew a day of judgment was coming that would be accompanied with fire, and they knew the arrogant and evildoers would be burned up. Nothing of evil will be left (4:1).

The Israelites knew it would be the Messiah who would bring this judgment at His coming. But they thought the Messiah would bring judgment against only non-Israelites. They seemed to have forgotten that Amos had warned them that the Day of the Lord was not something to wish for. It would be a time of judgment on both Jews and non-Jews. It would not be the time of light and prosperity that they thought. It would be a time of darkness and judgment—for both Jew and Gentile.

Earlier we saw the Israelites ask, "Where is the God of judgment?" (2:17). In Malachi 4 the God of judgment appears as the Messiah. He offers hope of healing for those who fear the name of the Lord. But to those who don't fear, He brings judgment and destruction with Him (4:5–6).

> "But unto [those] that fear my name shall the Sun of righteousness arise with healing in his wings."
>
> **—Malachi 4:2**

Malachi's prophecy is the last prophecy given in the Old Testament. Four hundred years will pass before God sends another prophet.

The Lord predicts the coming of that prophet through Malachi: "I will send my messenger, and he shall prepare the way before me" (Mal. 3:1). This prophet turns out to be the first prophet mentioned in the New Testament: John the Baptist (Mark 1:2). John faced the same kind of sinful people that Malachi faced. They hadn't improved during those four hundred years.

The Pharisees in the New Testament were similar to the Israelites in Malachi's time. The Pharisees thought that going through the correct rituals was more important than having a pure heart, and the Israelites thought they could do whatever they wanted and give sacrifices to make amends. Both groups thought they could win God's favor by simply going through the motions.

Unfortunately, not much has changed since then. The church has the same problems the Pharisees and the Old Testament Israelites had. We must be aware that simply going through the motions does not earn favor from God.

Thinking It Through 8.8

1. What was the main issue with sacrificing lame and blind animals?

2. Describe the type of fear you should have toward God.

3. What is the prophet's solution to Israel's sin problem?

4. What common misconception did the Israelites have about God's future judgment?

5. Explain why the prophet talks about fearing God when he urges the people to repent and be faithful.

GOD'S BIG PICTURE

Christ's death
conquered death.

Christ came to
establish His Church.

Christ is
coming again.

God has promised
a new creation.

JESUS: THE NAME THAT BIDS OUR SORROWS CEASE

Memorize Isaiah 53:1–12

Conflict and Resolution

Everybody tells himself some story about the world. The communist story goes like this:

- Rich people oppress poor workers.
- A communist revolution overthrows the rich.
- A new world of shared prosperity dawns.

The evolutionary story says something like this:

- Life and the universe develop by chance—but life is nasty, brutish, and short.
- Evolution brings self-consciousness and reason to one species of animals: humanity.
- Human evolutionary progress brings new worlds of prosperity.

These are stories Western people tell themselves about the world. Other peoples tell different stories. The Buddhist story is very different. So is the Hopi Indian story.

But every popular story about the world has at least one thing in common with the true story: there is a conflict, and there is a resolution.

Even the little stories we like in movies have conflict and resolution. *Finding Nemo* wouldn't be very interesting or enjoyable if Nemo never got lost (conflict)—or if he never got found (resolution). (Swimming around the ocean endlessly with Dory chattering away the whole time would get tiresome.)

Conflict is what drives good stories (in the context of the fallen world we live in). But it is deeply unsatisfying and even disturbing when one ends without resolution.

Resolution

This is where we are in the story of the Bible. The Messiah is still missing, and centuries of looking for Him have turned up empty. The people of Israel sin and sin and sin and sin, just like all the rest of the world.

God has done amazing things for them, and His plan has taken many steps forward. But to what end? The people still frustrate God and His leaders.

If God does just let the people scatter and die, that's no resolution. Or at least it's not the right one. It would be like letting Nemo die in the end. Even people who deny that God exists have a feeling deep inside their hearts that the outcome is supposed to be positive.

It's important for you to know that people who were much closer to the Jewish situation—who lived in it themselves—felt the same way.

This textbook has shown the problem as it existed throughout the Old Testament. As we looked at the prophets, we saw that they knew the solution to Israel's never-ending problems. They told us about the resolution to the conflict.

The Heart

The prophets showed us that the problem with Israel was something no one else could see. It was something internal. The problem with the Israelites was their hearts. They simply loved sin.

The prophets also showed us that there was nothing they could do about their hearts. They needed new hearts, and only God could give them new hearts that desired to obey His commands and do His will.

Jeremiah clarifies God's promise of new hearts to Israel by saying that these new hearts will be one of the benefits of a "new covenant" God is going to make with His people. The Old Covenant that God made with them at Sinai guaranteed basically one thing: you got special blessings if you were physically descended from Abraham and if you kept all God's laws. But you got cursing if you ever disobeyed just one of God's laws. But the Old Covenant did not provide the crucial blessing: new hearts for everyone. It couldn't fix the problem of sin; it could only reveal the problem of sin.

That crucial blessing, Jeremiah says, is what the New Covenant will bring. There were many participants in the Old Covenant who did not know the Lord. They proved it over and over again throughout their history. Just because Abraham was their great-great-great-grandfather didn't mean they had Abraham's faith. But in the New Covenant that God is going to make, everyone will know the Lord (Jer. 31:34). God will write His law on people's hearts so they both know it and desire to obey it (Jer. 31:33). God will forgive their sin and forget it (Jer. 31:34).

How can God make a New Covenant with wicked people, wiping away their sins and giving them new hearts? What about all the sins they've already committed? Who will pay for those?

Isaiah gives the answer to that question in Isaiah 53. He provides the key missing piece to the puzzle:

> He was wounded for our transgressions, he was bruised for our iniquities: the chastisement of our peace was upon him; and with his stripes we are healed. All we like sheep have gone astray; we have turned every one to his own way; and the Lord hath laid on him the iniquity of us all. (Isa. 53:5–6)

Jesus

Jesus. Jesus! **Jesus** is the missing piece. He is the resolution to the conflict in the story of Scripture. The terrible sins of Israel can't be paid for by Israel. Jesus will have to take them on His own sinless shoulders. He'll have to be bruised for those iniquities. He'll have to take the punishment God's sinful people deserve.

Jesus Christ of Nazareth, Son of Man, Son of God—that is the name the Bible has been pointing to all along.

If you think of the story of Scripture as one long rope made of many threads, a number of those threads are hanging loose at the end of the Old Testament. Jesus gathers them all into one.

- The Adam thread: Jesus is the Seed of the woman, crushing the head of the serpent and triumphing over him on the cross (Gen. 3:15). Jesus is the second Adam, taking up the perfect dominion of this world that Adam failed to fulfill. The New Testament also says that Jesus will fill the earth with His followers just as God commanded Adam to do with his own seed (Gen. 1:26–28).

- The Abraham thread: Jesus will bless the nations. The night before Jesus died on the cross, He told His disciples that the wine He poured them represented the "new covenant in [His] blood, which is shed for [them]" (Luke 22:20). Jesus' death and resurrection initiated the precious New Covenant spoken of by Jeremiah. As the New Testament tells the rest of the story, those amazing blessings (a new heart and forgiveness of sins) are not limited to Jews. Gentiles—including you!—can enjoy them too!

ADAM

Seed of the Woman

Serpent Crusher

Second Adam

Fills the Earth

ABRAHAM

Blessing of Nations

New Covenant

DAVID

Son of David

King of Kings

Messiah

JESUS CHRIST

- The David thread: Jesus is the Son of David who will rule over the world forever. Jesus is the true King, the King of Kings and Lord of Lords. God is in the process of putting all things "under his feet" (1 Cor. 15:25). Jesus is the King who will bring peace to the land by doing everything the Father says. He will even put Israel back in its own land; He'll rule from a new Jerusalem (Rev. 21:2).

Jesus ties up every thread in this textbook because He ties up every thread in the Bible. He's the perfect Priest who stands in between mankind and the Father. He's the perfect Prophet who says only what the Father tells Him to say. He's the perfect King who reigns in righteousness.

The Story and Your Worldview

Non-Christian stories about the world make some sense, or else no one would believe them. But in the end they don't work. The story of evolution is a fine example of that. It seems to explain a lot: how humans developed, where we're all going, and so on. But it leaves people unable to do something as simple as tell right from wrong. They have to steal from the Christian story to do that. What's "right" and what's "wrong" in a world ruled by random chance? Why is one random arrangement of atoms (the one in which the atoms in my fist hit the atoms in my sister, for example) better or worse than any other arrangement? And who says? If a big

lie helps our race come out on top in the survival of the fittest, who cares that it's a big lie?

Only the Christian story provides a worldview that makes sense of the world.

Creation: God created this world good. Evolution simply cannot explain why there's something rather than nothing.

Fall: Adam plunged this world into a curse by his sin. Evolution cannot explain why people do such wicked things.

Redemption: God is in the process of restoring this world. Jesus Christ pays for human sin and will rule this world in perfection forever. Evolution can't promise that the human race will last even another thousand years. If we all die out, what will human history mean? Nothing.

But in God's plan, every act in history has meaning. Everything contributes to God's story—His Plan A for the world. The Lord said through Isaiah,

I am God, and there is none else; I am God, and there is none like me, declaring the end from the beginning, and from ancient times the things that are not yet done, saying, My counsel shall stand, and I will do all my pleasure. (Isa. 46:9–10)

God's Ultimate Goal

C. S. Lewis wrote a hilarious poem called "Evolutionary Hymn." In it he criticizes evolution for being a blind process; no one can say where it will lead. Evolution hands you an aimless, purposeless life that will be forgotten a little while before the whole race is. Lewis captured that truth in a clever line:

> Never knowing where we're going,
> We can never go astray.

But the Christian story is different. It has a purpose. It tells us where we're going. It tells us our end goal because it tells us God's end goal. This goal shows up in Ezekiel:

> Therefore[, Ezekiel,] say unto the house of Israel, Thus saith the Lord God; I do not this for your sakes, O house of Israel, but for mine holy name's sake, which ye have profaned among the heathen, whither ye went. And I will sanctify my great name, which was profaned among the heathen, which ye have profaned in the midst of them; and the heathen shall know that I am the Lord, saith the Lord God, when I shall be sanctified in you before their eyes. (Ezek. 36:22–23)

God's ultimate goal in all He does is to glorify Himself, to lift up His name as the greatest in all the world. When Christ ties up all the loose threads of all world history and finally rules the whole world from David's throne, this is what will happen according to the Bible:

> Then cometh the end, when he shall have delivered up the kingdom to God, even the Father; when he shall have put down all rule and all authority and power. . . . And when all things shall be subdued unto him, then shall the Son also himself be subject unto him that put all things

The Verses of the Bible

Most Bibles printed today are full of big numbers and little numbers telling you where a new chapter or verse starts. Though these give some help in finding your place, it's helpful to realize that they weren't put there by God. Chapter numbers didn't arrive in the Bible until the 1200s. Verse numbers were added in the 1500s.

If the Bible is a long story, it doesn't make sense to divide it all up into little pieces, so a lot of modern Bibles are now put in a single-column paragraphed format—like a normal book. For some people, this takes a little getting used to, but it's a much better way to read the Bible.

There are even several editions of the Bible that leave out all chapter and verse numbers! It's easier to see the flow of the story when it isn't broken up and cluttered by unnecessary things on the page.

under him, that God may be all in all. (1 Cor. 15:24, 28)

If you want to live a life that means something, you have to have the same goal. God will be glorified whether you participate or not, but by God's grace Jesus has made a way for you to overcome the effects of the Fall. Jesus' death and resurrection can pay for your sins and infuse life into your stony heart. Don't finish the story of Scripture without purposefully stepping into the story yourself and becoming a disciple of the one whose name the whole Bible points to.

Thinking It Through Conclusion

1. How does Jesus tie up the threads of the Abrahamic Covenant? In other words, in what ways does He fulfill God's three major promises to Abraham?

2. Why can't God just forgive everyone and let us all into heaven?

3. What did C. S. Lewis mean when he wrote, "Never knowing where we're going, / We can never go astray"?

4. According to 1 Corinthians 15:20–28, what's the purpose of all history?

5. Do you, individually and personally, benefit from the New Covenant? If so, in what way(s)?

UNIT 8 REVIEW

Scripture Memory

Jeremiah 31:33–34	Haggai 1:5
Ezekiel 36:26–27	Esther 4:14
Daniel 7:13–14	Nehemiah 8:8
Ezra 7:10	Malachi 3:7
Zechariah 1:3	Isaiah 53:1–12

Understand the Story

1. Summarize the general promise and warning of Jeremiah's message.

2. What does Ezekiel say God will do so that His people will obey His rules?

3. What major theme unifies the whole book of Daniel?

4. Why are the lists of people at the beginning of the book of Ezra important?

5. How does Zechariah define repentance? What should motivate that repentance?

6. In what way does God appear throughout the book of Esther even though His name is never mentioned?

7. After observing two thousand years of Israelite history, what should you conclude about the ability of people to make themselves stay true to the Lord?

8. Why does God deserve honor from Israel? (Mal. 1:6)

Developing Observation Skills

9. One of the observation skills you've learned this year is to look for repetition. Based on Jeremiah 31:31–34, what repeated phrase makes clear that the New Covenant would be an unconditional covenant that God would surely bring to pass?

10. Ezekiel 36 is a parallel passage to Jeremiah 31 because it's about the New Covenant. What repeated phrase in Ezekiel 36 makes clear that the New Covenant would be an unconditional covenant that God would surely bring to pass?

11. Carefully describe the fourth beast in Daniel's vision (Dan. 7:7–8). How can you know the meaning of this vision? (Dan. 7:16–28)

12. Carefully describe Zechariah's vision in Zechariah 1:8. How can you know the meaning of this vision? (Zech. 1:9–15)

13. In Nehemiah 9 the whole history of the nation is recounted to God in a prayer. Nehemiah 9:32 starts with the words, "Now therefore." What was the plea of Nehemiah's prayer based on? What was it not based on?

14. Malachi uses similes and metaphors to describe the coming Day of the Lord in Malachi 4:1. What will the Day of the Lord be like for those who are proud and wicked?

Connecting the Story to the Big Story

15. What could and couldn't the Mosaic law do? How would the New Covenant provide the solution?

16. Connect the unconditional promise of the New Covenant with God's unconditional promise to Abraham (Ezek. 36:28; cf. Gen. 12:1; 17:8). When will these promises be fully fulfilled, and who will receive the full fulfillment of these promises?

17. Instead of taking a moralistic approach that assumes the book of Nehemiah merely teaches us how to be good leaders for a modern building project, how should you read the book of Nehemiah? In other words, what was the intended point of the author? How does the book of Nehemiah fit in with the one big story of Creation, Fall, Redemption?

18. What is the solution to Israel's problem?

Lessons for Life

19. The New Covenant promises hope (a new heart, the Holy Spirit within you, God's law within you, and final forgiveness), which enables you to fulfill your obligations (repentance and obedience). If you want to enjoy the New Covenant promises and fulfill your obligations, you must embrace the fear of the Lord. Write some key ideas that you would include in a plan of action to help you live in the fear of the Lord. Include the foundational beliefs that will drive your behavior.

20. To help you remember the big story of Scripture, create a brief summary of the big concepts you've learned this year.

SCRIPTURE READING & MEMORY

Section	Reading	Memory
Unit 1	**Creation & Fall**	
1.1	Proverbs 1:1–7, 20–33; 2:1–22	Proverbs 16:6
1.2	Ruth 2:4–16	Proverbs 1:7
1.3	See Exercise 1.3.	John 5:39
1.4	Genesis 1; Psalm 104	Genesis 1:26–28
1.5	Genesis 2:8–9, 15–17; 3:1–19	Genesis 3:15
1.6	Genesis 4	Genesis 4:7
1.7	Genesis 5:29–9:17	Genesis 6:5
1.8	Job 1–2	Job 28:28
Unit 2	**God's Covenant with Abraham**	
2.1	Genesis 12	Genesis 12:1–3
2.2	Genesis 14	Psalm 110:4; Hebrews 7:24–25
2.3	Genesis 15	Genesis 15:5–6; 17:1–2
2.4	Genesis 22:1–18	Genesis 22:16–18
2.5	Genesis 24	Genesis 24:60
2.6	Genesis 25:19–35:29	Genesis 35:2–3
2.7	Genesis 37; 39–45; 50:15–26	Genesis 50:20
2.8	Genesis 38	Genesis 49:10
Unit 3	**God's Covenant with Israel Through Moses**	
3.1	Exodus 1–2	Exodus 3:13–14
3.2	Exodus 7:14–12:36	Romans 9:17–18
3.3	Exodus 15:22–16:36	Exodus 15:26
3.4	Exodus 19:1–8; 20:1–20	Exodus 19:5–6
3.5	Exodus 19:1–8; 20:1–20	Deuteronomy 4:6–8
3.6	Exodus 32	Exodus 34:6–7
3.7	See Exercise 3.7.	Leviticus 10:10; 26:12
3.8	Numbers 22:1–21	Numbers 24:17
Unit 4	**The Weakness of the Old Covenant**	
4.1	See Exercise 4.1.	Deuteronomy 30:6
4.2	Joshua 6:1–8:29	Joshua 21:43–45
4.3	Joshua 3–4	Joshua 4:21–22, 24
4.4	Psalm 118	Psalm 136:1–4
4.5	Judges 4	Judges 2:10
4.6	Judges 6:1–8:3	Judges 8:34
4.7	Judges 11	Judges 10:13–14
4.8	Judges 13–16	Judges 14:4

Section	Reading	Memory
Unit 5	**The Promise of the Line of David**	
5.1	Ruth 1–4	Ruth 4:14
5.2	1 Samuel 1	1 Samuel 2:10
5.3	1 Samuel 8	1 Samuel 8:7, 19–20
5.4	1 Samuel 9–11	1 Samuel 15:22
5.5	1 Samuel 16	1 Samuel 17:46–47
5.6	2 Samuel 6:1–11; 1 Chronicles 13	1 Chronicles 15:13
5.7	2 Samuel 11:1–12:14	2 Samuel 7:16
5.8	1 Kings 8:22–53	1 Kings 8:60–61
Unit 6	**The Line of David: Failure & Hope**	
6.1	1 Kings 12	1 Kings 13:33–34
6.2	1 Kings 17–19	1 Kings 18:21
6.3	1 Kings 21	1 Kings 21:29
6.4	2 Kings 5	1 Kings 5:15b
6.5	2 Kings 6:24–7:20	2 Kings 7:17
6.6	Obadiah 1:1–21	Joel 2:1–2
6.7	2 Kings 11–12; 2 Chronicles 24:15–27	2 Kings 11:17
6.8	Amos 5:1–17	Amos 4:12
Unit 7	**The Line of David: Doomed to Failure?**	
7.1	Isaiah 6	Isaiah 1:18
7.2	Isaiah 55	Isaiah 55:6–7
7.3	2 Kings 19	2 Kings 17:22–23
7.4	Micah 1–2	Micah 6:8; 7:18
7.5	2 Kings 21:1–18	2 Kings 21:9
7.6	Nahum 1	Nahum 1:3, 7
7.7	2 Kings 22:1–23:30	2 Kings 22:17
7.8	Habakkuk 1:12–2:20	Habakkuk 2:4
Unit 8	**God's People Protected and Restored to the Land**	
8.1	Jeremiah 31	Jeremiah 31:33–34
8.2	Ezekiel 36:16–38	Ezekiel 36:26–27
8.3	Daniel 7	Daniel 7:13–14
8.4	Ezra 9:1–10:19	Ezra 7:10
8.5	Zechariah 1	Zechariah 1:3; Haggai 1:5
8.6	See Exercise 8.6.	Esther 4:14
8.7	Nehemiah 9	Nehemiah 8:8
8.8	Malachi 1:1–5; 3:13–4:6	Malachi 3:7
Conclusion		Isaiah 53:1–12

ACKNOWLEDGMENTS

Unit 1

1.1 [block quote, p. 4] George W. Knight, *The Pastoral Epistles: A Commentary on the Greek Text*, New International Greek Testament Commentary (Grand Rapids: Eerdmans, 1992), 450; [call-out, p. 4] Bruce Waltke, *Proverbs: Chapters 1–15*, New International Commentary on the Old Testament (Grand Rapids: Eerdmans, 2004), 181.

1.2 [right column, top, p. 7] Arthur Conan Doyle, *The Complete Sherlock Holmes* (Garden City, NY: Doubleday, 1930), 683; [right column, top, p. 7] Robert A. Traina, *Methodical Bible Study: A New Approach to Hermeneutics* (Grand Rapids: Zondervan, 1980), 32–33.

1.4 [call-out, p. 13] Stephen Dempster, *Dominion and Dynasty* (Downers Grove, IL: IVP Academic, 2003), 57; [call-out, p. 14] Andy Crouch, *Culture-Making: Recovering Our Creative Calling* (Downers Grove, IL: InterVarsity Press, 2008), 29; [block quote, pp. 14–15] Annalee Newitz, "Yes, Humans Are Animals—So Just Get Over Yourselves, *Homo sapiens*," Gizmodo, June 10, 2014, http://io9.gizmodo.com/yes-humans-are-animals-so-just-get-over-your-selves-1588990060.

1.5 [call-out, p. 17] Voltaire, quoted by J. I. Packer in *Still Sovereign*, eds. Thomas R. Schreiner and Bruce A. Ware (Grand Rapids: Baker Academic, 2000), 277.

1.7 [call-out, p. 24] Derek Kidner, *Genesis: An Introduction and Commentary* (Downers Grove, IL: InterVarsity Press, 1971), 87.

1.8 [box, p. 29] Charles Spurgeon, "Woe and Weal" (sermon, March 2, 1911), Spurgeon Gems, 2, http://www.spurgeongems.org/vols55-57/chs3239.pdf.

Unit 2

2.1 [call-out, p. 35] Vaughan Roberts, *God's Big Picture: Tracing the Storyline of the Bible* (Downers Grove, IL: InterVarsity Press, 2002), 63; [call-out, p. 35] Victor P. Hamilton, "Joseph," in *New Dictionary of Biblical Theology*, ed. T. Desmond Alexander and Brian S. Rosner, electronic ed. (Downers Grove, IL: InterVarsity Press, 2001).

2.3 [call-out, p. 42] Victor P. Hamilton, *The Book of Genesis: Chapters 18–50*, New International Commentary on the Old Testament (Grand Rapids: Eerdmans, 1995), 115; [call-out, p. 42] Paul R. Williamson, *Sealed with an Oath: Covenant in God's Unfolding Purpose* (Downers Grove, IL: InterVarsity Press, 2007), 77.

2.4 [call-out, p. 47] Roberts, *God's Big Picture*, 62; [call-out, p. 48] Gordon Wenham, *Genesis 16–50*, Word Biblical Commentary (Nashville: Thomas Nelson, 1994), 103.

2.6 [call-out, p. 56] V. Hamilton, "Jacob/Israel (Person)," in *New Dictionary of Biblical Theology*, electronic ed.; [call-out, p. 57] Stephen Motyer, "Israel (Nation)," in *New Dictionary of Biblical Theology*, electronic ed.

2.7 [call-out, p. 60] Dempster, *Dominion and Dynasty*, 88.

2.8 [call-out, p. 65] Bryan Smith, personal communication, May 2012.

Unit 3

3.2 [box, p. 75] Adaptation from Norman L. Geisler and Thomas Howe, *The Big Book of Bible Difficulties: Clear and Concise Answers from Genesis to Revelation* (Grand Rapids: Baker, 1992), 15–26; [call-out, p. 76] Dorian Coover-Cox, "The Hardening of Pharaoh's Heart in Its Literary and Cultural Contexts," *Bibliotheca Sacra* 163 (July–September 2006), 294; [call-out, p. 77] Jim Hamilton, *God's Glory in Salvation Through Judgment* (Wheaton: Crossway, 2010), 57; [call-out, p. 77] Roberts, *God's Big Picture*, 66.

3.3 [call-out, p. 79] Douglas K. Stuart, *Exodus*, New American Commentary (Nashville: Broadman & Holman Publishers, 2007), 364.

3.4 [bullet points, p. 83, and call-out, p. 83] Stuart, *Exodus*, 423; [call-out, p. 84] Eugene H. Merrill, "Royal Priesthood: An Old Testament Messianic Motif," *Bibliotheca Sacra* 150 (January–March 1993), 61.

3.5 [call-out, p. 86] Graeme Goldsworthy, *The Goldsworthy Trilogy* (Exeter, England: Paternoster Press, 2001), 78.

3.6 [call-out, p. 90] Williamson, *Sealed with an Oath*, 106; [block quote, p. 92] C. S. Lewis, *The Lion, the Witch, and the Wardrobe* (New York, HarperCollins, 1950), 146.

3.7 [diagram, p. 95] Jacob Milgrom, *Leviticus: A Book of Ritual and Ethics*, Continental Commentary (Minneapolis: Fortress Press, 2004), 95.

3.8 [call-out, p. 99] Gordon Wenham, *ESV Study Bible* (Wheaton: Crossway, 2008), 302.

Unit 4

4.1 [call-out, p. 108] Gordon McConville, *Grace in the End: A Study in Deuteronomic Theology* (Grand Rapids: Zondervan, 1993), 134; [call-out, p. 109] Paul Barker, "Introduction to Deuteronomy," *ESV Study Bible* (Wheaton: Crossway, 2008), 328.

4.3 [left column, middle, p. 114] "Vietnam Veterans Memorial," Vietnam Veterans Memorial Fund, http://www.vvmf.org/memorial.

4.4 [call-out, p. 117] Edward P. Blair, "An Appeal to Remembrance: The Memory Motif in Deuteronomy," *Interpretation* 15, no. 1 (1961): 43, http://int.sagepub.com/doi/pdf /10.1177/002096436101500104; [call-out, p. 119] Blair, "An Appeal to Remembrance," 43.

4.5 [call-out, p. 124] Daniel I. Block, "Deborah Among the Judges," in *Faith, Tradition, and History*, ed. A. R. Millard, J. K. Hoffmeter, D. W. Baker (Winona Lake, IL: Eisenbrauns, 1994), 241–42.

4.6 [call-out, p. 127] Daniel I. Block, *Judges, Ruth*, New American Commentary (Nashville: Broadman & Holman Publishers, 1999), 245; [call-out, p. 128] Alexander MacLaren, *Expositions of Holy Scripture* (Heritage Educational Systems, 2008), Judg. 7:1; [call-out, p. 128] J. Paul Tanner, "The Gideon Narrative as the Focal Point of Judges," *Bibliotheca Sacra* 149 (April–June 1992), 153.

4.7 [left column, top, p. 132] Block, *Judges, Ruth*, 375.

4.8 [call-out, p. 133] Block, *Judges, Ruth*, 194; [call-out, p. 133] Block, *Judges, Ruth*, 395; [bulleted list, p. 133–34] Block, *Judges, Ruth*, 421–22; [call-out, p. 135] David M. Howard, *ESV Study Bible*, 461; [call-out, p. 136] Robert Bell, *The Theological Messages of the Old Testament Books* (Greenville, SC: Bob Jones University Press, 2010), 126; [call-out, p. 136] Daniel I. Block, "Will the Real Gideon Please Stand Up? Narrative Style and Intention in Judges 6–9," *Journal of the Evangelical Theological Society* 40 (September 1997), 361–62.

Unit 5

5.1 [call-out, p. 143] Barry Webb, *Five Festal Garments* (Downers Grove, IL: IVP Academic, 2001), 45.

5.2 [call-out, p. 147] Dale Ralph Davis, *1 Samuel: Looking on the Heart* (Fearn, Scotland: Christian Focus Publications, 1996), 25.

5.3 [call-out, p. 149] Dempster, *Dominion and Dynasty*, 137; [call-out, p. 151] Robert D. Bergen, *1, 2 Samuel*, New American Commentary (Nashville: Broadman & Holman Publishers, 1996), 144; [call-out, p. 151] Roberts, *God's Big Picture*, 80.

5.4 [call-out, p. 153] Bergen, *1, 2 Samuel*, 121.

5.5 [box at bottom, p. 157] Bergen, *1, 2 Samuel*, 182; [call-out, p. 158] Bergen, *1, 2 Samuel*, 190; [call-out, p. 159] Smith, personal communication, May 2012; [call-out, p. 160] P. E. Satterthwaite, "Samuel," in *New Dictionary of Biblical Theology*, electronic ed.

5.6 [call-out, p. 164] J. A. Thompson, *1, 2 Chronicles*, New American Commentary (Nashville: Broadman & Holman Publishers, 1994), 129.

5.7 [call-out, p. 167] Williamson, *Sealed with an Oath*, 144; [call-out, p. 169] Dempster, *Dominion and Dynasty*, 141; [call-out, p. 172] Craig Bartholomew, "A God for Life, and Not Just for Christmas! The Revelation of God in the Old Testament Wisdom Literature," in *The Trustworthiness of God: Perspectives on the Nature of Scripture*, ed. Paul Helm and Carl R. Trueman, (Grand Rapids: Eerdmans, 2002), 41.

5.8 [call-out, p. 177] Paul R. House, *1, 2 Kings*, New American Commentary (Nashville: Broadman & Holman Publishers, 2001), 167–68; [right column, top, p. 178] Duane Garrett, *Proverbs, Ecclesiastes, Song of Songs*, New American Commentary (Nashville: Broadman & Holman Publishers, 1993), 289; [call-out, p. 179] John Newton, *The Life of John Newton* (Edinburgh, Scotland: Johnstone & Hunter, 1853), 30 (in the Olney hymns section); [block quote, left column, p. 180] Augustine, *On Christian Doctrine,* trans. J. F. Shaw (Mineola, NY: Dover, 2009), 2.6; [block quote, center column, p. 180], James Durham, *Commentary on the Song of Songs,* Fire and Ice, http://www.puritansermons.com/durham/durham402.htm; [right column, center, p. 180] Duane Garrett, *Song of Songs*, Word Biblical Commentary (Nashville: Nelson, 2004), 93.

Unit 6

6.1 [call-out, p. 187] Iain Provan, *1 & 2 Kings*, New International Biblical Commentary on the Old Testament (Peabody, MA: Hendrickson Publishers, 1995), 110; [call-out, p. 188] Bell, *Theological Messages*, 156; [left column, middle, p. 189] Provan, *1 & 2 Kings*, 110.

6.2 [call-out, p. 191] Peter Leithart, *1 & 2 Kings*, Brazos Theological Commentary (Ada, MI: Brazos Press, 2006), 126; [call-out, p. 192] J. Hamilton, *God's Glory in Salvation*, 182; [call-out, p. 193] Ronald Barclay Allen, "Elijah The Broken Prophet" *Journal of the Evangelical Theological Society* 22, no. 3 (Sept 1979): 200.

6.3 [call-out, p. 196] Philip Graham Ryken, *1 Kings*, Reformed Expository Commentary (Phillipsburg, NJ: P&R Publishing, 2011), 575; [call-out, p. 197] Provan, *1 & 2 Kings*, 13.

6.4 [call-out, p. 200] House, *1, 2 Kings*, 273.

6.5 [call-out, p. 202] Amy Balogh, "Elisha the Prophet," ed. John D. Barry et al., *The Lexham Bible Dictionary* (Bellingham, WA: Lexham Press, 2016).

6.7 [call-out, p. 213] *The Apocrypha and Pseudepigrapha of the Old Testament in English*, ed. R. H. Charles, (London: Oxford University Press, 1913) 2:321; [box, p. 215] *The American Heritage Dictionary*, s.v. "rhetorical question," https://www.ahdictionary.com/word/search .html?q=rhetorical+question.

Unit 7

7.2 [box, bottom, p. 228] Josephus, *Antiquities*, trans. William Whiston (London: Wordsworth Classics, 2006), 11.1.2.

7.3 [call-out, p. 232] Provan, *1 & 2 Kings*, 264.

7.5 [call-out, p. 239] John Calvin, *The Institutes of the Christian Religion,* (Raleigh, NC: Hayes Barton Press, n.d.) 456–57; [call-out, p. 240] D. A. Carson, *The Difficult Doctrine of the Love of God* (Wheaton: Crossway, 2000), 67; [block quote, pp. 241–42] D. A. Carson, *The God Who Is There* (Grand Rapids: Baker, 2010), 33–34.

7.6 [call-out, p. 245] Bell, *Theological Messages*, 432; [call-out, p. 246] David W. Baker, "Nahum," in *New Dictionary of Biblical Theology*, ed. T. Desmond Alexander et al. (Downers Grove, IL: InterVarsity Press, 2000), 252.

7.7 [call-out, p. 247] Roberts, *God's Big Picture*, 86; [call-out, p. 248] Dempster, *Dominion and Dynasty*, 153; [call-out, p. 150] Dempster, *Dominion and Dynasty*, 156.

7.8 [call-out, p. 252] John MacArthur, *ESV MacArthur Study Bible* (Wheaton: Crossway, 2010), 1289; [call-out, p. 253] Kenneth L. Barker, *Micah, Nahum, Habakkuk, Zephaniah*, New American Commentary (Nashville: Broadman & Holman Publishers, 1999), 302.

Unit 8

8.1 [call-out, p. 262] F. B. Huey, *Jeremiah, Lamentations*, New American Commentary (Nashville: Broadman & Holman Publishers, 1993), 447.

8.4 [left column, top, p. 274] Authur Conan Doyle, *The New Annotated Sherlock Holmes*, ed. Leslie S. Klinger (New York: W. W. Norton, 2005) 1:10; [right column, top, p. 276] Rich Christiano, *The Time Changer* (Nashville: Five & Two Pictures, 2002).

8.5 [call-out, p. 278] Joyce C. Baldwin, *Haggai, Zechariah, and Malachi*, Tyndale Old Testament Commentaries (Downers Grove, IL: InterVarsity Press, 1972), 64; [block quote, p. 280] Michael P. V. Barrett, *The Next to Last Word: Service, Hope, and Revival in the Postexilic Prophets* (Grand Rapids: Reformation Heritage, 2015), 62; [call-out, p. 281] J. Alec Motyer, "Haggai," in *An Exegetical and Expository Commentary: The Minor Prophets*, ed. Thomas Edward McComiskey (Grand Rapids: Baker Academic, 1998), 3:996.

8.6 [block quote, p. 283] C. S. Lewis, *The Chronicles of Narnia* (New York: HarperCollins, 1982), 281; [box, p. 287] Dempster, *Dominion and Dynasty,* 233.

8.7 [left column, top, p. 290] Charles Portis, Ethan Coen, and Joel Coen, *True Grit*, directed by Ethan Coen and Joel Coen, (Hollywood: Paramount Pictures, 2010).

8.8 [call-out, p. 292] Barrett, *The Next to Last Word*, 210; [call-out, p. 293] Barrett, *The Next to Last Word*, 239; [block quote, p. 299] C. S. Lewis, "Evolutionary Hymn," in *Poems* (San Diego: Harvest, 1992), 55.

PHOTO CREDITS

Key: (t) top; (c) center; (b) bottom;
(l) left; (r) right

Unit 1

15l Kzenon/Shutterstock.com; **15tc** Jacob Lund/Shutterstock.com; **15tr** Monkey Business Images/Shutterstock.com; **15bc** rocharibeiro/Shutterstock.com; **15br** Pressmaster/Shutterstock.com; **18** © iStock.com/Sasha Radosavljevic; **27–28** Illustrations by Chris Koelle from JŌB. © 2017 Chris Koelle. Used by permission.

Unit 2

53 Renata Sedmakova/Shutterstock.com

Unit 4

115 © 2016 Paul DeCesare | Express Image Media

Unit 6

206l Caesars Head State Park/The Times-News via AP; **206r** AP Photo/Eric Gay; **210l** Luis Santana /Tampa Bay Times via AP; **210r** David Joles /
Star Tribune via AP

Unit 7

231 © Z. Radovan, Jerusalem; **232l** www.BibleLandPictures.com / Alamy Stock Photo;
232r "Inside Hezekiah's Tunnel" by Ian Scott/Flickr/CC BY-SA 2.0

All maps from Map Resources